The Sixth Grandfather

The Sixth
GRANDFATHER

Black Elk's Teachings
Given to
John G. Neihardt

Edited and with an Introduction by

Raymond J. DeMallie

University of Nebraska Press

Lincoln and London

Publication of this book was aided by a grant from
the National Endowment for the Humanities.

The paper in this book meets the guidelines
for permanence and durability of the Committee on
Production Guidelines for Book Longevity of the
Council on Library Resources.

Library of Congress Cataloging in Publication Data

Neihardt, John Gneisenau, 1881-1973
The sixth grandfather.

Bibliography: p.
Includes index.
1. Black Elk, 1863-1950.   2. Oglala Indians – Religion
and mythology.   3. Oglala Indians – Philosophy.
4. Indians of North America – Great Plains – Religion and
mythology.   5. Indians of North America – Great Plains –
Philosophy.   6. Oglala Indians – Biography.   I. Black Elk,
1863-1950.   II. DeMallie, Raymond J., 1946-
III. Title.
E99.O3B536   1984   970.004'97 [B]   83-14452
ISBN 0-8032-1664-5

Second cloth printing: 1986

To the Sixth Grandfather:
The spirit of mankind

Contents

Illustrations and Maps

Foreword

The Sixth Grandfather is a book that needed to be written. It is a scholarly work done over a period of years and with singular dedication. Because *Black Elk Speaks* has attracted serious attention in the United States and in many other countries, certainly a full-length scholarly work on its creation is in order. But to Raymond DeMallie, *The Sixth Grandfather* has been much more than a research project. As an anthropologist, he has used his wide knowledge of the American Indian, and particularly the Lakota Sioux, both to prove a scholarly premise and to learn—insofar as that is possible in this still imperfect world—the truth. The special value of this book, to me, is this: it is an essay in understanding.

Upon their first, seemingly accidental, meeting, Black Elk told Neihardt that Neihardt "had been sent" to learn what the holy man would teach him. Through an awareness we cannot fully comprehend, the old Lakota somehow knew the essential truth about the poet; Black Elk believed that Neihardt could understand his teachings and had faith that this white man would communicate his vision to the world at large. To make the meaning of this vision a part of people's lives was a responsibility Black Elk felt had been placed upon him by the Grandfathers. Having himself only partially succeeded in carrying out the vision, he apparently decided to entrust it to the man who "had been sent" to him. "It is true and it is beautiful," Black Elk said, "and it is for all men." And so the interviews for *Black Elk Speaks* were planned.

John Neihardt was well pleased with the firsthand recounting by Black Elk and the other old Lakotas of historic events and the old Sioux way of life, which cast new light on matters already familiar to him as a student of western history. Above all, the beauty and meaning of Black Elk's vision astounded Neihardt, who felt it deserved a place among the great works of religious literature. When Black Elk finished recounting his vision, he stated, quite simply, that all his power had now been transferred to Neihardt, who had become his spiritual son.

The responsibility placed upon him was keenly felt by Neihardt. During the remainder of his life, he rarely spoke in public without referring to Black Elk. Through Neihardt's recitations, his adaptation of "Black Elk's Prayer" became known and loved by many.

DeMallie refers in his Introduction to this book—as did Vine Deloria, Jr., in an introduction to the 1979 edition of *Black Elk Speaks*—to assumptions by readers and researchers that have led to controversy over the authenticity of the subject matter of the book and the importance of Neihardt's role as its author. By the very title chosen for his book, *Black Elk Speaks,* Neihardt makes amply clear his desire to give full credit to Black Elk. Perhaps this title has itself contributed in some measure to the misunderstandings. One must realize that the process beginning with what Black Elk related in the Lakota language and resulting in Neihardt's writing of the book was not an easy one. To a listener, the interviews seemed at times tedious, for it took painstaking effort to learn, through an uninitiated interpreter, what Black Elk was trying to say.

The Sixth Grandfather may well guide the reader to a realization that at first blush seems deceptively simple: *Black Elk Speaks* is authentic; it does convey with faithful sincerity Black Elk's message. But in presenting this message to the reader, Neihardt created a work of art, and true art in all its forms is an intensification and greatly clarified form of communication.

In his research for this book, Ray DeMallie goes beyond the original typed transcriptions of the interview notes. Here presented for the first time, newly transcribed and annotated, is the entire body of shorthand notes of the Black Elk–Neihardt interviews, making available a wealth of material not used in *Black Elk Speaks*.

The Sixth Grandfather is a valuable contribution to scholarly research, in regard to *Black Elk Speaks* and also as a source for students of the American Indian and of a way of life and religion that were good. Not as a scholar, but as a believer, I commend this book warmly and affectionately as an essay in understanding.

HILDA NEIHARDT PETRI

Preface

In the great vision he received when still a small boy, Black Elk saw himself as the "sixth grandfather," the spiritual representative of the earth and of mankind. In Lakota religion the six grandfathers symbolized *Wakan Tanka*, the Great Mysteriousness, the powers of the six directions of the universe: west, north, east, south, above, and below. Understood as grandfathers, these spirits were represented as kind and loving, full of years and wisdom, like revered human grandfathers. They symbolized the six directions; but for Lakotas symbols were not merely empty signs. They expressed identity: the symbol and the symbolized were one. Thus the six grandfathers *were* the six directions. Black Elk became the sixth grandfather, the spirit of the "below" direction, the earth, the place where mankind lives, the source of human life. By becoming the sixth grandfather through the vision experience, Black Elk was identified as the spirit of all mankind. And the vision foreshadowed his life as a holy man—as thinker, healer, teacher.

In two important books, *Black Elk Speaks* (1932) and *When the Tree Flowered* (1951), John G. Neihardt immortalized Black Elk's teachings, preserving them as a legacy for future generations.[1] Neihardt's books are literary interpretations of what he learned from Black Elk. They preserve the details of Lakota culture and yet transcend them, securing a place for

1. John G. Neihardt, *Black Elk Speaks: Being the Life Story of a Holy Man of the Ogalala Sioux* (New York: William Morrow, 1932; reprint with a new preface by Neihardt and new introduction, illustrations, and appendixes, Lincoln: University of Nebraska Press, 1961, 1979); Neihardt, *When the Tree Flowered: An Authentic Tale of the Old Sioux World* (New York: Macmillan, 1951).

Lakota religion in the ranks of recorded tribal traditions to which people in contemporary industrial society continually look for inspiration.

To Lakota people today, Neihardt's records of Black Elk's teachings strike resonant chords that have elevated the teachings, as Vine Deloria, Jr., has suggested, to the status of an American Indian Bible. The books could also be considered an American Indian Rosetta stone, for they serve both Indians and non-Indians of today as an entrance into the traditional native American culture of the nineteenth century, a key to translation from modern American into older American Indian modes of thought. Shortly after the publication of *Black Elk Speaks,* Ella C. Deloria, linguist and ethnographer and herself a Yankton Sioux, wrote to Neihardt: "I have just finished 'Black Elk Speaks.' I want you to know that it makes me happy and sad all at once—sad for the days that are gone, and glad that a white man really lives who can enter into a right understanding of a Dakota's vision, and can translate it into so poetic a form."[2]

Black Elk's teachings, from which Neihardt wrote his books, were a kind of gift from Black Elk to Neihardt, his adopted son. The first set of teachings, recorded in summer 1931, concerns the great vision that Black Elk had and the story of his life, forming a microcosm of Lakota history from the 1860s through the Wounded Knee massacre in 1890. Black Elk recognized in Neihardt a kindred mystic, and he decided to transfer to him the sacred knowledge of the other world that he had learned in the visions of his youth. The second set of teachings, recorded in winter 1944, covers the general history of the Lakota people from mythical times through history. Most of this material relates to the period before the arrival of white men. Neihardt requested Black Elk to tell these stories so that he could write what he called a "cultural history" of the Lakotas, telling of their history from their own point of view. Thus the two sets of teachings are complementary.

Neihardt intended his books to be interpretations of Lakota culture and history that would preserve what was good and beautiful and true in traditional lifeways. He hoped to touch his readers with the emotional power of the inexorable struggle between the advancement of white civilization across the American west and the native peoples who had lived

2. Ella C. Deloria to John G. Neihardt, March 18, 1932. John G. Neihardt Collection, Western History Manuscripts Collection, University of Missouri, Columbia, Mo.

there for as long as anyone could remember. The historical force of this advancement, taken for granted in the concept of Manifest Destiny, took a bitter toll on the Indian people. Neihardt wished to bring this tragedy into focus by telling the story through the eyes of a single native person. *Black Elk Speaks* and *When the Tree Flowered* tell the same story: the former is a close rendering of the life of Black Elk and the latter is a freer one, based not only on Black Elk's life and teachings, but on those of another old Oglala man named Eagle Elk. As Neihardt wrote in the introduction to the British edition of *When the Tree Flowered* (entitled *Eagle Voice*), although the story is a composite, it is authentic, "giving a comprehensive view of the old Sioux world."[3]

Neihardt intended both of these volumes as contributions to American literature, presenting for the first time in the long history of literary interpretations of the American Indian a point of view developed out of the Indians' own consciousness. Over the years, however, the two books have been used for a variety of purposes for which they were not intended: for historical reference, for anthropological study of Lakota culture, for psychological analysis of the American Indian personality, for philosophical understanding of tribal religions. Of course there is an abundance of material in the two books for such analyses, but too often writers representing these diverse academic disciplines have failed to recognize that the books were written by Neihardt, not by Black Elk, and that they bear the stamp of Neihardt's genius and his sense of organization and detail. To treat Neihardt as a mere editor to Black Elk is a regrettable misunderstanding that fails to do justice to Neihardt's creative skill as a writer.[4]

On the other hand, some authors have tended to dismiss Neihardt's books as completely unusable for historical, anthropological, psychological, or philosophical study on the grounds that they can only be taken to represent Neihardt himself—that Black Elk was for Neihardt merely a

3. John G. Neihardt, *Eagle Voice: An Authentic Tale of the Sioux Indians* (London: Andrew Melrose, 1953), p. 4.

4. For a discussion of Neihardt's role in writing *Black Elk Speaks,* and the controversy the book engendered, see Lucile F. Aly, *John G. Neihardt: A Critical Biography* (Amsterdam: Rodopi, 1977), pp. 172–73; Sally McCluskey, "*Black Elk Speaks*: And So Does John Neihardt," *Western American Literature* 6(4) (Winter 1972): 231–42; and H. David Brumble III, *An Annotated Bibliography of American Indian and Eskimo Autobiographies* (Lincoln: University of Nebraska Press, 1981), pp. 28–30.

literary vehicle to express his own philosophy and around which to create his private fantasy world based on Lakota culture. These authors also make a regrettable mistake, for they fail to appreciate the sincerity of Neihardt's commitment to make the books speak for Black Elk faithfully, to represent what Black Elk would have said if he had understood the concept of literature and if he had been able to express himself in English. From his own perspective, Neihardt envisioned himself as Black Elk's literary spokesman, an interpreter of the old holy man's thoughts.

Untold numbers of readers of *Black Elk Speaks* and *When the Tree Flowered* have wished to understand more fully the relationship between Neihardt and Black Elk and the role that Neihardt played as Black Elk's amanuensis. They have also been curious to learn about Black Elk's life after the Wounded Knee massacre. How was it that a nineteenth-century Lakota mystic could live a full half of the twentieth century on the Pine Ridge Reservation in harmony with the encroaching white man's world?

The Sixth Grandfather is presented in order to help readers answer these questions. The title of the book is doubly appropriate. Black Elk, in his great vision, saw himself as the "sixth grandfather," the spirit of the earth, the power to nurture and make grow. Symbolically, Black Elk's teachings, transmitted through Neihardt, have had a marvelous generative power: they have grown and blossomed and become an inspiration for millions, Indians and non-Indians alike. Through Neihardt's writings, the sacred tree of Black Elk's vision has truly come to bloom.

This volume is a further contribution to the literature on Black Elk, presenting for the first time the teachings as given to Neihardt and as recorded by Neihardt's daughters Enid and Hilda, who acted as their father's secretaries during his interviews with Black Elk. Here are reproduced in full the notes of the interviews, the direct words of Black Elk as interpreted into English. The reader must understand, however, that these are not verbatim records of Black Elk's words, but that they are the combined efforts of the interpreters and of Neihardt to express in English the meaning of the old man's Lakota words. These are the most original records of Black Elk's teachings available, and they are the sources from which Neihardt wrote *Black Elk Speaks* and *When the Tree Flowered*. With access to this source material, readers can now compare for themselves Neihardt's literary treatment with the full recording in the interview notes. To aid the reader in this comparison, there is a detailed discussion in the Introduction to Part II of the differences between the accounts of Black Elk's childhood visions in the interviews and in *Black Elk Speaks*. Further, Appendix A, a concordance, indexes all the material in the interviews to the appropriate pages in the published books. In making such comparisons, it is impossible not to be struck by the brilliance and literary polish of Neihardt's transformation of Black Elk's tales. At the same time, the interview notes are invaluable for supplying a wealth of detail that Neihardt was forced to omit in order to keep his books to manageable length and to make them interesting.

To help readers understand Black Elk's narratives, the interview notes have been edited with footnotes to clarify obscure points; to identify persons, places, and events; to provide comparisons between the interviews and the published books; and to give bibliographical leads for further study of specific topics. These notes are not exhaustive but are intended to help the interested reader gain a fuller appreciation of Black Elk's teachings through comparative reading in other published sources.

Part I of this volume provides a biographical sketch for Black Elk to aid the reader in gaining a fuller understanding of the man and of his relationship to Neihardt. It tells the story of Black Elk's joining the Roman Catholic Church, his experiences as a missionary on other Indian reservations, his life as a catechist, his interviews with Neihardt, and his work during his last years in presenting an interpretive pageant each summer in the Black Hills to try to teach white audiences about the old Lakota ways.

Part II gives the text of the 1931 interviews, centering on Black Elk's life story, from which *Black Elk Speaks* was written. The introduction discusses Black Elk's place in the context of Lakota religious history, and it compares the vision accounts given in the interviews and in *Black Elk Speaks*.

Part III presents the text of the 1944 interviews, centering on Lakota history and culture, from which *When the Tree Flowered* was written.

Appendix A is a concordance of material in the interview notes and specific pages in *Black Elk Speaks* and *When the Tree Flowered*.

Appendix B gives the orthography used for rewriting Lakota words throughout the interview notes.

The intention of this book is to allow readers direct access to Black Elk, the historical personage; to make his life more fully understandable; and to publish at last the entirety of the teachings that he gave to John G.

Neihardt. Readers will also want to consult the important teachings concerning Lakota rituals that Black Elk gave, toward the end of his life, to Joseph Epes Brown; these were published as *The Sacred Pipe* (1953).[5]

Through his remarkable body of teachings, Black Elk truly lives. This is his legacy, passed on to us, the "future generations," that we might benefit from knowledge of the old Lakota world and of its sacred power, represented by the tree of his visions. As Black Elk said to Neihardt, "We want this tree to bloom again in the world of true that doesn't judge."

A NOTE ON THE EDITING

The records of Neihardt's interviews with Black Elk in 1931 and 1944, as well as correspondence between the two men and related manuscript material, are preserved in the Neihardt Collection, deposited in the Western History Manuscripts Collection of the University of Missouri at Columbia, Missouri. The 1931 interviews were first recorded in shorthand and the 1944 interviews were transcribed directly on a typewriter. Because of this difference, the two sets of interviews presented different editorial challenges.

Neihardt's 1931 interviews with Black Elk exist in two forms, Enid Neihardt's original shorthand record in four spiral notebooks and her typed manuscript, from which Neihardt wrote *Black Elk Speaks*. Both versions claim a kind of authenticity; although the shorthand notes are more primary, the transcript corrects obvious errors and failings that crept into the original notes owing to the press of time and to the difficult conditions under which they were made. The text presented in Part II combines the two versions, including all information from both.

My initial inclination was to publish an exact transcription of the stenographic record. But the notes from the first few interview sessions are too choppy and ungrammatical to be read easily. The notes become progressively smoother as Enid Neihardt perfected her recording system until by the middle of the interviews they are usually grammatical. Rather than needlessly subject the reader to the difficulties of interpreting the shorthand notes verbatim, I have relied on Enid Neihardt's transcript but

5. Joseph Epes Brown, recorder and ed., *The Sacred Pipe: Black Elk's Account of the Seven Rites of the Oglala Sioux* (Norman: University of Oklahoma Press, 1953, reprint with new preface by Brown, New York: Penguin Books, 1971).

have not attempted to rewrite the transcript to improve style. Rather, the text as established here reconstructs the interviews as precisely and completely as is now possible, at the same time taking readability into consideration.

In making the transcript, Enid Neihardt omitted or changed a small amount of material, usually only phrases she considered redundant, which is restored to the present text in brackets and printed in italics. The purpose of making this material explicit is to indicate that it was not part of the transcript from which Neihardt worked in writing *Black Elk Speaks,* and thus he did not have access to it—except, of course, in memory. Parenthetical insertions are part of Enid Neihardt's transcript. The shorthand notes continually shift from first person to third, from Black Elk speaking directly ("I . . .") to the interpreter's description ("he says that . . ."). In preparing the transcript, Enid Neihardt converted most of these to the first person; in this book others have been changed to the first person where appropriate. In the vision accounts and in prayers, the transcript alternates between "you" and "your" and "thou" and "thy" (the latter probably reflecting Christian prayer). These have been systematized to "you" and "your"—the forms that appear in the transcript in the great majority of cases. Simple errors in shorthand transcription have been corrected silently. The interview material is presented largely in chronological order; this represents only minor rearrangement because Black Elk related his life story basically in sequence. Miscellaneous, nonchronological material is grouped together in text no. 9. Finally, headings identifying the narrator and topic have been supplied.

Neihardt's 1944 interviews with Black Elk were recorded directly on the typewriter by Hilda Neihardt. These present fewer editorial problems than the earlier interviews. The text as established in Part III is taken directly from these notes. Again, I have supplied section headings. This material is presented in the sequence in which Black Elk related it, with only occasional shifting of paragraphs to keep related topics together. I felt it was important to maintain the original order of these interviews so that the reader could follow Black Elk's developmental history of Lakota society as he presented it.

In establishing the final text of both sets of interviews, I have regularized spelling and punctuation, broken up run-on sentences, supplied paragraphing, and corrected errors in spelling. I have also silently corrected tense and number, as well as occasional obvious inversions of subject and object and slips of the pen. Minimal grammatical editing has improved readability, but whenever the meaning was in question, grammatical changes have been indicated by brackets. Other editorial additions, to identify events, persons, places, and objects, are also enclosed in brackets. Lakota terms are given in italics in brackets to clarify Enid and Hilda Neihardt's writing of Lakota words. These retranscriptions follow the simplified orthography in Appendix B. When lengthier identification or discussion is required, that information appears in notes.

Acknowledgments

My greatest debt in preparing this book is to Hilda Neihardt Petri. Since 1978, when I proposed to edit for publication her father's interviews with Black Elk, she has supported my work and has helped in many ways to bring it to completion. In sharing memories of her father with me, she has made me appreciate the excitement of life with Neihardt. She has also given me a sense of the depth of Neihardt's affection and admiration for Black Elk, and of his commitment to presenting the old holy man's teachings to the world. Enid Neihardt Fink has also contributed in important ways to the project. Without her permission to use the private shorthand diary she kept in 1931 it would not have been possible for me to reconstruct a full and accurate chronology of Neihardt's first interviews with Black Elk. To both Hilda and Enid I express my warmest thanks.

I am grateful to Nancy C. Prewitt and her staff at the Western History Manuscript Collection, University of Missouri, for their assistance in my work with the Neihardt Collection. Philip Bantin, archivist of the Bureau of Catholic Indian Mission Records, Marquette University, Milwaukee, facilitated access to archival materials from Holy Rosary Mission. Monsignor Paul A. Lenz, executive director of the Bureau of Catholic Indian Missions, gave permission to quote from these archives. Sister Roberta Smith, archivist of the Sisters of the Blessed Sacrament, Cornwells Heights, Pennsylvania, located mission records for study and extended cordial hospitality. Brother C. M. Simon, S.J., and Mrs. Thelma Henry provided birth and baptismal records at Holy Rosary Mission.

The Venerable Vine V. Deloria, Sr., guided my translations of Black Elk's letters written in Lakota. He and his wife, Barbara, welcomed me into their home in Pierre, South Dakota, and transformed the work of translation into a joyful experience.

Mr. Bud Duhamel and Mrs. Emma Amiotte, both of Rapid City, South Dakota, have shared with me their memories of Black Elk, especially concerning his participation in the Duhamel summer pageant in the Black Hills. Reginald and Gladys Laubin, who also knew Black Elk at the pageant, invited me into their home in Moose, Wyoming, and likewise shared their memories. Charles E. Hanson, Jr., of the Museum of the Fur Trade in Chadron, Nebraska, recalled for me details of his meeting with Black Elk, adding a further dimension to my interpretation. Joseph Epes Brown, Professor of Religion at the University of Montana, kindly read Part I of the manuscript and gave valuable criticism and advice.

Many friends and acquaintances among the Lakotas have taught me about their traditional religion and culture and have helped me to develop an understanding of Black Elk in the context of reservation life.

I am grateful to the American Council of Learned Societies for a grant-in-aid during summer 1980 that allowed for transcribing the shorthand notes and preparing the final text of the interviews. The editing was completed during 1981–82 under the dual support of an American Council of Learned Societies Fellowship (made possible by a grant from the National Endowment for the Humanities) and sabbatical leave from Indiana University.

Father Peter John Powell of the Newberry Library, Chicago, read the manuscript, corrected some of my errors, and gave valuable advice. His unfailing faith in the project has sustained me throughout. Dr. Lucile F. Aly, Neihardt's biographer, shared knowledge and materials with me. Similarly, Father Michael F. Steltenkamp, S. J., who is writing a biography of Black Elk, discussed his work and shared ideas with me. Stuart W. Conner, of Billings, Montana, provided archaeological identification of petroglyph sites mentioned by Black Elk. Professor John H. Moore of the Department of Anthropology, University of Oklahoma, interviewed Walter Hamilton, Cheyenne Sacred Arrow Priest, to obtain information regarding a Cheyenne sacred arrow ceremony described by Black Elk.

To the Western History Manuscript Collection and Hilda Neihardt Petri, I am grateful for the use of photographs taken by Neihardt and his family. Harold D. Moore of the Buechel Memorial Lakota Museum in St. Francis, South Dakota, provided photographs from Father Eugene Buechel's collection. Professor Patricia Albers of the Department of Anthropology, University of Utah, located an excellent photograph of Black Elk at the Duhamel pageant in her incomparable collection of Indian postcards and allowed me to reproduce it. The South Dakota State Historical Society and the National Anthropological Archives of the Smithsonian Institution also provided photographs of Black Elk from their collections.

JoAllyn Archambault, Margaret C. Blaker, H. David Brumble III, Elaine A. Jahner, Harvey Markowitz, David Reed Miller, Douglas R. Parks, Brian D. F. Richmond, Joanna C. Scherer, Gloria A. Young, Kay Young, and Stephen Douglas Youngkin have all contributed in various ways to aid in the completion of this book. To them, and to the many others who have offered their support during preparation of *The Sixth Grandfather,* I am grateful.

I offer a final special note of thanks to Rita Harper, of Bloomington, Indiana, who transcribed the shorthand notes of the 1931 interviews, as well as Enid Neihardt's diary and the shorthand drafts of Neihardt's correspondence.

PART ONE

Nicholas Black Elk and John G. Neihardt: An Introduction

Black Elk was born in December 1863 on the Little Powder River, probably within the present borders of Wyoming.[1] His father and his father's
father were medicine men whose special healing powers brought renown
to the family. They were Oglala Lakotas, and Black Elk was brought up as
a member of Big Road's band, which camped and hunted in the most
westerly portion of Lakota country, beyond the Black Hills. The establishment of the Bozeman Trail through this territory in 1864 brought the
Oglalas into active conflict with the white men. These hostilities continually escalated into warfare until 1877, when the western Oglala bands
returned east of the Black Hills and joined their relatives on the Great
Sioux Reservation in present-day South Dakota.[2]

The world into which Black Elk was born was the old Lakota world, as
it was before the white men destroyed it—a sacred world in which the
Lakota people lived in daily interaction with the seen and unseen spirit
forces that comprised their universe. When he was only nine years old,
Black Elk was favored by the Thunder-beings (*Wakinyan*), embodiments
of the powers of the west, with a great vision that foreshadowed the
special powers he would have to use later in life to cure his people from
illness and aid them in war. The vision gave Black Elk remarkable pro-

1. Throughout the introduction I do not give citations for biographical and other
details taken from the interviews that constitute the remainder of this volume.

2. The history of relations between the Oglalas and the United States is summarized
in George E. Hyde, *Red Cloud's Folk: A History of the Oglala Sioux Indians,* rev. ed.
(Norman: University of Oklahoma Press, 1957 [original 1937]), and James C. Olson, *Red
Cloud and the Sioux Problem* (Lincoln: University of Nebraska Press, 1965).

The Northern Plains, 1860–90

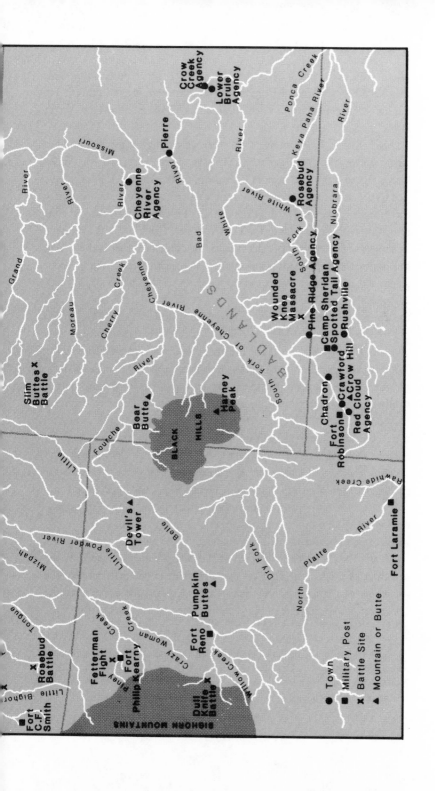

phetic powers that were beyond his conscious control, powers that were manifested spontaneously from time to time as he grew to adulthood. He felt himself set apart from other children, his life overshadowed by secret knowledge of the other world.

Black Elk was too young to take part in the fighting with the U.S. Army during the 1860s and 1870s. In 1877, after the Oglala war leader Crazy Horse was killed at Fort Robinson, Nebraska, Black Elk's people fled to Canada to seek refuge from the soldiers, and they remained there for about three years. During the summer of his sixteenth year, just after returning with his family to the United States, Black Elk was overcome by obsessive fear of the Thunder-beings. He could hear them calling him, but he was unsure what they wanted. When storms came he ran about frantically, hiding first in one lodge, then another. His behavior led Black Elk's family to realize that he had dreamed of Thunder. In Lakota belief the Thunder dreamer was required to enact Thunder's rituals on earth, to humble himself before the people and to manifest the power he had been given for curing or for war. The dreamer was obliged to do whatever the Thunder-beings required of him—even if they should demand that he murder a tribesman. But the usual task required was for the dreamer to sponsor a *heyoka* ceremony, in which he and other Thunder dreamers played the role of Thunder's messengers, acting clownishly, doing all things backward, making themselves the objects of the people's laughter. Anyone who failed to comply with the Thunder-beings' demands lived in dread of summer thunderstorms, because the punishment decreed for such failure was death by lightning. Hence Black Elk's pervasive fear.[3]

Finally, when he was seventeen, Black Elk relieved himself of his psychological burden by revealing his great vision to Black Road, a wise, old medicine man who could help him understand the will of the spirits. Black Road and the other medicine men of the village were astonished by the greatness of the vision. They advised him that, rather than sponsor the usual *heyoka* ceremony of Thunder dreamers, he should instead enact the horse dance, a spectacular public demonstration of the first portion of the

---

3. For information on the Thunder dreamers, see James R. Walker, *Lakota Belief and Ritual,* ed. Raymond J. DeMallie and Elaine A. Jahner (Lincoln: University of Nebraska Press, 1980), pp. 155–57; see ibid., pp. 54–61, for a bibliographic summary of sources on Lakota religion.

great vision. So it was that in spring 1881, Black Elk began his career as a medicine man by performing the horse dance ceremony at Fort Keogh, Montana, where his family was encamped with other Lakota refugees from Canada. By acknowledging the vision in this manner before his people, Black Elk at last put himself in harmony with the spirit world and publicly announced his spiritual calling.

After settling with the Oglalas at Pine Ridge Agency the following year, Black Elk undertook the ritual fasting and purification that were required before one would go up on a hill alone and cry for a vision. This was the age at which Lakota boys regularly sought visions to obtain spiritual gifts for success in life. Black Elk sought understanding, that he might control the powers given him in his childhood vision. Once again he was favored by the powers of the west, and as a result he sponsored the *heyoka* ceremony. Later he also performed the buffalo and elk ceremonies and repeated the horse dance so that the people at Pine Ridge would recognize his powers as a healer. Black Elk told Neihardt in detail of the first cure he accomplished, by means of which he assured himself of his ability to control and direct his spiritual gifts. Though still young, he soon became an important and sought-after medicine man among the Oglalas.

Reservation life presented hard challenges for the Lakotas. Buffalo, on which the Lakota economy had traditionally depended, were no longer available in large enough numbers to support the people, who were forced to depend on government rations. These they understood as given to them in recompense for the wrongs done them by the white people. Intertribal warfare ceased; with both war and hunting eliminated, the time-honored roles through which most Lakota men had achieved prominence were abolished. Many of the men turned to ranching and farming to try to support their families. At this time, Black Elk told Neihardt, he began to wonder whether it would be better for his people to abandon traditional Indian ways and to take up those of white men. In 1886, in order to learn more about the man's way of life, Black Elk seized the opportunity to travel as a member of Buffalo Bill's Wild West show. He signed two contracts with Buffalo Bill that year, one dated January 17 (but probably signed during autumn), the other dated December 17. He used his boyhood name, Choice (*Kahniǧapi*), his official designation in the Pine Ridge census at the time. Both contracts were for a period of two years, and every individual involved was to receive $25 per month in addition to all expenses of travel, food, clothing, medical attention, and incidentals.[4]

The wild west show adventure took Black Elk first to New York, where the show spent the winter performing at Madison Square Garden. Then, in spring 1887, Buffalo Bill took his troupe to England in time to participate in celebrating the Golden Jubilee of Queen Victoria's reign. From this period we receive the earliest glimpse into Black Elk's thoughts. Having been absent from the reservation for about two years, Black Elk wrote a letter in Lakota to give his people news of his whereabouts. The letter was printed in the *Iapi Oaye* (the "Word Carrier"), a monthly newspaper published in the Sioux language at Santee, Nebraska. Printed under the auspices of the Dakota Indian Mission of the Presbyterian and Congregational Churches, the paper was circulated widely and served as an important means of communication among the various Sioux agencies. The style of his letter suggests that Black Elk was not accustomed to expressing himself in writing, and translation presents some difficulties. Despite these limitations, the document is important for an understanding of Black Elk's own perception of his experience as he traveled for the first time in the white man's world:

Buffalo Bill's Wild West Show, Manchester, England

Feb. 15, 1888

Now I will tell about how I am doing with the wild west show. Always in my mind I hold to the law and all along I live remembering God. But the show runs day and night too, so at two o'clock we quit. But all along I live remembering God so He enables me to do it all.

So my relatives, the Lakota people, now I know the white men's customs well. One custom is very good. Whoever believes in God will find good ways—that is what I mean. And many of the ways the white men follow are hard to endure. Whoever has no country

---

4. The contracts are in Letters Received by the Commissioner of Indian Affairs, 1887–9555, enc. 1 and 2 (National Archives and Records Service, Washington, D.C., Record Group 75). From these contracts it is impossible to determine the actual dates on which they were signed; Black Elk probably joined the show during autumn 1886. Black Elk's boyhood name is recorded on the Pine Ridge census roll, 1890 (National Archives and Records Service, Record Group 75, Microcopy M595, roll 364).

will die in the wilderness. And although the country is large it is always full of white men. That which makes me happy is always land. Now I have stayed here three [two] years. And I am able to speak some of the white men's language. And a little while ago my friend gave me a translated paper [the *Iapi Oaye*] and I rejoiced greatly. Thus the Lakotas will be able to translate English.

Here the country is different; the days are all dark. It is always smoky so we never see the sun clearly. A little while ago this month, Feb. 7, 1888, a woman [one of the Indian women of the show] gave birth. This woman is called "Imim" and her father is called Little Chief. Now today they will baptize it, then February 15 at six o'clock that baby will have the law [be baptized]. So it is. With kindness I cause you to hear.[5]

When the wild west show closed in England in spring 1888, Black Elk became separated from the main party, and Buffalo Bill sailed for America without him. Stranded, Black Elk and two other Lakotas eventually joined another wild west show and traveled with it through Germany, France, and Italy. This gave Black Elk abundant opportunity to study the white man's way of life. In May 1889, Buffalo Bill returned to Europe, just a year after his departure, to open his show in Paris. Black Elk went to meet him there and received a ticket home. He returned to Pine Ridge in autumn 1889 and wrote a second letter which was printed in the December issue of the *Iapi Oaye:*

Black Elk's story

From Red Cloud [Pine Ridge Agency], my relatives the Lakota people, I am writing this letter in the language you understand. My relatives, I am Lakota. Back in about the year 1885 [1886] I stayed in New York; all along I remembered God. Across the ocean I came to what they call England. I stayed there one year, then again after crossing an ocean four days I came to what they call Germany. I stayed there one year. Then again sixty[?] days I crossed the ocean and I arrived there [England?] and I stayed one year. So thus all along, of the white man's many customs, only his faith, the white

---

5. *Iapi Oaye* (Santee Agency, Nebr.), 17(3) (March 1888):9. All translations from Black Elk's letters originally written in the Lakota language are mine, in collaboration with Vine V. Deloria, Sr.

man's beliefs about God's will, and how they act according to it, I
wanted to understand. I traveled to one city after another, and there
were many customs around God's will. "Though I speak with the
tongues of men and of angels, and have not charity, I am become as
sounding brass, or a tinkling cymbal. And though I have the gift of
prophecy, and understand all mysteries, and all knowledge; and
though I have all faith, so that I could remove mountains, and have
not charity, I am nothing. And though I bestow all my goods to
feed the poor, and though I give my body to be burned, and have
not charity, it profiteth me nothing" [1 Cor. 13].

So Lakota people, trust in God! Now all along I trust in God. I
work honestly and it is good; I hope the people will do likewise.
Then my relatives I will tell about something funny [ironic]. My
friend called Mexican Joe had a show that Lakotas joined—one
called High Bear, the other called Two Elk. We stayed in a place
called Manchester, England. I saw them in the show tent; they came
there and then I arrived. Then the tent burned and six horses died
and I also saw many other things burned.

Across the big ocean is where they killed Jesus; again I wished to
see it but it was four days on the ocean and there was no railroad. If
horses go there they die of thirst. Only those long-necks [camels]
are able to go there. [It would require] much money for me to be
able to go over there to tell about it myself.[6]

Black Elk's reference in the first letter to "holding to the law" refers to
his baptism as a Christian, probably in the Episcopal Church. This was
not a personal conversion, however; a stipulation of the contract with
Buffalo Bill was that all the Indians selected to join the show "shall be of
the same religious faith," and Buffalo Bill agreed to pay for a representative of that religious denomination to travel with the show and look after
the Indians' moral welfare.[7] This provided Black Elk with the opportunity to learn about Christianity; and his travels in the United States and
Europe allowed him to witness the daily realities of the white men's
civilization. The biblical passage from Saint Paul that Black Elk quoted in
his second letter suggests that he was favorably impressed by the con-

6. Ibid., 18(12) (December 1889):37.
7. See n. 4 above.

gruence between Christian belief and practice, for he found genuine hospitality among whites during the period in which he was lost from Buffalo Bill.[8] The second letter reveals Black Elk wrestling with fundamental Christian concepts, and expressing a desire to visit the Holy Land in order to study Jesus' life for himself. Such personal investigation lies at the heart of all Lakota attempts to understand the spiritual realm. Black Elk told Neihardt that while he was in Europe his own spiritual power disappeared, and perhaps this led him to Christianity. As soon as he returned to Pine Ridge, his power came back to him.

As a result of his trip abroad, Black Elk was able to understand some English, and he had a realistic perspective on the world. He took a job on Pine Ridge as store clerk; and, if the ghost dance, a millenarian American Indian religious movement, had not spread to the Sioux reservations at just this time, his life might have developed along a different path. Black Elk told Neihardt that although he at first stayed away from the ghost dances, he at last went to investigate this new religion for himself. At once he appreciated the parallel between the ghost dance and his great vision. The image of the sacred tree surrounded by the hoop of the people, just as he had seen in the other world so long before, struck him with such force that it flooded his life with renewed meaning. It was sent to him as a reminder, he thought, to get to work and help bring his people back into the sacred hoop of their traditional Indian ways.

The ghost dance proved a cruel disappointment to the Lakota people, but to none more than Black Elk. Rather than salvation, it brought death to as many as three hundred Lakotas at Wounded Knee, who were mowed down by gunfire in an unthinking, horrible slaughter. The disaster at Wounded Knee became a symbol to the Lakotas of the untrustworthiness of white men. Missionaries moralized it as the will of God, ending once and for all the pagan hold of idolatry on the Lakota people. But for many Lakotas it stood symbolically as an inpenetrable barrier between themselves and acceptance of white culture. The psychic cost was too high. One perceptive missionary commented, just after Wounded

8. Black Elk took these verses directly from the Dakota translation of the Bible, transposing them into the Lakota dialect. See Thomas S. Williamson and Stephen R. Riggs, trans., *Dakota Wowapi Wakan: The Holy Bible, in the Language of the Dakotas, Translated Out of the Original Tongues* (New York: American Bible Society, 1880), p. 273.

Knee, that the whole fiasco had left the Lakotas with a sense of dead indifference toward religion in general.[9]

Black Elk settled down in the Wounded Knee district of Pine Ridge Reservation and in 1892 married Katie War Bonnet.[10] Like so many other Lakotas who had been adapting well to civilization before the ghost dance, Black Elk seems to have turned his back on the white men's ways after the Wounded Knee massacre. Times were very hard. By the agreement of 1889 the Lakotas had surrendered over half of the Great Sioux Reservation, breaking up the remainder into five small, isolated reservations. All the intervening lands were opened to white settlement. Slowly the Lakotas tried to regain the economic progress they had achieved before the ghost dance. Black Elk continued to help his people in his role as medicine man and curer.[11]

During the years when Black Elk was away in Europe, Jesuits had established a Roman Catholic mission called Holy Rosary on the Pine Ridge Reservation in response to an invitation from Chief Red Cloud. Black Elk's practice of traditional healing ceremonies quickly brought him into conflict with the missionaries. He told Neihardt that once, when he was performing a ceremony, a Jesuit priest arrived and destroyed the sacred objects he used in his curing. The patient recovered, but the priest was killed soon after by falling from a horse.[12] It is easy to conjecture that

9. John P. Williamson, "Report of Missionary at Pine Ridge Agency," *Sixty-First Annual Report of the Commissioner of Indian Affairs to the Secretary of the Interior* (Washington, D.C.: Government Printing Office, 1892), p. 459. See Raymond J. DeMallie, "The Lakota Ghost Dance: An Ethnohistorical Account," *Pacific Historical Review* 51(4) (1982):385–405, for an interpretation that stresses the religious significance of the ghost dance.

10. Black Elk was twenty-eight years old, and his wife was twenty-four. Pine Ridge census roll, 1893 (National Archives and Records Service, Record Group 75, Microcopy M595, roll 365).

11. For a brief economic history of Pine Ridge Reservation, see Raymond J. De-Mallie, "Pine Ridge Economy: Cultural and Historical Perspectives," in *American Indian Economic Development,* ed. Sam Stanley (The Hague: Mouton, 1978), pp. 237–312.

12. The priest was probably Father Aloysius Bosch, S.J., who died in 1902 after being thrown from his horse. See *Red Cloud's Dream Come True: Holy Rosary Mission, 1888–1963* (Pine Ridge, S.D., 1963), p. 23, and Sister Mary Claudia Duratschek, *Crusading along Sioux Trails: A History of the Catholic Indian Missions of South Dakota* (Yankton, S.D.: Grail, 1947), p. 131.

it was the failure of white men to live up to the dictates of their own religion—even as exemplified in the simple virtue of charity—that embittered Black Elk toward whites during this difficult period in his life.

Nonetheless, he did not turn his back entirely on Christianity. It seems likely that his wife, Kate, joined the Roman Catholic Church. She bore Black Elk two sons, Never Showed Off in 1893 and Good Voice Star in 1895; they were both baptized as Catholics in 1895 and were christened William and John. William died in about 1897. In 1899 Kate gave birth to a third son, Benjamin, who was also baptized in the church.[13]

Black Elk continued to serve his people as a traditional religious leader during these years. In this capacity he performed the conjuring ceremonies called *yuwipi* in which the medicine man, wrapped in a robe and securely tied with thongs, is released mysteriously by spirit helpers. These spirits give messages concerning future events, cures, and lost objects and bring general well-being to those attending the ceremony. In darkness the spirits make their presence known through flashes of light, pounding, objects flying through the air, or the sound of eagles' wings or other animal noises. Black Elk told Neihardt that when he himself performed these ceremonies, women's voices could be heard singing all around the room. In later days it was reported that Black Elk had been famous for the love medicines he sometimes used in these ceremonies.[14]

Black Elk continued to be successful as a healer. His curing followed the shamanic tradition of his people, combining medicinal plants with psychological techniques that included a variety of tricks designed to assure the patient of the efficacy of the cure. Although denounced by missionaries as fraud, these psychological supports were essential to success in curing; they provided tangible proof of the medicine man's power, convincing the patient that the healer could cure him. Black Elk told Neihardt that one of his techniques—an impressive one indeed—was to bring up the little blue spirit that lived within him, spitting it into a cup of water during his healing ceremonies. Some Lakotas at Pine Ridge today say that one of Black Elk's demonstrations involved the creation of spon-

13. Birth and baptismal dates are taken from the Pine Ridge census rolls, 1893, 1896 and 1901 (National Archives and Records Service, Record Group 75, Microcopy M595, rolls 365, 367 and 368), and from the baptismal records of Holy Rosary Mission, Pine Ridge, S.D.

14. Wesley R. Hurt and James H. Howard, "A Dakota Conjuring Ceremony," *Southwestern Journal of Anthropology* 8 (1952):292.

taneous explosions, which he accomplished by placing charges of gunpowder in a fire. They say that this trick backfired on him once, causing an explosion directly in his face that permanently damaged his eyesight.

Shortly after the turn of the century, Black Elk turned his back on the entire practice of shamanic healing and joined the Roman Catholic Church. It seems impossible to understand fully the reasons for his decision. It was a slow process that stretched over two decades, for as early as 1888 he had begun his study of Christianity. Black Elk told Neihardt that, according to his great vision, when he reached age thirty-seven (1900) he was supposed to have used the soldier weed, a destructive power that would wipe out his enemies—men, women and children. But he confessed that he had refused to take the responsibility for such wholesale destruction, so he gave it all up and became a Catholic. Also at this time, about 1903, Black Elk's wife died, leaving him with two sons, John and Benjamin.[15] Whatever his immediate reasons, after having resisted the Jesuits for many years, Black Elk at last turned to Catholicism.

As Black Elk's daughter Lucy later told the story, the turning point had come in 1904. One day while Black Elk was treating a boy who was seriously ill, Father Joseph Lindebner, S. J., arrived. The priest, who was known to the Lakotas as Short Father (*Ate Ptecela*), had baptized the boy and now, judging him to be dying, had come to administer the last rites. Father Lindebner entered the tent and at once gathered up Black Elk's sacred objects; he jerked the drum and rattle from Black Elk's hands and threw them out of the tent. Grasping Black Elk by the neck he intoned: "Satan, get out!" Black Elk left the tent and sat dejectedly nearby. Lucy's account suggests that her father sensed that the priest's powers were greater than his own. When Father Lindebner finished his prayers he invited Black Elk to return with him to Holy Rosary Mission. There, after two weeks of instruction, he baptized Black Elk on December 6, giving him the Christian name Nicholas in honor of the saint whose feast day it was. Black Elk's conversion was unquestionably genuine. By accepting Catholicism he at last put himself beyond the onerous obligations of his vision, and he never practiced the Lakota religious ceremonies again.[16]

15. Pine Ridge census roll, 1904 (National Archives and Records Service, Record Group 75, Microcopy M595, roll 369).

16. The account of Black Elk's conversion as told by his daughter, Lucy Looks Twice, to Michael Steltenkamp, S.J., is quoted in Paul B. Steinmetz, S.J., *Pipe, Bible*

It is possible that one of the attractions that led Black Elk to Christianity was the access it provided to the social and material benefits of church life. From the beginning of the reservation period, the government had systematically suppressed all traditional social institutions—especially the tribal bands, the traditional chiefs, and the men's sacred and dancing societies—and tried to force the Lakotas to deal with the government as individual Indians rather than as a tribe. This attempt to destroy tribal solidarity lay behind all reservation policy. It countered every effort by the Lakotas to join together for political and social reasons, and it eliminated opportunities for individuals to exercise leadership abilities and attain personal prestige. Christian churches provided institutional structures that were not merely tolerated but encouraged by the government, allowing communities to organize themselves, with leaders and spokesmen who could represent their interests to the Indian agent as well as to other potential benefactors. Such men's and women's sodalities as the Roman Catholic St. Joseph and St. Mary societies could function as replacements for traditional men's and women's societies that had been fundamental social building blocks in earlier times. Annual religious congresses encouraged the Indians of each denomination to come together from all the reservations in South Dakota and adjoining states, creating large summer gatherings reminiscent of the encampments of the past. Church activities helped structure reservation life and provided individuals with avenues to achieve respect and attain influence. By the early 1900s, almost all Lakotas belonged at least nominally to one or another Christian denomination.[17]

Within the Catholic Church the men's sodality, the St. Joseph society, formed a substantial organizational support for the church. In order to join, prospective members had to apply first to the priest, then to the officers of the society. To be eligible, a man had to be a Catholic and learn

---

and Peyote among the Oglala Lakota, Stockholm Studies in Comparative Religion 19 (Motala, Sweden, 1980), pp. 158–59. Hilda Neihardt Petri recalled that her father repeatedly asked Black Elk to perform a *yuwipi* ceremony for him, but the old man steadfastly refused.

17. The first annual Catholic Indian Congress was held in 1891. Although this discussion emphasizes the positive aspects of mission activities, it is also true that there was real coercion on the part of the government to force Indians to join churches. For a history of Catholic missionization among the Sioux, see Duratschek, *Crusading along Sioux Trails.*

the basic prayers and precepts of the church. He had to hear Mass on Sundays and holy days, and he could not attend Protestant services. He also had to go to confession and receive the sacraments at least four times a year, and he had to respect all bishops and priests. Every member was enjoined to care for his family, have his children baptized, and educate them in Catholic schools whenever possible. Members were obliged to visit the sick, assist in burying the dead, and help the widows and children of deceased members. The use of intoxicating beverages was forbidden. Finally, members were given guidelines to follow their conscience in matters relating to Indian ways: "A member of the St. Joseph Society may go to Indian dances, but must govern his conduct properly; he shall not give away at dances things that his family needs, he shall not stay up too late at dances; and he shall not gamble away necessaries of life. All members have to abstain from all superstitious Indian customs."[18]

Black Elk became a staunch member of the St. Joseph Society in Manderson. In recognition of his zeal and of his excellent memory for Scripture and the teachings of the church, the priests soon appointed him to the position of catechist, an office that usually paid a stipend of $5 per month. At this time, Catholic missionaries were just beginning to experiment with appointing native catechists to help speed conversion and maintain the faith. Priests were able to celebrate Mass in the isolated communities on the reservation only about once a month, and in their absence catechists held Sunday services, led the prayers and hymns, read the Epistle and Gospel, and instructed the people—all in the Lakota language.

The missionaries supplied catechists with copies of *The Two Roads* picture catechism, printed in bright colors on a strip of paper one foot wide and five feet long. The catechism presented in pictorial form the basic concepts of Roman Catholicism, beginning with the Trinity and creation at the bottom and moving upward along two roads, a golden one leading to heaven and a black one leading to hell. The pictorial format avoided the problem of literacy and provided a degree of standardization of the catechists' teachings. Through the picture catechism the Lakota

18. "Rules for St. Joseph Society," in *Śina Sapa Wocekiye Taeyanpaha: The Catholic Sioux Herald* (Marty, S.D.: St. Paul's Catholic Indian Mission) 5(18) (November 1, 1936):7. See Louis J. Goll, S.J., *Jesuit Missions among the Sioux* (St. Francis, S.D.: St. Francis Mission, 1940), pp. 34–38.

catechists brought many converts into the church. In addition to their missionary role, the catechists also preached sermons, urging church members to remain faithful and uphold moral standards. They instructed children and taught them their prayers and rosary. They were responsible for visiting the sick, and in times of crisis they performed baptism and buried the dead. The missionaries quickly came to depend on these catechists, particularly because of their abilities to explain and persuade in the Lakota language, spreading the Word and keeping it alive. From the catechists' perspective, their role in the church provided them opportunities to help their people with practical as well as spiritual matters.[19]

The catechists took their work very seriously. From 1907 to 1912 Black Elk wrote letters in Lakota to the *Śinasapa Wocekiye Taeyanpaha,* the "Catholic Herald," a Sioux-language newspaper that began publication on the Devil's Lake Sioux Reservation in 1892. In these letters Black Elk reported news from Manderson, told of his church activities, and exhorted his people to be faithful to the church. On October 20, 1907, he wrote:

> My relatives, this year I have seen two events. Last July 14 I went to a large meeting of white men in Indianapolis, Indiana, and saw an event that nearly caused me to faint [in admiration]. Truly I saw how they were able to trust in God; truly, because they live with God, peace dwells with them. Therefore, my relatives, show respect to the priests who live with you and obey them, and hold on to what they tell you and stand firm. Thus peace will be with you, too. Then last September 20 there was a big meeting of the Catholic Church at Bull Head [South Dakota, on Standing Rock Reservation] and I went over there and the events that I saw were good. For this reason, my relatives, we must remember thoroughly all that the church reveals to us. In that way we will strengthen one another and good will be with us.[20]

Black Elk probably traveled to these meetings with Father Henry I. Westropp, a young Jesuit priest at Holy Rosary Mission who was especially zealous in his work with the native catechists. The trip to Indianapolis was for the purpose of attending the annual meeting of the

19. Duratschek, *Crusading along Sioux Trails,* pp. 206–7.
20. *Śinasapa Wocekiye Taeyanpaha* (Fort Totten, N.D.) 11(5) (December 15, 1907):4.

Federation of Catholic Societies to raise money for building mission churches in the reservation communities.[21] The meeting at Bull Head was the annual Catholic Indian Congress in South Dakota.

Father Westropp in 1907 proposed to Father William H. Ketcham, director of the Bureau of Catholic Indian Missions in Washington, D.C., that Oglala catechists be sent to missionize other Indian tribes; he argued that the cost would be small, that the catechists could speak to Indians of other tribes in sign language, and that they could start church societies like those at Pine Ridge. He wrote: "I think they could do more good in a way than many a priest." With some reluctance, Ketcham authorized the program and provided limited funds for a modest beginning. In 1908, Black Elk and Joseph Redwillow and their wives were sent to the Wind River Reservation in Wyoming to be missionaries among the Arapahoes. Father Westropp hoped the catechists would stay a year or more, but they returned before two months were up. The two catechists reported to Westropp that they had had a difficult time when they first arrived at Wind River, but that in the end they had been very successful. Westropp reported to Ketcham: "I still believe in the plan and I think now the ice is broken, they will have more success the next time. . . . Privately, I think that the Sioux have 'woke' the people up there a little."[22]

In the *Catholic Herald* of July 1908 Black Elk reported publicly on his first missionary journey:

> Last February 20 we went to the Arapahoe tribe in Wyoming and preached the gospel. Joe Canśaśa [Redwillow] and I held a large meeting with the people. We asked them to join the holy church of God but they did not give us any response, not knowing anything about the ways of the church. So the people did not know much of such things. With all our might we taught them about church work and now about half of the people believe and we organized a large St. Joseph society. And they had one good meeting for them and many men and women were baptized. . . .
>
> Now, my relatives, these people were suffering in spiritual dark-

21. See Goll, *Jesuit Missions among the Sioux,* p. 61.

22. Henry I. Westropp, S.J., to Father William H. Ketcham, Director, Bureau of Catholic Indian Missions, June 11, 1907, and April 2, 1908. Records of the Bureau of Catholic Indian Missions, Marquette University, Milwaukee, Wis. The total cost of this missionary venture was $70.

ness, but now they have joined the church. Therefore we should pray for them. . . .

Those of us here on earth who are suffering should help one another and have pity. We belong to one family and we have only one faith. Therefore, those who are suffering, my relatives, we should look toward them and pray for them, because our Savior came on this earth and helped all poor people. In the same manner we have one priest who has been with us two years. He is Father Westropp. He moves among the poor of us and seems to be everywhere and has enabled us to do a great deal of work. Moreover, he made a good meeting house and a good house [church?] for the Arapahoes. On our own reservation he has also built six good meeting houses. It seems that since then he has never been able to slow down anywhere, eager that the people may have the Kingdom of God; that is his great desire for us. In that way he seems to have taken some of the men and brought them to the mercy of God. He has many helpers. At Easter time a helpers' organization was started and they call it the St. Paul society. And they will defend the church and each year they will give a four-dollar offering. These things I want you to hear.[23]

Father Ketcham requested later that year that catechists be sent to the Winnebago Reservation in Nebraska. Father Westropp again sent Black Elk and Redwillow, suggesting that they stay as long as a year. They left early in November but returned only a month later. Ketcham was perturbed and wrote to Father Westropp in December to voice his concern that the would-be missionaries might simply be taking advantage of a good situation. "To an onlooker it would appear that I have become a bureau for travelling Indians," he wrote in frustration.[24]

Black Elk and the other catechists who participated in this missionary experiment seem to have perceived it as their primary duty to inform the people of the value of joining the Catholic Church and to induce them to form men's and women's societies that would serve as an institutional basis for future missionary work. Doubtless they considered this organizational aspect of church work to be the most essential, enabling Indians

23. *Śinasapa Wocekiye Taeyanpaha* 11(12) (July 15, 1908), reverse of supp. page.

24. Ketcham to Westropp, October 29, 1908, and December 12, 1908 (Records of the Bureau of Catholic Indian Missions). The cost of this trip was $60.

to deal more effectively with problems on their reservations. Refinement in dogma and belief could be left to the future work of priests. The trips the catechists took in the interests of the church were enjoyable interludes in the usual routine of life, as well as sources of income for their families.

Black Elk sent a letter to Father Ketcham, whom he had met at one of the summer congresses in South Dakota, in January 1909, asking for more money in connection with his missionary trip to the Winnebagos. Ketcham referred the letter to Westropp, who replied:

> The best reply to Uncle Nick's letter were a few kind words. To send him money would have been equal to committing suicide. To make him one present would plant a weed in his soul hard to weed out. Begging has become a passion with many of these fellows. They beg for grub to be sent out to them by express, though they will have to pay more for its carriage than it is worth. His trip to Winnebago netted him a nice little sum. Don't think that the harder of him for what I tell you. I am attending to him and he is on the way to prosperity—80 head of cattle coming to him within a year or so.[25]

Again Black Elk wrote to Father Ketcham on September 7, 1909, asking to be sent on further missionary work: "The Assiniboins in Canada want the prayer [the Catholic religion]. They want to see me very much." He also suggested spending two or three months traveling to the Sioux reservations to encourage children to join the Society for the Preservation of the Faith. In reply, Ketcham commended Black Elk for his zeal but informed him that he had no more money at present to continue such work.[26]

In summer 1909, Black Elk wrote again to the *Catholic Herald:*

> We are Indians who dwell on this earth, so I have seen the Arapahoes and Shoshones, [and the] Winnebagos who dwell to the south in the Omaha country. On account of the church I have traveled among the Rosebud, Cheyenne River, Standing Rock people, Pine Ridge people, and the white people. Therefore I

25. Westropp to Ketcham, January 29, 1909 (Records of the Bureau of Catholic Indian Missions).

26. Nic Black Elk to Ketcham, September 7, 1909; Ketcham to Black Elk, October 29, 1909 (Records of the Bureau of Catholic Indian Missions).

would like to say a few things. People from all over are going to come to the congress you are going to have of the universal church; when they speak words from God we should hold them strongly. There are many Indians in the U.S. but only a few belong to God's church; many are living unhappy lives. For this reason we should take in firmly what the priests tell us: these are God's words and so mankind should benefit from them in the name of our Savior. Those of you who belong to the church in this country, stand steadfast in it. Remember that God's Son suffered and died. It is not a matter of the children of God giving things to one another, for we are to have them forever. We are here on this earth temporarily and for he who walks the straight path and dies, there is rest waiting for him. Those who receive the blood of God's Son unworthily will die and suffer. My relatives, this is very difficult, so think of these things.[27]

Father Westropp took Black Elk with him on a visit to the Sisseton Reservation in the next year, 1910, attempting to renew the people's interest in Catholicism; early missionaries had converted a number of the Sissetons, but no priest had lived among them during the reservation period. This visit was to prepare the way for establishment of a permanent mission. There is no doubt as to Black Elk's real commitment to the work. Again in a letter to the *Catholic Herald,* written November 2, 1911, he voiced deep concern that the Lakotas should be sincere in their acceptance of Catholicism:

I am engaged in difficult work which is good onto death; let us not talk of our ways of the past, but think about the new ways our Savior has given to us. If you do this there will be peace and kindness. So it is.

Remember the words you have said in making declarations. You speak the words but your lives are lives of the old way. Therefore my relatives unify yourselves. Perhaps you cannot live lives split in two, which does not please God. Only one church, one God, one Son, and only one Holy Spirit—that way you have only one faith, you have only one body, and you have only one life and one spirit. Thus

27. *Šinasapa Wocekiye Taeyanpaha* 13(12) (July 15, 1909):3.

we have three but really we have One—thus he who unifies himself will have victory. So it is; read carefully.[28]

Black Elk wrote once again to Father Ketcham on January 9, 1912, to inform him that despite ill health he hoped to be able to continue his work for the church:

> Would like to notify you that I have live [sic] up to nineteen twelve and would like to notify you about my condition. Last nineteen hundred & four I became a catechist and during that time & at the present date. I have had quite a number join our flock and I expect to have quite a number more in the future but I am in a critical condition at present. Therefore I gave you thanks in Christ and wish for you to remember me in your prayers. I am now going to make my head way to Hot Springs for a treatment. I will be in Hot Springs 13th of this month. Therefore I beg you to find me a little help and would like to hear of you, too, and if our Savior gives me help on my sickness and restores my health I will again look into our business among my Catholic Sioux's. I sincerely wish to hear from you soon. In the name of our Savior we praise you.
> Yours in Christ,
> Nicholas Black Elk

Father Eugene Buechel, S.J., at Holy Rosary Mission, forwarded Black Elk's letter to Father Ketcham, adding the following comments:

> The enclosed letter has been written by Nick Black Elk, one of our Catechists, or rather somebody wrote it for him. It is also true that he is sick & went to Hot Springs. In case you should feel inclined to help him a little be sure to send the money to the *sisters* of the Hospital. Black Elk is an efficient Catechist, but like many fullbloods a very poor manager. He will always be a beggar, no matter how much money one would give him. At the end of last [Catholic Indian] Congress I gave him $10.00 for extra work done. The next day he begged again for he had distributed the money among the visitors from Standing Rock. He never has anything and always

28. Duratschek, *Crusading along Sioux Trails*, p. 262; *Śinasapa Wocekiye Taeyanpaha* 16(6) (January 15, 1912):4.

asks for something. Poor fellow! And yet he can do a great deal and has done much in the past.[29]

From Father Buechel's letter, a clearer picture of Black Elk as a catechist begins to emerge. On the one hand, holding to Christian doctrine, he practiced the virtue of charity to its fullest. On the other hand, he was able at the same time to fulfill the traditional role of a Lakota leader, poor himself but ever generous to his people. Churches, with the access they provided to resources, gave many Lakotas means to help their people in both the material and the spiritual senses. At the same time, these leaders gained prestige by earning the people's respect. In a significant sense, effective leadership for the Lakotas shifted during the early reservation period from political to religious spheres.

In 1906 Black Elk married Anna Brings White (also known as Brings White Horses), a widow who lived with her five-year-old daughter, Emma Waterman, in the Manderson area. That year she gave birth to another daughter, Lucy Black Elk. In 1914 a son named Nick, Jr., was born. Paralleling Black Elk's role as a catechist, Brings White became active in the church as a member of the St. Mary society. Together the two grew to be respected leaders in the Catholic community of Pine Ridge Reservation. Johnnie Black Elk, the older surviving son by Black Elk's first wife, died in 1909. In 1915 Ben was sent east to be educated at Carlisle Indian School. That summer he was placed on a farm in Pennsylvania as part of the school's "outing system," to provide students with practical work experience. Concerned for his son's spiritual well-being, Black Elk wrote to Carlisle School to learn whether Ben was attending Mass regularly.[30]

The illness that in 1912 had forced Black Elk to Hot Springs for treatment was tuberculosis. He suffered from it throughout his life, and it

29. Nicholas Black Elk to Ketcham, January 9, 1912; Eugene Buechel, S.J., to Ketcham, January 19, 1912 (Records of the Bureau of Catholic Indian Missions).

30. Pine Ridge census roll, 1907 (National Archives and Records Service, Record Group 75, Microcopy M595, roll 369); vital dates taken from tombstones, St. Agnes cemetery, Manderson, S.D.; Letters Received by the Commissioner of Indian Affairs, 1915–118828, Carlisle File 820 (National Archives and Records Service, Record Group 75); Stephen McNamara, S. J., "Black Elk and Brings White," *Indian Sentinel* (November 1941):139–40; marriage records, Holy Rosary Mission, Pine Ridge, South Dakota.

must have affected his personality. It was a continual drain on his strength. No doubt he accepted it as part of the cost of reservation life, for tuberculosis reached epidemic proportions on Pine Ridge in the early twentieth century.[31]

Father Westropp had raised enough money by 1913 to construct a Catholic church on the Sisseton Reservation, where his visit with Black Elk three years before had met with real success. No priest was available for the mission, so Father Westropp sent Black Elk and Ivan Star, another Pine Ridge catechist, to teach the gospel and keep the church alive. When Father Westropp returned to Sisseton in 1914 he found that the catechists had done their work well: already the congregation numbered 130. Black Elk was especially close to Father Westropp and traveled with him frequently. When Father Westropp was reassigned to missionary work in India in 1916, it was a personal loss for Black Elk. Thereafter he seems to have ceased his missionary travels, focusing his attention instead on his people at home.[32]

In 1917 Black Elk requested that his son Ben be sent home from Carlisle School—perhaps fearing that he would join the army and go off to the world war. The Pine Ridge Indian agent, J. R. Brennan, wrote to the superintendent of the school on Black Elk's behalf: "The father of Ben Black Elk, a pupil of your school, whose enrollment expires this year, asked that his son be allowed to return home at once. The father is practically blind, and needs the son to help him in what farming he is attempting, and in the care of his stock. If you can excuse the boy, and send him back home at this time, I think he will be of assistance to his father."[33] Black Elk's request was granted, and Ben was sent home in July.

The Jesuit fathers at Holy Rosary Mission continued to depend on Black Elk as a leader among the catechists on Pine Ridge. During Holy Week 1922, Father Placidus F. Sialm gave the first of an annual series of retreats for Oglala catechists at the mission. He told one anecdote from that retreat over and over throughout his life; it signified for him, per-

31. See James R. Walker, "Tuberculosis among the Oglala Sioux Indians," *Southern Workman* 35 (1906):378–84.

32. Duratschek, *Crusading along Sioux Trails*, pp. 285–86.

33. J. R. Brennan to John Francis, Jr., Superintendent, Carlisle Indian School, May 2, 1917 (Pine Ridge agency records, "Correspondence—Carlisle Boarding School," Federal Archives and Records Center, Kansas City, Mo., Record Group 75).

haps, a turning point in the Lakotas' acceptance of the church. In Father Sialm's words: "On the third day of that retreat, Nick Black Elk came to me with this very worthy resolution: 'We catechists resolve never to commit a mortal sin.'" That year Father Sialm organized the first annual Corpus Christi Sunday procession at the mission church in Oglala community. Over one thousand Lakotas participated as Father Sialm, arrayed in the full splendor of his priestly garb, carried the consecrated host while four Lakota men held a canopy above him; further back in the line, Black Elk led the older Indians, all of them dressed in their native finery. It was a symbolic union of old and new, to bring the living presence of Christ to bless the Oglalas and their country. Black Elk's own life was fitting testimonial to this union of Christian and native traditions.[34]

The *Indian Sentinel,* a quarterly fund-raising publication of the Bureau of Catholic Indian Missions, in 1925 published a photograph of Black Elk (taken circa 1910), dressed in his usual vested suit with collar and tie, instructing his daughter. Her hands are folded in prayer as he displays a rosary, holding out the crucifix to her. The following year the *Sentinel* ran as its cover illustration a stylized drawing based on the photo—with Black Elk dressed in native buckskins and eagle feather warbonnet. These illustrations, widely circulated on the Indian reservations, cannot have failed to express their intended message to the Lakotas, as they did to whites. Black Elk symbolized the dawning of a new day for the Indians.[35]

Black Elk was apparently called on regularly to represent the old-time Oglalas at Pine Ridge on special occasions. He seems to have maintained his reputation as a showman, begun during his travels with Buffalo Bill. It seems likely that he was involved in early Indian shows in the Black Hills, some of the first tourist entertainments in South Dakota. In 1925 he probably attended the dedication of Mount Rushmore as a national memorial. Carving of the gigantic monument had not yet begun, but on October 1 a ceremony was held there to publicize the project and attempt to gain popular support.[36]

34. Placidus Sialm, S.J., "Camp Churches" (manuscript in the Records of the Bureau of Catholic Indian Missions), pp. 62, 86. See also Sialm, "A Retreat to Catechists," *Indian Sentinel* 3(2) (April 1923):78.

35. *Indian Sentinel* 5(2) (Spring 1925):81; 6(4) (Fall 1926), front cover.

36. This event did not get widespread news coverage. Photographs of an unidentified Indian man on top of Mount Rushmore, taken on this occasion, appear in the *Black Hills Engineer,* Mount Rushmore Memorial Issue 18(4) (November 1930):338–39.

Father Buechel built a catechist's house near the church in Oglala community, north of Holy Rosary Mission, in 1926, and he called Black Elk there to take over the work. The Black Elks' house became a kind of mission center, with neighbors often gathering to pray and sing hymns. Black Elk assisted the priest in instructing the children, and he conducted services on Sundays when the priest was unable to come. He was counselor and advisor to his people, visiting the sick and bringing others to the church by the power of his preaching and the persuasion of his example. One missionary estimated that Black Elk was personally responsible for at least four hundred conversions through his work as catechist.[37]

Over the years Black Elk came to head a large and respected family. His children married and had children of their own. Black Elk's son Ben settled at Manderson, where the family raised some horses and cattle. Although his eyesight continued to deteriorate and his health began to fail, Black Elk nonetheless enjoyed a happy and rewarding life, adjusting to the changing times with courage and ingenuity. He was a shining example to whom the missionaries could point with pride: his life fulfilled their conviction that through the acceptance of Catholicism, the Indians could be led out of heathenism into the enlightenment of civilization. From all outward appearances, Black Elk had made the transition with remarkable success.

A series of critical turning points in Black Elk's life permanently altered its direction. The first was his vision, the next his trip with the wild west show to Europe; then there was the ghost dance, and finally his acceptance of Catholicism. In 1930 one more critical event occurred that, like the others, had important repercussions throughout the rest of his life. An unfamiliar car drove up to Black Elk's house in Manderson in August; and Black Elk sensed a powerful presence. The visitor was John G. Neihardt, poet laureate of Nebraska, who was visiting the Sioux country preparatory to writing the final volume of his epic poem *A Cycle of the West,* which would tell the story of the ghost dance and culminate in the massacre at Wounded Knee, symbolizing the completion of the white men's conquest of the New World. Accompanied by his son Sigurd and by Emil Afraid of Hawk as interpreter, Neihardt hoped to talk to Black Elk about the ghost

37. Sialm, "Camp Churches," p. 88; Joseph A. Zimmerman, S.J., "Catechist Nick Black Elk," *Indian Sentinel* (October 1950):101–2.

dance religion, to try to understand its emotional overtones and, as he later wrote, "the deeper spiritual significance of the matter."[38] Neihardt probably did not know that both Black Elk and Afraid of Hawk were Roman Catholic catechists, pillars of the church at Pine Ridge. Under such circumstances the likelihood that Black Elk would talk about non-Christian spiritual matters would be slight, and Afraid of Hawk warned Neihardt that the old man would probably refuse to talk to him.

But Black Elk responded to Neihardt with remarkable intensity. He announced: "As I sit here, I can feel in this man beside me a strong desire to know the things of the Other World. He has been sent to learn what I know, and I will teach him."[39] A more suspicious person might have questioned both Black Elk's truthfulness and his sincerity, but the rapport that grew almost immediately between the two men left no room for suspicion. Neihardt described the meeting in a letter written soon afterward:

> He [Black Elk] struck me as being a bit uncanny in his intuitions; not that he favored me, but that he seemed to know what was inside the visitor. He told me—the sphinx-like old chap—that, as he sat there, he felt in my heart a very strong will to know the things of the other world and that a spirit, which stood behind me, had forced me to come to him that I might learn a little from him. In spite of the sound of this statement, he was very modest, modest as a man may be who is sure of what he knows and that what he knows is worth knowing. I had no difficulty whatever with him. He seemed to be expecting me and welcomed me as though he had seen me often. He began by saying that he must tell me his whole story in so far as it could be done in the time we had, but that it would take a long, long time to tell it all. First, he said that he could not speak to me without giving me some reason to know that he had authority to speak. "I am just a common man, but I have a gift of vision, which has been hereditary in my family and I must tell you of my people before I tell you of my life so that you may trust me."[40]

38. Neihardt, "Preface," *Black Elk Speaks* (1979 ed., cited hereafter), p. xv. Neihardt referred to his interpreter as "Flying Hawk," but cf. Sialm, "Camp Churches," p. 60.

39. Neihardt, "Preface," p. xvii.

40. Neihardt, "Letter to Julius T. House, August 10, 1930," in *Present-Day American Literature* 4(3) (1930):95–97; copy courtesy of Lucile F. Aly.

It was as if something long bound up inside the old man had broken free at last, an impulse to save that entire system of knowledge that his vision represented and that for more than twenty-five years he had denied. Since becoming a Catholic Black Elk had strictly put away the old ceremonies and his healing rituals. He had accepted the white man's religion and the white man's ways, and this would not change. But the vision, and his failure to live up to it, must have been a heavy burden. This burden he could at long last transfer to another man—someone who could record the old Lakota ways as testament and memorial to a way of life now gone forever.

Later, Neihardt wrote: "The sun was near to setting when Black Elk said: 'There is so much to teach you. What I know was given to me for men and it is true and it is beautiful. Soon I shall be under the grass and it will be lost. You were sent to save it, and you must come back so that I can teach you.'"[41] Black Elk asked Neihardt to return in the spring, when he would be ready to teach the spiritual knowledge of his people. As a compact between them, Black Elk gave Neihardt a present:

> Before I left, Black Elk presented to me a beautiful old sacred ornament that he had used a long while in the sun dances in which he has officiated as priest. This ornament consists of a painted rawhide morning star to which are attached by thongs an eagle feather and a strip of buffalo hair. He told me the meaning of this. He said that the morning star signified the desire for and the certainty of more light to those who desire, that the eagle feather signified high thinking and feeling, as the eagle flies high, and that the buffalo hair signified plenty of that which is needed by men in this world. And as he gave me the sacred ornament, he said that he wished me all these things.[42]

41. Neihardt, "Preface," p. xviii.

42. Neihardt, "Letter to House." The sacred ornament is a circle with notches cut around the circumference, made from an old rawhide parfleche. The front side is painted deep blue, and the reverse shows part of the original painted design of the parfleche. Suspended from the center are a dark mottled eagle wing feather and some shed buffalo hair woven with thread to form a pendant. In *Black Elk Speaks*, p. xvii, Neihardt wrote that Black Elk also interpreted the eagle feather as signifying *Wakan Tanka*.

Neihardt returned to his home in Branson, Missouri, determined to find some way to undertake the work with Black Elk. He wrote to William Morrow, the New York publisher, and explained the proposed project. Morrow gave him a contract to write a book about Black Elk in October and provided him with an advance to pay for the costs of another, longer visit to Pine Ridge. On November 6, 1930, Neihardt wrote to Black Elk to arrange for the interviews:

Dear Friend,

Your letter of November 3 has just reached me, and I am very glad to hear from you! . . .

Now I have something to tell you that I hope and believe will interest you as much as it does me. After talking with you four and a half hours and thinking over many things you told me, I feel that the whole story of your life ought to be written truthfully by somebody with the right feeling and understanding of your people and of their great history. My idea is to come back to the reservation next spring, probably in April, and have a number of meetings with you and your old friends among the Oglalas who have shared the great history of your race, during the past half century or more.

I would want you to tell the story of your life beginning at the beginning and going straight through to Wounded Knee. . . .

So, you see, this book would be not only the story of your life, but the story of the life of your people. . . .

I would, of course, expect to pay you well for all the time that you would give me. . . .

This is not a money-making scheme for me. I can make money much faster and easier in other ways. I want to do this book because I want to tell the things that you and your friends know, and I can promise you that it will be an honest and a loving book.[43]

The stage was set. Black Elk would tell of his visions and of his life experiences, and some of his friends would tell about episodes in Lakota history of which Black Elk himself could not speak from firsthand experience. Standing Bear, one of Black Elk's closest friends, would draw a

---

43. Neihardt to Black Elk, November 6, 1930; original shorthand draft in the Neihardt Collection; printed in part in *Black Elk Speaks,* pp. 277–79.

pictographic record of the Wounded Knee massacre, as well as other related scenes, to illustrate the book.

Neihardt left Branson for his eagerly awaited meeting with Black Elk on May 1, 1931. This time he took along his two older daughters: Enid, an accomplished stenographer, who served as his secretary, and Hilda. Neihardt gave a reading in Lincoln, Nebraska, the following day. On May 4 the Neihardts visited the old family home in Bancroft, then went on to Wayne to stay with Julius T. House, one of Neihardt's closest friends, who had published in 1920 the first study of the life and work of Nebraska's poet laureate. On the next two days Neihardt lectured at Nebraska Normal College in Wayne, and on May 7 they were back on the road. They drove through rain over slick, muddy roads and arrived in Gordon, Nebraska, just south of the boundary of Pine Ridge Reservation the next day.[44]

On Saturday, May 9, the Neihardts began the last leg of their journey. They made one final stop, to visit the Wounded Knee battlefield and the hill where the bodies of the victims lay in their long communal grave. This spot was to form the backdrop for the final scenes of Neihardt's *Song of the Messiah*, to be the final volume of *A Cycle of the West*, and it was important that he know the landscape thoroughly. Then they drove north, toward Manderson, where they met two of Black Elk's sons, who were borrowing beds for their visitors' use. As the Neihardts followed the boys to Black Elk's house in the hills beyond the town, Hilda noticed men busily hauling barrels of water from the creek. On a knoll in front of the house a large new tipi of white duck had been erected, with the flaming rainbow of Black Elk's vision painted above the doorway and the vision power symbols painted on the sides. The material for the lodge had been provided by Roy Wooden, the trader in Manderson. Nearby, the Neihardts noticed a startlingly new privy, obviously constructed for their convenience. Around the house and the tipi a circle of freshly cut pine trees, uniformly small, had been thrust into the ground. Partway down the slope in front

44. Julius T. House, *John G. Neihardt: Man and Poet* (Wayne, Nebr.: F. H. Jones & Son, 1920), Details of the 1931 visit are taken from Neihardt's "Preface"; Enid Neihardt's stenographic diary and shorthand drafts of Neihardt's correspondence in the Neihardt Collection; and interviews with Hilda Neihardt Petri.

of the tipi was a small circular dance bowery, also constructed of fresh pine boughs.

When the visitors entered Black Elk's one-room log cabin, they found the entire household bustling with activity. There was no formal welcome. The visitors were expected and they had arrived. The tipi—a gift to Neihardt—had been set up to lodge the visitors during their stay, but the night was so chilly that they preferred to sleep in the house. Neihardt requested that Black Elk send word to some other elderly men in the neighborhood to come and tell of their experiences, in order to fill out Black Elk's story. They would begin in the morning.

It is impossible to know fully what the two men's expectations were at the outset. In terms of his own career, Neihardt was primarily concerned with coming to an intuitive understanding of the ghost dance in order to give life to the *Song of the Messiah*. At the same time, he had his contract with William Morrow for a book based on Black Elk's life story; and the small advance the publisher had given him allowed him to make the journey and bear the expenses of providing food to Black Elk and his family and friends while the interviews progressed. But the material that he was to be given by Black Elk and his friends was, as he later confessed in a letter to Morrow, "richer than I had expected it to be."[45]

Black Elk, for his part, was tying together the ends of his life. Now, at age sixty-seven, he was returning to the days of his youth to tell about his great vision, and the sacred power from the six grandfathers, which he had put behind him when he converted to Roman Catholicism. Surely the decision to disclose the sacred teachings and to preserve them for the benefit of posterity—rather than to let them die, completely replaced by the white man's religion—had not been made lightly. Black Elk sensed an interest and a power in Neihardt that was kindred to his own, and he felt compelled to respond to it. As Enid Neihardt noted in her diary on that day of their arrival at Black Elk's home, "We found that he had made many arrangements for us and apparently he considered this as one of the great things of his life."

The next morning, May 10, they started work at the break of day. Several elders began to arrive to participate in the talks, including Fire Thunder, Standing Bear, Chase in the Morning, and Holy Black Tail

45. Neihardt to William Morrow [June 1931]. Shorthand draft, Neihardt Collection.

Deer. Hilda remembers that many others came uninvited and that each one sat on the ground a respectful distance from the house with his back to the proceedings. Then Ellen, Ben Black Elk's wife, would ask Neihardt if the newcomer could be fed. After this invitation had been extended, the man would join the group. The women of Black Elk's family prepared three meals that day, feeding all who came.

Meanwhile, the work began very slowly. The girls perceived it as real drudgery. Black Elk would make a statement in Lakota, which his son Ben then translated into English. Ben spoke the idiomatic "Indian English" typical of the time—a dialect that had arisen out of the need for Indian students in off-reservation boarding schools, coming from many tribes and speaking many different languages, to communicate with one another in English. Neihardt would repeat Ben's translation, rephrasing it for clarity in more standard English. When necessary, the sentence was repeated to Black Elk in Lakota for further clarification. As each sentence came forth in revised form from Neihardt's repetition, Enid wrote it down in shorthand. The method took time to perfect. At the start of the morning, Enid wrote in her notebook: "To begin with my father name Black Elk, his father name Black Elk, his son name Black Elk, 3rd one Black Elk. 4th of the name Black Elk. His father was Medicine Man as far back remember." This reflects the halting beginning of the interviews, but shortly the channel of translation and communication began to improve, and soon the narrative was coming in grammatical sentences. The quality of the stenographic record improved steadily throughout the first few days of interviewing. What was written down was not, strictly speaking, a verbatim record of Black Elk's words, but a rephrasing in comprehensible English. While this could sometimes be one or two steps removed from the old man's actual words, in the long run it was likely to generate fewer misunderstandings and to be more faithful to the intended meaning than a strictly verbatim recording. In a sense, Neihardt was already "writing" Black Elk's story by rephrasing his words in English.

The material recorded on that first day came in large part from the other men present. As they were older than Black Elk, they were better able from firsthand knowledge to describe the historical context of the great vision, which had occurred in 1873. They told of fighting the whites in Wyoming during the 1860s when the hated Bozeman Trail was blazed through the middle of their best hunting grounds and the soldiers built forts in the Sioux country to defend the road. Then Black Elk told of his earliest mystical experiences during childhood, hearing voices when he was only four years old and seeing a portent of his great vision when he was five. By then the day was over, and the stage was set for revealing the great vision.

But the next day Neihardt had to leave. He was scheduled to speak at the normal college in Chadron, Nebraska, on May 12. So the Neihardts set off on the road again. The girls enjoyed the plains scenery and the novelty of prairie dog towns; Neihardt stopped to shoot two prairie chickens for their dinner. Two days later, on May 13, they returned to Black Elk's home in the evening, ate supper, and slept for the first time in their tipi.

In the morning they began to record the great vision, but they did not make much progress. The Indians had made hoops and spears for the old game that had once been a favorite pastime of boys and that had also been played ceremonially by men to bring good fortune in the buffalo hunt. Much of the day was spent playing the game; the girls went horseback riding in the hills around Manderson. There was a bustle of activity all day as preparations were made for the great feast to be held on the following day. Neihardt bought a fine little Holstein bull from Lucy, Black Elk's daughter, and the men butchered it in the traditional manner, crowding around to eat pieces of the liver steaming hot from the dead animal. Neihardt tasted it out of politeness and pretended to enjoy it immensely. Mischievously, Enid offered him more—which he firmly refused. The Indian men enjoyed it as a rare treat, reminiscent of buffalo hunts in the old days.

Over two hundred people, from throughout the entire district, began to gather for the feast on May 15. A number of local whites attended the celebration, including Dorothy Cook, a reporter for the *Lincoln State Journal*.[46] The Neihardt girls made a last-minute trip to town to buy prunes for the women to make *wojapi*, an Indian pudding of sweetened fruit, thickened with flour. This was cooked in large cans, while pots of highly sweetened coffee simmered by the fire. The meat had been cut up, and most of it was roasted over an open fire. The rest was made into soup in the traditional manner: the beef paunch, filled with water and strips of meat and suspended from a tripod, served as a kettle and the soup was

---

46. Dorothy Cook, "J. G. Neihardt Made a Member of the Sioux Tribe," *Nebraska State Journal* (Lincoln), Sunday, June 7, 1931, p. 26.

cooked by dropping heated stones into it. This was how men out on war parties had made soup.

All the Indian people who could do so dressed in their traditional finery, painting their faces in the old way for this special occasion. Black Elk wore a brilliant cerise shirt, beaded cloth leggings, a dancer's porcupine hair-roach, and around his head a band of fur with a single eagle feather affixed to the front. Standing Bear wore his yellow-painted beaded buckskin war shirt and leggings, and a double-trailer war bonnet of eagle feathers. Holy Black Tail Deer, Chase in the Morning, and others of the old men also wore their war bonnets. Some of the spectators had only everday clothes of blue denim overalls to wear, but even they painted their faces red, the sacred color. One old man painted his face half red, half yellow.

The ceremony began late in the morning as Black Elk lit his long-stemmed pipe and presented it in prayer to the six directions, invoking the blessing of the six grandfathers on the proceedings. This was the day Black Elk would take Neihardt as his son, making the relationship between them public, preparing him to receive the teachings of his holy vision. After the prayer, Black Elk smoked the pipe and presented it to Neihardt for the ritual four puffs; then it was passed around the circle of the old men, who witnessed and validated the proceedings.

In early afternoon the men carried a drum into the pine bowery down the hillside, and six singers dressed in everyday clothes formed a circle around it. The crowd drifted toward the sound of the drum. One by one the old men rose to recite their coups (literally, "kill talks"), testifying to their right to dance and participate in the ceremonies. Standing Bear rose first and told about his part in the fight on the Greasy Grass River (the battle of the Little Big Horn) in 1876: "We were in camp on the Greasy Grass when something happened. The soldiers were coming. I went to get my pony. It was a gray pony. Then the Indians charged. The bullets were raining. It was so smoky and dusty we could see nothing. Then suddenly I met one of the soldiers face to face, and I pulled my pistol out and shot him."[47]

Holy Black Tail Deer made the next kill talks. Dorothy Cook wrote: "His story was told in the Sioux tongue but an interpreter sat near the

47. These kill talks are recorded in steno notebook 1, "Black Elk's Vision," Neihardt Collection.

edge of the circle and explained his words. He told a dramatic tale of his early youth. . . . With vivid gestures and appropriate actions he half acted and half told the story of his youthful bravery, his commanding voice punctuated occasionally by loud drum beats by way of applause. The crowd murmured its approval when he concluded his tale."[48]

Enid Neihardt recorded Holy Black Tail Deer's words in her notebook:

> There was a man lying there amidst the bullets, and I saved him. Afterward I ran my horse up against a bank and they retreated, and I tried to get on top of a bank, and some men pushed me over and I got scalps of the men. Then I returned. I saved two of my friends and then I scalped the enemy, and when I got home the people said: "We knew you were going to do this because you are brave." This happened when I was about fifteen years old. At this present time a fifteen-year-old boy couldn't do this, but when I was that age, boys were men at this age.
>
> [I was] about twelve years old at that time, and there was a fight between the Crows and Sioux, and they had quite a skirmish. The Sioux were camped, and the Crows were upon them before they knew it. I was out looking for horses. There was a blind man in camp, and I went and rescued him from among the bullets. The people said about this: "We knew you were going to do it."

After reciting his coup, each man had to make a present to the singers, who had sung in his honor.

Black Elk got up to make the last kill talk. The singers sang this song:

> With great difficulty they are bringing him.
> (Meaning that he is wounded.)
> Black Elk the great—with great difficulty
> they are bringing him.

The song memorialized Black Elk's participation in the fight against the soldiers after the Wounded Knee massacre. Then Black Elk gave his talk:

> The Oglalas were camped somewhere I don't know, but up the Wounded Knee Creek there was something going on, so I went up on my pony. I got up on top [of] the hill, and it was terrible! Sol-

---

48. Cook, "J. G. Neihardt Made a Member of the Sioux Tribe."

diers were standing there mowing the women and children down!
[*There I stood and cried.*] So I decided that I must defend my people
some way, and I just went over. I depended on my vision, and so I
went down and showed the soldiers what power I had; and the
bullets were raining, and again I came within three hundred yards
of them and I wasn't shot. Soon we made a retreat. I did all I could
do to defend my people. It was hopeless. So I decided to take it just
as it was. It was a butchering, and I cried because I couldn't defend
my people in time.

When he finished, Black Elk gave a dollar to the singers.

After the kill talks ended, the people were told to climb up the hill for
the ceremony in which the Neihardts were to be adopted into the tribe.
Neihardt and his daughters were deeply moved when the older men
announced that they wanted them to be members of the Oglala tribe from
then on.

The men made long speeches about each girl, concluding with these
words: "And we know that when in the future there may be only one
Indian left alive, she will be a friend to him." Then they were given names
to mark their new identities, each name referring to an aspect of Black
Elk's holy vision. Enid recorded in her diary that she was called She Walks
with Her Sacred Stick (*Sagye Wakan Yuha Mani Win*). "This means that
I shall be very prosperous in the future and shall have a large family and I
would probably be married soon, too." Hilda was given the name
Daybreak Star Woman (*Anpo Wicahpi Win*). Enid wrote: "Indians get
their whole knowledge and wisdom from this star and Hilda is to have lots
of knowledge and wisdom." The singers, accompanied by a chorus of
women, sang in the girls' honor.

The old men then made a speech about Neihardt, naming him Flaming
Rainbow (*Peta Wigmunke*). Enid scribbled in shorthand on the back of
her notebook as the name was bestowed: "Whenever the rain is over there
is always the rainbow with a beautiful sight. Your thoughts are beautiful
and from your thoughts the rainbow goes out and they get knowledge out
of it. Gives acclaim to his work. His world is like the garden and his words
are like the drizzly pour of rain falling on the thirsty garden. Afterwards
the rainbow stands overhead. The rainbow is like his thoughts and whenever the rain passes over there will be a rainbow. (All colors = thoughts.)"

We can begin to glimpse Black Elk's perception of Neihardt by understanding the significance of this naming ceremony. By bestowing the

name Flaming Rainbow on him, Black Elk was making him share in the vision. The flaming rainbow was the power that marked the entryway to the home of the six grandfathers; it was their guardian and their symbol. As Flaming Rainbow, Neihardt was to enact the role of this power on earth by making the vision "go out"—like the flames from the rainbow—so that people would understand its meaning.

At this point in the interviews, surely Neihardt could not fully comprehend the meaning of the vision, but he did understand the obligation that Black Elk was placing on him to serve as his spokesman through his writing. Neihardt had told Black Elk that in his youth he had been a lyric poet, which the old man translated in Lakota as *iyapi kaǧe*, "talk maker," and which Neihardt thereafter expressed in English as "word sender." But, Neihardt told Black Elk, in his maturity, seeking a higher purpose, he had become an epic poet; this the old man translated as *hanbloglaka*, "vision telling," the traditional mystical speech of Lakota holy men when they told about their sacred vision experiences.[49] Such speech always embodied the specific symbols of a man's vision, obliquely expressed, and was the source of power when repeated in ceremonial context.

For Black Elk, Neihardt as an epic poet was not only a relater of visions, but one who could use vision power to do good. In this way Black Elk undoutedly saw his own vision as an integral part of Neihardt's ongoing lifework. As Neihardt later wrote, Black Elk "was utterly unaware of the existence of literature"—nor did he understand it.[50] But he was literate in Lakota, and he appreciated the Bible as a written source of religious inspiration. Neihardt perceived Black Elk's religion in terms of art; Black Elk perceived Neihardt's art in terms of religion. Both tried to use their special skills to enrich human life by merging it into something greater than the individual.[51] In Lakota fashion, Black Elk conceptualized the relationship between himself and Neihardt in terms of kinship, and he

49. These Lakota terms are recorded in Enid Neihardt's typed transcripts of the Black Elk interview notes, Neihardt Collection.

50. Neihardt to Morrow [June 1931].

51. Neihardt conceptualized the relationship between religion and art as follows: "It is important to note how Art blends, by imperceptible degrees, into Ethics; while in the realm of its origin it is obviously one process with essential Religion. . . . And is not every religious dogma an art form originally intended to function as the medium of this same passionate desire for loss of self in the great process of which we are a part?" John G. Neihardt, *Poetic Values: Their Reality and Our Need of Them* (New York: Macmillan, 1925), pp. 105–6.

thereafter called Neihardt "son" or "nephew"; Neihardt usually called Black Elk "uncle." Flaming Rainbow was now not only an adopted Oglala, he was also a man with a sacred duty.

After the naming ceremony, dancing began immediately in the bowery. Dorothy Cook, the newspaper reporter, wrote:

> . . . the drummer took his place within the circle of little pines and the dances began. Among the many that they performed, the favorite was the modern Rabbit dance. This is the only one in which the steps are performed by couples. The man standing to the right of his partner with his arm about her shoulders and hers around his waist, they progress in an inefficient, roundabout manner by taking two steps forward and one back with an occasional whirl. It is a love dance, and simple as the steps are, there seems to be a great deal of merriment over its execution. The words to the song, repeated over and over are "Come let us dance together for this is the only time that I can see you." The sight of Nebraska's dignified poet laureate being dragged thru the steps of the Rabbit dance by a large and blandly smiling Indian woman brought shrieks of laughter from the bystanders. Enid, who had been sitting crosslegged beside the interpreter writing what he said in shorthand, was seized by an Indian named Standing Bear, while another, Chase-In-The-Morning, took her sister to join in the dance.[52]

Although Indian dancing was the major form of recreation on the reservation, the Bureau of Indian Affairs placed severe restrictions on when and where such dances could be held. Government officials blamed the rabbit dance in particular for encouraging licentiousness. In fact, at the 1929 annual Catholic Indian Congress, Father Buechel had denounced the rabbit dance as one of the "chief evils threatening the family" among the Oglalas, and the delegates (of whom Black Elk was one) had pledged to abstain from participating in it. Neihardt, however, was armed with letters of support from the Board of Indian Commissioners and the Secretary of the Interior, and the agent at Pine Ridge had given him special permission to sponsor this celebration.[53]

52. Cook, "J. G. Neihardt Made a Member of the Sioux Tribe." The article incorrectly gives Chase in the Morning's name as "Shines-In-The-Morning."

53. Frank T. Dietz, S.J., "Catholic Indian Congress of 1929: Sioux Catholic Congress Inspiring," *Indian Sentinel* 9(4) (1929):151–52, 183; permission letters include Ray

The dancing recessed late in the afternoon for the feast but resumed toward dark. The old men danced the war dance, acting out their coups and giving more kill talks, and by firelight the rabbit dance continued far into the night.

The next day everyone was tired. Neihardt wrote that the entire bull had been eaten, with the exception of the hoofs and horns—and later the hoofs were eaten, too.[54] Enid's diary entry for the day begins: "Today everyone was recuperating over yesterday's wonderful time." Everyone was sleepy, so they worked only for a while on the vision, and the girls went horseback riding.

Neihardt's interviews with Black Elk as the old man related his vision were not private. The other old men stayed around to listen and to eat, serving as witnesses to the truthfulness of Black Elk's story. Working intensively for three days, May 17–19, they finally completed Black Elk's great vision. All the listeners were excited and amazed by the great vision. Black Elk had not revealed it before, so even Standing Bear and Ben Black Elk were hearing it for the first time. Ben could hardly find the English words to translate his father's account, for this was all new to him. "I always knew the old man had something," Hilda remembers Ben saying. "Ain't it wonderful!"

The economic burden of feeding so many began to weigh on Neihardt's slim financial resources, so on May 20 the party moved down to Standing Bear's property, in a wooded area a short distance away, where they cooked their lunch. There they began Black Elk's story of his youth; Standing Bear was the only other old man present.

May 21 was a full day, and the interview took place in the draw behind Black Elk's house. That day Enid wrote in her diary: "We learned a lot from the old men, Black Elk, Iron Hawk, and Standing Bear. They are telling us about the life of Black Elk and how it corresponds to Black Elk's vision. We did a steady job of it all day, only stopping in the noon time to get something to eat." May 22 was much the same. Enid wrote: "We rose this morning with the familiar blasts of Ben's voice saying: 'Come and get

---

Lyman Wilbur, Secretary of the Interior, to Neihardt, May 1, 1931, and Malcolm McDowell, Secretary, Board of Indian Commissioners, to B. Courtright, Superintendent, Pine Ridge, May 8, 1931 (letter enclosing copy of telegram), Neihardt Collection.

54. Neihardt to Ray Lyman Wilbur [June 1931]. Shorthand draft, Neihardt Collection.

it or I'll throw it out!' Well, it was worth getting alright. We did another day of talking. This time the real old men, Iron Hawk, Standing Bear, and Black Elk were the talkers. We got some fine things today from the old men. We camped down in the draw back of Black Elk's place. . . . This was a really hard day. I believe I worked harder today than any other day so far."

The story must have been completed up through the Custer battle in 1876 by Saturday, May 23. Evidently the other old men had all gone back to their homes, for the remainder of the story is told by Black Elk alone, and there is no further mention of any of the others in Enid's diary. That morning they worked out under the pine sunshade at Black Elk's house. Enid wrote: "We got a few good things today, but not nearly so many as we got the day before. The main thing was history today and Black Elk is not nearly so good at remembering his history as he is in telling things about himself. When he talks about his vision he is marvelous!" That afternoon Black Elk began to tell about the horse dance.

The next day brought a break in the routine. The Neihardts rose early and drove with Black Elk to the Wounded Knee battlefield. There the old man told about the events of 1890, pointing out where each action had taken place. He also showed them the scar on his body received there from a soldier's bullet. They made camp for the day along Wounded Knee Creek, and Black Elk completed the story of the horse dance. Neihardt keenly appreciated the pageantry of the prancing ranks of variously color-ed horses (representing the four world directions), and he felt that it would make an excellent subject for a movie. Black Elk offered to provide an entire village as a background and to stage the dance if Neihardt could get the backing. The old man saw it as an opportunity to spread the message of his sacred vision on a larger scale than he had ever thought possible—and besides, Neihardt held out hope that there would be mon-etary profit in it with which Black Elk could support his family.[55]

That day Neihardt and Black Elk both talked about their outlook on life. Neihardt was growing closer and closer to this old Oglala man; though their races were different, Neihardt sensed that their philosophies were remarkably similar. He later wrote to his publisher: "There was a very peculiar merging of consciousness between me and Black Elk, and his

55. Neihardt to William Morrow [June 1931]; Neihardt to Nicholas Black Elk, June 27, 1931. Shorthand drafts, Neihardt Collection.

son, who interpreted for me, commented on the fact. Very often it seemed as though Black Elk were only repeating my own thoughts or my own poetry although he knows no English and is utterly unaware of the existence of literature. Also, at various times, he would say, 'He has guessed this already,' and once he said, 'This man could make an ant talk. I think he could make an ant talk.'" To House, Neihardt wrote: "A strange thing happened often while I was talking with Black Elk. Over and over he seemed to be quoting from my poems, and sometimes I quoted some of my stuff to him which when translated into Sioux could not retain much of its literary character, but the old man immediately recognized the ideas as his own."[56]

In the quiet bottomland of Wounded Knee Creek, Neihardt told Black Elk about a dramatic incident he had experienced some years before. In writing *The Song of Hugh Glass* (1915), he had been required to identify the location on the upper Grand River where Glass had been mauled by a bear in 1823 and to describe in detail the features of the terrain as Glass crawled more than one hundred miles to Fort Kiowa, downstream on the Missouri. Because Neihardt could not afford to visit the area, he had been forced to rely on intuition for his description. In 1923 he joined a group of friends who had been inspired by the poem to erect a monument to Glass at the site of his mishap. Neihardt feared they would be disappointed in him when they discovered that the landscape differed from the description in the poem. To his surprise, the old bank of the Grand (its location had subsequently shifted) was exactly as he had described it.[57]

Black Elk was not surprised by the story, and certainly he found it to be no mere coincidence. He said:

> [*When a man sits down making something, in his mind it will be full of all kinds of thoughts equal to the books you have written. You are what they call a man thinker. As you sit there, in your mind there is a kind of a power that has been sent you by the spirits; and while you are doing this work in describing this land, probably there is a kind of a power that did the work for you, although you think you are doing it yourself. Just like my vision; a man goes without food twelve days he'll probably die, and during*

56. Neihardt to Morrow [June 1931]; Neihardt to Julius T. House [June 3, 1931]. Shorthand drafts, Neihardt Collection.

57. John G. Neihardt, *The Song of Hugh Glass* (New York: Macmillan, 1915). See Aly, *John G. Neihardt*, pp. 83–84.

this time probably they were feeding me. But all this while I was in a form
of the vision. It seems that I was transformed into another world.]58

Just as Black Elk held the power to heal from the spirits, so he understood
that Neihardt held his power to write as a gift from the spirits.

Neihardt told Black Elk that when he was eleven years old he had
experienced a powerful dream that in many ways mirrored the old man's
vision. Like Black Elk, Neihardt had fallen suddenly ill. In the dream he
saw himself flying through space, arms and hands forward, much as Black
Elk had followed the two messengers to the rainbow tipi of the six grandfathers. In Neihardt's dream there was empty vastness and dreadful speed,
a great voice driving him on. The dream recurred three times during the
night; in the morning his fever was gone and he was well again. Neihardt
interpreted this dream as a mandate for his lifework, driving him to strive
for literary success—a spiritual striving that reflected his conception of
the higher purpose of human existence. Nearly twenty years later,
Neihardt wrote a poem entitled "The Ghostly Brother" that identified the
cosmic force of the dream with a spiritual alter ego, a fate or guide: "I am
you and you are I." The poem expresses tension between the two egos, the
spiritual leading forward, urging the other to follow "through the outer
walls of sense," and toward a higher reality, while the earthly fears the
challenge and begs to stop and enjoy life's worldly comforts. The poem is
an important expression of Neihardt's personal quest for meaning in life,
and he understood it in much the same way that Black Elk had understood
his vision—as Neihardt wrote, furnishing "the dynamic plan for Black
Elk's life."59

Black Elk listened carefully to Neihardt's story, which perhaps helped
the old man to understand in his own terms how it was that Neihardt had
come to him. He said:

[*This was a power vision that you had. The dream when you were*
eleven years old. It was your brother ghost who had the power to describe

58. Steno notebook 3, "Wounded Knee," Neihardt Collection. Italics in brackets
indicate material not transcribed from shorthand by Enid Neihardt; see A Note on the
Editing, in Preface.
59. The poem is printed in John G. Neihardt, *The Quest* (New York: Macmillan,
1928), pp. 175–78. For Neihardt's own account of the dream, see John G. Neihardt, *All Is*
But a Beginning: Youth Remembered, 1881–1901 (New York: Harcourt Brace Jovanovich,
1972), pp. 47–49.

*that land that you did not see and had been helping you to do all these
other things. I think this was an Indian brother from the happy hunting
grounds who is your guide. The work you were assigned was man thinker.
For my part, I am sorry; I should have done my deed, and because I did
not do it I have been punished. I should have gone through my vision and
performed everything on earth and then I would have prospered. At the
same time, the tree that was to bloom just faded away; but the roots will
stay alive, and we are here to make that tree bloom.*][60]

He revealed his own understanding of the significance of Neihardt's visit
and of the book he would write:

> [*Before I ever saw you I wondered about the dream; and your brother
> ghost has put you here to do good to your people, and through you your
> people have their knowledge. Furthermore, this vision of mine ought to go
> out, I feel, but somehow I couldn't get anyone to do it. I would think about
> it and get sad. I wanted the world to know about it. It seems that your
> ghostly brother has sent you here to do this for me. You are here and have
> the vision just the way I wanted, and then the tree will bloom again and
> the people will know the true facts. We want this tree to bloom again in
> the world of true that doesn't judge.*][61]

Neihardt replied, *"All great spiritual visions triumph in this world by
being diffused,"* and Black Elk answered, *"Yes, that is true."*

Enid noted in the record: *"When we're through with the story, Black Elk
wants to put in just a few words."*

This conversation was undoubtedly an important breakthrough in
understanding between the two men. Neihardt was not merely collecting
material for his poem or for the book he would write about Black Elk. He
was sharing in the spiritual burden that had been placed on the Oglala
holy man so long before by the six grandfathers—and that Black Elk had
denied for so long—to spread the message of his vision as a means to
bring about human happiness and harmony, to better men's lives. For
Black Elk, as for Neihardt, it was a striving after higher purpose. Neihardt
later wrote of his experience at Pine Ridge: "There were times when I felt
very humble before these old men, and especially when Black Elk, who is

60. Steno notebook 3, Neihardt Collection.
61. Ibid.

in spirit a great poet, was describing the great vision upon which his whole life has been based."[62]

During the afternoon clouds began to build, and it looked as if it might rain, so the party returned to Manderson. Early the next morning, May 25, they started out for a trip to the badlands country, in the northwestern portion of Pine Ridge Reservation. By noon they had arrived at the property that Black Elk owned in the badlands. From there the Black Hills were blue silhouettes rising against the western sky, and the party could make out Harney Peak, the highest in the Black Hills, the center of the world to which Black Elk had been taken in his vision. They lunched on prairie chickens Neihardt had shot on the way; then Black Elk talked for four hours, continuing his life story. Afterward they decided to visit the stronghold, the badlands fortress where the ghost dancers had gathered to protect themselves from the soldiers. Enid wrote in her diary: "Before we went we had a prayer made by Black Elk, which was a prayer to the six grandfathers of his vision, wishing that they should help Daddy to make a success of this book and hope that we would be together again in the near future."

Enid recorded the old man's words as they sat gazing across the rugged badlands toward the Black Hills.[63]

The more I talk about these things the more I think of old times, and it makes me feel sad, but I hope that we can make the tree bloom for your children and for mine. We know each other now, and from now on we will be like relatives; and we have been that so far, but we will think of that deeply and set that remembrance down deep in our hearts—not just thinly, but deeply in our hearts it should be marked. From here we can see the Black Hills and the high peak to which I was taken to see the whole world and [the spirits] showed me the good things; and when I think of that it was hopeless it seems before I saw you, but here you came. Somehow the spirits have made you come to revive the tree that never bloomed. We see here the strange lands of the world [the badlands], and on this side you see the greenness of the world [the plains] and down there the wideness of the world [the prairies], the colors of the earth. And

62. Neihardt to Ray Lyman Wilbur [June 1931].
63. The following is from steno notebook 3, Neihardt Collection.

you will set them in your mind. This is my land. Someday we'll be here again; thus I will do a little prayer before we go home, and you will have that down in your heart that you will make a success out of this. So we shall name that butte Remembrance Butte. You will remember the six grandfathers, and the sixth one [*is myself and perhaps I am the sixth one*] that stands before you, and I am speaking of the truth that really happens. And furthermore, that Remembrance Butte will always be remembered because this is the land that I have assigned to my children. This was the land that was my favorite, and in this land my children will prosper; and with this proposition I hope you will have success in it. Perhaps some day we will be here again, and whenever we see this butte we will always think of what it means.[64]

The six grandfathers set upon this world many things, all of which should be happy. Every little thing is sent for something, and in that thing there should be happiness and making each other happy. With the tender grasses showing their tender faces to each other, thus we should do, and this was the wish of the six grandfathers.

As Black Elk began his prayer, he had his son Ben stand at his right hand to represent his generations on into the future; Neihardt with Enid and Hilda stood on Black Elk's left, representing their generations. Then he prayed:

Hey-a-a-hey! (four times)
Grandfather, the Great Spirit, behold us on earth,
      the two-leggeds. The flowering stick
      that you have given to me has not bloomed,
      and my people are in despair.

64. "The greenness of the world" (*awanka toyala*, extended green) refers to the rolling expanse of the great plains; "the wideness of the world" (*oblayela*, flatness) refers to the level prairies. See Melvin Randolph Gilmore, "On the Ethnogeography of the Nebraska Region," manuscript in the Nebraska State Historical Society, Lincoln. Black Elk and Neihardt never returned to this spot together. In 1942 the federal government confiscated the badlands portion of the reservation for military use as an aerial gunnery range. Families living in the area were forced to move. Today, much of this land has become part of the Badlands National Monument, administered jointly by the National Park Service and the Oglala Sioux Tribe.

To where the sun goes down to the six grandfathers where
        you have placed them, thus guarding the whole universe
        and the guidance of all beings.
And to the center of the earth you have set a sacred stick
        that should bloom, but it failed.
But nevertheless, grandfathers, behold it and guide us; you
        have beheld us. I myself, Black Elk, and my nephew,
        Mr. Neihardt. Thus the tree may bloom.
Oh hear me, grandfathers, and help us, that our generation
        in the future will live and walk the good road with the
        flowering stick to success.
Also, the pipe of peace we will offer it as we walk the good
        road to success.
Hear me, and hear our plea.[65]

Everyone was deeply moved by the earnestness of the old man's prayer. When he had finished, they went on to the stronghold, then returned to Manderson after dark.

The next morning they sat out under the pine sunshade to work; the women brought their dinner so as to interrupt the session as little as possible. During the afternoon they continued the work at the sacred butte near Black Elk's house where he regularly went to pray. Enid wrote in her diary that the scenery was beautiful, much like the badlands. But after they had been there an hour and a half a rainstorm drove them back home. That night, after supper, the girls joined in a rabbit dance.

There was another hard day of work on May 27. Again they stayed at home and worked under the pine shelter, and again that evening they had a dance after supper, with Black Elk singing and dancing for them. The girls enjoyed it immensely.

The next morning most of Black Elk's household went to Holy Rosary Mission for the Catholic Indian Congress, which was being held this year on the Pine Ridge Reservation. Because Black Elk was one of the senior catechists, his absence was no doubt conspicuous. Nonetheless, he stayed at home with Ben and that day at last finished telling his life story up through the ghost dance troubles. With the story completed, Black Elk had finally transferred his spiritual burden to Neihardt: it would never trouble him again. He said that while he talked he had the queer feeling

65. Steno notebook 3, Neihardt Collection.

that he was giving his power away, and that he would die soon after. Neihardt later wrote to his publisher: "At various times Black Elk became melancholy over the thought that at last he had given away his great vision, and once he said to me, 'Now I have given you my vision that I have never given to anyone before and with it I have given you my power. I have no power now, but you can take it and perhaps with it you can make the tree bloom again, at least for my people and yours.'"[66] Hilda recalls that Black Elk said to Neihardt: "I have given you my power, and now I am just a poor old man."

Black Elk told Neihardt very little about his later life, his experiences in the Catholic Church, his travels to other Indian reservations as a missionary, and his work as a catechist at Pine Ridge. Neihardt was curious about why Black Elk had put aside his old religion. According to Hilda, Black Elk merely replied, "My children had to live in this world," and Neihardt did not probe any further. For Neihardt, the beauty of Black Elk's vision made the formalism of Christian religion seem all the more stultifying, and he seems to have accepted Black Elk's pragmatic explanation at face value.

The next day, May 29, the Neihardts loaded their car with the painted tipi cover and many other presents from their friends in Manderson and headed for the Black Hills. The old man and his son came along in Ben's Ford. The culmination of the visit was to be a climb to the top of Harney Peak, where Black Elk would pray to the six grandfathers that the tree of his vision would bloom at last. Hilda recalls that somewhere along the way they passed through a small town where a county fair was in progress. In a mischievous spirit, they put Black Elk on the ferris wheel. Much to the old man's consternation, the wheel became stuck with Black Elk high in the air. When it came down, he hollered " 'top!"—but to no avail; he was to get the full ride.

That evening they all took in a movie, an old-fashioned black and white melodrama. Although Hilda doubted that the old man was able to follow the story, he reacted visibly to the image of the scantily clothed, seductive heroine that appeared upon the screen. Grasping the arms of his theater seat he mumbled, "*Śice, śice!* [Bad, bad!]."[67]

66. Neihardt to William Morrow [June 1931].

67. Neihardt related this incident of the movie in his newspaper column, "Of Making Many Books," *St. Louis Post-Dispatch,* July 3, 1931 (clipping in the Neihardt Collection).

That night they rented a tourist cabin in the Black Hills at Sylvan Lake, the foot of the trail leading up Harney Peak. They climbed to the top the next morning, with Black Elk walking eagerly but stopping frequently to rest. Neihardt later wrote to Morrow: "On the way up he told his son that if he had any power left surely there would be a little thunder and some rain while he was on the Peak. This is a curious thing and equally interesting for it, but at the time we were going up and after we were on the Peak, the day was bright and clear. During his prayer on the summit, clouds came up and there was low thunder and a scant, chill rain fell, but the old man seemed broken and very sad."[68] When they arrived at the top, Black Elk stepped behind a large rock, removed his white man's clothing, and donned long red underwear—a substitute for the body paint regularly used by Sioux of the time while dancing, although the Neihardts felt that the underwear was a concession to the presence of the girls. According to Enid's diary, he wore over this a black (probably dark blue) breechcloth trimmed with green. On his feet were high, patterned stockings and fully beaded moccasins that he had gotten from the trader in Manderson. He wore a headdress of buffalo hide with a single eagle tail feather fixed transversely at the front and several others hanging down from the back; the feathers were tipped with plumes dyed pink. In his left hand he carried a simple T-bowl catlinite pipe, the pipestem ornamented with colored ribbons symbolizing the four world directions and a single eagle tail feather symbolizing *Wakan Tanka*. His prayer, Neihardt wrote, "was a beautiful thing,"[69] and Enid recorded it in full in the journal (see below, pp. 294–96).

Arriving back at Sylvan Lake too late to be served dinner in the lodge, they bought roast beef sandwiches to eat in their cabin. After a short rest they drove to Hill City, where Neihardt filled Ben's car with gas and oil. Enid wrote in her diary, "We told them goodbye and sadly parted." Neihardt wrote to Ben, after he returned home, "We were really very lonesome."[70] The Neihardts spent the night in Deadwood, intending to go on to the Custer battlefield in Montana; but car trouble delayed them,

68. Neihardt to William Morrow [June 1931].

69. Neihardt to Julius T. House [June 3, 1931].

70. Neihardt to Benjamin Black Elk, June 27, 1931. Shorthand draft, Neihardt Collection.

and after waiting two days in Spearfish for parts to be sent from Denver they drove directly back to Branson.

Back home, Neihardt was anxious to get to work. He had written to House from Spearfish, "This is going to be the first absolutely Indian book thus far written. It is all out of the Indian consciousness."[71] He planned to call Black Elk's story "The Tree That Never Bloomed."

The vision Black Elk had experienced was exciting to Neihardt. Hilda remembers him exclaiming time and again, "I know of nothing in the whole history of religious literature to equal it!" He was anxious to share what he had learned with his readers, for he had found in Black Elk a critical perspective on the whole of civilization. In his first newspaper column after his return,[72] he wrote:

> Recently, as a result of four weeks spent with the old men of the Ogalala Sioux, this writer was able to feel with extraordinary intensity the profound and perhaps fatal truth about our civilization in its dominant aspects. During that time he was able to lose himself in the consciousness of those essentially primitive men, and it so happened that the whole mood of the experience was determined by one of them in whom the highest spiritual conceptions of his race have flowered in beauty and wisdom.
>
> The empty country and the social vacuum made it an easy matter to forget the flood of vicious and silly books that constitute so great a portion of contemporary literature, which is nothing if not an expression of the dominant contemporary consciousness. Actually, the too familiar twentieth century world passed away like a dream, to be remembered only at intervals when one was forced to buy something from a store conducted by a very "shrewd" business man indeed,[73] or when the old Ogalala seer happened to say something like the following: "The Great Spirit made the Two-Legged to live like relatives with the Four-Legged and the Wings of the Air and all

71. Neihardt to Julius T. House [June 3, 1931].

72. Neihardt, "Of Making Many Books."

73. Hilda Neihardt Petri recalls her father's rage when an unscrupulous reservation merchant suggested that he sell bootleg whiskey at the feast and naming ceremony, offering to split the profits with Neihardt.

things that live and are green. But the white man has put us in a little
island and in other little islands he has put the four-legged beings;
and steadily the islands grow smaller, for around them surges the
hungry flood of the Wasichu (white men) and it is dirty with lies
and greed."[74]

At such a time one could insist with pathetic truth that there are
many, many, many good men and women among the "Wasichu."
"Of course," was the reply, "but surely they, too, shall drown."

For Neihardt, Black Elk's teachings were no mere antiquarian record of
the past; rather, they served as commentary on the present, drawing a
general message for mankind out of the specific details of Oglala history
and culture.

As soon as the Neihardts had reached home, Enid began to make a
typewritten transcript of the interview notes. In the process she rear-
ranged the material roughly in chronological order and smoothed out the
grammar when necessary—particularly in the notes for the early sessions,
which reflected the confusion of establishing an efficient recording system. Otherwise her transcript follows the stenographic notes exactly.
Occasionally she deleted a phrase or brief passage, in most cases probably
because the information seemed redundant.

Meanwhile, Neihardt wrote to William Morrow to suggest producing
a motion picture version of Black Elk's horse dance. He asked the publisher, "Does this idea strike you as having any possibilities? If so is there
some way that you and I could work together in promoting the idea with
the proper people? If we were successful, this might help a great deal in
pushing the book." Evidently Morrow was interested in the idea.
Neihardt sent the publisher's reply to Black Elk: "You will see that my
publisher thinks the best chance is to try to make a picture of the whole
book rather than of the Horse Dance alone. I think perhaps this will be the
best way, because there will be a story to tell and people like stories.
Anyway, you may be sure that my publisher means business and knows
how to do business. If anything comes of this, you can depend upon me to
see that you get what is just as your portion."[75]

But nothing came of the plan. William Morrow died during the win-

---

74. See below, "The Indians and the white people," pp. 288–90.
75. Neihardt to Morrow [June 1931]; Neihardt to Nicholas Black Elk, June 27, 1931.

ter; and although his publishing house did publish *Black Elk Speaks,* Neihardt missed Morrow's personal support. On his own, he was unable to find backing for a motion picture venture.

Part of Neihardt's enjoyment of his visit with Black Elk came from the attraction he felt for the country on Pine Ridge Reservation; he wanted to be able to return to it. He wrote to House: "As a matter of fact I am planning simply on buying a section of land near Manderson for a ranch. It is very beautiful, has a half mile of Wounded Knee Creek in it and is full of prairie chickens and jackrabbits. We could all live very happy there and may do so." This section bordered on Black Elk's allotment, and Ben Black Elk promised to get the section numbers that identified the land so Neihardt could investigate buying it. Although Neihardt wrote to the superintendent at Pine Ridge concerning the matter, nothing came of it. The Depression and war years were to be hard ones for the Neihardts, during which additional financial obligations would be impossible.[76]

Despite these disappointments, Neihardt remained confident of the book he would write. In June he wrote to Black Elk to reassure him: "Enid is now copying on the typewriter the notes she took of your story, and very soon I shall be able to get to work on the book. It is going to be a really big book, and you are going to be happy about it I know. Keep this in mind when you feel lonesome or sad and it will cheer you up. The finest things in your life are going to be saved for other men. This ought to make you happy."[77]

Neihardt wrote *Black Elk Speaks* in longhand, on oversize sheets, working primarily from Enid's transcript. For historical data on battles, and for some of the information on Crazy Horse and other chiefs, he referred to the source material he had amassed during his work on *The Song of the Indian Wars.* Neihardt was an extraordinarily faithful spokesman for Black Elk; what he wrote was an interpretation of Black Elk's life, but not one that was embellished in any way. Instead, he tried to write what he thought the old man himself would have expressed. The book is Black Elk's story as he gave it to Neihardt, but the literary quality and the tone of the work are Neihardt's. Much later Neihardt commented in an inter-

76. Neihardt to Julius T. House [June 3, 1931]; Neihardt to Benjamin Black Elk [June 1931]; Neihardt to B. G. Courtright, Field Agent, Pine Ridge [June 1931]. Shorthand drafts, Neihardt Collection.

77. Shorthand draft, Neihardt Collection.

view: "*Black Elk Speaks* is a work of art with two collaborators, the chief one being Black Elk. My function was both creative and editorial. . . . The beginning and ending [of the book] are mine; they are what he would have said if he had been able. . . . And the translation—or rather the *transformation*—of what was given me was expressed so that it could be understood by the white world."[78]

In line with his assertion that this was to be "the first absolutely Indian book," Neihardt minimized everything that reflected Black Elk's knowledge and experience in the white man's world previous to his travels with the wild west shows. The book retains the intensely personal quality of the interviews; Black Elk becomes both the spokesman for and the symbol of the Indian people as his life experiences reflect their gradual defeat by the inevitable force of white civilization. The book is written in deceptively simple language. Neihardt told Black Elk at the outset that he would "use as much of your language in it as possible." Lucile F. Aly, Neihardt's literary biographer, notes that the simplicity of the style reflects our expectation of Indian speech patterns. The use of Indian expressions like "yellow metal" for gold and "four-leggeds" for horses reinforces the illusion of Indian speech. But she also notes that the simple, concrete style frequently reflects underlying abstraction. Similarly, Neihardt's dependence in the book on "flattened" adjectives like "good" and "bad" again reinforces the impression of Indian style and simultaneously suggests Indian stoicism. Only a literary master like Neihardt could use these techniques with such precision as to prevent them from degenerating into stereotypical "Indian talk" of the Hollywood movie variety. And Neihardt succeeded brilliantly. As Aly notes, this was not a totally new style for him; similar language appears both in his early Indian stories and in *The Song of the Indian Wars*.[79]

It was Black Elk's great vision that must have presented Neihardt the greatest challenge as a writer. This was, after all, the core of what Black Elk had wanted to tell Neihardt in order to record it for posterity. The historical events and autobiographical anecdotes were all incidental to Black Elk's purpose: to save his vision for mankind. But from a literary perspective the problem was what should be saved, the details of the vision or its meaning? Black Elk never stated succinctly what he considered the mean-

78. McCluskey, "*Black Elk Speaks:* And So Does John Neihardt," pp. 238–39.
79. See Aly, *John G. Neihardt*, pp. 175–76.

ing to be; he left this for Neihardt to interpret. In one sense the meaning is that the powers of the Lakota universe exist and have the ability to aid mankind in all endeavors, to protect people from disease and from their enemies and to bring joy and contentment. These powers were not simply replaced by the Christian God whom Black Elk came to accept; instead, they represented an alternate approach to the unknowable, another path to the "other world." Therefore the vision was good and true and important to save for mankind, as a lesson and perhaps as a plan—to make the "tree blossom," bringing Indians and non-Indians together in the harmony of a common circle. It is this universalistic message that Neihardt chose to emphasize, generalizing the vision as a means to understanding humanity writ large. Thus he presented the vision as an integral whole, of and for itself, drawing no parallels to other religious systems, and letting the vision's very uniqueness speak for its universal value.

To that end, Neihardt presented the vision in his narrative at the chronological moment in Black Elk's life when it occurred, developing the theme of the vision as a pattern for Black Elk's life. Neihardt resisted the publisher's attempt to relegate the vision to an appendix.[80] Although it was long and involved, and posed the danger of boring or losing the reader, it was essential for understanding the mission and purpose of Black Elk's life. It was necessary to abridge the vision so that it would be appreciated by a non-Indian reader, however, cutting it down to essentials so that it would fit into a manageable chapter. Cultural details were not so important to Neihardt as were the mood and the message. Accordingly, he decided to minimize the imagery of warfare and killing—the power to destroy that complemented the power to make live. By so doing, Neihardt set off Black Elk's vision from other published Lakota vision accounts, most of them centered on the bestowal of power for success in warfare. Though warfare was integral to traditional Lakota culture, it was not the aspect of that culture to emphasize in order to develop the universalistic message of the vision. So Neihardt cut and edited, focusing the published story of the vision on the powers to heal that Black Elk used later in life to help his people. Black Elk himself had rejected the power to destroy when he turned his back on the vision and embraced Catholicism, and this alone gave Neihardt justification for accentuating those aspects

80. Ibid., p. 171.

of the vision that were most important for understanding Black Elk as a healer.

One other important decision colored Neihardt's presentation of the great vision. This was a Thunder-being vision—a vision of the powers of the west, the vision of a *heyoka*. Although in it Black Elk was presented with powers from all six directions (the four quarters—north, east, south, and west—as well as earth and sky), the first grandfather's house to which he was taken was the cloud tipi of the Thunder-beings, a conventional Lakota vision symbol for the west. But later in his life, when Black Elk went on a vision quest at the age of eighteen, he had a second Thunder-being vision (which Neihardt called "the dog vision"), after which he at long last performed the *heyoka* ceremony. To have emphasized the extent to which the first vision was a Thunder-being vision would have forced either cutting the later vision or presenting repetitious material. Because the reader's patience was likely to be taxed by these vision accounts, Neihardt chose to minimize the Thunder-being powers of the great vision. This was doubly appropriate because the west presented Black Elk with destructive powers. Minimizing the association of the great vision with Thunder-beings simultaneously minimized the warlike symbolism and heightened the emphasis on the vision's curative, life-giving powers.

Neihardt's interpretation of Black Elk's vision is valid and consistent. It hews closely to the way Black Elk himself interpreted his vision later in life. It seems likely that for Black Elk, minimization of warlike themes in the vision resulted from his Christian perspective. Neihardt's motives for minimizing them, on the other hand, stemmed more from humanitarian than dogmatic concerns. Although motivated differently, both men developed the same meaning out of the vision. While working on the book, Neihardt expressed his intentions in a letter to Black Elk: "We are going to do something real with this book about 'The Tree That Never Bloomed' and I am sure that you are going to be a good deal happier because of this book. Keep a good heart and be patient until next spring when the book appears. I have to work hard on the book and be patient too, and I can do both with a strong heart because I know that the book is wise and good and that thousands of people will find good in it."[81]

Black Elk's great vision forms the heart of *Black Elk Speaks* just as it formed the core of the teachings Black Elk gave to Neihardt. From the

81. Neihardt to Nicholas Black Elk, June 27, 1931.

idyllic union of man with the cosmic forces of the universe that is represented by the vision, all develops in a downward spiral as human life fails to match supernatural expectation. In the vision Black Elk saw the troubled times ahead, but he was also given powers that were to protect his people from danger. *Black Elk Speaks* emphasizes Black Elk's sense of failure, his inability to use the spiritual powers given to him, and his sense of personal responsibility for the downfall of his people. Lest the reader miss the tragedy of the destruction of the Lakotas' way of life that is mirrored in Black Elk's own failure, Neihardt concluded the work with this now-famous passage:

> I did not know then how much was ended. When I look back now from this high hill of my old age, I can still see the butchered women and children lying heaped and scattered all along the crooked gulch as plain as when I saw them with eyes still young. And I can see that something else died there in the bloody mud, and was buried in the blizzard. A people's dream died there. It was a beautiful dream.
>
> And I, to whom so great a vision was given in my youth,—you see me now a pitiful old man who has done nothing, for the nation's hoop is broken and scattered. There is no center any longer, and the sacred tree is dead.[82]

The author's postscript relating the ceremony on Harney Peak does little to buoy hope. There the old man prayed that the sacred tree might bloom again and the people find their way back to the sacred hoop and the good red road. He cried out, "O make my people live!"—and in reply a low rumble of thunder sounded, and a drizzle of rain fell from a sky that shortly before had been cloudless. Whether this sign was a hopeful one or, more likely, a tragic recognition of the power that Black Elk had been given but failed to use is one of the dynamic issues that makes the book a literary success. *Black Elk Speaks* can be best characterized as an elegy, the commemoration of a man who has failed in his life's work, as well as of a people whose way of life has passed.

There is no doubt that Black Elk expressed the sense of despair that Neihardt attributes to him in *Black Elk Speaks*. When the time came in his

---

82. Neihardt, *Black Elk Speaks,* p. 276. Although these are Neihardt's words, not Black Elk's, this is the most frequently quoted passage from the book.

life to implement the power to destroy that had been given him in the
vision, he chose to turn his back on it and joined the Catholic Church
instead. He rejected the traditional Lakota value of warfare for the Christian virtue of charity. True to his new religion, he did no longer practice
his native healing rituals. But Black Elk's attitude toward his people's
future held more hope than thoughts of doom. The sense of irreversible
tragedy that pervades *Black Elk Speaks* reflects Neihardt's interpretation.
Lakota culture does not emphasize the irreversible, but rather the op-
posite: what once was is likely to be again. This was the hope that Black
Elk voiced again and again in talking to Neihardt, that together they
could "make the tree bloom." With its unrelenting sense of defeat, *Black
Elk Speaks* became an eloquent literary restatement of the theme of the
vanishing American.

Did Neihardt misunderstand Black Elk? On the one hand, it seems
likely that Neihardt did not fully appreciate the Lakota attitude of prayer.
Sorrow and despair were outward expressions of traditional Lakota
prayer, for the efficacy of prayer depended upon making oneself humble
and pitiable before the powers of the universe. But this was a ritual
attitude, not an expression of hopelessness. On the other hand, Neihardt
perceived Black Elk through the lens of his own lifework, *A Cycle of the
West*. The purpose of this epic poem, Neihardt had written, was "to
preserve the great race-mood of courage that was developed west of the
Missouri River in the 19th century."[83] The corollary to the triumph of the
"westering white men" was the inevitable defeat of the Plains Indians. It is
not that Neihardt misunderstood Black Elk, but that he perceived his life
as embodying the whole tragic history of defeat whose emotional tone he
was trying to convey in verse in *A Cycle*.

Because it was written in the first person, *Black Elk Speaks* opens Black
Elk's innermost life for public inspection, although it does so with a
pervasive sense of dignity. The book's success is due in large part to
Neihardt's empathy with Black Elk's "otherworldliness"—a spirituality
that set him apart. The mystic in Neihardt and the mystic in Black Elk
were kindred souls. At times in the book, Black Elk's "other world"
becomes the "outer world" of Neihardt's poetic imagination. Black Elk in
the book is left poised, seemingly helplessly, on the brink of civilization;

83. John G. Neihardt, *The Song of the Indian Wars* (New York: Macmillan, 1925),
p. 7.

the pitiful old man at the end of *Black Elk Speaks,* sorrowing over the destruction of his people, is a powerful literary figure. And in one sense this is an accurate reflection of Black Elk's sense of failure to use his vision powers as he was directed. Yet this image is far removed from Black Elk's daily life as patriarch, rancher, catechist, and community elder—one of the most successful old-time, uneducated Indians in adapting to the exigencies of life on the Pine Ridge Reservation. In a practical sense, far from failing, he had made a successful life for himself and his family.

The extent to which Neihardt succeeded in making mysticism the central theme of Black Elk's entire life intensified the degree to which the old holy man came to be interpreted as saintly, as a person far removed from life's normal cares. Again, this is an effective literary device, a powerful one for generalizing Black Elk into the very symbol of his people, but it leads away from understanding Black Elk as a person and toward the creation of Black Elk as a myth.

Literature and biography are very different genres, however; as Neihardt said, *Black Elk Speaks* was intended as a work of art, transcending the ordinary to make a larger statement about humanity. In the process the book becomes an interpretation of the whole of Lakota culture, for Neihardt had an intuitive appreciation and understanding of other modes of thought, and he had a gift for translating between cultures. Neihardt was satisfied that the book preserved "the finest things" in Black Elk's life. And to Ben Black Elk, Neihardt wrote: "There seems to be good reason to believe that a great many people are going to know about your father within the next two years, and I think this book is going to make him a happier man."[84]

When *Black Elk Speaks* appeared in 1932, it received strongly positive reviews. Some critics praised it as the most insightful work ever published on native shamanism and found it to be an important revelation of the nature of "primitive psychology." Others attributed the philosophy of the book to Neihardt himself, refusing to credit an uneducated Indian with such sophistication. They read into it a social commentary on the times. But despite the positive publicity, the book failed to capture the popular reader. Financially it was a total failure, and eventually it was consigned to the remainder tables. Not until its reissue in 1961 by the University of

84. Neihardt to Nicholas Black Elk [June 1931]; Neihardt to Benjamin Black Elk, June 27, 1931.

Nebraska Press did the book at last find its public, rapidly becoming not only Neihardt's best-known work, but one of the most successful books of all time on American Indians.[85]

Black Elk Speaks met with a mixed reaction at Pine Ridge. The Bureau of Indian Affairs field agent on the reservation, B. G. Courtright, was very enthusiastic. When Neihardt sent him a copy of the book, he replied: "It is a beautiful work. . . . I have shown the book around in the office, and it is meeting with distinct favor. It is beautifully written. I am writing to Black Elk and Standing Bear to congratulate them on their material. The charm and delight of the book, however, remain distinctly yours."[86]

Despite such secular acclaim, the book put Black Elk in an awkward position in relation to the Catholic Church. His reputation on the reservation was built as a Catholic catechist, not as a native religious leader. The Jesuit priests at Holy Rosary Mission were shocked and horrified at the suggestion that one of their most valued catechists still harbored beliefs in the old Indian religion. For them to accept *Black Elk Speaks* at face value necessarily called into question the genuineness of their success in converting the Lakotas to Catholicism. Rather than accept the book as a true representation of Black Elk, they blamed Neihardt for telling only part of Black Elk's story. The priests objected most strongly to the epilogue portraying Black Elk as a believing, practicing "pagan," praying to the six grandfathers when he knew well that the Christian God was the only source of salvation. Ben Black Elk told the missionaries, no doubt truthfully, that he and his father had not realized that Neihardt intended to include the prayer on Harney Peak in the book. Although the old man was embarrassed in front of the priests who had been his confessors and advisors for many years, he never denied the sincerity of his final appeal to the six grandfathers.[87]

Black Elk was an old man and, as he said to Neihardt, he did not expect to live much longer. During winter 1933 he had a serious accident when

85. Aly, *John G. Neihardt,* pp. 172–73; McCluskey, *"Black Elk Speaks:* And So Does John Neihardt," p. 231.

86. B. G. Courtright to Neihardt, February 22, 1931 [1932], Neihardt Collection.

87. See Sialm, "Camp Churches," pp. 60–63; Duratschek, *Crusading along Sioux Trails,* pp. 207–8.

the team of horses he was driving ran away with him; he was thrown from the wagon and run over, and two ribs were broken. In the hospital, he received the last rites of the Catholic Church. He survived, but as Ben Black Elk wrote to Neihardt the next summer, "Father got well but he aint the old man he used to be."[88] After Black Elk recovered he felt moved to reassert his devotion to the Catholic Church. Whether this was his own idea or that of the priests is not entirely certain, but the resulting document has all the indications of sincerity. It was dictated and written down in the Lakota language, then translated into English. Typed copies of both versions were signed by Black Elk and witnessed by his daughter, Lucy Looks Twice, and by Father Joseph A. Zimmerman, S.J. Father Sialm, who had been close to Black Elk over the years, commented: "This Declaration should stand in every new edition of *Black Elk Speaks.*"[89] The document, preserved in the records of Holy Rosary Mission, reads as follows:

Holy Rosary Mission
Pine Ridge, S. Dak.
January 26, 1934

BLACK ELK SPEAKS AGAIN—THE FINAL SPEECH

I shake hands with my white friends. Listen! I will speak words of truth. I told about the people's ways of long age and some of this a white man put in a book but he did not tell about current ways. Therefore I will speak again, a final speech.

Now I am an old man. I called my priest to pray for me and so he gave me Extreme Unction and Holy Eucharist. Therefore I will tell you the truth. Listen, my friends!

For the last thirty years I have lived very differently from what the white man told about me. I am a believer. The Catholic priest Short Father baptized me thirty years ago. From then on they have called me Nick Black Elk. Very many of the Indians know me. Now I have converted and live in the true faith of God the Father, the Son, and the Holy Spirit. Accordingly, I say in my own Sioux

---

88. Benj. Black Elk to Neihardt, June 4, 1934. Neihardt Collection.
89. Sialm, "Camp Churches," p. 63.

Indian language, "Our Father, who art in heaven, hallowed be thy name," as Christ taught us and instructed us to say. I say the Apostles' Creed and I believe it all.

I believe in the seven sacraments of the Catholic Church. I have now received six of these: Baptism, Confirmation, Penance, Holy Eucharist, Holy Matrimony, and Extreme Unction.

For very many years I went with several priests to fight for Christ among my people. For about twenty years I helped the priests and I was a catechist in several communities. So I think I know more about the Catholic religion than many white men.

For eight years I participated in the retreat for catechists and from this I learned a great deal about the faith. I am able to explain my faith. From my faith I know Who I believe in so my work is not in vain.

All of my family is baptized. All my children and grandchildren belong to the Catholic Church and I am glad of that and I wish very much that they will always follow the holy road.

I know what St. Peter has to say to those men who forsake the holy commandments. My white friends should read carefully 2 Peter 2: 20–22. I send my people on the straight road that Christ's church has taught us about. While I live I will never fall from faith in Christ.

Thirty years ago I knew little about the one we call God. At that time I was a very good dancer. In England I danced before Our Grandmother, Queen Victoria. At that time I gave medicines to the sick. Perhaps I was proud, I considered myself brave and I considered myself to be a good Indian, but now I think I am better.

St. Paul also became better after his conversion. I know that the Catholic religion is good, better than the Sun dance or the Ghost dance. Long ago the Indians performed such dances only for glory. They cut themselves and caused the blood to flow. But for the sake of sin Christ was nailed on the cross to take our sins away. The Indian religion of long ago did not benefit mankind. The medicine men sought only glory and presents from their curing. Christ commanded us to be humble and He taught us to stop sin. The Indian medicine men did not stop sin. Now I despise sin. And I want to go straight in the righteous way that the Catholics teach us so my soul will reach heaven. This is the way I wish it to be. With a good heart I shake hands with all of you.

> [signed] Nick Black Elk
> Lucy Looks Twice
> Joseph A. Zimmerman, S. J.
> (Wanblee Wankatuya [High Eagle])[90]

It is unknown whether this document received any publicity on the reservation. In a printed letter sent to friends of the mission dated Feast of Christ the King 1940, Father Zimmerman wrote of Black Elk and *Black Elk Speaks:* "So staunch is his profession of Christianity that after the book was published he made in English and in Sioux formal statements of his Catholic faith signing them before witnesses lest he should be regarded as still a pagan." After discussing Black Elk's career as a catechist, Father Zimmerman continued: "Old age, blindness and the seven miles between him and the nearest Catholic church prevent him from often hearing mass, so at times I promise to say mass at his home. Then he sends out word and gathers in the entire neighborhood, and as in his old time catechist days leads them in hymns and prayers."[91]

Black Elk's declaration of faith apparently quieted the minds of the Jesuit fathers concerning the sincerity of his belief in Christianity. They blamed Neihardt's poetic romanticism for presenting Black Elk's life without mention of what, to them, was its fulfillment: his conversion and

90. Records of the Bureau of Catholic Indian Missions. This is a my retranslation from the original Lakota text; the translation made in 1934 tends to slant the document slightly more in Christian idioms. The biblical verses to which Black Elk refers (2 Peter 2:20–22) read: "For if, flying from the pollutions of the world, through the knowledge of our Lord and Saviour Jesus Christ, they be again entangled in them and overcome: their latter state is become unto them worse than the former. For it had been better for them not to have known the way of justice, than after they have known it, to turn back from that holy commandment which was delivered to them. For, that of the true proverb has happened to them: The dog is returned to his vomit: and, The sow that was washed, to her wallowing in the mire."

91. Archives of the Sisters of the Blessed Sacrament, Cornwells Heights, Pa. An extract from this letter is printed in Duratschek, *Crusading along Sioux Trails,* pp. 207–8. Photos of Black Elk as an old man, holding out a rosary to a small child (similar to the pose that appeared in 1926 on the cover of the *Indian Sentinel*), were used for many years in the mission's fund-raising publications to symbolize the Lakotas' transition from Indian religion to Christianity.

his work as a Catholic. From Neihardt's perspective, he had come to write what Black Elk wished to teach him about the Lakota people before the Wounded Knee massacre; from Black Elk's perspective, he had invited Neihardt in order to instruct him in the old Lakota religion. There has been a misunderstanding of purpose: Neihardt conceived of the project as writing Black Elk's life story, whereas Black Elk conceived of it as making a record of the Lakota religion.

The Jesuits seem not to have been the only residents of Pine Ridge who were disturbed by *Black Elk Speaks*. Apparently other Catholic catechists were opposed to—or perhaps jealous of—the book, and they may have interpreted Black Elk's accident as divine retribution for his backsliding to the old religion. Ben Black Elk wrote to Neihardt in June 1934: "Emil A. [Afraid of] Hawk has been loading the old man about lots of things. The old man felt uneasy for a while. But he is perfectly satisfied, very glad to hear you are coming again." There was perhaps no more powerful symbol of the Black Elk family's respect for Neihardt than this: when Ben's wife gave birth that year to a boy, they named him John Neihardt Black Elk.[92]

Later that summer of 1934, Neihardt returned to Pine Ridge with his daughters Hilda and Alice and spent the entire summer camping on Ben Black Elk's land along Wounded Knee Creek. The purpose of this long visit was to provide Neihardt an opportunity to complete *The Song of the Messiah* in the area where the final action of the poem takes place, at Wounded Knee. When he left for Branson that fall, the poem was nearly finished.

Neihardt's return visit evidently alarmed the missionaries, although there is no indication that any of them spoke to him about their concerns. In any case, on September 20, 1934, after Neihardt had returned home, Black Elk dictated a letter to the missionaries, written down in English by his daughter, Lucy Looks Twice, clarifying his relationship with Neihardt.[93] He stated that when *Black Elk Speaks* was being written, Neihardt had promised him half the profits from the project; now Neihardt told him he had not made a cent on the book. Black Elk then stated that he had requested Neihardt to include at the end of the book the story of his conversion to Catholicism and of his work for the church but

92. Benj. Black Elk to Neihardt, June 4, 1934.

93. Records of the Bureau of Catholic Indian Missions. It is possible, of course, that Lucy Looks Twice rather than her father, Black Elk, was the actual author of the letter.

that Neihardt had not done so. This is a difficult document to assess; it is not signed by Black Elk, and the motive for writing it is not clear. Probably it was composed to satisfy the priests and quiet their suspicions. The missionaries may have blamed Neihardt for some backsliding on Black Elk's part: for years Black Elk had refrained from Indian dancing (which the Jesuits in those days unequivocally equated with Satan's influence), but in his old age he had taken it up once again, receiving enthusiastic support from Neihardt.

The following spring, Alex Duhamel, a businessman from Rapid City, South Dakota, invited Black Elk to participate in an Indian pageant as a tourist attraction. With a group of friends and relatives, Black Elk would camp out for the summer in the Black Hills. The inducement was irresistible. Black Elk continued with Duhamel's Sioux Indian Pageant every season for most of the rest of his life. In the spring, Black Elk's party moved to the Black Hills, picking up children en route who had been attending boarding schools during the year. They camped at Duhamel's Sitting Bull Crystal Caverns, a beautiful area nine miles south of Rapid City and the site of a large natural cavern that the Duhamel family had developed into a tourist attraction. It was an ideal location, directly on the highway between Rapid City and Mount Rushmore—which, as the colossal carving neared completion, drew more and more tourists from all over the world. A brightly painted wooden tipi-like log structure was built beside the road to sell tickets. Nearby, a large circular wooden dance house was constructed to Black Elk's specifications to shelter the pageant during rainy weather. A group of small, canvas-covered tipis provided by Duhamel was located on the flat land beyond. The Indians lived in canvas-wall tents, pitched out of sight. They were provided with wood, water, food, and, at the end of the season, a percentage of the pageant profits.[94]

The pageant was held twice daily, at 8:30 A.M. near the Indian village and at 8:00 P.M. at the National Guard camp west of Rapid City. In case of rain the evening performance was moved into the city auditorium. In the

94. Information on the pageant is based on an undated printed program entitled *Duhamel's Sioux Indian Pageant* and on my 1979–81 interviews with Bud Duhamel and Emma Amiotte, both of Rapid City, S.D., and with Reginald and Gladys Laubin, Moose, Wyo. It is not certain whether this was Black Elk's first year with the pageant or whether he had participated in it earlier. According to the program, the pageant was begun in 1927.

afternoons the Indians were brought down to the city, where they danced in the street in front of Duhamel's Trading Post, across from the Alex Johnson Hotel. The trading post installed exhibit cases for a large display of Indian artifacts; the story of the Custer fight was depicted in pictographs around the walls, and there was a large mural of the fight painted by Rudy Adams, a Sioux boy who had composed the work under the direction of some of the warriors who had participated in the fight.

The goals of the pageant were represented as educational rather than sensational. One program lists seventeen different acts, including a variety of social and religious dances, a Lakota speech, demonstration of sign language and blanket signals, preparation of a corpse for burial, burial on a scaffold, and the peace pipe ceremony. After the performance the tourists mingled with the Indians, visited in the village, and had an opportunity to examine the costumes and accoutrements closely. Many tourists enjoyed the Duhamel pageant as an introduction to American Indian life, but other visitors went there to learn more. Some were seriously interested in Indian culture, like Reginald and Gladys Laubin, students of Indian dance and traditional arts and crafts, who visited the pageant in order to talk with Black Elk and the other old men. And Lakotas from other reservations came to visit and join in the dancing.

Black Elk supervised the painting of one of the canvas tipi covers with a rainbow over the doorway and a horse on the south side of the tent, symbols of his great vision.[95] He was the main attraction of the pageant, billed as its medicine man, and in conjunction with this the audiences were advised to read Neihardt's *Black Elk Speaks*. In a series of vignettes in the pageant, Black Elk demonstrated traditional religious activities including the offering of the pipe, the burial enactment, and the sun dance. In one scene a sick boy was brought in on a horse-drawn travois by sorrowing parents who asked Black Elk to cure him. Black Elk was stripped to the breechcloth; his face was painted red with yellow streaks around the sides, and across his torso and limbs were yellow streaks representing lightning. He wore a medicine man's buffalo horn headdress and sacred ornaments around his neck. He sang his healing songs, accompanying himself by beating a square hand drum with a tin can rattle. As he

95. The tipi is illustrated in Reginald and Gladys Laubin, *The Indian Tipi: Its History, Construction, and Use,* 2d ed. (Norman: University of Oklahoma Press, 1977), p. 251.

prayed, Black Elk repeatedly touched the boy's body with the rattle, invoking the rejuvenating power it symbolized: the sound of rain striking the hard earth. After an appropriate interval, the boy suddenly leaped up and ran off, apparently well again. In the sun dance, dancers were tied to the center pole by ropes attached to halters worn around the back. The dancers blew on their eagle bone whistles, straining on the ropes, giving a good impression of a real sun dance. Finally the ropes would be jerked free of the halters, the dancers staggering backward as if they had just torn their flesh free.[96]

As part of the publicity for Duhamel's pageant, Black Elk again made a formal visit to Mount Rushmore during summer 1936. Gutzon Borglum was preparing to unveil the second head, that of Thomas Jefferson, at a dedication to be attended by President Franklin D. Roosevelt. Black Elk and a group of Oglalas went there from the pageant on August 28, two days before the official dedication, and requested to be allowed to ascend the mountain to hold a ceremony of their own; permission was readily granted. The party, accompanied by Ben and his sister-in-law, Emma, rode in a crude wooden gondola seven hundred feet up the mountain on the aerial tramway. Local reporters came along, and Black Elk announced to them that as they rode through the air he would sing his sacred songs. Several times he cleared his throat as if about to sing. Finally, they asked him what was wrong. Emma put the question to the old man in Lakota. "Granddaughter," he replied, "tell them I'm too scared—I can't even sing!"[97]

On top of the mountain, Black Elk, wearing a buffalo headdress, carrying his pipe in his right hand, once more prayed to the six grandfathers. Ben told the reporters that Black Elk

> prayed for the preservation of his people and for "unity of my people and the whites in the name of brotherhood," that Borglum and his men be protected in their work. He also called the attention of the gods to the need of rain, and asked that "greenness and abundance" be forthcoming. He called for preservation of the greatness of the memories of the men whose granite likenesses are

96. Pageant descriptions are from Emma Amiotte.
97. Interview with Emma Amiotte.

being carved on the mountain, and asked that their greatness be carried on through "changes of nations and races."[98]

When the prayer had ended, the party descended on the tramway and visited the sculptor in his studio before returning to the pageant camp.

Black Elk's motivation in publicly performing these sacred rituals appears to have been to teach white audiences that the old-time Lakota religion was a true religion, not devil worship as the missionaries claimed. In this spirit Black Elk gave Reginald Laubin permission to use his invocation with the pipe—the offering of the pipe to the six directions—to open the concerts of traditional Indian dances that he and his wife Gladys presented to audiences around the world. Black Elk told the Laubins that he believed this would help bring about a better understanding of his people.[99] Watching these traditional rituals, spectators could judge for themselves their moral worth. This was the logical extension of Black Elk's wish to make his vision "go out," to share the traditional ways with white men. Today such ecumenical sharing between native and Christian religious traditions is taken as a given by Catholic Lakotas, but in Black Elk's day it was an idea yet unborn.[100] Jesuit missionaries remained firm in their conviction—at least until the 1960s—that Indian religion necessarily represented an earlier, more primitive stage in human history that would have to be completely replaced by Christianity in order for the people to raise themselves to the enlightenment of civilization.

In yet another context, therefore, we find Black Elk and Neihardt close to one another in ideas but having arrived there from different premises. Black Elk, like other Lakotas, could express his firm belief in the truth of the Catholic religion without the necessity of rejecting Indian beliefs. The two systems were not compartmentalized; rather, they were stages in his life. Unlike the missionaries, however, Black Elk did not conceive of the two religions as forming a developmental sequence. Both were intimately bound up in his being, and both sets of beliefs molded his character and personality.[101] Neihardt, on the other hand, arrived at the same position

98. "Sioux Prays to Gods from Rushmore Peak," *Rapid City Daily Journal,* August 28, 1936, p. 10.

99. Personal communication from Reginald and Gladys Laubin, March 14, 1983.

100. Steinmetz, *Pipe, Bible and Peyote among the Oglala Lakota,* pp. 153–61.

101. Today old people on the Pine Ridge Reservation who knew Black Elk personally remember him primarily as a Roman Catholic catechist, not as a Lakota holy man;

without concern for religion as dogma. His approach was that of the mystic who experiences the radiant "white light" of understanding that unites all peoples. This was the message he developed in *The Song of the Messiah:* the defeat of the Lakotas at the hands of the soldiers was only outward. The ghost dancers and the white men shared the same longing for happiness and goodness but failed through historical circumstances to be able to communicate. But the theme of the poem, as Neihardt said, was "the triumph of spirit through apparent defeat." It is a subtler interpretation of Sioux history than that presented in *Black Elk Speaks,* one that reflects Neihardt's developing perspective on the meaning of the "race-mood of courage" that he saw evolve through time from the physical to the spiritual. The message is an optimistic one for humanity, although it does little to console the Lakotas for the loss of their world. Like Black Elk, Neihardt seems trapped between what appears so self-evidently right and good and the exigencies of life as each individual must live it. Neither man, however, would surrender to mere exigency, and each in his own way strove for the higher understanding that promises to unite all mankind in common endeavor.[102]

After the publication of *The Song of the Messiah* in 1935, Neihardt turned to *The Song of Jed Smith,* the last volume to be written in *A Cycle of the West.* This work led him away from the Lakotas and occupied him until 1941, when at last the epic poem was completed. During this time he did not return to Pine Ridge, but in 1940 he received a letter from his Indian father:

Oglala, S.D.
Dec. 16, 1940

Dear Son:
Well you'll be surprised to hear from you [sic] because I dont know why you never write to me but I still remember you folks so here I am writing to you and your family. First of all I will say we're all

---

this reflects the thoroughness with which he put aside traditional religious practices and the zeal with which he preached Catholicism. Younger Oglalas, who know Black Elk through the writings of Neihardt and Brown, seem largely unaware of his activities as a Catholic.

102. For critical discussion of *The Song of the Messiah,* see Aly, *John G. Neihardt,* pp. 177–90.

getting along fine even up to Ben & his family. Well the weather is
pretty cold up here but quite a few snow. For 5 yrs successive Ive
been to the Bl[ack] Hills for the summer & pretty busy putting up a
show for Duhamels so I really forget to write to my friends.
Well theres [not] any news except that we're hearing about the war
all the time. I hope you enjoy your holidays and may the Great
Spirit bring lots of blessings.

I'm yours truly father
Nick Black Elk Sr.
Oglala S.D.[103]

Despite the optimistic tone of the letter, Black Elk, suffering from
tuberculosis, was becoming progressively infirm. When his wife died the
following year, he was hospitalized for a time at the Sioux Sanitarium in
Rapid City. He no longer had the strength for church work, but he
continued to participate in the summer pageants. During the winters he
lived with one or another of his children, returning in his last years to live
with Ben and his family at Manderson.[104]

For the Neihardts, the war years were difficult. Neihardt and his wife,
in debt and in danger of losing their home in Branson, moved to Chicago
to look for employment. After a succession of miscellaneous jobs,
Neihardt met John Collier, the commissioner of Indian Affairs, whose
office had been moved from Washington to Chicago for the duration of
the war. In 1944 Collier appointed Neihardt director of the Bureau of
Indian Affairs' Bureau of Information, and his duties included editing the
monthly newsletter *Indians at Work*. Neihardt held this position through
the end of the war, and when the bureau was transferred back to Washington in 1946, he and his wife were financially able to return to
Branson.[105]

While employed by the bureau, Neihardt was assigned to write a
cultural history of the Oglala Sioux, building on his earlier work. Black
Elk may have suggested the project. In an undated draft of a letter addressed "Dear Uncle Black Elk," Neihardt mentions sending Black Elk
stamped envelopes so he could write to him more easily. Neihardt wrote:

103. Neihardt Collection.
104. McNamara, "Black Elk and Brings White," pp. 139–40.
105. Aly, *John G. Neihardt*, pp. 227–44.

"I want you to tell me something about the great work you want to do with me before we are both laid in the ground."[106]

During winter 1944 Neihardt had the opportunity to return to Pine Ridge to gather material for the history. He expressed the intention of getting a fuller picture by interviewing a number of old Oglalas, women as well as men. Accompanied by his daughter Hilda, Neihardt arrived at Pine Ridge late in November 1944; they lodged at the agency hotel. For four days, November 27–29 and December 1, they interviewed Eagle Elk, who at age ninety-three was probably the oldest man alive on the reservation. He told the story of his life, a dramatic tale that included incidents of war expeditions against other tribes and against white soldiers, as well as a detailed account of his participation in the sun dance. Hilda served as secretary, typing the interview notes directly on a portable machine, bypassing the shorthand stage. This was an efficient system that made it easier to review what had been recorded.

After completing the work with Eagle Elk, Neihardt returned to Black Elk. This time William Bergin—ironically, also a Catholic catechist—was interpreter.[107] During seven days of interviews, December 5–8 and 11–13, Black Elk related the history of the development of Lakota culture, exactly the material Neihardt needed for his proposed study. Although from a white man's perspective this history is really myth—a series of nonchronological anecdotes full of mystical happenings—from the Lakotas' perspective it is the only true history because it explains the moral framework within which Lakota culture developed and flourished. It can best be characterized as sacred history. Black Elk began by telling about the dispersal of the seven bands of Lakotas; the naming of the directions; the introduction of the bow and arrow, fire, and the knife; the establishment of kinship relations; the domestication of dogs; and the prophecies that led the Lakotas from one stage of their history to the next. In addition, Black Elk told the story of Falling Star, a long traditional myth, as well as a variety of other tales about war and hunting.

From these interviews, a different perspective on Black Elk's personality emerges. Far from the sad, defeated old man of *Black Elk Speaks,* he

---

106. Undated letter draft, Neihardt Collection.

107. Neihardt to Mona Neihardt, November 29, 1944. Photostatic copy, Neihardt Collection. Leo C. Cunningham, S. J., "Who's Who among Catholic Indians: William Bergin, Sioux," *Indian Sentinel* 10(2) (Spring 1930):76.

appears vibrant and strong, a proud preserver of the cultural traditions of his people. In these interviews Black Elk never refers to his own visions and sacred experiences; this is instead public material, the tribal legacy. The interviews can perhaps be thought of as summarizing those things that Black Elk tried each summer to teach to white people through his dramatic presentations at the Black Hills pageant.

When Black Elk had finished relating this new set of teachings, Neihardt returned to Chicago. It is not known why he abandoned his plan to interview a greater number of individuals. Perhaps he felt that he had all the material he could use for another book on the Sioux.

Neihardt returned twice more to Pine Ridge in the interests of the Bureau of Indian Affairs. The first time was to attend the great Sioux victory celebration, marking the end of World War II, at Pine Ridge on September 15, 1945. On behalf of the bureau, Neihardt spoke to the gathering. His theme was that the Lakotas had never truly been defeated in the past; rather, their downfall had been caused by the destruction of the buffalo herds. They had proved their fighting mettle once again by their service in the war. After Neihardt had returned to Chicago, Black Elk wrote him a letter dated October 11, 1945, expressing the Indians' gratitude: "The Sioux's sure liked the way you gave that speech at that celebration. They sure felt lot of encouragement by you & wish you could help them more in future."[108]

Neihardt's next visit to Pine Ridge was from September 19 to October 11, 1946. Although he was no longer regularly employed by the bureau, he had been hired to undertake a special investigation of reservation conditions. Hampered by an unseasonably early blizzard, he was able to spend only eight days driving around the reservation districts; the remainder of the time he interviewed Indians and agency personnel in Pine Ridge town. His investigation centered on the functioning of tribal government, as well as education, law and order, and a general survey of social conditions. Undoubtedly Neihardt once again visited Black Elk on this occasion, but no written records seem to have been preserved. It would have been their last meeting.[109]

In 1947 Neihardt received a letter from Joseph Epes Brown, then a

108. Letter in Neihardt Collection.
109. Aly, *John G. Neihardt,* p. 245. A typed copy of the report is in the Neihardt Collection.

college student; Brown had been deeply moved by *Black Elk Speaks* and wanted to meet the old Oglala. Although Neihardt warned Brown that Black Elk might not talk to him, the holy man welcomed him, and Brown spent eight months living with him at Manderson in winter 1947–48, returning for visits in the summers of 1948 and 1949. Brown had not gone to see Black Elk with the intention of writing a book, but Black Elk told him that he wished to record one more set of teachings, this time the sacred rituals of the traditional Lakota religion. These were ceremonies that he demonstrated in part to white visitors at the Black Hills pageant, and he wanted them preserved for posterity. Again Ben Black Elk served as interpreter. The material that Brown recorded became *The Sacred Pipe: Black Elk's Account of the Seven Rites of the Oglala Sioux,* published in 1953. These teachings seem to represent the end point in Black Elk's synthesis of Lakota and Christian beliefs, for in them he structures Lakota rituals in parallel fashion to the Catholic sacraments. Perhaps this was Black Elk's final attempt to bridge the two religious traditions that his life had so intimately embodied.

Black Elk remained a member of the Catholic Church until the end of his life. He had witnessed the power of the white man's religion, and he had chosen to embrace it even though it meant abandoning traditional religious ceremonies, particularly the healing rituals of his visions. Nonetheless, he lived with the sadness that came from remembering all that his people had lost because of the whites: namely, the spiritual power that had bound them inextricably to the world around them.

In his old age, when interacting with whites—and probably with other Indian elders as well—Black Elk turned his attention increasingly to Lakota tradition. Apparently this began with Neihardt's first visit in 1930. Reginald and Gladys Laubin, who met Black Elk in 1936 at the Black Hills pageant and visited with him each year until his death, commented that although they had been aware that Black Elk had once been converted to Catholicism, he never mentioned that aspect of his life. They wrote, "We had the feeling he was interested mainly in early days."[110]

In about 1948, Charles Hanson, Jr., a young man visiting at Pine Ridge, went to meet Black Elk. When he arrived, the old man was lying on a bed; he sat up when his son Ben announced that a visitor had come. Black Elk made a short speech by way of greeting, which Ben translated

110. Personal communication, March 14, 1983.

into English. As they left the room, Ben apologized that the interview couldn't have been longer, but his father was very old and very tired. He went on to say that many of their conversations then were about the old religion, and that Black Elk now felt he had made a mistake in rejecting it for Christianity. Perhaps, after all, the Lakota religion would have been better for his people.[111]

In 1947, Neihardt began to work on the interview notes recorded at Pine Ridge in 1944. Since terminating his appointment with the Bureau of Indian Affairs, he was no longer required to write a cultural history; and he decided instead to use the material in a more literary fashion. The writing of *When the Tree Flowered* occupied him for four years, and the book appeared in 1951. Neihardt used this work, which retells the entire story of the Lakotas' struggle with the whites, in part as an attempt to compensate for the popular failure of *Black Elk Speaks*. More important, perhaps, Neihardt believed that the material he had collected formed a tale worth the telling. He wrote to Hilda: "It's, above all, a good story, a *romance*."[112] The plot of the book follows the life of Eagle Elk but incorporates experiences from Black Elk's life as well, most notably his trip to Europe with Buffalo Bill. In many ways the book presents a more human story than does *Black Elk Speaks:* the fictionalized narrator, Eagle Voice, is fully developed as a literary character, and the book balances love, war, humor, the sacred, and pathos. In an almost incidental fashion, the narrative incorporates Black Elk's historical and mythical tales and his accounts of Lakota social and political life.

The style of *When the Tree Flowered* is conversational, with Neihardt portraying himself as interviewer, sitting in the tent with Eagle Voice, while the old man tells the story of his life and his people. This book is more descriptive than *Black Elk Speaks,* and it focuses more on making the reader understand than on merely setting a mood. It is important that Eagle Voice is depicted as a vibrant man, one who does not suffer any sense of personal defeat and whose memories, though bittersweet, are not full of regret. The book develops the theme of the prophetic visions of Wooden Cup, who long before the whites invaded Lakota country

111. Personal communication from Charles E. Hanson, Jr., Museum of the Fur Trade, Chadron, Nebraska, February 19, 1983.

112. Letter to Hilda Neihardt Petri, quoted in Aly, *John G. Neihardt,* p. 270.

prophesied their coming; the disappearance of the buffalo; the binding of the earth with iron bands (railroads); the destruction of the people's sacred hoop; and the imposition of little square gray houses. But, says Eagle Voice (p. 8), "I think I did not believe what Wooden Cup said, for I was young and the world was new."

Throughout the book, Neihardt continually evokes the bittersweet mood by correlating the erosion of Lakota culture with Eagle Voice's own aging and with the increasing confusion and disorganization of his world. When Eagle Voice speaks of the old customs, he comments: "All this was many snows ago, before the sacred hoop was broken, and when the people still were good" (p. 32). As he remembers the passing time, the battles and troubles as well as the happy times, he says: "I did not know then that the hoop was breaking and would never come together again" (p. 223). The book offers a highly personal feeling for the perspective of a man grown old that seems to reflect Neihardt's own life. By this time *A Cycle,* his lifework, had long been completed. He was sixty-six when he began writing *When the Tree Flowered,* and by the time he finished it he was nearly seventy. The changes that had been wrought in the world during his lifetime approached the magnitude of those that faced his fictional Lakota narrator. The personal empathy is unmistakable.

When the Tree Flowered carries the story of the Lakotas beyond Wounded Knee, unlike *Black Elk Speaks.* In the chaotic aftermath of the massacre, Eagle Voice meets the girl he had loved when he was a boy— now a woman whose husband and son have been killed by the soldiers. In time the two marry, but the narrator tells little about the details of domestic life. Eagle Voice later summarizes his life on Pine Ridge Reservation (p. 248): "It was a good road that we walked together, Grandson. Sometimes we were hungry, but it was a good road. Our children came to us, and when we were old, we saw our grandchildren too. It was a good road."

When the Tree Flowered presents the traditional Lakota culture and religion as past, to be honored and remembered in the telling. But it suggests an optimistic picture of contemporary Lakota life—based on strengths inherited from the past. It reflects Neihardt's positive outlook on the Lakotas as a people who would survive the dramatic changes in their outward cultural life. In this sense it carries forward the message of *Black Elk Speaks,* putting it in a fuller social context and reintegrating the power of the sacred into everyday life.

By the time *When the Tree Flowered* had been completed, Black Elk was dead. He passed away at Manderson on August 19, 1950, after having received the sacraments of Holy Communion and Extreme Unction. He was buried at St. Agnes Mission Chapel, in the desolate graveyard on a hill overlooking the valley. His tombstone bears the inscription "Chief Black Elk"; but his true monument is the body of teachings he gave so that future generations would not forget the spiritual world in which he had grown to adulthood. The two books have brought countless readers to know Black Elk, to share in a vision of that world as given to us through John G. Neihardt.

And now the last part of the legacy, the entirety of the teachings as Black Elk gave them to Neihardt, is allowed to "go out." For readers who wish to go beyond Neihardt's introduction to Black Elk's world and to explore it for themselves—guided by the understandings that Neihardt developed in his books—the material in the present volume is made available. It represents the final transfer of the burden passed on by Black Elk to Neihardt. Those of us who never had the opportunity to meet Black Elk, or to know his spokesman Neihardt, have at least this record of their meetings, to share in the excitement of their common endeavor, to study and contemplate, and to try to understand.

PART TWO

The 1931
Interviews

The full text of Neihardt's 1931 interviews with Black Elk preserves a wealth of detail that does not appear in *Black Elk Speaks*. In order to create a literary work, Neihardt could not avoid such omissions, especially when detail failed to advance the narrative. Likewise, he omitted material relating to European culture that seemed out of context with Black Elk's telling of his life story from an Indian perspective. All of this omitted material forms an important resource for the study of Lakota culture, and access to the entirety of the interview notes will enable literary scholars to analyze more accurately Neihardt's creative role in writing *Black Elk Speaks*.

There is also material in *Black Elk Speaks* that does not appear in the interview notes, much of it relating to the Sioux wars with the U.S. Army. Here Neihardt was forced to rely on published sources in order to fill in the background of Black Elk's story. This additional material includes information on Crazy Horse (*Black Elk Speaks,* pp. 84–87), the Reynolds fight (p. 91), the sun dance on the Rosebud (96–98), Gall at the Custer battle (110), and details concerning the winter of 1876–77 and the death of Crazy Horse (136–47). In addition, the book's three introductory paragraphs (pp. 1–2) and the three concluding paragraphs (276) were composed by Neihardt as expressions of Black Elk's thoughts. Finally, the story of High Horse's courting (67–76) does not appear in the notes; but Neihardt's 1944 interviews make it clear that this was one of Black Elk's stories. Ironically, many of the passages that do not reflect the direct words of Black Elk are among those most frequently quoted from *Black Elk Speaks*. This points up the inappropriateness of using *Black Elk Speaks*

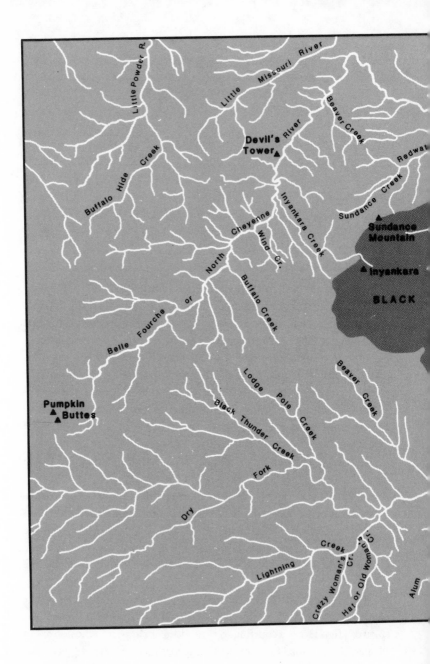

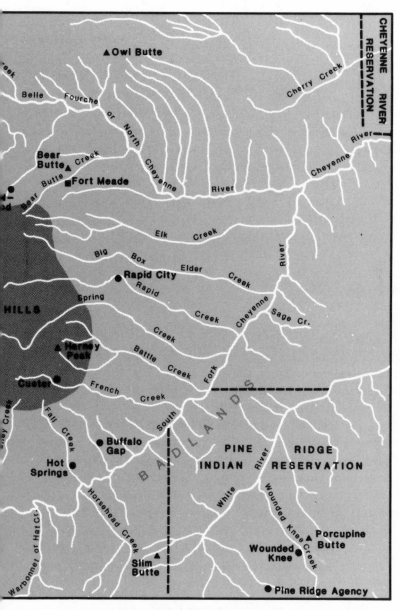

The Black Hills Area, 1890

in any comparative study as representative of traditional Lakota culture and religion.

The far-reaching influence that Black Elk's teachings have on the ideas and attitudes of countless individuals today, Indians and non-Indians alike, testifies to basic religious and philosophical dilemmas generated by a sense of increasing alienation from the natural world. For many, Black Elk suggests a perspective on a prior, more satisfying relation between man and nature. For others, his teachings are a blueprint for religious revitalization. Indeed, Black Elk's teachings appear to be evolving into a consensual American Indian theological canon. In this regard, one question has been raised again and again: What is Black Elk's place in the history of Lakota religion? Does he truly represent the old Lakota way, or was his thinking profoundly affected by Catholicism? Discussion of this question usually dissolves into political rhetoric rather than objective assessment. In order to arrive at a resolution it is necessary to begin by reviewing what is known about the fundamentals of late nineteenth-century Lakota religion.[1]

The preeminent tangible symbol of traditional Lakota religion was the circle. The Lakotas perceived everything in the natural world as circular (except rock), for roundness was indicative of life itself. For this reason the circle was held to be sacred (*wakan*). Sun, sky, earth, moon, a human body, a tree trunk, day, night, a year, a man's life—all these were sacred circles. In respect for this natural order, the Lakotas made circular tipis, pitching them in camp circles, and sat in circles for ceremonial occasions. The wholeness of the circle, without beginning or end, represented the wholeness and oneness of the universe.

All life forms that comprise the universe, from the stars in the sky to the grasses on the earth, were considered as one. They embodied *wakan*, and this concept of *wakan* was the dominant intangible symbol of Lakota

---

1. The following discussion draws most heavily on Walker, *Lakota Belief and Ritual;* Walker, "The Sun Dance and Other Ceremonies of the Oglala Division of the Teton Dakota," American Museum of Natural History, *Anthropological Papers* 16, pt. 2 (1917), pp. 50–221; Frances Densmore, *Teton Sioux Music,* Smithsonian Institution, Bureau of American Ethnology, Bulletin 61 (1918); and the unpublished writings of George Sword in the Colorado Historical Society, Denver, and in the American Museum of Natural History, New York (I am currently translating these for publication). Much of what is said here of traditional Lakota religion also accurately characterizes Lakota beliefs today.

religion, the core of Lakota belief. According to one Oglala, *wakan* was "anything that is hard to understand."[2] It was the animating force of the universe, the common denominator of its oneness. The totality of this life-giving force was called *Wakan Tanka,* Great Incomprehensibility, the whole of all that was mysterious, powerful, sacred, holy. The *wakan* permeated all of life, all of the universe, making everything one. For this reason, "religion" for the Lakotas was not a separate institution distinct from the rest of daily life, but rather it was integral to all human experience.

The concept of *Wakan Tanka* was amorphous. *Wakan Tanka* was never born and so will never die. *Wakan Tanka* created the universe and at the same time was embodied in the universe. One Lakota explained: "The *Wakan Tanka* are those which made everything. They are *Wakanpi*. *Wakanpi* are all things that are above mankind. . . . *Wakan Tanka* are many. But they are all the same as one."[3]

Among the Lakotas, knowledge of the *wakan* beings belonged to the holy men, *wicaśa wakan,* individuals who shared to a greater or lesser extent in the universal power. Through their personal experiences in prayer, fasting, and ceremony they sought understanding of the *wakan*. Some holy men conceptualized *Wakan Tanka* as sixteen benevolent *wakan* beings, many nonhuman but nonetheless sharing human characteristics. These included sun, moon, wind, Thunder-beings, earth, rock, White Buffalo Woman, and a variety of invisible spirit forms.

In human terms, the oneness of the *wakan* beings was symbolized in kin relationships that bound all together and provided accepted patterns for interaction. Human relationships—parents and children, grandparents and grandchildren, brothers and sisters, husbands and wives— were reflections of these greater, more fundamental relationships established by the *wakan* beings.[4] The sacred pipe, brought to the Lakotas by White Buffalo Woman, one of the *Wakan Tanka,* was the tangible symbol of these relationships. When humans smoked the pipe together they bound themselves in recognized relationships that carried with them obligations for peace, friendship, and cooperation. In offering the smoke to *Wakan Tanka,* they likewise bound themselves to the *wakan* beings in

2. Good Seat, quoted in Walker, *Lakota Belief and Ritual,* p. 70.
3. Little Wound, quoted in ibid., p. 69. *Wakanpi* literally means "they are *wakan*."
4. See Brown, *The Sacred Pipe,* p. 15, n. 5.

recognized relationships, calling on the powers for pity and aid. For the Lakota people, prayer was the act of invoking relationship: the term *wacekiye* meant "to call on for aid," "to pray," "to claim relationship with." The pipe symbolized the relationship established by *Wakan Tanka* with the Lakotas, and it was therefore used in all ceremonial contexts.

Lakotas possessed a great diversity of rituals that brought power into their lives. Some of these were said to have been taught by White Buffalo Woman, whereas others had their origins in men's visions, but all rituals were patterned after the instructions given by *wakan* beings. Basic to every ritual was the sweat lodge, or lodge of purification (*ini kaǧapi*), which cleansed both a man's body and spirit and prepared him to participate in other rituals. Public rituals included great tribal festivals like the sun dance; celebrations of changes in life status, like the girls' puberty ceremony, called the Buffalo Sing (*Tatanka lowanpi*); and rites of togetherness like the *hunka* ceremony, in which one person ritually adopted another, thus bringing two families (or bands, or tribes) together as one. Many rituals expressed individuals' dream experiences, including the *heyoka* ceremony for Thunder-being dreamers, and ceremonies for dreamers of the elk, buffalo, wolf, deer, or horse. Some rituals were for healing, notably those of the bear dreamers, who used their *wakan* power to doctor wounds. Still other rituals, like the *yuwipi* ceremonies of stone dreamers, could predict the future or locate lost objects. Finally, some rituals were completely personal and secret, like those of the Bone Keepers, who made powerful love medicines.

For the Lakotas, belief and ritual were completely intertwined. Belief formed the intellectual and emotional underpinnings of religion, a system of knowledge representing mankind in relation to the universe. Belief made men's lives and the world in which men lived intelligible and acceptable, and it defined the moral structure for society. Ritual provided the means for actualizing religious power and for expressing belief. The Lakotas spoke of the purpose of ritual in terms of "pleasing" the *wakan* beings, which they believed formed the structure and substance of their world. But ritual was no mere reflection of belief; it was also the means to further belief, for through ritual people came to expand their knowledge.

In Lakota culture, the quest for knowledge of the *wakan* was largely a personal enterprise, and it was predominately the work of men. Each individual formulated a system of belief by and for himself. There was no standard theology, no dogmatic body of belief. Fundamental concepts were universally shared, but specific knowledge of the *wakan* beings was not shared beyond a small number of holy men. Through individual experience, every man had the opportunity to contribute to and resynthesize the general body of knowledge that constituted Lakota religion.

The vision quest, *hanble ceyapi,* "crying for a vision," was undertaken by every Lakota man as essential to achieving success in life's concerns. Before the quest, the candidate was taken into the sweat lodge by a holy man. There in the close darkness, cold water poured on heated rocks released the spirit or breath of the rock in clouds of steam. The ensuing heat caused the participants to sweat profusely—purifying a man's body, as one Lakota explained, "of all that makes him tired, or all that causes disease, or all that causes him to think wrong."[5] After this purification the vision seeker went away from the village to a hill to pray for a vision in solitude. His body was naked, clothed only in a breechcloth, and a furred buffalo robe was draped about his shoulders; his hair was unbraided. The seeker cried aloud for the vision, tears streaming down his face. All these tangible signs—nakedness, unbraided hair, tears—were symbols of humility. The vision seeker made himself pitiable so that the *wakan* beings would be moved to hear his prayers, to acknowledge their relationship with him.

Above all, the vision seeker was instructed to be alert, attentive, ready to receive the power of the *wakan.* The injunction *Wacin ksapa yo,* "Be attentive!" suggested a focusing of mind, or, as Black Elk repeatedly expressed it to Neihardt, "clearness of understanding" (*waableza*), preparing the will to receive wisdom.[6] Attentiveness must be maintained not only during the vision itself; it was important that it remain afterward as well. Although power originated in the vision, a man developed this power by lifelong contemplation of the vision's meaning. As one Lakota put it, mastery of the vision required "effort and study."[7]

After the vision quest, the seeker returned to the sweat lodge with the holy man who prepared him and related his experience. Couched in ritualized expressions, the "telling of the vision" (*hanbloglaka*) became for the dreamer a ritual speech the repetition of which brought forth the powers granted in the vision. For the dreamer this "vision talk" was an important

---

5. Sword, quoted in Walker, *Lakota Belief and Ritual,* pp. 83–84.
6. See the discussion in Brown, *The Sacred Pipe,* p. 64, n. 5.
7. Densmore, *Teton Sioux Music,* p. 85.

part of every subsequent ritual, validating the right to perform such ceremonies and actualizing the powers.

The vision experience invested a man with a supernatural aura, a *wakan*
quality that set the visionary apart from others. The special knowledge
and power granted by the vision placed on him the sacred duty to use
these gifts for the benefit of the people. In some cases this may have
involved no more than carrying into battle sacred objects and adornments
that would protect the dreamer from the arrows and bullets of the enemy.
In other cases the dreamer might have been commanded to hold some
ritual such as the *heyoka* ceremony, or else he would be punished for failure
to comply. Some individuals' visions showed them various herbs to cure
disease or heal wounds. A smaller number of special men received instructions for performing ceremonies of all kinds to bring the people well-
being. For them, fulfillment of their sacred duty became the dominating
theme of their lives. Black Elk was such a man.

In most respects, Black Elk's religious experiences were entirely representative of late nineteenth-century Lakota culture. It was not unusual for
a boy to have his first vision before undertaking a formal vision quest.
Many Lakotas who later became famous holy men or great warriors
experienced such unsought visions during youth. But the man who wanted power and the ability to use it effectively always undertook the formal
vision quest, repeating it many times during his life. These experiences
perfected and extended his knowledge of the *wakan*.

A comparison of Black Elk's great childhood vision with that of another Lakota, White Bull, is instructive for showing both as transformations of the same theme. Both men, at the age of nine, had visions of the
Thunder-beings. For White Bull, the vision occurred one day while he
was out of camp, trying to shoot swallows with his bow and arrows as the
birds darted overhead. In Lakota culture, swallows were held to be especially sacred, messengers of the Thunder-beings. Suddenly White Bull
fainted, and his body lay as if dead while his spirit traveled in the vision.[8]

White Bull saw a man coming from the west who was painted with red
lightning streaks and riding a black horse. The rider attacked an enemy

8. Stanley Vestal, *Warpath: The True Story of the Fighting Sioux Told in a Biography of
Chief White Bull* (Boston: Houghton Mifflin, 1934), pp. 12–15, and original notes of
interviews with White Bull, Walter S. Campbell (Stanley Vestal) Collection, Western
History Collections, University of Oklahoma, Norman, Okla.

and, as he pierced him with a lance, the victim transformed into a plant. Then the rider struck a white-faced cow with a club; suddenly the scene transformed into a large group of men and women performing the *heyoka* ceremony around a kettle in which the meat of the cow was boiling. A second rider, painted like the first and mounted on a roan, came out of the south. He charged the kettle, spearing the cow tongue as he passed. Then he transformed into a skeleton lying on the ground, and While Bull heard a voice: "If you do not become a clown [*heyoka*] when the cherries are ripe, you will be lying like this one." Next, a third rider on a white horse came from the north, and finally, a fourth rider on a sorrel horse came from the east. The four riders led White Bull to a tipi where four men wearing furred buffalo robes were beating a yellow drum. They sang four songs. When they finished, the rider on the black horse—now transformed into White Bull himself—led them all in a charge toward the west; then, transformed into swallows, they flew back to the tipi. They repeated this charge, to the north, east, and south, with White Bull leading each time, mounted on the appropriately colored horse. White Bull interpreted this vision as giving him power for victory in battle. The dream, he said, "made him brave" and prepared him for war. Later he performed the *heyoka* ceremony as he had been commanded.

Although White Bull's vision had many similarities to Black Elk's, he did not interpret it as a mandate to become a holy man. In part this reflected the times. White Bull was born in 1849; when the vision came to him in 1858 the Lakotas were still living in the old way. Buffalo were plentiful, and the northern Lakotas (White Bull was a Minneconjou) had not yet become involved in war with the whites. The road to success for a young man was still through fighting enemy tribes and gaining war honors, and it was for this kind of endeavor that White Bull found power in his vision. Even more important, perhaps, was personality. White Bull seems not to have been the visionary type—he was a man of action, not a philosopher.[9] Black Elk, on the other hand, was predisposed to inwardly directed contemplation and philosophizing. Although they shared similar experiences of the *wakan*, White Bull and Black Elk interpreted them very differently. Instead of orchestrating a horse dance to demonstrate his power before the people, White Bull used his inspiration to take the

---

9. This is Vestal's estimation. See *Warpath,* p. 15.

warpath against enemy tribes, demonstrating his power through successes in battle.

Comparison of White Bull's and Black Elk's visions reveals both the conventionality and the relativity of sacred symbols in Lakota religion. The horseback riders, painted with lightning streaks and racing across the skies, are conventional enbodiments of the Thunder-beings. The colors of their horses and their association with the four directions are also conventional, although the buckskin horses of the south in Black Elk's vision are roans in White Bull's. Spearing the enemy (symbolic of lightning striking), thereby causing transformations, is common to both men's visions. When Black Elk strikes the enemy at the headwaters of the Missouri the enemy transforms into a turtle; White Bull's enemy transforms into a plant, probably an herb to heal wounds. The animal for Black Elk's *heyoka* ceremony is an oddly colored dog (the dog was the conventional sacrificial animal). But White Bull sees an oddly colored cow, perhaps a domestic cow—a rare animal to the Lakotas at that time, and one not conventionally associated with the Thunder-beings.

Black Elk's great vision is constructed out of the elements and in the patterns of Lakota culture. That it is so rich and complex can be accounted for by the length of time over which it occurred: White Bull's experience lasted only part of an afternoon, whereas Black Elk's filled twelve days. The greatness of Black Elk's vision lies not in its uniqueness, but in its very representativeness. It synthesizes religious themes in Lakota culture and balances all aspects of the Lakota world: destruction and renewal, the powers of earth and sky and of land and water, the four directions, the living and the nonliving (both dead and unborn). Perhaps its most striking feature is the representation of the circle of life as enclosing a central tree, symbolizing regeneration, with crossed roads from south to north and west to east, the former symbolizing life and harmony and colored red, the latter symbolizing warfare and destruction and colored black. Although these are conventional symbols—the central tree was the sun dance pole itself—they are given greater prominence and more precise definition in Black Elk's vision than in the recorded teachings of other holy men. That the circle and the central tree, as axis mundi, are pan-cultural archetypes leads directly to many parallels with other religious traditions. But there is nothing in Black Elk's great vision that is foreign to Lakota culture. The same is true of the *heyoka* vision of his vision quest, which, in effect, is a restatement of the Thunder-being powers of the earlier vision, a command to fulfill the role assigned to him.

Black Elk's ghost dance visions are also rooted in Lakota culture, but their symbols reflect the pantribal teachings of the ghost dance religion. In his visions, the fearful river, the emphasis on redemption, and the Messiah are Christian in their origin—although Black Elk tied them back into his traditional Lakota religious system by interpreting the Messiah as yet another transformation of the red man of his great vision who had transformed first into a buffalo, then into an herb. Yet Black Elk's hesitancy about the ghost dance, his feeling that he should not fight the whites to defend it, his lack of faith in the efficacy of his ghost dance visions, and the ease with which after Wounded Knee he abandoned the ghost dance and its teachings, suggest how superficially this new ritual and its supporting belief system were grafted onto the older Lakota religious tradition. Clearly, Black Elk perceived the old religion as truer and more powerful.

For the Lakotas, the powers granted in visions can be thought of as the ability to recognize and utilize transformations of the natural world. Implicit to this belief system is a conception of interdependence that is more fundamental than mere interrelationship: the universe is one, and its varying life forms are different configurations of the universal animating power. Thus what appears to Black Elk first as a man painted red may actually be a spiritual power (*wakan*) that in varying guises could be man, buffalo, or herb. What the vision teaches is the key to these transformations. Here the basic concept relates to the mind or willpower (*wacin*) and to belief (*awacin*). The first grandfather told Black Elk, "You shall know the willpower of myself," which might be translated, "You shall acknowledge me," "You shall clearly understand me," "You shall believe in me." Belief and knowledge are equated, the gift of the spirits. (Compare Black Elk's injunction, "If you think about it, you can see that it is true."[10]) This is the "clarity of understanding" that fills the dreamer with power, for such knowledge is not accessible in any other way: it is personal knowledge, gained through experience and not through general philosophical truths. Its truth is individual, not universal. After receiving his vision, Black Elk said, he began to compare everything on earth with it, measuring and testing it, exploring the interconnections of its meaning in his

10. Neihardt, *Black Elk Speaks,* p. 5.

mind. When at last he performed the horse dance, the presence of the Thunder-beings in the storm that came as if to watch the proceedings, and the reflection of the vision in the clouds as if to form a model to be emulated on earth, gave Black Elk all he required to convince him that the vision was valid. The mere recollection of the vision began to bring him power.

Further testing of the vision came in matching the vision herbs with earthly ones. Black Elk tells of his search for the daybreak star herb, and of how the tangible manifestation of a variety of birds circling over the spot where the herb grew, as if leading him to it, provided both certainty in identifying the herb and confidence in its efficacy. Still, Black Elk sensed a flickering uncertainty in his ability to use it effectively. His dramatic telling of the first cure provides an invaluable insight into how the holy man comes to recognize the reality of his power. For Black Elk this was a physical sensation first, a queer feeling in his legs that seemed to raise him off the ground. He had earlier experienced this sensation when, as a child, he participated in the bear medicine ceremony as a helper. Now, performing his own ceremony, invoking his own powers, the feeling grips him totally and convinces him that what he is doing is real, that he is indeed *wakan*. He senses the blue spirit that lives inside him heaving in his chest, giving him power. He feels, as he says, "like a man"—that is, in control of himself, able to direct the power within him to help his people. This feeling develops into an omnipresent sense of duty. He senses the people weighing heavily upon him, and he sorrows that they seem to stray from the oneness and goodness of his vision. The appeal of the ghost dance was the recognition of its outward similarity to his great vision and the joyful hope that at last the vision was coming true, symbolized by the budding of the tree.

Of the many traditional Lakota rituals, Black Elk describes in detail only the bear medicine ceremony in which he participated as a child and those that he performed to enact his vision: the horse dance and the *heyoka*, buffalo, and elk ceremonies. In Lakota belief such public displays of ritual were required before a man could control the powers that had been given him. Black Elk's vision enactments number four, a sacred number that perhaps evokes the powers of the four winds. In addition, Black Elk discusses ritual smoking of the pipe, the sweat lodge, and the vision quest, and he mentions the sun dance and soul keeping rituals.

These public tribal rituals are the subject of the more detailed teachings that he later gave to Joseph Epes Brown, published as *The Sacred Pipe*.

Black Elk's teachings reflect the Lakota ritual attitude of prayer. His prayer on Harney Peak provides a good example. By making himself pitiable, with tears streaming down his face, Black Elk invoked the mercy of *Wakan Tanka*. In order to beg the powers to fulfill their relationship to mankind, the supplicant must emphasize his helplessness and his total dependence on the universal power for aid in accomplishing anything. Hence in the prayer Black Elk speaks of his own difficulties and of the despair of his people. He recalls his vision, naming over again the central symbols—the six grandfathers, the sacred hoop, the tree that failed to bloom, the powers of the four quarters. Offering his pipe, symbol of man's relationship to the powers, he begs that his people may live, stating this as his desire and asking that it be fulfilled. The prayer is addressed to the Great Spirit, *Wakan Tanka*, represented by the six grandfathers. Once again, the tangible recognition of Black Elk's power by the Thunder-beings in the form of thunder and rain validates the reality of his power and the efficacy of his prayer.

It is unquestionably reasonable to assert that Black Elk's teachings represent to a great extent traditional Lakota belief and ritual. But it would not be reasonable to assume that Black Elk's long active involvement with Roman Catholicism did not influence the way he spoke about traditional religion. In expression and attitude it is possible to abstract elements of Black Elk's teachings that seem to reflect Christian influence. Such expressions as phrases from the Bible ("like chickens under the wing," for example) are readily transparent and not especially significant, whereas less obvious attitudes may reveal deeper Christian influence.

As a starting place, it can be noted that the universalistic message of Black Elk's teachings reflects an ecumenical attitude that is foreign to traditional Lakota religion. Black Elk interprets the sacred hoop as symbolizing all the continents of the world and embracing peoples of all colors—even though, as he remarked to Neihardt (perhaps jokingly), at first he was not certain whether he saw any white people in his vision. At a personal level, Black Elk took this to mean that during his lifetime he would make friends with all the different peoples he had seen in the vision. At a more general level, he seems to have interpreted it as a promise of salvation for all peoples within the harmony of the sacred circle. Salvation, of course, is a Christian concept. Traditional Lakotas felt no such need, for they considered themselves the original and best people.[11] The emphasis on salvation may arise in part out of Black Elk's fear that the Indian people would pass away completely, overpowered by the whites. In part it may reflect his later interpretation in light of the Christian doctrine of salvation.

With the same universalistic perspective, Black Elk interpreted the sixth grandfather—the spirit of the earth (whom he himself represented in this world)—as the spirit of mankind in general, a Christ-like union of God and man. Yet it is instructive that at the time of the ghost dance, he did not immediately identify the Messiah with Christ (defined as white) or with the sixth grandfather (defined as Lakota, Black Elk himself). If the ghost dance ritual or some of its teachings had survived among the Oglalas, doubtless Black Elk would have integrated them into the Lakota religious tradition. Later, probably after his acceptance of Christianity, he came to regard the Messiah whom he had seen in his ghost dance vision, in the splendid image of the Transfiguration, as "the Son of the Great Spirit himself." This became a significant link for him between his own visionary experiences and the teachings of Christianity.[12]

As a corollary of Black Elk's universalism, he completely rejected the powers for destruction granted by his vision. Although the spirits had told him that there would be "war in the four quarters," and that he would have to depend on war and on the power of the soldier weed, Black Elk turned his back on all this in favor of peace. This, as he explained to Neihardt, was the immediate reason for his joining the Catholic Church. Thereafter his interpretations of Lakota life minimized warfare, focusing instead on the integrative themes in Lakota culture, interpreting the harmony of the circle much in the sense of the Christian concept of love.

A significant issue of Christian influence on Black Elk's teachings involves his understanding of *Wakan Tanka*. In translating the Bible into the Sioux language, Christian missionaries used the term *Wakan Tanka* (written as a single word, *Wakantanka*) to refer to God the Father, the

11. See James R. Walker, *Lakota Society,* ed. Raymond J. DeMallie (Lincoln: University of Nebraska Press, 1982), p. 3; Walker, *Lakota Belief and Ritual,* p. 115.

12. Compare the discussion in Steinmetz, *Pipe, Bible and Peyote Among the Oglala Lakota,* pp. 155–56. Steinmetz suggests (p. 159) that Black Elk integrated Lakota religion with Catholicism "on a deep emotional and unconscious level."

Three in One. It is likely that Black Elk's acceptance of Catholicism influenced him to reinterpret the six grandfathers (west, north, east, south, sky, and earth) as the Six in One—the fifth grandfather (sky) representing the Great Spirit, the creator of all. Personification of *Wakan Tanka* as a single being has no parallel in recorded Lakota religious tradition. *Wakan Tanka* traditionally was a collective concept, embodying various *wakan* beings in many different aspects. From the prayers given by Black Elk, it is not possible to infer directly his understanding of *Wakan Tanka*. In the prayer offering performed in connection with the telling of his vision, for example, Black Elk recited an ancient Lakota prayer addressed to the Great Spirit: "You have been always. . . . There is no other one to pray to but you. . . everything has been made by you." These are traditional Lakota prayer formulas and do not imply a singular conception of *Wakan Tanka*. Here, for example, are prayers of the *hunka* ceremony as recorded by Edward S. Curtis:

> Great Mystery [*Wakan Tanka*], you have existed from the first; . . .
> Wing Flapper [ritual term for the Thunder-beings], you have
>   existed from the first; . . .

Again:

> No other creature may be mentioned save you, Wing Flapper,
>   who first existed. . . .
> This day no other creature may be mentioned beside you,
>   Spotted Eagle, most powerful. . . .
> Sunrise, no other creature may be mentioned. . . .
> South, no other creature may be mentioned. . . .
> No one else may be mentioned.
> Great Mystery, you were the first to exist.
> This earth you created and placed here; . . .[13]

Both these *hunka* prayers and Black Elk's offering prayer ascribe the role of creation to *Wakan Tanka*, but the real significance here seems to be that the process of creation was the differentiation of *Wakan Tanka* into the entities that comprised the universe as the Lakotas knew it.

13. Edward S. Curtis, *The North American Indian*, vol. 3 (1908; reprint, New York: Johnson Reprint Corporation, 1970), pp. 72, 76–77.

It is impossible to assert with certainty that Black Elk reinterpreted the traditional Lakota concept of *Wakan Tanka* as the Christian Godhead. It is clear, however, that he equated the power of the Indian people as Indians with the natural world—that is, the manifestations of *Wakan Tanka*. As the wild animals disappeared, Black Elk said, so the Indian people would also disappear. The white men had taken the Indians' world, leaving them only little islands. As the Indians fled to these islands, Black Elk explained, they left their old religion behind. When the people danced the ghost dance, he said, they cried for their old ways and their old religion. To judge from Black Elk's own life experiences, after the ghost dance he and his people felt that their religion was lost to them forever, and they turned to Christianity.

Conversion to Christianity must not be misunderstood as indicating loss of faith in traditional religion. In his statement of faith dictated in 1934, Black Elk used the Lakota term "to turn myself around" (*migluhom-ni*) to express the English concept of conversion. For Black Elk, as for most Lakotas, the acceptance of Christianity seems to have been a pragmatic decision, not an emotional conversion. As one old holy man commented, "The spirits do not come to help us now. The white men have driven them away."[14] After the Christian religions came to be firmly established on the reservation, and Christian rituals and prayers became routine, it seems that for many Lakotas the sharp differences between traditional religion and Christianity began to blur. Looking back on Black Elk a quarter of a century after his death, Frank Fools Crow, his nephew and an important religious leader on Pine Ridge, commented:

> Black Elk was very interested in the teachings of the Roman Catholic Church, and spent many hours talking to the priests about it. When he and I were discussing it one day, Black Elk told me he had decided that the Sioux religious way of life was pretty much the same as that of the Christian churches, and there was no reason to change what the Sioux were doing. We could pick up some of the Christian ways and teachings, and just work them in with our own, so in the end both would be better.[15]

14. Afraid of Bear, quoted in Walker, *Lakota Belief and Ritual,* p. 202.

15. Thomas E. Mails, assisted by Dallas Chief Eagle, *Fools Crow* (Garden City, N.Y.: Doubleday, 1979), p. 45.

This undoubtedly oversimplifies Black Elk's personal struggle with the doctrines of Catholicism, but it is a clear statement of the ecumenical spirit with which Lakotas today approach religion.

Despite his acceptance of the Catholic Church and his refrainment from traditional rituals thereafter (except as demonstrations), Black Elk refused to accept the missionaries' dictum that the Lakota religion was evil, the work of the devil. As he commented to Neihardt, if anyone had power from the devil, it must be the white men. Although Black Elk seems to have believed sincerely in the white man's religion, as he testified in his 1934 statement of faith, he nonetheless still believed that the Lakota religion was good and true and that there was something in it of value not only to the Lakotas but to all mankind. It was in this spirit, surely a Christian spirit of proselytization, that he gave his teachings to Neihardt and Brown to be sent out to all the world.

As Black Elk grew to old age, the world around him changed dramatically. His experiences convinced him that at least some white people valued the old Lakota teachings and the old religion. A deepening sense of regret, of loss of what had been the source of the Lakotas' most fundamental and irreplaceable spiritual strength seems to have overcome the old man. This was undoubtedly exacerbated by the burgeoning social problems endemic to reservation life that made the most dismal prophecies of Black Elk's great vision painfully real. In the end he grieved that it had been a great tragedy for his people to abandon their old religion; yet, they had done so out of necessity, and they had to live with the new.

Today there has been a great reawakening of traditional ways and religious beliefs and rituals among the Lakotas. For Christian and traditionalist Lakotas alike, the teachings of Black Elk have taken on new life. The six grandfathers, the power symbols of the six directions, the sacred hoop with its crossed red and black roads, the sacred tree—these and many other of Black Elk's teachings have taken root in new soil, nourishing the spiritual needs of a people searching after their own uniqueness, their own identity in the modern world.

Once again the tree of Black Elk's vision is budding.

BLACK ELK'S VISION

Much of the popular interest in Black Elk's teachings stems from the appeal of his great vision. Scholars have found in it a rewarding subject for study, treating it as an open door to the traditional Lakota world.[16] Neihardt's literary retelling of the vision in *Black Elk Speaks* (pp. 20–47) makes far more dramatic and powerful reading than the stenographic record, but the latter is essential for an understanding of the vision within the context of Lakota culture. It places Black Elk firmly within the symbol system of Lakota religious tradition, and it provides the detail necessary for cultural understanding. Analysis of the published account of the vision is a literary task, whereas analysis of the stenographic record is an ethnographic study from which a great deal can be learned about Lakota religion.

Comparison of the differences between the vision as told in *Black Elk Speaks* and the stenographic record reveals Neihardt's concerns as he wrote the book. Because the vision is so essential, and because a good deal has already been written about it, it is worthwhile to make this comparison in detail. For ease of reference, the comparison is presented according to the eleven sections into which I have divided the text of the vision account. Black Elk's dog vision is also considered here.

1. *The two men take Black Elk up into the clouds.* The content of this brief introduction is substantially identical in the two versions, although one difference should be noted. In the notes the men tell Black Elk: "Your Grandfather is calling you," referring to the first (western) grandfather; *Black Elk Speaks* has "Your Grandfathers are calling you!" (p. 22), generalizing to all six grandfathers. The cloud house where the grandfathers sit in council is in the west, and it symbolizes the home of the western grandfather. Throughout the stenographic notes, Black Elk varies between referring to the grandfather(s) in the singular and in the plural. It seems that he understood himself to have been called by the western grandfather (for it was to that direction that he went) but that the western grandfather represented all six grandfathers. This rich web of symbolism is overlapping and enigmatic: Black Elk also identifies the fifth grandfather, representing the above (*Wakan Tanka*), as he in whose oneness all six grandfathers are actually embraced.

16. For a good example of this, see Paul A. Olson, "*Black Elk Speaks* as Epic and Ritual Attempt to Reverse History," in *Vision and Refuge: Essays on the Literature of the Great Plains,* ed. Virginia Faulkner with Frederick C. Leubke (Lincoln: University of Nebraska Press, 1982), pp. 3–27.

2. *Black Elk is shown the horses of the four directions.* Only minor differences between the notes and the published version occur in this section. According to the stenographic record, "One of the men said"; *Black Elk Speaks* has the two men speaking as one (p. 23). In the book, Neihardt confused some of the symbols of the horses. The notes make clear that two sets of horses (west and north) wore necklaces—one made of buffalo hoofs (west), the other of elk teeth (north). The other two sets of horses (east and south) had horns. *Black Elk Speaks* mistakenly has the elk teeth necklaces on the eastern horses (p. 23), and does not mention the eastern horses' horns. According to the notes, "birds" (of unspecified kind, probably swallows) flew above the heads of the western horses, geese above those of the north, eagles above those of the east. Surely some sort of bird flew above the southern horses as well, though this is not recorded. *Black Elk Speaks* mentions only the geese above the northern horses (p. 23). These symbols are also confused in the drawing by Standing Bear that depicts Black Elk killing the spirit in the Missouri River (on the dust jacket of the 1932 edition of *Black Elk Speaks,* or facing p. 13 in the 1979 edition), which shows horns on all four sets of horses and birds over the heads of all except those of the north.

In *Black Elk Speaks* the horses of the four directions are presented to Black Elk by the bay horse (p. 23); in the stenographic record it is the two men who show him these horses.

3. *The bay horse leads Black Elk to the cloud tipi of the six grandfathers.* In this section Neihardt followed the notes closely, although he erred in attributing both songs to the second grandfather (p. 27); the first song was sung by the first grandfather (west) and refers to the Thunder-being nation, whereas the second song was sung by the second grandfather (north) and refers to the white geese nation.

4. *Black Elk walks the black sacred road from west to east and vanquishes the spirit in the water.* At the beginning of this section the bay horse faces the four directions and reviews the powers given to Black Elk; in *Black Elk Speaks* Neihardt omitted the north from this sequence (p. 30). In the book, Black Elk rides off to face the spirit in the water alone (p. 31), but in the stenographic notes he goes with twelve other riders, including Left Hand Charger and Red One Horn; the book also omits the sacred song sung before charging the spirit. In the book, Neihardt comments that the spirit, after Black Elk strikes it, turns into a "harmless turtle" (p. 33); the

notes simply read "turtle." Neihardt probably misunderstood the turtle as a symbol. Lakota cosmology envisions cosmic warfare between the powers in the skies (the Thunder-beings) and those in the waters. Representing the Thunder-beings as he rides, Black Elk enacts this ancient conflict, and his attack symbolizes lightning striking the spirit in the water. The turtle is one of those underwater powers, and transformation of the spirit into a turtle doubtless also symbolizes the impossibility of killing the foe, because the conflict between these natural forces is eternal. Black Elk commented that this was a prophecy that in the future he would kill an enemy in battle. Neihardt omitted this and followed Black Elk's interpretation of the event as rain falling on earth, killing the drought (see below, p. 122).

5. *Black Elk walks the red sacred road from south to north.* Much of this section is very confusing in the notes, reflecting problems of translation from Lakota to English. Because of uncertainty as to which spirit is speaking to Black Elk at any given moment, in most of sections 5 through 8 Neihardt in *Black Elk Speaks* merely identifies the speakers as "a Voice." The notes for the episode in which Black Elk is given the power of the sacred days, refered to by colors—"greenward" (probably blue), white, and yellow, with red implied—are especially garbled, again indicating failure of translation (see below, p. 124). Certainly Black Elk's meaning is not fully expressed. *Black Elk Speaks* omits the songs sung in the first and third ascents, as well as the calling of the unborn generations. Most other details are identical in the two versions.

6. *Black Elk receives the healing herb of the north, and the sacred tree is established at the center of the nation's hoop.* In this section Black Elk relates demonstrations of the powers of the four directions; *Black Elk Speaks* includes only the demonstration of the powers of the north by which Black Elk is presented with an herb identified as the four-rayed herb (pp. 38–39). Neihardt's understanding was that all the healing herbs given to Black Elk in the vision were one and the same: the four-rayed or daybreak star herb, which bore flowers in the four sacred directional colors—blue, red, yellow, and white (see below, p. 134). *Black Elk Speaks* omits the powers of the other three directions from this section.

7. *Black Elk kills the dog in the flames and receives the healing herb of the west.* Neihardt omitted the entire episode from *Black Elk Speaks* in which Black Elk, together with One Side, One Red Horn, Left Hand Charger, and Brave Thunder, attacks the being in the midst of flames; after Black

Elk kills it he recognizes it as a dog. Black Elk told Neihardt that this means that in war one kills one's enemies like dogs. This is the conventional Thunder-being dream that compels the dreamer to perform the *heyoka* ceremony. This episode is repeated later in the vision that Black Elk experienced on his vision quest, at age eighteen. *Black Elk Speaks* includes the latter part of this section, in which Black Elk receives the herb from the west and cures the black horse (pp. 40–42).

8. *Black Elk is taken to the center of the earth and receives the daybreak star herb.* In this section, *Black Elk Speaks* again omits reference to One Side, who accompanied Black Elk in the vision. One passage of the book that represents Black Elk's thoughts as he stood at the center of the world (p. 43) has an analogue in the stenographic notes for section 6 (see below, p. 129):

> And while I stood there I saw more than I can tell and I understood more than I saw; for I was seeing in a sacred manner the shapes of all things in the spirit, and the shape of all shapes as they must live together like one being. And I saw that the sacred hoop of my people was one of many hoops that made one circle, wide as daylight and as starlight, and in the center grew one mighty flowering tree to shelter all the children of one mother and one father. And I saw that it was holy.

Although this clearly expresses the universalism of Black Elk's vision, the phrasing Neihardt's. Otherwise, the published version of this section is substantially the same as the stenographic record.

9. *Black Elk receives the soldier weed of destruction.* In *Black Elk Speaks* Neihardt eliminated the entire episode, in which Black Elk is shown the spirit of war and is told that he will have to depend on it in the future. At this time Black Elk received the soldier weed and the power to wipe out his enemies; he also met the four warrior riders who represented warfare throughout the universe in the fourth ascent. Although visually this is one of the strongest images in the vision, Neihardt chose to omit it as discordant with the universalistic message of the vision—just as Black Elk ultimately rejected this portion of his vision by failing to enact it on earth. To have done so would have made him a chief, but Black Elk turned his back on this possibility in the interests of peace. Black Elk's description, at the end, of how he was dressed, and of his horse, is the only part of this section included in *Black Elk Speaks* (p. 44).

10. *Black Elk returns to the six grandfathers.* Neihardt shortened this section drastically, omitting the goose power song and most of the review of the powers of the six grandfathers as each presented a cup of water to Black Elk. He eliminated the vision of the unity of people on earth that Black Elk saw in the cup of the western grandfather, as well as the gift of cocoons (symbols of the whirlwind) that the northern grandfather placed on Black Elk's wrists (power that he later used in his healing). With this gift, the northern grandfather tells Black Elk, rather enigmatically, "hundreds shall be sacred, hundreds shall be flames"; in *Black Elk Speaks* this comment is attributed to the fifth grandfather, the sky (p. 45). Neihardt also omitted the northern grandfather's gift of the little blue man with the bow and arrow, swimming in the cup of water. Black Elk was instructed to swallow the man along with the water; thereafter this spirit lived within him and helped him in his curing. Black Elk told Neihardt that he could make the man come up and swim around in a cup of water during his curing ceremonies. The ability to perform feats like this, calculated to induce trust in the healer's power, was a highly valued spiritual gift.

In *Black Elk Speaks* (p. 45) Neihardt attributes the healing song of the fourth (southern) grandfather to the oldest grandfather, the fifth (sky). The song included toward the end of the vision account (p. 46) comes not from the vision itself, but from the prayer ceremony that goes with the vision. This song was not specifically Black Elk's.

Finally, in *Black Elk Speaks,* after the cloud tipi disappears, Black Elk sees "only the tall rock mountain at the center of the world" (p. 46). This confuses the two mountains in the vision: the grandfathers' cloud tipi, according to the stenographic notes, was on Pike's Peak, but the center of the world, to which Black Elk was taken afterward, was Harney Peak in the Black Hills. Neihardt condensed the two into one.

11. *The spotted eagle guides Black Elk home.* The two accounts do not significantly diverge in this brief section.

The dog vision. When Black Elk underwent the traditional young Lakota man's vision quest at age eighteen, he saw repeated in his vision the episode of the killing of the dog from his great vision (episode 7 above) and understood from this that it was his duty to perform the *heyoka* ceremony. Neihardt recounts the second vision in detail in *Black Elk Speaks* (pp. 187–191), following the stenographic notes closely. The only significant divergence is that, whereas in the interview notes a single dog is killed, which then transforms into a man, in the published version there are two dogs, which transform into white men. It seems likely that Neihardt made this change for literary effect, for there appears to be no confusion in the stenographic version, which portrays as it stands a representative *heyoka* dream.

Through the stenographic record there emerges a clearer, more detailed picture of Black Elk's religious life than can be gained from reading *Black Elk Speaks*. The intricacy of the images of the west is impressive in an artistic sense, with many natural phenomena symbolizing the Thunder-beings: thunder and lightning, horses, dogs, swallows, butterflies, dragonflies. Each functions as a specific representation of the western powers. Black Elk stands between these natural forces and his people, as a conduit for *wakan* power and an intercessor for the people. This is suggested in the drawing by Standing Bear that depicts Black Elk, with all the forces of Thunder at his back, facing the open hoop of his people (facing p. 173 in the 1979 edition of *Black Elk Speaks*).

Study of the interview notes in full not only helps explicate Black Elk's traditional religious life, it also provides a wealth of information on historical and cultural topics, thus carrying on the spirit of the dialogue between Neihardt and Black Elk: the quest for understanding.

[1]

Boyhood (1863–72)

THE OLD MEN TELL THEIR AGES

Black Elk [*Hehaka Sapa*], age sixty-seven: I was born on Little Powder River in 1863, the Winter When the Four Crows Were Killed ([on] Tongue River).[1]

Standing Bear [*Mato Najin*], age seventy-two: I was born on Tongue River in the Winter When the Children Died of Coughing (1859).

Fire Thunder [*Wakinyan Peta*], age eighty-two: I was born at the mouth of Beaver Creek in Wyoming during the Year When the Indians Died of Cramps (1849).

Holy Black Tail Deer [*Sinte Sapa Wakan*], age seventy-four: I was born

---

1. The Lakotas measured time and dated events by reference to winter counts, annual calendars that named each year after a memorable event. Originally recorded as pictographs, these year names were later transcribed in written form. The Lakotas referred to a year, from first snow to first snow, as a "winter." Throughout the interviews, Black Elk and the other old men used these winter count names to date past events. For three Oglala winter counts and a discussion of the literature on the subject, see Walker, *Lakota Society*, pp. 111–57.

The stenographic record incorrectly gives Black Elk's age at seventy-two. No Ears's winter count gives 1864 as the "Winter When the Four Crows Were Killed" (Walker, *Lakota Society*, p. 144). This corroborates the date given by Black Elk, when the discrepency between calendar years and Lakota "winters" is taken into account. "Winters" span two calendar years; hence a difference of a calendar year one way or the other is to be expected in dating entries in winter counts. The 1900 Pine Ridge census gives Black Elk's age as thirty-seven, further corroborating his birth in 1863 (National Archives and Records Service, Record Group 75, Microcopy M595, roll 368). Black Elk's tombstone incorrectly gives his date of birth as 1858.

in the western Black Hills on the Wyoming side on Bear Creek in the Year When Yellow Blanket Was Killed (1857).[2] (Yellow Blanket was a Crow Indian who was scouting for a war party and they chased him and killed him.)

BLACK ELK TELLS OF HIS PARENTAGE

To begin with, I am the fourth of the name Black Elk. My father was a medicine man and was brother to several medicine men. My father was cousin to Crazy Horse's father. (Sioux medicine man—wapiapi [*wapiyapi*], "fixing up."[3]) My grandfather was killed by Pawnees. My mother's name was White Cow Sees. I remember my grandmother on my mother's side—her name was Plenty Eagle Feathers. My mother's father was Refuse To Go.[4] At this time my grandmother and grandfather on my father's side died. I was three years old when my father was in the Fetterman fight [near Fort Philip Kearny, December 21, 1866]—he got his right leg broken. Just about the year of the Big Foot massacre [at Wounded Knee Creek, December 29, 1890] my father died and was buried out in these hills in 1889.

2. The stenographic record gives the year as 1854—obviously incorrect if Black Tail Deer was seventy-four. White Cow Killer's winter count gives the date for this event as 1858–59. See Garrick Mallery, *Pictographs of the North American Indian*, Smithsonian Institution, Bureau of American Ethnology, Annual Report 4 (1886), p. 143. Again it is essential to bear in mind that the Lakota "winter" covers two calendar years. The 1897 Pine Ridge census gives Black Tail Deer's age as forty, corroborating his birth in 1857 (Microcopy M595, roll 367).

3. The Lakotas use the word *wapiyapi* (from *piya*, to make anew) to designate a healer. *Pejuta wicaśa* (literally, medicine man) refers to a healer who uses roots and other medicines to cure; this term is also used for white men's doctors. *Wicaśa wakan*, or *wakan wicaśa* (holy man), is a healer whose power comes from the mystical experiences of his vision. There are no sharp distinctions among these three designations; rather, they can be thought of as emphasizing different aspects of a healer's power: *wapiyapi* implies conjuring, *pejuta wicaśa* emphasizes the use of medicinal cures, and *wicaśa wakan* brings to mind visionary power and wisdom. See Sword in Walker, "The Sun Dance and Other Ceremonies of the Oglala Division of the Teton Dakota," p. 152, and in Walker, *Lakota Belief and Ritual*, pp. 91–92.

4. Later in the stenographic record Black Elk's grandfather's name is given as Keeps His Tipi. These are undoubtedly alternate translations of his Lakota name, which may have been *Iglaka Tehila*; this was also the name of a small Oglala band. See Stephen Return Riggs, *Dakota Grammar, Texts, and Ethnography*, ed. James Owen Dorsey, Contributions to North American Ethnology 9 (Washington, D.C., 1893), p. 163.

FIRE THUNDER TELLS OF THE FETTERMAN FIGHT

I was sixteen years old at the Fetterman fight.[5] We camped on Tongue River. A man by the name of Big Road was the chief of our band at this time. Red Cloud was, of course, over all of us. We decided to go on a warpath, several different bands all taking part on horseback. We were out to fight anything, but particularly we were after the soldiers. We started out, camping twice from Tongue River the same day. We were going toward the Piney Creek Fort [Fort Philip Kearny]. We had come out to attack the fort. Sent ten men ahead to coax them out of the fort and then we were going to hide there nearby. There is a hill there and this band of ours divided into two parts and stood on either side of this hill.

We waited there for an hour or so and heard a shot soon and knew that meant the soldiers were coming. This happened right on the north side of Piney Creek. I was on the west side of the hill. The riders were coaxing the soldiers back. Some got off their horses, leading them, pretending they were worn out. The Indians came first downhill and the soldiers followed, firing on the running Indians all the time. My weapons were six-shooters and bow and arrows, which I had traded for. As the Indians got down the hill, got to a little flat, the soldiers in between them began to holler.

I was riding a sorrel horse and just as I was about to get on my horse, the soldiers stopped and began to fight the Indians back up the hill. I hung on to my sorrel. As they charged I pulled out my six-shooter and began killing them. There were lots of bullets and lots of arrows—like locusts. The soldiers did not kill all the Indians that were killed, as the Indians killed each other as well as the soldiers. I saw them shot through the arms

5. On December 21, 1866, Sioux and Cheyenne decoys lured Lt. Col. W. J. Fetterman and his eighty men out of Fort Philip Kearny and into ambush; all the soldiers were killed. For a history of the struggles between whites and Indians in Wyoming during the 1860s, see Grace Raymond Hebard and E. A. Brininstool, *The Bozeman Trail: Historical Accounts of the Blazing of the Overland Routes into the Northwest, and the Fights with Red Cloud's Warriors,* 2 vols. (Cleveland: Arthur H. Clark, 1922). Also see Hyde, *Red Cloud's Folk,* pp. 147–49, and Olson, *Red Cloud and the Sioux Problem,* pp. 50–51. The best firsthand Lakota accounts are those of White Bull in Vestal, *Warpath,* pp. 50–69, and in James H. Howard, trans. and ed., *The Warrior Who Killed Custer: The Personal Narrative of Chief Joseph White Bull* (Lincoln: University of Nebraska Press, 1968), pp. 37–38. An excellent summary account from the Cheyenne perspective, but that draws on all other sources as well, is Father Peter John Powell, *People of the Sacred Mountain: A History of the Northern Cheyenne Chiefs and Warrior Societies, 1830–1879, with an Epilogue, 1969–1974,* 2 vols. (San Francisco: Harper & Row, 1981), 1:451–61.

and legs. They charged up the hill [*little by little*], losing men as they went. There were only a few left. There was no place to hide so they got on the hill and surrounded them. As they charged up the hill some of the soldiers let go of their horses and the Indians tried to capture some of the horses.

I tried to catch a horse, but I thought it was a good day to die so I just went ahead fighting. I wasn't after horses—I was after white men. Just as I was going up the hill I saw there were seven horses left, so I just caught one of them, as it came right by me. We were told to crawl inch by inch onto the soldiers, so I got off my horse. When we got closer someone hollered: "Let's go; this is a good day to die. If we don't, someone is going to die today, and at home our women are hungry!" Then they all hollered "Hoka He!" Then we all jumped up and went for them.

I was pretty quick on my feet and was first to get there [*and I scalped a soldier lying there*]. I killed five or six of these soldiers myself—three with my six-shooter and three with arrows. Some of the soldiers that we were among now were dead and [*a few*] of them were alive. They all got up and fought hard. There were none of them left at the end of the fight. The only living thing was a dog. We didn't kill the dog because he looked too sweet.

After the fight was over, we picked up our wounded and started back to the Tongue and just left the dead lying there. It was pretty cold weather to bury anything—the ground was frozen solid. We did bury a few by just turning them over in the hollow ground. There was a terribly big blizzard that night and we lost most of our wounded going home, and most of the [remaining] wounded died when they did get home. This was the same time when Black Elk's father was wounded.

BLACK ELK TELLS HOW CREEPING CURED THE SNOWBLINDS

I was at this time not allowed to play outside. [*I liked to play outside. Raised in a tipi.*] At this same winter they broke camp. They went somewhere, but I was too young to remember exactly where. During this winter everyone got snowblind. They couldn't see anything. There was only one who wasn't snowblind, so he led the rest. This was in March, and we were moving west. Holy Black Tail Deer was nine years old then at the same camp. We were trying to find elk, and I remember that we moved camp after this and there was a big famine and we started out for meat. My uncle went with us hunting and they finally brought meat back. We were hunting all over after the rest of our band which had broken camp a little before. We roamed all over and I was the lookout sitting in a travois, my mother on a horse. We went to a creek and camped here and the men went out hunting, bringing back meat.

One day in camp a [*great*] medicine man by the name of Creeping came. [*He went around from camp to camp*] curing snowblinds. He would put snow before the eyes and blow on the back of the head and this blew dirt out of their eyes and they were thus cured. He was curing people all day long. This medicine man had a way of loading a gun just once and singing this sacred song of his and the gun would go off each time he sang the song regardless of the fact that there seemingly could be no loading in the gun. Here are the words of the song:

> Who is this that you face the dragonfly?
> They are the people I belong to.

Second song:

> Boys, face me, like butterfly I am, myself.

These two songs gave him the power to cure snowblindness. He acquired these songs during one of his dreams as a dreamer of the Thunder-beings, heyoka kaga [*heyoka kaġa*], fool impersonation.[6]

---

6. *Heyoka kaġa* (literally, to make *heyoka*) was a ceremony performed by Lakotas who had dreamed of the Thunder-beings (*Wakinyan*). Such visions bestowed great power, but the individual (either male or female) lived in dread of thunder and lightning until he had enacted ("made") his vision publicly before the people. The *heyoka* himself plays the role of sacred clown, performing everything backward in order to make people laugh. The *heyoka* ceremony (*heyoka woze,* or *heyoka* ladling) centers on the ritual boiling of a dog; pieces of cooked meat are removed with bare hands by the *heyoka* dancers, and they splash boiling water about. Black Elk's visions gave him power from the Thunder-beings (the west), and he lived in fear of thunderstorms until he had begun to enact his visions on earth. An excellent discussion of the *heyoka* by Thomas Tyon, an Oglala, appears in Walker, *Lakota Belief and Ritual,* pp. 155–57. Also see James Owen Dorsey, *A Study of Siouan Cults,* Smithsonian Institution, Bureau of American Ethnology, Annual Report 11 (1894), pp. 468–71; Densmore, *Teton Sioux Music,* pp. 157–72; Ella Cara Deloria, *Speaking of Indians* (New York: Friendship Press, 1944), pp. 53–55.

STANDING BEAR TELLS HOW THE INDIANS
FELT ABOUT THE WHITES

The way I felt about this question is that I felt that the white men would just simply wipe us out and there would be no Indian nation. I felt this when I was a [*boy, old enough to realize*].

BLACK TAIL DEER TELLS HOW THE INDIANS
FELT ABOUT THE WHITES

From what I heard from old people, I thought I would just have to do my part. We roamed the country freely, and this country belonged to us in the first place. There was plenty of game and we were never hungry. But since the white men came we were fighting all the time. The white man was just going to kill all of us. I was so scared that I rode one horse all night just guarding. I learned a great deal because my parents taught me everything. The band I was in got together and said they were not going to let the white men run over them and down deep in my heart I was going to defend my fellow men to the last. At the age of ten or eleven I had a six-shooter and a quiver full of arrows to defend my nation.

FIRE THUNDER TELLS HOW THE INDIANS
FELT ABOUT THE WHITES

When I was old enough, about fourteen, I remember that the white men were coming and that they were going to fight us to the finish and take away our land, and I thought it was not right. We are humans too and God created us all alike, and I was going to do the best I could to defend my nation. So I started out on the warpath when I was sixteen years old.

BLACK ELK TELLS ABOUT BOYS' GAMES

When we were youngsters nobody taught us, but it was just in our blood to be prepared. In the different bands, the Indian boys used to play battle with mud on the ends of sticks, which they threw at each other. Throwing each other off horseback was another game we had. This was done by wrestling. The boys were six or seven years old when they played these games on horseback. I just thought that when we grew older we might win out. Boy battles on horseback were called "throwing them off their horses." They grabbed each other after charging—trying to pull each other off the horses. Once while playing this game—I was naked, as we always were while playing this game, and I fell right down into the center of a cactus.[7]

STANDING BEAR TELLS ABOUT FIGHTING THE WHITE SOLDIERS

We went into battle naked because it is more handy. You can get around quickly and are more swift in every way. With clothes on you would be much slower. We had the pony's bridle fastened to our belt to keep the pony from getting away when the rider would fall off.

We wouldn't have fought the white men if they hadn't fought us. We would have allowed them to live among us in peace. The white cavalry did not know how to fight. They stuck together and thus made an easy target for us. When we started fighting, we would probably be under the horse's belly and after we were on the ground we would jump around, and it was pretty hard to hit us. We'd zigzag toward them. It was open order fighting. We fought in circles because when we go around them it would scare the soldiers and then we would charge on them at this time. Some would go one way and the others would go another way, thus disorganizing the soldiers. We would hang on our ponies at times with one leg. This is a real trick to know how to do. Then we would shoot under the horse's neck, while the other leg is cramped up on the side.

BLACK ELK TELLS ABOUT CAMPING ON THE ROSEBUD

Then we camped on the Rosebud. I heard that a war party was going out. After this shortly, [I] heard that they were having the Wagon Box fight. This was in the middle of the summer. Fire Thunder was in the Wagon Box fight (the Attacking of the Wagons) [August 2, 1867].

FIRE THUNDER TELLS ABOUT THE WAGON BOX FIGHT

The band was camped on the Rosebud. We heard that there were three parties of soldiers—one on the Little Big Horn [Fort C. F. Smith], one at

7. For references to Lakota games, see below, December 6, n. 11.

Piney Creek [Fort Philip Kearny], and one at the head of Powder Creek [Fort Reno]. Then after a meeting of the council, we decided that we were going to go on a warpath against the soldiers at Piney Creek and Little Big Horn the next day. They sent no scouts, for the whole party saw the covered wagons. The wagons were in a circle with their stock in the middle. We charged on this group of soldiers and they drove us back aways.[8]

BLACK ELK TELLS OF HEARING VOICES

When I was four years old, I played a little here and there and while playing I would hear a voice [*singing*] now and then, but I did not catch it very well then.

FIRE THUNDER TELLS OF THE ATTACK
ON THE WAGON TRAIN

While playing around I heard that Indians attacked a train of freight with a lot of groceries in it, not knowing where it was. [*At the head of Tongue River.*] There were some soldiers' wagons going north. So the Indians got scared and left everything, took one wagon and left.[9]

8. After holding their sun dances, the Sioux and Cheyennes split up to attack the forts. A large party of Cheyennes, with some of the Sioux, attacked a haying crew near Fort C. F. Smith on August 1, 1867. They were driven off by the soldiers' new breech-loading Springfields, the first repeating rifles the Indians had experienced. See Olson, *Red Cloud and the Sioux Problem*, p. 63.

The next day, August 2, the main body of the Sioux with some of the Cheyennes attacked a wood-cutting crew west of Fort Philip Kearny. The soldiers took refuge within a circle of wagon boxes and again were able to save themselves with their new repeating rifles. See Hebard and Brininstool, *The Bozeman Trail*, 2:39–87; Hyde, *Red Cloud's Folk*, pp. 159–60; Olson, *Red Cloud and the Sioux Problem*, p. 64. The best firsthand Lakota accounts of the Wagon Box fight are by White Bull in Vestal, *Warpath*, pp. 70–83, and Howard, *The Warrior Who Killed Custer*, pp. 38–39. For the Cheyenne perspective, see Powell, *People of the Sacred Mountain*, 2:747–54.

9. American Horse's winter count for 1867–68 records: "They captured a train of wagons near Tongue River. The men who were with it got away." Mallery, *Pictographs of the North American Indian*, p. 144. The freight train undoubtedly supplied the Union Pacific work crews.

STANDING BEAR TELLS OF THE DEATH
OF HIGH SHIRT'S MOTHER

That winter [1867] I was eight years old (the Year High Shirt's Mother Was Killed by a Falling Tree) at this camp on Powder River.[10] In the fall we camped. There were lots of cottonwood trees here. It was windy all day and all night. While sleeping that night I was awakened by a noise, so I heard someone say that an old woman had gotten killed by the falling of a tree. [*The wind blew the tree over on the tipi.*]

BLACK ELK TELLS OF HIS FIRST VISION

The first time I rode a horse I was five years old and my father[11] made me some bows and arrows. This was in the spring. I was out in the woods trying to get a bird and just as I was going into the woods there was a thunderstorm coming and I heard a voice over there. This was not a dream—it actually happened. I saw two men coming out of a cloud with spears. As I was looking up to that, there was a kingbird sitting there and these two men were coming toward me singing the sacred song and that bird told me to listen to the two men. The kingbird said: "[*Look,*] the clouds all over are one-sided, a voice is calling you."[12] I looked up and the two men were coming down singing:

> Behold him, a sacred voice is calling you.
> All over the sky a sacred voice is calling you.

I stood gazing at them and they were coming from the north; then they started toward the west and were geese.

This vision lasted about twenty minutes.

10. The stenographic record gives Standing Bear's age at the time as five, an obvious inconsistency. White Cow Killer's winter count gives 1869–70 as the date for the death of High Shirt's mother. See Mallery, *Pictographs of the North American Indian*, p. 145.

11. *Black Elk Speaks*, p. 18, has "Grandfather."

12. "One-sided," *wasanica*, implies a sacred (not an ordinary) manner, beneficial to mankind. That it is a kingbird (flycatcher) who makes this announcement to Black Elk is not mere happenstance, for the Lakotas call this bird *wasnasnaheca*, a word that may suggest *wasanica*, although it is not identical to it.

(Note. This vision happened in the Year of Red Cloud's Treaty [1868].)[13]

At this time [1869] I was six years old. It seemed that at times I would hear someone calling me, and then at other times I would forget entirely about this voice.

[*After the vision I felt that someone was calling me always after that. That winter High Vertebra (Hump) was killed* (1870).[14]]

When I was about seven years old [1871] there were a good many Flatheads killed.[15]

I remember that there was a man by the name of Yellow Bear who was talking with some chiefs in a tipi. A man came in and shot Yellow Bear right on the spot [1872].[16]

13. The 1868 treaty ended the so-called Red Cloud war. The army capitulated to the chief's demands, closing the Bozeman Trail and abandoning Forts C. F. Smith and Philip Kearny. The treaty also established the principal foundation for all further legal relations between the Sioux and the United States. See Hyde, *Red Cloud's Folk,* pp. 162–84, and Olson, *Red Cloud and the Sioux Problem,* pp. 66–82.

14. Hump was killed in a fight with Shoshones during the summer of 1870; the event was commemorated in many winter counts. See Mallery, *Pictographs of the North American Indian,* p. 145, and Walker, *Lakota Society,* p. 146. Also see Hyde, *Red Cloud's Folk,* pp. 192–93, and Mari Sandoz, *Crazy Horse: The Strange Man of the Oglalas* (New York: Alfred A. Knopf, 1942), pp. 261–63.

15. The fight with the Flatheads to drive them from Lakota hunting grounds is described in Stanley Vestal, *Sitting Bull, Champion of the Sioux,* rev. ed. (Norman: University of Oklahoma Press, 1957 [original 1932]), pp. 118–24, and Vestal, *Warpath,* pp. 117–24.

16. American Horse's winter count records the killing of Yellow Bear by John Richard in spring 1872. See Mallery, *Pictographs of the North American Indian,* p. 145. The best account of this event was dictated by William Garnett to Judge Eli Ricker in 1907 and is printed in Donald F. Danker, "The Violent Deaths of Yellow Bear and John Richard Jr.," *Nebraska History* 63(2) (Summer 1982):137–51.

[2]

The Great Vision (1873)

When I was nine years old, many Pawnees got killed and the camp was now going toward the Rocky Mountains.[1] I was now able to shoot a prairie chicken, a grouse, and other things quite well. I was also training in slinging the mud at this time.

Close to the Crow camp on the Little Big Horn I was riding along and I heard something calling me again. Just before we got to Greasy Grass Creek [the Little Big Horn], they camped again for the night. There was a man by the name of Man Hip who invited me for supper. While eating I heard a voice. I heard someone say, "It is time, now they are calling you." I knew then that I was called upon by the spirits so I thought I'd just go where they wanted me to. As I came out of the tent both of my thighs hurt me.

The next morning [*they broke camp and*] I started out with some others on horseback. We stopped at a creek to get a drink. When I got off my horse I crumbled down, helpless, and I couldn't walk. The boys helped me up and when the camp camped again, I was very sick. They went on,

---

1. The event is recorded in Cloud Shield's winter count for 1873–74: "They killed many Pawnees on the Republican River" (Mallery, *Pictographs of the North American Indian,* p. 145). On August 5, 1873, the Oglalas and Brulés attacked the Pawnees during their summer buffalo hunt; the Lakotas killed one hundred or more of their enemies. See George E. Hyde, *Pawnee Indians* (Denver: University of Denver Press, 1951), pp. 244–47, and Paul D. Riley, "The Battle of Massacre Canyon," *Nebraska History* 54 (1973):220–49.

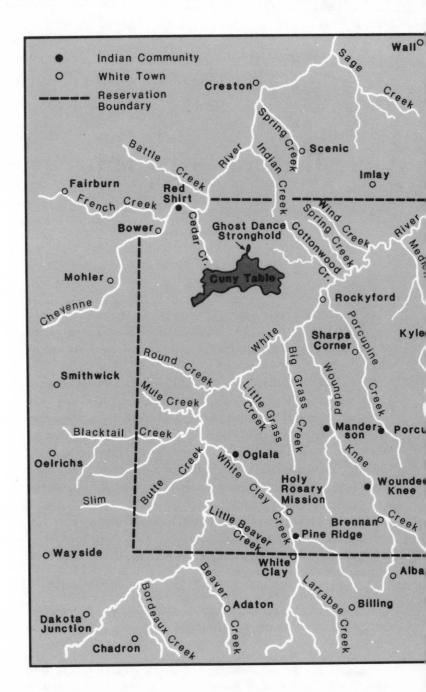

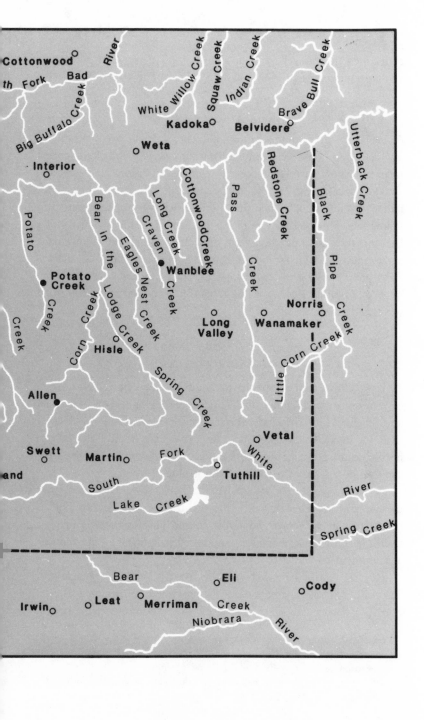

taking me to the Sioux band camp and I was still pretty sick. Both my legs and arms were swollen badly and even my face. This all came suddenly.

THE TWO MEN TAKE BLACK ELK UP INTO THE CLOUDS

As I lay in the tipi I could see through the tipi the same two men whom I saw before and they were coming from the clouds.[2] Then I recognized them as the same men I had seen before in my first vision. They came and stood off aways from me and stopped, saying: "Hurry up, your grandfather is calling you." When they started back I got up and started to follow them. Just as I got out of the tipi I could see the two men going back into the clouds and there was a small cloud coming down toward me at the same time, which stood before me. I got on top of the cloud and was raised up, following the two men, and when I looked back, I saw my father and mother looking at me. When I looked back I felt sorry that I was leaving them.

BLACK ELK IS SHOWN THE HORSES
OF THE FOUR DIRECTIONS

I followed those men on up into the clouds and they showed me a vision of a bay horse standing there in the middle of the clouds. One of the men said: "Behold him, the horse who has four legs, you shall see." I stood there and looked at the horse and it began to speak. It said: "Behold me; my life history you shall see. Furthermore, behold them, those where the sun goes down, their lives' history you shall see."

I looked over there and saw twelve black horses toward the west, where the sun goes down. All the horses had on their necks necklaces of buffalo hoofs. [*I saw above the twelve head of horses birds.*[3]] I was very scared of those twelve head of horses because I could see the light[ning] and thunder around them.

Then they showed me twelve white horses with necklaces of elks' teeth and said: "Behold them, those who are where the giant lives [the north]."[4] Then I saw some white geese flying around over the horses.

2. For comparison of the stenographic notes on the vision with the account in *Black Elk Speaks,* see pp. 94–98.

3. Probably swallows, symbolic of the Thunder-beings.

4. For the Lakotas, elks' teeth, because of their durability, were symbolic of long life. See Shooter in Densmore, *Teton Sioux Music,* p. 176.

Then I turned around toward the east, where the sun shines continually. The men said: "Behold them, those where the sun shines continually." I saw twelve head of horses, all sorrels [*and these sorrels had horns and there were some eagles flying above the sorrels*].

Then I turned to the place where you always face, the south, and saw twelve head of buckskin horses. They said: "Behold him, those where you always face." These horses had horns.[5]

[*At the beginning of the vision they were all horses, only two* (sets) *had necklaces* (the blacks and the whites) *and two had horns* (the sorrels and the buckskins).]

When I had seen it all, the bay horse said to me: "Your grandfathers are having a council, these shall take you; so take courage." Then these horses went into formation of twelve abreast in four lines—blacks, whites, sorrels, buckskins. As they stood, the bay horse looked to the west and neighed. I looked over there and saw great clouds of horses in all colors and they all neighed back to this horse and it sounded like thunder. Then the horse neighed toward the north and the horses came through there and neighed back again. These horses were in all colors also. Then the bay looked toward the east and he neighed and some more horses neighed back. The bay looked southward and neighed and the horses neighed back to him from there.

The bay horse said to me: "Behold them, your horses come dancing." I looked around and saw millions of horses circling around me—a sky full of horses. Then the bay horse said: "Make haste." The horse began to go beside me and the forty-eight horses followed us. I looked around and all the horses that were running changed into buffalo, elk, and all kinds of animals and fowls and they all went back to the four quarters.

THE BAY HORSE LEADS BLACK ELK TO THE CLOUD TIPI OF THE SIX GRANDFATHERS

I followed the bay horse and it took me to a place on a cloud under a rainbow gate and there were sitting my six grandfathers, sitting inside of a rainbow door, and the horses stopped behind me.[6] I saw on either side of

5. Birds—probably hawks—undoubtedly flew above the heads of these horses also.

6. The cloud tipi is the house of the Thunder-beings (the first grandfather). George Sword (unpublished writings) described a similar lodge seen in a vision. Likewise, the rainbow is symbolic of the Thunder-beings.

me a man whom I recognized as those of the first vision. The horses took their original positions in the four quarters.

One of the grandfathers said to me: "Do not fear, come right in" (through the rainbow door). So I went in and stood before them. The horses in the four quarters of the earth all neighed to cheer me as I entered the rainbow door.

The grandfather representing where the sun goes down said: "Your grandfathers all over the world and the earth are having a council and there you were called, so here you are. Behold then, those where the sun goes down; from thence they shall come, you shall see. From them you shall know the willpower of myself, for they shall take you to the center of the earth, and the nations of all kinds shall tremble.[7] Behold where the sun continually shines, for they shall take you there."

The first grandfather then showed me a wooden cup with water, turning it toward me. He said: "Take courage and be not afraid, for you will know him. And furthermore, behold him, whom you shall represent. By representing him, you shall be very powerful on earth in medicines and all powers. He is your spirit and you are his body and his name is Eagle Wing Stretches."

When I looked up I saw flames going up from the rainbow. The first grandfather gave me a cup of water and also a bow and arrow and said: "Behold them, what I give you shall depend on, for you shall go against our enemies and you shall be a great warrior." Then he gave me that cup of water and said: "Behold, take this, and with this you shall be great." (This means that I should kill all sickness on earth with this water.)

After this he got up and started to run toward where the sun goes down and as he ran he changed into a black horse as he faced me. The five men left said: "Behold him." And this black horse changed into a poor horse.[8]

7. "Willpower" (*tawacin*) is an important concept for understanding Lakota religion, for it is the power of mind—which is not merely passive, but creative—that is enriched ("made wise") by the vision experiences. Here the western grandfather promises that Black Elk will share in his willpower, thus giving him power to use on earth. To receive such power—or to activate it once one has it—requires "clarity of understanding" (*waableza*), a focusing of mental energies on the psychic gifts of the spirits. It is probably this to which the Lakotas refer when they say that mastery of a vision requires "effort and study" (Densmore, *Teton Sioux Music*, p. 85). See Brown, *The Sacred Pipe*, p. 64, no. 5.

8. Throughout the interviews the term "poor" is used in the sense of "emaciated."

The second grandfather rose and said: "Take this and make haste." So I took an herb out of the second grandfather's hand. And as [*I turned to the dying horse*] I held it toward the black horse [*and this holy herb*] cured the black horse, making him strong and fat once again.

The second grandfather represented the north. He said: "Behold the mother earth, for you shall create a nation." (This means that I am going to cure lots of sickness with this herb—bring children back to life.) The bay horse stood with the black horse and said to me: "Father, paint me, for I shall make a nation on the earth." [The] second grandfather of the north said again: "Take courage and behold, for you shall represent the wing of the great giant that lives."9 The second grandfather stood up and ran toward the north and as he turned around he changed himself again into a white goose. I looked toward where the black horses were and they were thunders and the northern white horses turned into white geese. The second grandfather said: "Behold then, your grandfather, for they shall fly in circles from one end of the earth to the other." [*Through this power of the north I will make everybody cry as geese do when they go north in the spring because the hardship is over.*]

First grandfather's song:

> They are appearing, may you behold.
> They are appearing, may you behold.
> The thunder nation is appearing, may you behold.

Second grandfather's song:

> They are appearing, may you behold.
> They are appearing, may you behold
> The white geese nation is appearing, may you behold.

The third grandfather, where the sun continually shines, says: "Younger brother, take courage, for across the earth they shall take you. Behold them" (pointing to the morning star and below the star there were two men flying), "from them you shall have power. All the fowls of the universe, these he has wakened and also he has wakened the beings on the earth" (animals, people, etc.). As the third grandfather said this, he held in his hand a peace pipe, which had a spotted eagle outstretched on the

9. The "great giant that lives" is *Waziya*, personification of the north. His "wing" (winged) is the white goose.

handle of the pipe; apparently the eagle was alive for it was moving. He said: "Behold this, for with this you shall walk across the earth. Behold this, for with this whatever is sick on this earth you shall make well."

Then the third grandfather pointed to a man who was solid red in color and said: "Behold him." Then the red man lay down and changed into a buffalo before he got up.[10] When he was standing up, the third grandfather said "Behold him" again. The buffalo ran back to the east and when he looked at the horses in this direction they all turned into buffalo.

The fourth grandfather said to me: "Younger brother, behold me; a nation's center of the earth I shall give you with the power of the four quarters. With the power of the four quarters like relatives you shall walk. Behold the four quarters." And after he said this I looked and saw that at each of the four quarters there was a chief. [*At the time I grew up to manhood there was no war and the Indians all became white men and if there had been the right feeling among the Indians I would have been the greatest, most powerful medicine man of the ages.*]

The fourth grandfather had a stick in his hand and he said: "Behold this, with this to the nation's center of the earth, many you shall save." I looked at the stick and saw that it was sprouting out and at the top there were all kinds of birds singing. The fourth grandfather said: "With this you shall brace yourself as a cane and thus your nation shall brace themselves with this as a cane and upon this cane you shall make a nation. Behold the earth, for across it there are two roads. Behold the sacred road from where the giant is to where we always face. Behold, this road shall be your nation. From this road you shall receive good." (Meaning red sacred road from north to south, a good road for good spirits.)

Next the fourth grandfather pointed to the road from where the sun shines continually to where the sun goes down and said: "Behold the black road, for it is the road of the Thunder-beings" (road of fearfulness); or, "Behold the black road for it shall be a fearful road. With this road you shall defend yourself." (Whenever I go to war I shall get powers from this fearful road and will be able to destroy any enemies. From the red road I get power to do good. From east to west I have power to destroy and from north to south power to do good.)

"Behold the earth with four ascents you shall walk." (This power will

10. The same transformation of a red man into a buffalo is repeated for the north (second grandfather); see below, p. 128.

be with me for four generations.)[11] The fourth grandfather turned around and started to the south and then he rolled on the ground and became a horse and he rolled once more and became an elk. He then stood among the buckskins and they too turned into elks.

The fifth grandfather represented the Great Spirit above. He said: "Boy, I sent for you and you came. Behold me, my power you shall see." He stretched his hands out and turned into a spotted eagle. Then he said: "Behold them; they, the fowls of the universe, shall come to you. Things in the skies shall be like relatives" (meaning stars). "They shall take you across the earth with my power. Your grandfathers shall attack an enemy and be unable to destroy him, but you will have the power to destroy. You shall go with courage. This is all." Then the eagle flew up over my head and I saw the animals and birds all coming toward me to perform a duty.

Then the sixth grandfather said: "Boy, take courage, you wanted my power on earth, so you shall know me. You shall have my power in going back to the earth. Your nation on earth shall have great difficulties. There you shall go. Behold me, for I will depart." (The sixth grandfather was a very old man with very white hair.) I saw him go out the rainbow gate. I followed him out the rainbow gate. I was on the bay horse now that had talked to me at the first. I stopped and took a good look at the sixth grandfather and it seemed that I recognized him. I stood there for awhile very scared and then as I looked at him longer I knew it was myself as a young man. At the first he was an old man, but he got younger and younger until he was a little boy nine years old. This old man had in his hand a spear.

BLACK ELK WALKS THE BLACK SACRED ROAD FROM WEST TO EAST AND VANQUISHES THE SPIRIT IN THE WATER

I remembered that the grandfather of the west had given me a wooden cup of water and a bow and arrow and with this bow and arrow I was going to destroy the enemy with the power of the fearful road. With the wooden cup of water I was to save mankind. This water was clear and with it I was to raise a nation (like medicine).

11. In *Black Elk Speaks,* p. 29, Neihardt writes (speaking for Black Elk), "I think he meant that I should see four generations," explicitly identifying "ascents" with "generations."

My horse turned around and faced the west and all the black horses went and stood behind me in four ranks, twelve abreast—blacks, whites, sorrels, buckskins. They turned around toward the north. "Behold your wind from the north; this wind and an herb they have given you. With this herb and the wind you shall go back to the earth." (With the herb I was to have power to save horses and the wind was included. Whenever I would own a horse, it would be able to run for weeks and weeks without getting out of wind.) We swung around to the east in formation. The grandfather of the east let the pipe go which he was holding and it flew to me: "Behold it, for with this you shall be peaceful with the nations. Behold it, for you shall possess this for the nations on earth." I took the pipe. The eastern grandfather said again: "Behold him who shall appear; from him you shall have power." The morning star was coming up in the east as I looked this way. As I faced them, I noticed that the sorrels of the east had stars on their foreheads and they were very bright. Then we faced the south and the eastern grandfather said: "Behold your black sacred road you shall walk." As I turned around the buckskins lined up into formation and turned around facing the east to take me down the road of destruction. "As you walk your nation, the beings all over the universe shall fear you."

They began to go toward the east. They were all following me. I was the leader. I could see ahead of me a lot of birds in the air and behind me they were all fearful of me. There were twelve riders—all right-handed except one and he was called Left Hand Charger. The rider of the white horse was called One Horn Red[12] and they gave me the name of Eagle That Stretches Its Wing.

Going east from the highest peak in the west—Pike's Peak. As we went along I noticed that everything on the earth was trembling with fear. I looked back and saw my twelve horseback riders and the horses' manes and tails were decorated with hail and the men had hail all over them. I was riding along as the chief of all the heavens and I looked down and saw the hail falling from these men and horses. I could see the country as I went and I remember well seeing in the forks of the Missouri River a man standing amid a flame with the dust around him in the air. I knew then that this was the enemy which was going to attack me. I could see all kinds of creatures dying beneath me, as he had destroyed everything.

12. Later the same name is translated "Red One Horn."

As we neared this place we sang a sacred song concerning the peace pipe and the eagle, and all the riders had this for a weapon. [*The sorrels sang first.*] The song that represents the four quarters:

> I, myself, have sent them a-fleeing
> Because I wore the feather of an eagle.
> I, myself, sent them a-fleeing.

> I, myself, have sent them a-fleeing
> For I wore the relic of the wind.
> I, myself, have sent them a-fleeing.

[The] Thunder-beings sang then:

> I, myself, send them a-fleeing
> For I wore the relic of the hail.
> I, myself, send them a-fleeing.

Then the ones on the west sang:

> I, myself, send them a-fleeing.
> I, myself, send them a-fleeing.

Then the water splashed up as a result of something scared of me, and the flames came rolling out of this same place. The twelve riders from the west attacked this man but could not destroy him. He attacked them and forced them back toward the south. The white riders from the north attacked him but failed also to kill him. The eastern riders attacked him and also failed [*as he drove them back. They stood facing north*]. The buckskins from the south also attacked him and failed. After they all had attacked this man and failed, I looked at the splashing water and saw a man painted blue coming out. Then they all hollered: "He is coming!" and ran. They said: "Eagle Wing Stretches, make haste, for your nation all over the universe is in fear, make haste." I could hear, at this time, everything in the universe cheering for me. At this time my bow and arrow turned into a big spear. With the spear and the cup of water in the other hand, I immediately charged on the enemy myself. As I attacked, everybody cheered for me, telling me to "Make haste!" Just as the man got to the water, I swooped down on him and stabbed him through the heart. You could see the lightning from my spear as I stabbed him. I took him and threw him quite a distance. Just as I took the spear out, the man turned into a turtle. After I had killed the enemy the horse troops came by and hit [couped] the enemy [*and then they went back*]. Everything that had been dead came back to life and cheered me for killing that enemy. (This means that sometime in the future I was going to kill an enemy in some future battle.)

BLACK ELK WALKS THE RED SACRED ROAD
FROM SOUTH TO NORTH

[*I was taken to the four parts of the earth.*] I now came down to the earth and we traveled along the Missouri River. Soon we saw a camp in a circle. One of them pointed to the camp and said: "Behold that nation; yours it is." They stopped on the south side and gave me the stick with the branches on it. They said: "Behold this stick; with this stick you shall walk with your nation where the big giant lives [north]." I was to give this stick to my people so that they will depend on it and with it they shall walk that red road and also with the pipe. They showed me the people that I was going to raise. The [southern] spirit said: "Behold them, your nation and your people, make haste."

Before me they showed me a tipi of the village, which was on the east side by itself. Here I could see women, children and men dying. The [southern] spirit said: "Behold them and make haste." I saw a man whose body was turning gray and whose mouth had red flames coming out of it. I was very much frightened at the sight and tried to get away. [*As I went down there*] the wind was blowing from the south to the north now. I passed in front of the tipi and all the people got up. The [southern] spirit said: "That's the way you shall save men." I was to be a sacred man when I got back to earth (wakan shasha [*wakan wicaśa*], "holy man").

Then they took me back to the middle of the camp where people gathered all around me. The [southern] spirit then said: "Give your nation the sacred pipe and also your sacred flowering stick." I presented the pipe and stick to the people and they all rejoiced. They were going to depend on that stick for peace and health. [The southern] spirit said: "Your nation shall walk that red road" (from south to north) "toward where the giant lives." The northern grandfather then said: "Give your sacred herb to your people; also give them your sacred wind so they shall face the wind with courage. Also they shall walk as a relative of your wind. Behold your people for they shall break camp and go forth. Behold them." (Breaking camp here means that they shall be prosperous always.)

These men were going to pray to the spirits and call upon them. They were ready to pray for [sic] the spirits. One among the people hollered out: "Hey, hey, hey, hey!" One of the grandfathers said to the people then: "Behold your grandfathers, for they shall walk forth with you." The people broke camp and one of each of the horses went forward. The black horse rider took the herb with him; [the] white horse rider took the sacred wind with him; the sorrel rider took the sacred pipe; the buckskin rider took the flowering stick. All of the people were going along. Four more riders, one from each quarter, came forth and presented me with a hoop, and with that hoop I was to make a nation and under that we were to prosper.

The circle represented the old people that represented the nation. The center of it represented the prosperity of the nation. I was to raise a nation either in prosperity or in difficulty. In presenting the sacred hoop to me [*each is a nation*], the spirit from the west said: "Behold this sacred hoop; it is the people you shall have" (meaning that I would own these people[13]). In his left hand the spirit held the hoop and in his right hand he held the bow and arrow. He said: "You shall have this nation and with this bow and arrow on earth your worst enemy you shall conquer." At the same time he held this wooden cup of water, and he said: "With this the wildest enemies will be tame." (I could capture anything without being hurt. With that bow and arrow my people should be able to do the same things as I can. They used that on Custer and there wasn't one of them who did not have an arrow in his skin. This worked in the Custer fight very well.)

(The Thunder-beings [*lightning*] have the power to kill and the water the power to heal. We could depend on the water to live on and the lightning to kill with. From this water all the herbs grow. Water is the great power. The water in the wooden cup represented a big lake.[14] When I was conquering the spirit at the head of the Missouri River I was getting power from the water [*and now I get power from the water the same as then*]. Everything is dependent on water. If I had not conquered the bad spirit, I would not have had the power. I had conquered the power of the water in conquering this bad spirit. The three forks of the Missouri River is the

13. "Owning the people" is a metaphor that indicates the duties of a chief, who is responsible for the welfare of his people.

14. In *Black Elk Speaks*, p. 26, Neihardt interprets the water in the cup as the sky.

source of the Great Water. When I had conquered the bad spirit I had gained control over the power of the water. At this place there had been many people who had died without water and I came and destroyed the enemy and the people were then all living well again. I was killing drought and also I could bring my people out of any difficulty that they might have.)

(Any man who sees the morning star will see something more, meaning that he will be worth something, and if he does not see the morning star, he is not worth anything ever.)

(I think about this dream often. [*It is in me.*] And many times I feel bad about it and other times I feel good about it. It was a power dream and it will never be forgotten until I die. You take a bunch of honey bees. You know that it always has a king of the hive in it. All the bees obey the king and he wants to get along with all the bees. My vision is something like that. I am liked by all people and can influence them. Everybody has respect for me—even the white people. The moment I see anybody I want to get along with him and I always do get along with him.)

The [southern?] spirit said furthermore to me: "With their power the four quarters shall return to their places on the four quarters." The spirit of the west [south?] said: "Behold the man who sits where the sun goes down; with his power also the greenward day [the blue day?]." (Rain comes mostly from the west here. [*West represents spring and summer.*]) The southern spirit said: "Behold [*him*] where the giant lives for you shall have his power also—a white day" (representing winter). They all returned to their four quarters now. The southern spirit said: "Behold him where the sun shines continually, for you shall have his power [the red day?]. Behold him where you always face, for you shall have his power and also the yellow day." ([*Yellow day represented*] autumn and furthermore the night.[15] The nighttime is the best time to think with the stars out.) The southern spirit said: "Behold your morning star, for your nation shall have a knowledge from that morning star. Now the people shall walk with their power, the power they have received."

15. This discussion of "sacred days" is, clearly, confusing and incomplete. Later Black Elk is told that he will have "twelve sacred days" (two from each grandfather), the same number of days that his great vision lasted. See the discussion of "red and blue days" in Brown, *The Sacred Pipe,* p. 19, n. 8.

In my nation they made four chiefs and four advisors. The people were in formation for moving farther, walking thus:

> First, the four spirit horsemen leading [the] people.
> Second, the four chiefs leading [the] people.
> Third, the four advisors leading [the] people.
> Fourth, the old men with canes.
> Fifth, the old women with canes.
> Sixth, myself, following them in the rear.

The southern spirit said again to me: "Behold the four old men; present thy sacred hoop to them, for they are really the grandfathers and great grandfathers way back which the tribe came from." They were in order, the younger generations and then the older generations following. They are marching. The southern spirit said: "Thus I will walk in the rear; sending a voice out, I thus walk." ([I was] leading my people so that they will all be prosperous. As I walk I am going to pray to the Great Spirit.)

> I wore an ornament of the sacred hoop.
> This nation shall send a voice for their children.
> (Means these people will prosper and increase.)

Song about the people increasing. Words sung by the southern spirit:

> A voice I am sending as I walk. (twice)
> A sacred hoop I wore.
> Thus, a voice I send as I walk. (twice)
> (To future generations.)

The first child they called for was by the name of Spotted Deer Woman [*calling unborn children*]. The next one I called for was Young Buffalo Woman. [*The people are on a good road now and walking toward where the child lives. These people shall go up four more generations.*] "Behold your nation as they walk and to the first ascent they shall step as they walk" (meaning they are going to take them to the first ascent [*and show them another such and so on*]). When they get to the first generation (ascent) all the creatures on the earth and in the air shall rejoice because the first ascent represents the people here on earth and they are going to multiply and increase and at the same time prosper. One of the old men said (showing me the sacred hoop): "Behold a good nation, a sacred nation, again they will walk toward good land, the land of plenty, and no suffering shall there be. A nation you shall create and it shall be a sacred nation" (meaning that I was given the power to raise a nation).

Song in [the] first ascent:

> May you behold this I have asked to be made over.[16] (twice)
> A good nation I have asked to be made over.
> May you behold this I have asked to be made over. (twice)
> A sacred nation I have asked to be made over.
> May you behold this I have asked to be made over. (twice)

After singing this song, the people went on. When they got to the end, the men and women began sending voices for their children and again they stopped (at the [*end of the*] second generation).

(Black Elk says at this point he has a queer feeling all the time he is telling this, and that he is giving his power away. He feels that he will die very soon afterward. His dream has been coming true. The first and the second ascents were both good and the third is to be a fearful thing and perhaps we're in that time now—something is going to happen. In the third ascent people are going to transform themselves into all kinds of beasts. He knew something was going to happen in the war [World War I], so he didn't allow his son to go even though he wanted to. In Black Elk's days he has seen the second generation and in the third he thinks something fearful is going to happen.)

The man of the south says: "Behold, you shalt prevent the making of the clouds."[17] (They were now at the second ascent and I was given the power to defend my people at all dangerous times and to keep them from destruction.) [The] south man says: "Behold your nation they have given you, for they shall be like unto the animals and the fowls; thus they shall walk." As they started, the men and women were sending voices for their children again. At this moment the whole people walking on the good road transformed into buffalo and elk and even fowls of the air and were

16. "To make over" implies a spiritual strengthening, the making of new life for the people.

17. Although the referent of "clouds" is uncertain, Black Elk later identifies the white cloud that he saw coming in his vision as the encroachment of the white people on the Lakotas (see below, p. 134).

traveling on the good road toward the north. [*Meaning that the Indian generations have dreams and are like unto the animals of this world. Some have visions about elks, birds, and even gophers or eagles. People will be like the animals—take the animals' virtues and strength.*]

As the beasts walked along I saw that the Indians from thence on would be like unto the animals and will have rules of their own. As I noticed this, all the animals became restless and were all in fear and were afraid that they weren't what they were. This nation was walking in a sacred manner. Just before the people stopped I could hear them calling for their chiefs. They were scared and wanted the chiefs to come at once. [*They were calling on the third ascent and above.*] After sending voices for their chiefs they stopped. The southern spirit said: "Behold your nation walking in a sacred manner; from thence they shall walk in difficulty. Now you shall go forth to the center of the nation's hoop. Behold this, for you shall go forth to the center of the nation's hoop; with this you shall have power."

(The third ascent represented all kinds of animals and fowls, and from there on every man has his own vision and his own rules. The fourth ascent will be terrible.)

(They [the white men] couldn't get along with us and they did not look after us. The birds and other animals are the only race that we really get along with. We, [the] Indian race, and the beings on this earth—the buffalo, elk, and birds in the air—they are just like relatives to us and we get along fine with them, for we get our power from them and from them we live. The white people came on this continent and put us Indians in a fence and they put another fence somewhere else and put our game into it. When the buffalo and elk are all gone, the Great Spirit will look upon the whites for this and perhaps something will happen.)

"Behold when you shall go forth to the center of the nation's hoop you shall run to the four quarters."[18] (Nobody shall be sacred before me. Wherever I go, in front of me there will be no hard task for me. Every task I undertake I will push through. It won't be hard for me either.)

---

18. The exact significance of "run to the four quarters" is unclear, but it suggests the Thunder Bow ceremony, in which the participants race to the four quarters. See Helen Heather Blish, "The Ceremony of the Sacred Bow of the Oglala Dakota," *American Anthropologist* 36 (1934):180–87.

Then the spirit sang a powerful song:

> The four quarters may you run to.
> (Meaning that I will get power from them.)
> No man will be sacred before you.
> They have said to me.

At this time, everything that was given to me by the spirits I had. The man of the south said again to me: "Behold your grandfathers who have given you the sacred relics. Whenever you look upon an enemy, it shall tremble" (meaning that I shall conquer any kind of opposition). "Remember this" (meaning the cup of water I got), "for from this the people shall have strength and power."

As they stood ready to go on the fourth ascent of the earth, the south spirit said: "Look upon your nation." The beasts transformed themselves into humans and they were all very poor. ("Oh, gee! It was a sight," says Black Elk.) There were lots of sick children—all pale and it looked like a dying nation. They showed me a circle village and all the people were very poor in there. All the horses were hide and bones and here and there you could hear the wail of women and also men. Some of them were dying and some were dead. Quite an epidemic there. Again the southern spirit said: "Behold your nation." (Meaning they were going to show me something terrible. I am now ready to return to the earth after being in the air with the fowls. The three ascents were all spiritual, but now I am to see the fourth quarter and in this they were showing me the difficulties.)

BLACK ELK RECEIVES THE HEALING HERB OF THE NORTH AND THE SACRED TREE IS ESTABLISHED AT THE CENTER OF THE NATION'S HOOP

As I looked down upon the people, there stood on the north side a man painted red all over his body and he had with him a lance (Indian spear) and he walked into the center of the sacred nation's hoop and lay down and rolled himself on the ground and when he got up he was a buffalo standing right in the center of the nation's hoop. The buffalo rolled and when he got up there was an herb there in his place. The herb plant grew up and bloomed so that I could see what it looked like—what kind of an herb it was from the bloom. After the buffalo's arrival the people looked better and then when the buffalo turned into an herb, the people all got up and seemed to be well. Even the horses got up and stretched themselves and neighed. Then a little breeze came from the north and I could see that the wind was in the form of a spirit and as it went over the people all the dead things came to life. All the horses pulled up their tails and neighed and began to prance around.

[The southern?] spirit said: "Behold you have seen the powers of the north in the forms of man, buffalo, herb and wind. The people shall follow the man's steps; like him they shall walk and like the buffalo they shall live and with the herb they shall have knowledge. They shall be like relatives to the wind." (From the man in the illustration they should be healthy, from the buffalo they shall get meat, from the herb they shall get knowledge of diseases. The north wind will give them strong endurance.)

[The southern?] spirit speaks again: "Behold him they have sent forth to the center of the nation's hoop." Then I saw the pipe with the spotted eagle flying to the center of the nation's hoop. The morning star went along with the pipe. They flew from the east to the center. "With this your nation's offering as they walk. They will be like unto him. With the pipe they shall have peace in everything. Behold your eagle, for your nation like relatives they shall be. Behold the morning star, relative-like they shall be, from whence they shall have wisdom." Just then the morning star appeared and all the people looked up to it and the horses neighed and dogs barked.

(The flowering stick was in the middle of the nation's hoop again.) [The southern?] spirit said: "Behold the circle of the sacred hoop, for the people shall be like unto it; and if they are like unto this, they shall have power, because there is no end to this hoop and in the center of the hoop these raise their children." (The sacred hoop means the continents of the world and the people shall stand as one. Everything reproduces here inside the hoop.)

They put the sacred stick into the center of the hoop and you could hear birds singing all kinds of songs by this flowering stick and the people and animals all rejoiced and hollered. The women were sending up their tremolos. The men said: "Behold it; from there we shall multiply, for it is the greatest of the greatest sticks." This stick will take care of the people and at the same time it will multiply. We live under it like chickens under the wing.[19] We live under the flowering stick like under the wing of a hen.

19. See Matt. 23:37; Luke 13:34.

Depending on the sacred stick we shall walk and it will be with us always. From this we will raise our children and under the flowering stick we will communicate with our relatives—beast and bird—as one people. This is the center of the life of the nation.

The sacred stick is the cottonwood tree ("rustling tree," waga chun [*waǵacan*]).[20] The nation represents this tree [*and if they grow up they will multiply like birds, etc.*]. This tree never had a chance to bloom because the white men came. The trunk is the chief of the people. If this tree had seen a bloom probably I or some of my descendants would be great chiefs.

The people camped there. I was on the bay horse again on the west side and was with another man. (This man is still living today and probably I could have made him a medicine man, but I never did it as yet, because I have never seen him.[21] This man lives at Grass Creek and he knows nothing about this, nevertheless. This man's name was One Side.) One Side had [a] bow and arrow in one hand and a cup of water in the other. I saw that the people were getting ready for a storm and they were fixing their tipis to make them stronger for the storm. The storm cloud was approaching and swallows were coming under the cloud and I, myself, and One Side were coming on top of the cloud. (We were traveling on the fourth ascent and I saw the people on the third ascent from the fourth ascent.)

It was raining on earth now. A spirit [southern?] said to me that they had shown me everything there was to do on earth and that I was to do it myself now. He sang this song and it went like this:

> A good nation I will make over.
> The nation above has said this to me.
> They have given me the power to make over this nation.

The cloud then swept over the village and they [the people?] stood in the west. When they turned around, the cloud was all gone. The cloud christened them with water. They all hollered: "Eagle Wing Stretches, A-ha-hey!" (meaning "Thanks to Eagle Wing Stretches!"). The people on earth started on the good road again, the red road, and I was forced to give

20. The cottonwood is also the tree used as the center pole in the sun dance and the ghost dance.

21. This is unclear because Black Elk later describes the *heyoka* ceremony that he and One Side performed together, an earthly enactment of this portion of the vision. See below, pp. 232–35.

all my relics to the people with the exception of the bow and arrow. The horses were all very fat now, so the people began to break camp. The people accepted what I gave them and I went ahead on the good road. (The bow and arrow represent lightning.)22

BLACK ELK KILLS THE DOG IN THE FLAMES AND RECEIVES THE HEALING HERB OF THE WEST

[The] western spirit said (people turning toward the west): "Behold where the sun goes down, you shall walk. Everything that lacks strength you shall make over as you walk." I was on the bay horse and One Side on a bay also; we led the blacks, whites, sorrels, and buckskins westward. As they went into formation one of the black horse riders, Left Hand Charger, said: "Behold your grandfathers; they will seek your enemy. Take courage, you shall be the leader." Just as he said this he called for someone by the name of Red One Horn and someone by the name of Brave Thunder and they all three hollered for Black Elk [*Eagle Wing Stretches*].

Soon I could see a flame coming up from the earth. They went around it and Left Hand Charger went around the left instead of right and we followed. (They were on the west side of the flame when they stopped.) When we got around it, it was a sight. You could hear the crashing of the thunder and lightning. Left Hand Charger was ready to charge and he saw the flame of it. The horse's tail was lightning and the flames were coming out of his horse's nose. As I went I could see nothing but I could only hear the thunder and lightning and of course I could see the flames. All the rest of the troops went around the enemy. Left Hand Charger made a vain attempt to kill the enemy. A spirit said: "Eagle Wing Stretches, take courage; your turn has come."

We got ready and started down on the cloud on our bay horses. One Side and I were coming down together. I could see the lightning coming off of my arrows as I descended. Just as we were about to hit the earth, we struck something. I could hear thunder rolling and everyone cheered for me saying, "Unhee!" ("Kill!") I could hear my people on the good road saying, "Who killed that enemy?" I heard someone say then that Eagle

22. Throughout the vision the bow and arrow seem to be equivalent to a bow lance, and they are depicted as such in Standing Bear's drawings. As symbols of lightning they represent the destructive power of the Thunder-beings.

Wing Stretches has done it and they all cheered again, "Un hah hey!" I made a swoop again on the west side of the enemy, whatever it was, and when I killed it, I looked at it and it was a dog which had a very funny color. One side of him was white and the other side was black. Each one of them struck the dog (couped), meaning that they all had a hand in killing it.

(This meant that when you go to war you should kill your enemy like a dog. Whenever an Indian gets hungry he kills the dog and then whenever you call someone a dog it means you don't like him and you want to fight.[23] [*If I had gone to war much, I would have been able to do much damage to the enemy, but the enemy couldn't fight back.*])

The western spirit said: "We are now going to show you a flipping. Behold him, for you shall make him over." (They showed me a black horse that was brown-like and he was very poor, like skin and bones.) Then the west spirit presented me with an herb and said: "Take this and go forth in haste." I took the herb and made a circle over the horse and as I did this they all said: "A-hey, a-hey!" (calling for spirit power). After I had made the circle over the horse, the horse neighed and began to roll. It was a beautiful shiny stallion. His mane was streaming in the form of a cloud all around him and he had dapples all over him. Every time he snorted there was a flash of lightning and his eyes were as bright as stars. Then the stallion went forth and stopped suddenly, facing the west. He neighed and you could see the dust flying over there as he neighed. In this dust there were a million horses coming. These horses were happy and full of pep. This stallion dashed toward the north and stopped and neighed. Then you could see millions of horses coming out of the dust from this stallion neighing dust in front of him. The stallion then dashed at the east and faced it and neighed and saw some more horses and then he did the same thing toward the south.

Then the black spirit [western grandfather] said: "Behold them, for these are your horses. Your horses shall come neighing to you. Your horses shall dance and you shall see. Behold them; all over the universe you have finished." Then there appeared before him four beautiful virgins

23. For the Lakotas, the dog is an ambivalent symbol—on the one hand positive, the friend of man, the animal sacrificed in ritual contexts; on the other hand negative, the symbol of cowardice, licentiousness, and animosity. This may explain why the dog in the vision is half white and half black. For further discussion of dogs see below, December 5.

standing there dressed in red. One of the virgins held the sacred pipe. "Behold your virgins all over the universe; through them the earth shall be happy. From all over the universe they are coming to see them."

The black spirit sang a song [*the horse dance*]:

My horses prancing they are coming from all over the universe.
My horses neighing they are coming, prancing they are coming.
All over the universe my horses are coming.

The dappled black stallion sang this song now:

They will dance, may you behold them. (four times)
A horse nation will dance, may you behold them. (four times)

The horse's voice went all over the universe like a radio and everyone heard it. It was more beautiful than anything could be. All the fowls, beasts, and every living thing heard this horse sing. The birds, horses, tree leaves, and everything [*in the universe*] danced to the music of the horse's song. It was so beautiful that they just couldn't help dancing.

After singing, the black stallion spoke saying: "All over the universe everything is finished and your nation of nations is rejoicing." (Meaning that everything is living—trees, flowers, grass, and every animal is living now.) In the vision I was representing the earth and everything was giving me power. I was given power so that all creatures on earth would be happy.

At the end of the fourth ascent I could see the horses all going back to their homes. The black stallion started back to the west where his home was. The birds and everything sang and the women sang and the tree leaves sang as they went to the four quarters.

The black horse rider from the west speaks: "All over the universe they have finished a day of happiness." As he said this the day was very beautiful, the day was green, the birds were singing, the creeks were singing as they flowed clearly along. You could see the people down there very happy. The deer and the buffalo were leaping and running. The country was all very beautiful—fruit was growing up in great abundance.

BLACK ELK IS TAKEN TO THE CENTER OF THE EARTH
AND RECEIVES THE DAYBREAK STAR HERB

[The] western black spirit said: "Behold this day, for this day is yours." [*I will have the power to shed many happy days on people, they tell me.*] "Take courage, for we shall take you to the center of the earth." They [the spirits] said: "Behold the center of the earth for we are taking you there." As I looked I could see great mountains with rocks and forests on them. I could see all colors of light flashing out of the mountains toward the four quarters. Then they took me on top of a high mountain where I could see all over the earth. Then they told me to take courage for they were taking me to the center of the earth. All the sixteen riders of the four quarters were with me going to the center of the earth and also this man by the name of One Side.

We were facing the east and I noticed something queer and found out that it was two men coming from the east and they had wings. On each one's breast was a bright star. The two men came and stood right in front of us and the west black spirit said: "Behold them, for you shall depend upon them." Then as we stood there the daybreak star stood between the two men from the east. There was a little star beside the daybreak star also.[24] They had an herb in their hands and they gave it to me, saying: "Behold this; with this on earth you shall undertake anything and accomplish it." As they presented the herb to me they told me to drop it on earth and when it hit the earth it took root and grew and flowered. You could see a ray of light coming up from the flower, reaching the heavens, and all the creatures of the universe saw this light. (Herbs used by Black Elk are in four colors—yellow, blue, red, white flowers all on one bush. The four-colored flowers represent the four quarters of the earth. This herb is called daybreak star herb.)

[The] western black spirit said: "Behold all over the universe." As I looked around I could see the country full of sickness and in need of help. This was the future and I was going to cure these people. On the east and north people were rejoicing, and on the south and west they were sick and there was a cloud over them. They said: "Behold them who need help. You shall make them over in the future." After a while I noticed the cloud over the people was a white one and it was probably the white people coming.

The western black spirit sang:

---

24. *Anpo wicahpi* (daybreak star) and *anpo wicahpi sunkaku* (daybreak star's younger brother).

> Here and there may you behold. (twice)
> All may you behold.
> Here and there may you behold. (twice)

They had taken me all over the world and showed me all the powers. They took me to the center of the earth and to the top of the peak they took me to review it all. This last song means that I have already seen it. I was to see the bad and the good. I was to see what is good for humans and what is not good for humans.

BLACK ELK RECEIVES THE SOLDIER WEED OF DESTRUCTION

[The] black horse rider says: "Now your grandfathers, toward them may you walk" (meaning they are going back to the six grandfathers under the flaming rainbow). "You shall now walk toward your grandfathers, but before you there is a man with power. You shall see. Behold him!" I looked down upon the earth and saw a flame which looked to be a man and I couldn't make it out quite. I heard all around voices of moaning and woe. It was sad on earth. I felt uneasy and I trembled. We went to the north side of the flaming man. I saw that the flame really was a man now. They showed me the bad in the form of this man who was all in black and [had] lightning flashes going all over his body when he moved. He had horns. All around, the animals and everything were dying and they were all crying. (The black man represented war in general.)

They said: "Behold him. Some day you shall depend upon him. There will be dispute all over the universe." As they said this the man transformed into a gopher and it stood up on its hind legs and turned around.[25] Then this gopher transformed into an herb. This was the most powerful herb of all that I had gotten. It could be used in war and could destroy a nation. (This was used in war and it was very destructive. If you

---

25. The pocket gopher was symbolically associated with warfare for the Lakotas. They believed that gophers could shoot people with their whiskers, causing scrofula. See Tyon in Walker, *Lakota Belief and Ritual,* pp. 169. The pulverized dirt around gopher holes was used as war medicine; the medicine man Chips gave some to Crazy Horse for protection in battle.

touch this herb it will kill you at once. Nothing grows anywhere near it because it is killed immediately if it does.)

"Behold him. There will be dispute of nations and you will defend your people with this herb." (I was not old enough when I was supposed to use this herb or else I could have used it and killed many enemies. It was too terrible to use and I was glad that I did not get to use it. This herb is in the Black Hills. Every animal that nears it dies. Around where it grows there are many skeletons always. This medicine belongs only to me—no one else knows what this herb looks like. It looks like a little tree with crinkly leaves, reddish in color. I call this herb a soldier weed.)

Four riders came up—bay, gray, sorrel, white. The bay rider had a buffalo bonnet on and the latter [bonnet] was alive. You could see its eyes and nostrils flaming. The horns were long and curled and there were animals of all kinds standing on the horns. The gray rider had on a warbonnet which had many curved horns to the earth. There were only eagles on these horns. The white rider had on a spotted eagle for a bonnet and he had a lance also. The sorrel rider had a lance in his hand and it was a serpent. He had an eagle bonnet. These riders were on the left side of the soldier medicine. Then the four riders sang this song:

> My grandfathers, they have caused me to be sacred.
> They have caused me to be sacred.
> May you behold me.
> May you behold me.

As they finished the song, the four riders turned around and made a charge. There was so much smoke that I could not see the riders. I heard rapid gunfire and women and children wailing and the horses screaming in fear, dogs yelping. I heard them hollering for victory.

(I am glad that I did not perform this killing, for I would have not only killed the enemy but I would probably have killed the women and children of the enemy, but I am satisfied that I have not been well off. Perhaps I would have been a chief if I had obeyed this, but I am satisfied that I didn't become a chief.)

(Explanation of why they wore [the] helmets they did. The buffalo head meant great endurance. Some animals there had no power and had no right to be on the helmet. The eagle and the horse also had great endurance. These were to represent the people's endurance. The snake meant poison to the people. War itself is terrible.)

The smoke cleared away now and the warriors were in the fourth ascent. You could hear war all over the world. As they appear[ed], smoke covered up the herb and there was nothing but a skeleton as the smoke cleared away. This war was happening all over the world and the fourth ascent is yet to come. Then when the four riders reached the fourth ascent they turned into black-tailed deer. (Some black-tailed deer are sacred and if you try to kill them you cannot do it.[26]) These deer had wounds on their sides which shone out like lightning. Here they showed me the power of the medicine and how to use it. Then the deer turned around and faced the herb from the east side. The black-horned man was standing there again and he changed himself into a gopher, then into an herb, and next into a skeleton.

(At the age of thirty-seven, Black Elk was to use this herb and it made him sad to think of what harm it would do to women and children. At this time he gave it up for the Catholic religion.)

(While performing his duties as a medicine man, Black Elk would hear women singing all over the room.)

[The] black spirit says: "Behold your herb; with it everything you face will be like it and the world will tremble" (meaning that whenever I have the herb I will be able to destroy). (Dispute of four ascents means war in the four quarters.) "There shall be a dispute of the winds, and then you shall depend upon the herb."

During this whole time I did not notice how I was dressed. But now I noticed that I was painted red and all my joints were black. There was a white stripe between the joints all over my body. And whenever I would breath, I would be breathing lightning. My bay horse had lightning stripes on it. The horse's mane was like clouds.

BLACK ELK RETURNS TO THE SIX GRANDFATHERS

They took me back to where the grandfathers were now: "Behold, you shall go back to where your grandfathers are." Then I saw the rainbow flaming and I saw the six grandfathers sitting there. (I [had] seemed to be traveling with them, but I found that I was traveling toward them instead.) Then I saw the first two men (turned to geese) that I had seen in

26. See Dorsey, *A Study of Siouan Cults,* pp. 480–81, and Tyon in Walker, *Lakota Belief and Ritual,* p. 167.

the beginning of the vision. They were flying in four formations (circles)—one over the east, one over the west, one over the north, one over the south. The nation of geese sang this:

> In four circles they are flying
> In a sacred manner.
> May you behold them.

As they went around, the geese called thus: "B-p-p-p, b-p-p-p!" *[On earth Black Elk is to make the goose sound and he will get the goose power.]* The western spirit said: "Behold them, for they shall have a sacred voice for you." Here I was presented with the power of the goose voice.

They were taking me back now. Now I could see the house of the first grandfather. It was walled and roofed with cloud and above was lightning and underneath were the fowls of the air. Under the fowls are the beasts of the earth and men. The people on earth were rejoicing and the birds and animals and lightning and thunder were like laughter. They were saying: "Eagle Wing Stretches is coming home." Just before I entered the house, the black spirit said: "Behold your grandfathers; a great council they are having." The door was facing the side where the sun shines continually.

As I entered the door the grandfathers cheered for me and the lightning and the birds, beasts, and men cheered for me. I could hear many voices cheering. They were praising me. Some of them said: "He has triumphed!" As I entered, all the grandfathers were sitting with their arms and palms out and said: "He has triumphed!" I could see nothing but millions of faces behind the grandfathers. The west spirit said (pointing to all the people trying to see me): "Behold your nation!"

(All the six men had wooden cups of water in front of them.) I took the cup of water from the west spirit and I could see a buffalo in the water. He presented it to me saying: "Behold the cup; in this cup your nation and you shall feed from it." (Meaning that this cup will be used for me and my nation—that they will all be relatives to each other, and the water is the power to give them strength and to purify them. This water will make the people happy.)

Again I looked toward the people and took good notice this time. I saw there were some animals [people?] in there of different tribes that I was to get along with on earth. I wasn't quite sure yet whether I saw a white man or not. (What I saw there actually happened, for now I have friends of all the different tribes, even of the whites. There will probably never be a time again when the Indians will fight each other; but the whites will fight each other and the Indians may have to fight in with the whites.) The people were happy, as I could see, after I took the cup.

The second (northern) grandfather spoke: "Grandson, all around the universe you have seen the powers and for what you have done your people rejoiced. You have given the men of earth the power they have given you, and with courage they are facing the wind" (meaning the wind of life). "Hundreds shall be sacred; hundreds shall be flames." He came forward and put butterflies' cocoons onto my arms—a red one on the right wrist and a brown one on the left wrist. (Brown is sacred and red is lightning power.) "All over the universe, all your grandfathers, the two-leggeds and on-earth walking, the day-fliers, they have had a council and appointed you and have given you their power. Now you shall go forth to the place from whence you came. Your people are in great difficulty. Behold them!"

As they [the grandfathers] said that I turned around and I could see that it was my own people. Everyone was happy and all the horses were happy except one who was sick. I took good notice and it was myself and I had been sick twelve days. This was probably the twelfth day when I was just going back to my body. I was shown the village and the second grandfather presented me with a cup of water, saying: "Behold this cup." In this cup I saw a man painted blue and he had a bow and arrow and he was in distress. He wanted to get out of the water and get away, but I was told to drink it down. They said: "Make haste and drink your cup of water." I took it and drank the man too. This blue spirit was a fish and I had drunk it down. From this I received strange power and whenever I was conjuring [*wapiya*] I could actually make this blue man come out and swim in the cup of water I used. (The fish represents the power of the water.)

The black spirit says: "Stand over to the third grandfather." (As each grandfather finished talking he would melt into the earth and come up again. Each time a grandfather spoke I was nearer to the earth.)

The third grandfather speaks: "Behold, there are two days relative-like they have given you." Pointing the cup of water to me he said: "Behold this; like unto this you shall live." There was a star in the third cup of water. He said again: "On earth the beings will be glad to see you. So take courage. Now you shall go forth back to your mother earth." Through this morning star in the cup of water I was to get all my wisdom to know everything.

The black spirit said to me again: "Stand over to the fourth grandfather." The fourth grandfather said (as he presented me with the cup I noticed the red road across the cup): "The road of the generations you shall walk. The ascents of your days shall be sacred. Take courage, your grandfathers shall watch over you in all the four quarters of the earth." The fourth grandfather sang this song:

> There is somebody lying on earth in a sacred manner.
> I made him walk. (five times)
> There is somebody, on earth he lies.
> In a sacred manner I have caused him to walk.

(Black Elk uses this song in treating the sick.)

The black spirit says to me: "Stand over by the fifth grandfather." Then I noticed a cup which represented the Great Spirit. In this cup there was a spotted eagle outstretched. "Your grandfathers, whatever they have decided upon, you have finished. Take this." The eagle began to make beautiful sounds and I noticed his eyes were sparkling and he (the eagle) was dancing. "Every day this eagle shall be over you. He has eyes that will see everything (living eyes), and through them you shall also see. To your nation in a sacred manner you shall go."

[The] black spirit again asked me to stand over to the sixth grandfather. The sixth grandfather showed me a cup full of water and in it there were many small human beings. He said: "Behold them, with great difficulty they shall walk and you shall go among them. You shall make six centers of the nation's hoop." (Referring to the six cups of water, meaning that the six centers of the nation's hoop were the different bands or tribes: 1) Hunkpapas, 2) Minneconjous, 3) Brulés, 4) Oglalas, 5) Shihela [*Šahiyela*, Cheyennes], 6) Idazipcho (Black Kettle) [*Itazipco*, Without Bows].27)

27. Note that Black Elk incorporates the Cheyennes into the hoop of the Lakota nation. The sixth hoop is evidently intended to consolidate the Sans Arcs (*Itazipco*, Without Bows), Blackfeet (*Siha sapa*), and Two Kettles (*Oohenunpa*), the three smallest of the seven Teton groups. The translation Black Kettle is apparently Ben Black Elk's attempt to express in English the conglomerate nature of the sixth hoop. See below, p. 171, n. 12. Most Lakota accounts give seven as the number of divisions of the Lakotas, but in telling of his vision Black Elk organized everything in sixes, reflecting the cosmic order revealed to him through the six grandfathers.

"Behold them, this is your nation and you shall go back to them. There are six centers of your nation and there you shall go. Now in a sacred manner you shall walk. Your grandfathers shall make four goals" (four quarters).

Now the cloud house began to sway back and forth and everyone was moving around in it. The rainbow over the house was moving up and down. "Behold, the rainbow of your grandfathers shall be set where the sun shines continually." Then I could hear all living voices outside the rainbow tipi calling to me as I came out of the tipi: "Eagle Wing Stretches is coming out, so behold him!" Now I noticed that the sixth grandfather was myself, who represented the spirit of mankind.

"Your grandfathers have given you a good twelve days of happiness, and you shall have twelve sacred days. A day is appearing—behold its face as you come forth. It is so (hetchetu alo [*hecetu yelo*]). Your grandfathers shall go forth. You shall lead them. The living creatures of the earth's generations walk together as relatives."

When they showed me the star it was daybreak and then the sun came up and after it appeared they told me to go forth and I stood outside the rainbow tipi and this was the happiest moment of the vision. I looked to the four quarters of the earth and I saw all the riders. There were colors and lightning in the west and I saw black horses. In the north there were all kinds of birds flying and all different colors of horses. The same was true of the east. All sorts of horses started to mill around and in the south the buckskins were milling around. On earth the animals all rejoiced in happiness.

When I came out of the rainbow tipi the sixth grandfather was gone and I stood there in his place. The western grandfather led me out and the horses all neighed as I came out. As each grandfather came out of the rainbow tipi he was cheered for. They all took their places—north, south, and east. As the eastern man came out he took the rainbow with him and set it on the east side. The last grandfather was on earth and I did not know it and when I started to come back I was suddenly left alone. I heard a voice saying: "Look back and behold it." I looked back and the cloud house was gone. There was nothing there but a big mountain with a big gap in it. (Black Elk knows where this mountain is—Pike's Peak.)

THE SPOTTED EAGLE GUIDES BLACK ELK HOME

I could see nothing but dust flying on the four quarters of the earth. I looked up and could see right above me a spotted eagle hovering over me and this was evidently who had told me to look back. I started back to the camp with the eagle guarding me. No one was with me then but the eagle, but I knew that I was coming back to the center of the nation's hoop by myself. I could see the people following me. Soon I saw my own tipi at home and I walked fast to get there. As I entered the tipi I saw a boy lying there dying and I stood there awhile and finally found out that it was myself.

The next thing I heard was somebody saying: "The boy is feeling better now, you had better give him some water." I looked up and saw it was my mother and father stooping over me. They were giving me some medicine but it was not that that cured me—it was my vision that cured me. The first thought that came to me was that I had been traveling and my father and mother didn't seem to know that I had been gone and they didn't look glad. I felt very sad over this.

[3]

Youth (1873–75)

I remember when Black Elk was sick. I was about thirteen years old and it was at the headwaters of the Greasy Grass and during his sickness I visited him and he was unconscious twelve days. Everyone around was in perfect health and so was Black Elk until he got sick all at once while he was riding home with some boys. The next thing I heard was that he was dying and just breathing barely. Everybody in the whole village was excited over it and sent for medicine all over, but they could not tell what sickness it was Black Elk had. When I saw Black Elk he was lying perfectly still and the people all said it was a queer sickness, but still nobody knew what it was. The next thing I heard was that he was well again and everyone wondered at it and then we moved camp from the mouth of the Greasy Grass to the mouth of Willow Creek about two days after he came to. (The vision was in the month of June.)[1]

Then we camped there and Black Elk's father came over to my tipi for a visit and as we sat down to eat supper we talked about things in general and Black Elk, Sr., said: "My boy was very sick all at once and it was a strange sickness and he was unconscious for twelve days and it looked like he would not come to and I prepared for it, but all of a sudden he came to, but ever since my boy hasn't been acting well. He has queer ways. He is

1. Part of this section relating to the preparations for the buffalo hunt and the scouts' ritualized reporting of the location of the herds is attributed to Black Elk in *Black Elk Speaks*, pp. 53–57. Other good accounts of Lakota buffalo hunting are in Densmore, *Teton Sioux Music*, pp. 436–47, and Walker, *Lakota Society*, pp. 74–94.

not the boy he used to be. It is strange the way he acts. Poor boy, I thought lots of him and I feel sorry about the way he is feeling now. It seems that he doesn't think of his home very much. He stays out alone. He had been very sick but he seemed to get well so quickly and is able to get around."

The next morning the crier came around saying that we should break camp again. The advisors were in the council tipi. The crier said: "The advisors come forth to the center of the nation's hoop and bring your fire along." (Bringing your fire along meant that they had to carry their fire, for they had no matches.) "Now take it down, down!" (Take down the tipis.) Everyone began to take down their tipis and pack them on the travois. There were scouts sent out ahead of them to find buffalo. The crier says: "Many buffalo I have heard, many buffalo I have heard. Your children, you must take care of them." (Meaning to keep the children close to them while traveling so they wouldn't scare the buffalo).

As they broke camp they were in formation—(either four or six) advisors ahead on foot with a crier behind them; the chiefs; the people. When they get to a place where there were many Indian turnips, they would stop to take a rest.[2] The crier says: "Take off the loads and take your sticks and dig turnips for yourselves and let your horses rest." The advisors sit on the hill and smoke two or three times. Then the crier says: "Put on your loads." Then they all began loading on again and proceed to travel on again. The advisors look for a good place to camp for the people. At noon they had lunch while resting. They find a place where there is plenty of wood and water. Then the criers say: "Make camp." As a rule they camp in a circle (putting the ponies with the travois in a circle around the camp.)

Before we camped, I made up my mind I would see Black Elk. I was a bigger boy now and went back to where the smaller boys were, near the rear. Black Elk was riding a bay horse and I went back and spoke to him saying: "How!" and Black Elk answered me thus. I rode up to Black Elk and said: "Younger brother, after all, you got well?" Black Elk replied to me: "Yes, I'm not sick at all now." As I walked along with Black Elk it seemed that he was more like a man than a boy even though he was only

2. The turnips, *Psoralea esculenta*, called *tinpsila* by the Lakotas, were dug during June and early July. Some were eaten fresh, but most were dried for later use, when they were boiled with dried meat. See Melvin Randolph Gilmore, *Uses of Plants by the Indians of the Missouri River Region*, Smithsonian Institution, Bureau of American Ethnology, Annual Report 33 (1919), pp. 92–93.

nine years old. Other boys were playing [a] game of throwing off the
horses as they went along, but Black Elk wasn't doing this.

When we camped I noticed people were getting ready to camp so I
went over to where my tipi was and told Black Elk I'd see him again and I
went my way and he went his. When I got back I heard that some of the
men had gone to the top of a big hill (scouts). These men were now
returning and I looked over there to see three riders coming over the hill;
then I knew they were scouts seeing that no one was around. When they
formed in a circle, the council tipi was put up in the middle. The three
riders were going toward the council tipi and all the people were going
over there and I wondered if something was not coming and I went over
there myself to see what it was. When I got over there the advisors were in
the tipi and listeners were standing all around. The crier came out and
said: "Come forth and make haste. I have protected you; in return you
shall give me many things" (speaking for the scouts).

The scouts stopped in front of the camp and sat themselves down at the
door of the council tipi. One of the advisors filled his pipe with kinnikinnick. There was a buffalo chip right in front of one of the advisors and he
set the pipe on it which he had filled. The advisor said: "The nation has
depended on you; whatever you have seen, maybe it is for the good of the
nation that you have seen. Report what you have seen."

The chief offered his pipe to the four quarters of the earth—west,
north, east, and south. Then the chief lit the pipe and held it in his hand
with the stem out. Then he rose and offered the three scouts smoke. The
three scouts smoked it, meaning that they were telling the truth—like
taking an oath. He said: "At what place have you stood and seen the
good? Report it to me and I will be glad. You have been raised on this
earth and every corner of it you are supposed to know. Therefore, tell me
the truth."

The scout did not know the rules of the people, so he took [sic] his
thumb up and the chief said: "Uh, huh," meaning that he should use the
first finger in telling the truth. The scout said: "You know where we
started from. We went and got on top of the hill and there we have seen a
herd of buffalo" (pointing to the direction). As the scout said this, the
chief rose and said: "Maybe on the other side of the herd you have seen
good. Report it." The scout said: "On the other side of that herd there is
another herd of buffalo we have seen." Then [the] chief rose and said:

"Maybe you have seen something good on the other side of this herd. Report it to me and I shall be glad." The scout said: "On the other side of this herd we have seen another herd of buffalo." Then the chief said the same thing again: "I will be thankful to you. Tell me fully what you have seen out there. It shall be the truth." [And] the scout said: "On the other side of that last herd there is nothing but buffalo all over the country." The chief said: "Hetchetu alo" [It is so indeed].

When the advisors were through questioning him the crier went out and announced to the people the report and said further: "Your knives must be sharpened, your arrows shall be sharpened. Make ready, make haste, your horses make ready. We shall go forth with your arrows. Plenty of meat we shall make." Everyone began sharpening their knives and arrows. They were all getting ready for the great killing of meat.

I was now old enough myself to get around and hunt, so I went along. We had soldier bands [*akicita*]. The soldier bands went first when they started out to kill buffalo. They went in formation—everyone was to go behind the soldier band. If they went ahead of the soldier band they would be knocked unconscious. The soldiers went twenty abreast and the hunters followed four or five abreast. Everyone had to respect the soldiers, for whenever they said they would do something they meant it— they kept order. We were started toward the herd and everyone was to hunt alike. If a man went around ahead after the buffalo he would get knocked off his horse and would not get a buffalo.[3]

The advisor would be along and he would go around and find the best men in the bunch with good horses and bring them forward and [he] said to them: "Good young warriors, my relatives, your work I know is good. What you do is good always, so today you shall feed the helpless and feed the old and feeble and perhaps there is a widow who has no support. You shall help them. Whatever you get you shall donate to the poor."

Then they were all put into formation. They all went around the buffalo. The announcer said: "Hoga hey!" [*Hoka he!*] (meaning they were to go or charge). Then they all started for the buffalo—every man for himself. They were dressed as light as possible—had only a robe over them and after charging on the buffalo they fling the robe back and they are partly naked, as they fastened their robe around their waists. The

---

3. For further discussion of the *akicita,* see below, pp. 320–23 and Walker, *Lakota Society,* pp. 76–80.

quiver of arrows was on the left side of each warrior. When they got close to one they shot the buffalo behind the left shoulder. After getting the buffalo, they yelled, "Oohee!" (meaning that they had gotten one buffalo). Some of the arrows would go in up to the feather and some of them not striking bones went right straight through the buffalo's body. Everyone enjoyed this immensely.

I was supposed to be a man now and I made up my mind I'd get one myself. I had a pony and bow and arrows so I went right down and I made up my mind to get a yearling. One of them went down the draw and I went after it. I took an arrow and shot, but the first shot did not affect him. I went again but my horse went right after him and I shot an arrow through him on the left side this time. The arrow went in about a foot and probably I hit his heart and he began to sway back and forth while running and I could see the blood coming out of his mouth. I was overjoyed. This was my second buffalo, but the first was just a calf. I was supposed to say "Yuhoo" once, but I kept on saying it. They thought I was killing a lot of them from the way I yelled.

This was the first one I butchered myself. I got off my horse and began butchering. All over the flat there were men butchering buffalo. Some of the old people weren't able to shoot buffalo, but they went along to help butcher. You could hear the women rejoice over what the warriors had given them. The women followed the hunters and helped the men butcher the buffalo.

BLACK ELK TELLS OF THE HUNT
AND OF GAMES OF ENDURANCE

Of course I had been sick and I was well enough to go now. But I was not old enough to hunt. We scouted around and watched the hunters and when we would see the buffalo coming, we would signal to the people saying "Yuhoo, yuhoo!" meaning that there was meat coming in plenty. Sometimes we little fellows would get hungry and whenever we got very hungry we would run up to meet the hunters and we helped ourselves to the liver from the hunters' buffalo. They carried the meat on the saddle with pieces of buffalo hide, hanging it over the horses' backs so that it would not fall off. Some of the horses had a lot of meat on them, so they drove them back walking. In the meantime the women at home got out and cut some long poles and forked sticks and thus made drying racks for the meat. When they got back with the meat they threw it off the horses onto leaves of the spring trees. [*All the helpless who had meat distributed to them came home singing to the people who had given them this meat.*]

When they returned from hunting, the advisors would get back into their tipi and from all directions of the tipi the people brought meat to the counselors and the counselors all said: "Hyya-a-a!" [*Haye,* "Thanks!"] Then the counselors sang for the people who had brought them the meat. When the counselors had used all the meat they needed and had some left over the crier would go out saying: "All come home, it is more than I can eat." And people from the camp around would come with their cups and take what they needed from the leftover of the counselors' meat. Then the women thinned out the meat and put it on the racks to dry. You could see red meat all over the village. They then tanned the hides of the buffalo. The people fed all night long.

The day after this, I took part in an act that they had then. We boys went out in a place by ourselves and made grass tipis [war lodges], first fixed them so that they were warm. When we had fixed these tipis, we began to crawl on our home village, one to a tipi, and we were going to steal from them some of their meat (playing war). We had an advisor. His order was for us to go out and steal some dried meat. We all went. The dried meat was way up where we couldn't reach it. We saw the meat hanging up there and I wanted a tongue which was drying there, so I looked over there and began to crawl up to it. It was way up in the air. It was a tree leaning over and the rack was way up in this tree. Just as I was in the act of getting that meat someone said "Ye-a-a!" but the fellow was crying at the dog and I thought he was crying at me. I fell down on the ground and got hurt and I went away crying, and I had gotten nothing out of it. This fellow heard me and they wondered and said, "Someone is scared." By this time I was quite a ways from there and brought home nothing. The people had plenty but it was just fun to do this for us boys. When we brought this meat back to the grass tipis we began to fry it. Every evening we'd gather over there in our play tipis and steal meat just for the fun of it.

Then at other times we'd bring meat from the camp and they would get a stick and make us bite a piece off of it and if we bit a small piece we were to bring a small piece of meat, and if longer were to bring a bigger piece of meat. The advisor would know by these sticks how much we were to bring. When the boys come back, the ones who brought a small piece, their parents thought little of them and the boys who brought a large piece, their parents thought more of them.

Then we would get around and have a feast. The advisor would say, "We are going to dance now." We dressed without shirts and had on robes instead. We were naked on the breast. I remember we used to get sunburned on the breast and would be all chapped up. When the advisor would see our breasts, the one who had the biggest chapped breast would lead the dance. This was called the chapped breast dance. We had on a robe made of buffalo skin [and] a necklace that would begin ringing when we would dance. Then we all said, "Whoop, whoop!" while dancing. The song sung was like this:

> I have a chapped breast
> My breast is red.
> My breast is yellow

At this age the boys learned how to endure lots of things. This was my first experience of endurance. The older boys taught us lots of endurances. They put a heart of a sunflower on my wrist, which was lit at the top and which was burning downward. If I could stand for it to burn down to the skin I would be classed as a man and if we should fret we would be classed as a woman. Some of them said they couldn't stand the endurance and when it began to burn them they would say "Ow-h-h!" and knock it off. I stood the test without a move. We would take large ones at different times and sometimes several at once.

BLACK ELK TELLS ABOUT HIS ILLNESS

I felt that my mother and father did not welcome me and when I came to, I found out that my whole body was swollen and puffed. As I thought about it, I knew that I had gone someplace. Standing Bear's uncle was a medicine man called Whirlwind Chaser and he was treating me at this time. When I came to I felt better and wanted to go out and run around right away, but my parents wouldn't let me. Next morning I was myself again and the vision was, of course, still in my mind. When they broke camp I thought it over and thought it was a wonderful place I went to. I thought the people should know it and I felt as though I wanted them to know about it. I pondered over it and at times I did not want to think about it. The medicine man got a great name because I was cured by him all at once, but anyway it was the power of the vision that cured me. Everyone felt happy that I was living, but they did not know where I had been. They had to give this medicine man a horse for treating me. I had quite a few uncles and cousins and they were all so surprised at the way I got cured. All of a sudden it seemed I had strength enough to get around and to do almost anything. Everyone was talking about it.

That night Whirlwind Chaser (Standing Bear's mother's brother— my father and Standing Bear's father were cousins-in-law) came over to see me. They told him to be seated so he sat down. He told my father this: "Your son there is sitting in a sacred manner. I can see that there is a special duty for him to do. Just as he came in I could see the power of lightning all through his body."

The next day they went out hunting and my mind was full of thoughts and I wanted to forget about it but I couldn't. I took part in playing with the boys. But after that I did not play with the boys any more. Twelve days after I felt that I did not belong ιo the people—they were strangers to me. I wanted to be away from the people and often would go away from them. I would come home to get something to eat, but did not eat much. I would look to the four quarters of the earth and think of my vision. I couldn't stay at home at all. The only person I wanted to see often and talk to was my grandfather (mother's father). My grandfather's name was Keeps His Tipi. I wanted to talk to this man all the time and this is the only man who really cared to talk with me. I only wanted to ask my grandfather a question, but I wouldn't tell this vision to him.

I didn't want to see this medicine man again because I was afraid he would tell the people. I would lie down and hide my face when this man came along until he had passed by. This man, I thought, might tell it.

BLACK ELK'S GRANDFATHER EXPLAINS
THE MEANING OF *Wasichu*

One day I saw my grandfather in a tipi and I wanted to ask what the scouts meant when they returned from a scouting hike when they said: "The big talkers [are] coming step by step." So I asked my grandfather this question: "Grandfather, why do they say, 'The big talkers are coming little by little and step by step,' and what do they say when they talk?" Grandfather replied: "My grandfathers used to say this before the whites had ever come and I couldn't get the meaning of it, but now I know what they meant. The only thing I knew about the big talkers is that they used to mean the buffalo are coming little by little. At that time there were no white men, but someone might have at least heard of them and about them." They called the buffalo wasichu [*wašicu*] at this time before the white men came.

(Origin of the word wasichu meaning white man. Undoubtedly when the first ships came from Europe to America they carried salt pork which they gave to the Indians. "Wasichu" means "fat-takers" and this seems to have referred to the salt bacon. But at the same time the Indians noticed that the white men were always trying to find out something, poking their noses into other peoples' business and talking a great deal—perhaps trying to make the Indians understand. For this reason the word which means "fat-takers" came to carry an overtone signifying the "big-talkers." But in ancient times the word was used to refer to buffalo in very large numbers. They did not refer to small herds of buffalo by this word, but when the whole prairie was filled with buffalo the scouts would return and report wasichu. What they meant in ancient times by this word seems to have been connected with the conception of fat, meaning, as we might say, a fat lot of buffalo or a great fatness.[4])

When I was about five or six years old I knew that the wasichu meant white men, but at the same time when they say wasichu they meant

4. The term *wašicu*, in older Lakota culture, seems to have referred to certain kinds of spirits. George Bushotter, a Lakota, wrote in 1887: "In ancient times when the people first saw white men they always thought this of them, it is said—that they must be earth people or sprung from some sort of animal; and then some thought they must come out of the water, having grown there." These spirits were called *mniwašicu*, literally, water spirits (George Bushotter, "Lakota Texts," no. 93, translated by J. Owen Dorsey, National Anthropological Archives, Smithsonian Institution, Washington, D.C.). This accords with early historic accounts in which the Sioux were said to have addressed the whites as "spirits" (see, e.g., Edmund C. Bray and Martha Coleman Bray, eds., *Joseph N. Nicollet on the Plains and Prairies: The Expeditions of 1838–39 with Journals, Letters, and Notes on the Dakota Indians* [St. Paul: Minnesota Historical Society, 1976], p. 266). The etymology of the term *wašicu* is unknown, but many folk etymologies have developed in recent times. "Fat-takers" and "big-talkers" are not linguistically valid etymologies, although they are graphic expressions of more contemporary Lakota attitudes toward white men. See the discussion of *wašicu* in Eugene Buechel, S. J., *A Dictionary of the Teton Dakota Sioux Language,* ed. Paul Manhart, S.J. (Pine Ridge, S.D.: Red Cloud Indian School, 1970).

buffalo. From there on I had wondered about this and had never made it out why they would call the white men this also. They use to warn the women to keep the children quiet while the wasichu were around so as not to scare them.

[I] said to my grandfather: "I thought you meant there were white men coming, but now I know you meant there were a lot of buffalo coming."

BLACK ELK'S GRANDFATHER MAKES HIM
A BOW AND ARROWS

Then my grandfather made me a bow and arrows [some of] which were blunt and some were sharpened wood. My grandfather showed me how to use them so that I would be a man at an early age. So I took my bow and arrows and went out. At first I felt queer with this bow and arrows and wondered if it wasn't the same one that the grandfather in the vision had given me. I started out to the timber to kill birds. It was pretty warm then, but I wore the calf robe that I had. I came to a bush where there was a woodlouse (wren) and I was going to shoot it but then I remembered the vision again. Just as I was going to shoot I felt queer about this and remembered that I was to be relative-like to the birds and I didn't shoot the bird because I was relative to it, I thought. I started toward the creek and went along the creek and saw a green frog sitting there and I wanted to shoot it and I did shoot him. Then I went over there and picked it up and I thought: "I have killed him now." This was the first shot I made with my bow and arrows.

We didn't move camp for several days because we had plenty of work to do with the fresh meat. All this time I had a funny feeling. After I shot the frog I felt as though I wasn't walking on the ground.

THE VISIT TO FORT ROBINSON

Then there came a day when all this disappeared from me and I forgot all about that vision for a while and I was among the boys again like I used to be. Just at the time I got back among the boys they broke camp and then the six bands went different places, scattering. Then the Oglala band started for the Soldiers' Town, Fort Robinson.[5] As they pulled out, I was among the boys and I was a pretty good shot and could get a bird whenever I wanted to. When we broke camp we were at the mouth of the Willow Creek and we made camp again close to Powder River. We were on horseback now and this was in the Month When the Cherries Were Ripe (July). The queer feeling had left me and I thought no more about the vision and I no longer felt bashful. I rode around with the other boys.

The next camp was this side of Powder River. The next camp was at the headwaters of the north fork of the Good River (Cheyenne) [the Belle Fourche]. There are two buttes here—a big and a little one and they called this "Sits-With-Young-One" [Pumpkin Buttes]. Because there were only a few boys in this small band, we all played together and had games of all kinds. We made camp on Driftwood Creek. The next camp after that was at the Plain of the Pine Trees. We were hurrying to the Soldiers' Camp for some of our relatives were there and we wanted bread and coffee!

Whenever a thunderstorm came up I felt glad. The next camp was at Plum Creek. At this time the plums weren't very ripe, but they were just turning. My grandfather went out and came back that evening with some big red plums. We had quite a feast on this. My grandfather made me quite a few arrows and took great interest in me. Most of the boys lost their arrows, but I kept mine very carefully.

We made our next camp at Hat Creek (War Bonnet Creek). This was very close to the Soldiers' Camp and they must have heard of our coming and my aunt and other relatives came to meet us and they brought us coffee and bread. We had a real feast on coffee and bread. I got pretty sick that night and I threw up all night. I got sick again so they put me back in the travois. They were afraid that I would die surely this time. Next day I was traveling in a pony drag. We traveled downstream on the War Bonnet Creek. On this side of the War Bonnet Creek there is a hill called Hip's Hill where we made camp again. By that time most of the Indians from the Soldiers' Camp were among us. I was still riding in the pony drag.

5. Red Cloud Agency, where the Oglalas received their government annuities, was established during summer 1873 near the White Cliffs on White River in northwestern Nebraska. The next spring, Camp (later Fort) Robinson was established near the agency. See Olson, *Red Cloud and the Sioux Problem*, pp. 158, 168.

The next day we reached the Soldiers' Camp. There were only about twenty tipis of the Oglalas that were traveling to the fort—the main band stayed back. When we reached the camp we scattered out among the relatives of ours. I had an aunt there and I made camp there right beside her tipi. Part of the Oglalas camped by the White Butte at Fort Robinson. (This was six [seven?] years after the Battle of the Hundred Slain. Black Elk's father was wounded in this battle.)

We stayed all winter [1873–74] at Fort Robinson. I was now ten years old. The only thing we did here was to make Indian sleds and coast down the hills [*and we also whipped the tops on the ice*]. The sleds were made out of jaws and ribs of buffalo, tied together with rawhide.

This is the first time I had been close enough to the white men to see what they were like. What I thought about them was that they were fighting men and perhaps they were going to fight us too. They scared me a little, but I got over the scare and I wasn't afraid. While we were here wintering someone killed a rider[?] and they couldn't find out who it was. He was shot through the window of the house. The fellow rapped at the door and shot him [February 9, 1874].[6] Some thought it was Kicking Bear, but it was never proven. They had a flag on a pole and some of the Indian boys went up and chopped the flagpole down during the daytime [October 23, 1874]. There was about one troop of soldiers there and they surrounded the Indians and it seemed that they were going to fight. Right in the center Red Cloud was standing trying to prevent a fight without any weapons, and he did evidently prevent the fighting. (Red Cloud's Brulés were there.) They both wanted to fight, but Red Cloud did all he could and stopped them from fighting. He made speeches to both the Indians and the whites.[7]

6. Frank S. Appleton, Indian agent J. J. Saville's clerk, was killed by an Indian supposed to have been a Minneconjou. The Indian wakened the clerk during the night; when Appleton opened the door, the Indian shot him, evidently mistaking him for the agent. See Hyde, *Red Cloud's Folk,* p. 212, and Olson, *Red Cloud and the Sioux Problem,* p. 164.

7. Black Elk related this event out of chronological sequence; it occurred after the visit to the Black Hills described in the next section. The Indians opposed the erection of the flagpole presumably because they considered it to symbolize domination by the soldiers; the pole was chopped to pieces before it was erected. Black Elk's use of the term "boys" here probably reflects the Lakota word *koškalaka,* meaning "young men," that is, warriors; Lakotas frequently translate this word as "boys." In *Black Elk Speaks,*

CAMPING IN THE BLACK HILLS

In the moon when the ponies shed [May 1874] we broke camp again and we started for the Black Hills to cut tipi poles for the tipis. There were about thirty tipis in the band now. We went down the Horse Headcutting Creek [Horsehead Creek] and made camp midway. Then we made camp at the head of the Horse Headcutting Creek. As I looked up I heard the shrill whistle of an eagle and I wondered if this eagle wasn't the one of my vision, which was guarding me. I thought also that the people around me might be the nation of my vision. Whenever I saw a cloud appearing it seemed that someone was coming to see me and that some day it would be a duty for me to do something for my nation.

We broke camp here and left the south fork of the Good River and made camp at the foot of the Black Hills at Buffalo Gap. We camped quite early in the afternoon here. My father was lame and my father and I went out into the timber on top of a big hill and we looked down toward the Cheyenne River and my father looked all around and said: "There are some deer coming. We'll catch them and in whatever direction they go you stay here and I'll round them up and you wait for me here."

I did not want my father to go, so I said before I knew it: "No father, you stay here, they are bringing them toward us and we'll get them here." When I realized what I had said, it made me feel queer for I thought this was also a part of my vision. My father looked at me in a queer manner but he did not say anything. Then he said: "All right, son, you take the horses back a little ways out of the way." So father lay down in some high grass and watched. When they came closer we saw they were antelopes. I went back and held the horses so that they wouldn't run. I was quite a ways from my father and I heard two shots and knew that my father had gotten two antelopes. After the second shot my father gave me a signal to go up with the horses, so I went back with the horses again. My father was going down to the antelopes and found out that he had shot four antelopes with two shots. While father was butchering the game, I began to eat the kidneys and liver.

---

p. 63, Neihardt mistakenly identifies this incident as the mischievous prank of a playful boy. See Hyde, *Red Cloud's Folk,* pp. 220–22, and Olson, *Red Cloud and the Sioux Problem,* 169–70. Black Elk's reference here to "Red Cloud's Brulés" is confusing and apparently was intended to be "Oglalas."

When I filled up I was rather sorry that we had killed these animals and we ought to do something in return—make an offering to the wild things of the earth. I suggested this to my father and said: "Father, why shouldn't we offer one of these things to the wild things?" Father stared at me and [he] had a queer feeling about it. We did this, however. We laid the antelope facing the east and my father made an offering prayer as follows:

> Hey-a-a-a-a (four times). (Facing where the sun goes down—raised
> his hand higher saying this line.)
> Grandfather, the Great Spirit, behold me.
> To all the wild things that eat flesh,
> This I have offered that my people may live and the children
> will grow up in abundance.

As we started down the hill, I could hear the whistle of an eagle above us and he was probably the one who had gotten part of the meat. After we returned with the meat this vision was all out of my mind again. We were in a hurry to get home with the meat.

(Before storms from there on I knew that the thunderstorms were coming. I could hear a thundering noise in the earth as I walked along that the Thunder-beings were coming, but I was always glad to see the storm come.)

When we returned with the meat everyone rejoiced and all cheered and shared the meat with us.

My uncle, Iron Bull, a little boy my age, came running up from the creek saying that we should go fishing. When boys fish they say: "I offer this to you who are down in the water with wings of red, so come hither." We have a boy who [*calls the fish and catches them and*] puts the fish on a stick with a fork on the end so that it will not fall off and then he kisses it. If you don't kiss the fish you don't get any. They should all be very quiet except the fisherman. We caught them right along this way. We used venison for bait (the pancreas). If we didn't have this we used grasshoppers. There was another boy [*the caller*] who, when he would say this line to the fish, he would pull them out one after the other. We got about thirty fish on two sticks, and went home with them. Whenever we caught a small fish that is no good, we would kiss it and throw it back in the water, meaning that he should tell the bigger fish to come along. The reason we talk to the fish was that we should be like relatives to all animals as I had seen in my vision. We were ready to go home and the bait we had left we offered to the fish in payment for the fish we had gotten. The next time we went fishing we would be lucky.

In olden times whenever we'd go out before we were men we'd go out and bring in game to show that we would be good providers. I knew that my mother was glad to see me home when I'd bring something home, so I wanted to get something bigger. I made up my mind to do this so that everyone would think lots of me.

We moved camp from here and camped at Split Toe Creek. Then we broke camp from here and camped at Spring Creek up into the hills on the south side toward Rapid Creek. From Spring Creek we camped at Rapid Creek. That evening before the sun set there came a big storm, but I was glad to see it, and right before the storm you could see all kinds of split-tail swallows all over above us. The boys wanted to hit them and I did not like to see them do it. I got a stone and acted as though I was going to hit them, but had no intention of doing anything. No matter how hard they tried, the boys couldn't hit them. After thinking over the vision I knew that they couldn't kill them, so I was satisfied.

Next morning men got on horses and got [*axes*] ready to get tipi poles. They followed the Rapid Creek into the hills and into the thick of the forest and began cutting tipi poles. There were lots of slim poles, for no one at this time had bothered them at all.[8] They brought them back and began to strip and dress the poles. Some of us knew how to strip them and some did not, so the work was rather slow. Men had gone out on a hunt so we had plenty of meat—bear meat, etc. We were sitting around camp boiling bear meat. Next morning we were all through with the poles and we began building a sweat tipi for a medicine man by the name of Chips. He was the first man who made a sacred ornament for Crazy Horse to use in the war and probably this is where Crazy Horse was made bullet-proof and got his [*bullet-proof*] power.[9]

8. The tall, straight lodgepole pines that grew in the Black Hills were used by the Lakotas and other plains tribes for tipi poles. See Gilmore, *Uses of Plants by the Indians of the Missouri River Region,* p. 63.

9. Chips (or Horn Chips) was one of the most renowned medicine men among the Lakotas. See Sandoz, *Crazy Horse,* pp. 163, 242–43; Steinmetz, *Pipe, Bible and Peyote among the Oglala Lakota,* pp. 21–22; William K. Powers, *Yuwipi: Vision and Experience in Oglala Ritual* (Lincoln: University of Nebraska Press, 1982), pp. 8–13.

STANDING BEAR TELLS OF THE MOVEMENT
OF BANDS IN SPRING 1874

In this year I was over with the Minneconjous and they were camped near the mouth of the Good [Cheyenne] River on the Missouri. We were heading for the Black Hills. It was in May in the spring and Crazy Horse was on the west side of the Black Hills. Sitting Bull was on the north side of the Grand River near the Missouri River. The rest of the Minneconjous were on the north side of the Black Hills on Forest Creek. We moved from the mouth of the Cheyenne upstream to the forks and then we struck out for Forest Creek. Then when we got there, we heard there were white men in the Black Hills exploring.[10] (They had a chief there with the Minneconjous called Hump and he was killed. He was very noted and just as noted as chief Crazy Horse and was a friend of the latter. When Hump got killed it was in the battle of the Shoshones [1870]. Next to Hump was Lame Deer who probably took the former's place.[11] At this time I was four [six?] years old, just old enough to know about it.) We stayed here and hunted around for awhile there. We had a council and were going to [that part of] the Missouri River which is west of where Sitting Bull was.

BLACK ELK TELLS OF CHIPS'S WARNING AND
THE RETURN TO FORT ROBINSON

We made this sweat tipi.[12] The boys asked me to go out and shoot some squirrels. They were hard to hit and as we were shooting them I felt uneasy, so I sat down and wondered. When I sat down someone said: "Go

10. On July 2, 1874, Lt. Col. George A. Custer left Fort Abraham Lincoln, Dakota Territory, with a scientific exploration party and military escort of over a thousand men. They reconnoitered the Black Hills from north to south and returned to Fort Abraham Lincoln on August 30 with enthusiastic reports of gold "from the grass roots down" that triggered a flood of white prospectors into the hills. See William H. Goetzmann, *Exploration and Empire: The Explorer and the Scientist in the Winning of the American West* (New York: Alfred A. Knopf, 1967), pp. 419–21; Hyde, *Red Cloud's Folk*, pp. 217–19; and Olson, *Red Cloud and the Sioux Problem*, pp. 172–73.

11. Hump's death is recorded in No Ears's winter count for 1870 (Walker, *Lakota Society*, p. 146). According to White Bull, Lame Deer was one of the leading chiefs of the Minneconjous. See Vestal, *Warpath*, p. 48. He was killed on May 7, 1877, when his camp near the Rosebud River was attacked by troops under Gen. Nelson A. Miles. See Powell, *People of the Sacred Mountain*, 2:1129–34.

12. The *initi,* or sweat lodge, is a low, dome-shaped structure constructed of willow saplings covered with hides. See Brown, *The Sacred Pipe,* p. 33.

at once, go home." I thought it was from the camp so I asked the others to go back to the camp, not telling them what I heard. At this time I knew nothing about Chips being in the sweat house. When I got back everyone was getting excited, saddling up their ponies, and I heard that while Chips was in the tipi he said that we must go at once that something was going to happen here. (Black Elk evidently heard the same words that Chips heard.)

We got ready and proceeded down to where our other big camp was and we fled all that night because it was nearly sundown when we broke camp. We fled on the back trail toward Spring Creek. We followed the creek down and went south a ways to [the south fork of the] Cheyenne River. I got sleepy and I had to ride in the travois. We got to the south fork of the Good [Cheyenne] River in the morning. We were in haste so we didn't have much breakfast. We followed upstream from there on all day long until we got to the mouth of Horse [Horsehead] Creek, which was a good day's ride. When we stopped in the evening we were going to stop there, but the scouts reported that there were soldiers coming toward the Black Hills.[13] [*We had some time and then*] we came on. It was nighttime but we had to flee anyway, so we kept on going. From Horse Creek we headed toward White River (Smoky Earth River) and when we got there it was daybreak. We went up the White River toward Robinson, making one camp on the way. Near Fort Robinson we came to a butte called Hill Surrounded where some Indians were stationed.[14]

When we got back to the people at Fort Robinson we told them that we saw some whites going toward the Black Hills. It was heard that the soldiers were up there to get the white and yellow metals in the hills. Everyone thought that something should be done about it and they must get together and decide on something. They called the Indians who stayed around the fort "Sticks around the Fort," and they thought of them as sticking up for the whites.[15] Crazy Horse was on the west and Sitting

13. This is apparently another reference to Custer's exploring party.

14. Hill Surrounded, about eight miles east of Fort Robinson, Nebr., is also known as Crow Butte or Dancer's Hill. In 1944 Black Elk told Neihardt the story of how the Sioux trapped a Crow war party on top of the butte; see below, December 8.

15. "Sticks around the Fort" is frequently given as a translation of *Wagluhe*, Loafers, a band formed during the 1850s of Oglalas camped around Fort Laramie. There were many intermarriages between the women of this band and the white soldiers. Hyde, *Red Cloud's Folk*, pp. 86, 314; and William K. Powers, *Oglala Religion* (Lincoln: University of Nebraska Press, 1977), p. 31.

Bull was on the north and everyone thought they should get together and do something about the gold-diggers in the Black Hills. Red Cloud's people said that the soldiers had come up there to drive the gold-diggers out, but the northern Indians did not believe it.[16]

They had a sun dance here at Fort Robinson for the people's health and for an abundance of meat. Some of them were dancing before they were going to war. I remember that only two men [?] danced this sun dance because one of them was dancing on one leg and had lost one in the battle of the Hundred Slain. The other man had two good legs but he had lost one eye in some battle. So the two men danced with three eyes and three legs.[17]

We youngsters went down to the creek while they were sun dancing and we got some elm leaves and put them in a sack and we would fill our mouths with slippery elm leaves and we'd slash this stuff on the people when they were trying to look their best in the sun dance. We even would do this to some of the older people. Everyone was supposed to be teasing each other and everyone was happy that day. This was a kind of an endurance. Men should stand lots of endurance in the sun dance and we boys were to test the endurance of their minds.

At the sun dances the children are taken, and the priests (medicine men) pierce their ears if they [the parents] think a lot of their children and they must give away a pony for each piercing. These ponies were given to the poor. Or a person who has performed a brave deed has the right to pierce a child's ear the same as a medicine man has.[18]

After the sun dance was over we moved over to Crawford on the White River. At this time my present wife's father died there of sickness and they put him up on four poles because Indians are supposed to be relative-like

16. The 1868 treaty guaranteed that the United States would protect Sioux territory from trespass by whites. After Custer's 1874 expedition reported gold in the Black Hills it became impossible—short of using military force—to keep white prospectors out of the area, despite President Grant's promise to the Sioux chiefs to do so. See Olson, *Red Cloud and the Sioux Problem,* pp. 171–74.

17. According to *Black Elk Speaks,* p. 80, this sun dance occurred in June 1875. It was the first Lakota sun dance reported to have been held at the agencies. See George E. Hyde, *Spotted Tail's Folk: A History of the Brulé Sioux* (Norman: University of Oklahoma Press, 1961), p. 209. The two mutilated dancers were apparently not the only ones to participate in the ceremony.

18. In traditional times, ear piercing was an important ritual, essential for identity as a Lakota. See Rocky Bear in Walker, *Lakota Belief and Ritual,* pp. 191–93.

to the animals of the earth and when an animal dies, his bones are just scattered and probably his spirit is on earth. So an Indian when he dies should be put up there so that when his body dries up his spirit will remain on earth in the happy hunting grounds. When you bury a person, he is completely dead and he will not come out of the ground. They think that the dead persons look after their relatives on earth. They make this offering to the spirit of the sun.[19]

THE STORY OF WATANYE

There was a man by the name of Watanye and he had very bad sore lips, sore all around and were sore for quite a while. He did not dare to laugh because it split his lips and if you tried to make him laugh he would just walk away and not laugh. But one day when I was a boy I went fishing with Watanye in a little Black Hills creek where there were a lot of speckled trout. We were fishing with spears. As we walked along the stream we saw a big fish about this long (above elbow) lying in the water almost on top. I started to spear him and Watanye said: "Spear low, because they always drop." I threw my spear and missed the fish and tumbled over head first into the water. It was clear water and much deeper than it seemed. When I came up I saw Watanye doubled up and heard him going "Hunh, Hunh." The blood was streaming from his lips. I had made him laugh at last. He ran away as fast as he could and for a long time afterward he would not let me come near him because every time he saw me he had to laugh.[20]

19. For Lakota burial customs see Luther Standing Bear, *Land of the Spotted Eagle* (Boston: Houghton Mifflin, 1933), pp. 211–13, and Royal B. Hassrick, *The Sioux: Life and Customs of a Warrior Society* (Norman: University of Oklahoma Press, 1964), pp. 293–98.

20. In the stenographic record this is entitled "Incidental story of Black Elk's boyhood," and Black Elk related it just before his recollections of the Custer battle. The date of the incident is unknown. In *Black Elk Speaks,* p. 66, Watanye is said to have been the original narrator of the story of High Horse's courting, which is not part of the stenographic record. See below, December 7.

[4]

Walking the Black Road
(1875–76)

BLACK ELK TELLS ABOUT THE 1875
BLACK HILLS COUNCIL

Now I began to want to stand endurance, so I took part in all kinds of games to prepare myself for fighting. We camped all this fall [1875], and I was now eleven years old. This winter [1875–76] was called The Selling of the Hunting Ground.[1] We were here [near the present location of

---

1. In summer 1875 the secretary of the interior appointed a commission to treat with the Sioux for the relinquishment of the Black Hills. Headed by Sen. William B. Allison, the commissioners met with representatives from all the western Sioux bands at a site on the White River about eight miles east of Red Cloud Agency, September 20–28. The two sides were unable to reach an agreement, and the commissioners returned to Washington without the chiefs' signatures. The next year, after the loss of Custer and his men, the president appointed a second commission, headed by George W. Manypenny, to inform the Sioux that unless they agreed to relinquish the hills they would receive no further government annuities. This time the commissioners met each of the Sioux groups separately, counseling with the Oglalas at Red Cloud Agency on September 7–20, 1876. Under pressure, and with protest, the chiefs signed the agreement. See Olson, *Red Cloud and the Sioux Problem,* pp. 201–13; Hyde, *Red Cloud's Folk,* pp. 239–48, and *Spotted Tail's Folk,* pp. 211–15, 229–32.

The two councils were held for the same purpose, almost exactly one year apart, and Black Elk, Iron Hawk, and Standing Bear seemed to have merged the two in their memories. The descriptions they give in the following accounts are of the 1875, not the 1876, council. Although both Lakotas and whites refer to the 1876 agreement as a "treaty," it was not a treaty per se because the United States ceased making treaties with Indian tribes in 1871. Nonetheless, the government accords agreements the same binding force as treaties.

Crawford, Nebraska] all winter [that is, the previous winter, 1874–75] with the Brulés [Oglalas?], and we stayed all the next summer here also.[2] In the fall we broke camp and started toward the Little Big Horn. While we were at Fort Robinson we could see immigrants coming up to the Black Hills for gold and this was in the year of the treaty of 1876. This is the year when Custer got wiped out—1876.

I was there at the time of the powwow for the arrangement of the treaty of 1875. All I could remember [is] that in the middle of the circle of the tipis they put up a shade of canvas and underneath this were the white and Indian councilors and all around them were Indians on horseback. This was on the north side of White River,[3] at the mouth of [Little] White Clay Creek. I was only a boy then, so this was all I saw of the making of the treaty. I wondered about the treaty so I asked my father what it was. He told me that the soldiers had wanted to lease the Black Hills. The general said to the Indians that if they did not lease the Black Hills to the Grandfather at Washington, the Black Hills would be just like snow held in the hand and melting away. In other words, they were going to take the Black Hills (Kha Sapa [*He Sapa*]) away from us anyway.

(Questioned what they think of the Black Hills, Black Elk says:) As a boy I thought the Indians should stick to the Black Hills and I told the boys around me, "When we grow up, boys, we'll have to help hold the Black Hills."

Black Elk thinks that the highest peak in the Black Hills—Harney Peak—is the one to which the spirits took him in the vision to see the whole earth. The spirits had told him that the people[4] would prosper there.

STANDING BEAR TELLS ABOUT THE BLACK HILLS

At this time I was about fifteen years old and I heard Sitting Bull say that the Black Hills was just like a food pack and therefore the Indians should

2. The chronology is somewhat garbled here. The reference to the Brulés is probably an error, most likely intended for "Oglalas." The Brulés were camped that winter on Chadron Creek, farther down White River, near Spotted Tail Agency (Hyde, *Spotted Tail's Folk,* p. 204).

3. The stenographic record incorrectly has "north side of the south fork of the Good River."

4. The stenographic record has "spirits," an apparent scriptographic error; cf. above, p. 44.

stick to it. At that time I just wondered about what he had said and I knew what he meant after thinking it over because I knew that the Black Hills were full of fish, animals, and lots of water, and I just felt that we Indians should stick to it. Indians would rove all around, but when they were in need of something, they could just go in there and get it.

BLACK ELK TELLS OF JOINING CRAZY HORSE'S CAMP AND THE KILLING OF THE CROW HORSE THIEF

This was in the fall of the year (1875) and we broke camp and we wanted to join Crazy Horse's band on the Tongue River. The first camp we made was at Horse [Horsehead] Creek and the next camp was on War Bonnet Creek; the next camp was at Sage Creek. We crossed the Bozeman Trail[5] before coming to War Bonnet Creek. We next camped at Beaver Creek. Next we camped on Driftwood Creek. We broke camp here and we went on the Plain of the Pine Trees again. Then I went up into the Black Hills alone and had another vision under a tree and found out that the duty I was to do was to come to me and that I would probably save the Black Hills. It looked as though it were impossible, but I was anxious to perform my duty on earth.

We next camped at Taking the Crow Horses Creek. The next camp we made was on the Powder River. Buffalo were in abundance here and we went out hunting. Thus there was again plenty of meat in the band. Then something happened while we were here. There was a man by the name of Fat and he had a good horse which could run well. I had a pony that seemed as though it couldn't run at all. I wanted to race with him but he wouldn't do it because he thought my horse couldn't run. I made a bet with him that he was to make me something to eat when he got into camp. We made a race and this man was sure he was going to beat me. My horse probably had power and I beat him. Fat was very surprised at the pony. I used the help I got from the north in the vision in this act. I got something to eat from Fat because of this, anyway.

5. This is an error because the Bozeman Trail is far west of War Bonnet Creek. Black Elk is probably referring to the Thieves' Road, Custer's 1874 trail through the Black Hills, or possibly to the route of the 1875 Black Hills exploration led by Col. Richard I. Dodge (see Hyde, *Red Cloud's Folk*, p. 234, and Olson, *Red Cloud and the Sioux Problem*, p. 200).

The next camp we made was on Kills Himself Creek and buffalo were in abundance here so we camped awhile and the crier went around saying that we should make lots of meat for winter was coming. Everyone was getting ready for the morning hunt the next day. We stayed here over ten days and dried our meat, made hides, etc. We were going to break camp and join Crazy Horse now. The Stick around the Fort people [*Loafers*] were here and most of them hurried back to the fort when they found out the band was going to join Crazy Horse.

We broke camp and followed upstream (northwest) on the Kills Himself Creek and camped at the head of this creek. We had no advisors, as we were a little band. One of my boy pals, Steal Horses, and I went ahead of the band. We were going through a trail and we could see the footprints of somebody going ahead so we followed the tracks. As we crossed the Kills Himself Creek, there was a knoll on the [other] side and there was an Indian lying down and he was apparently dead. His name was Root of the Tail; he was an old man and he died quite awhile before. He had started out afoot and wanted to see some of his relatives over on Tongue River and he died going. The best thing we could do was to cover the old man up and leave him alone there.

My uncles were over there and one of them, Iron Crow, was there at Tongue River. I was anxious to see my cousin Crazy Horse but he wasn't there. He must have been on a warpath against the Crows.

(At this time the Indians put their arms over each other's shoulders to greet each other.)

In the winter the Indians left, scattering all along the way so that they would all have plenty. At this time they were near the enemy's land and they must be ready all the time for anything that might happen. They would herd their ponies in the daytime and corral them at night. The women would go out in the daytime and chop up the bark of the cottonwood trees and feed their ponies with this which made them very fat and sleek. The guard had a tipi right at the mouth of the corral so that no enemy could get the horses. Crows were known as the greatest horse thieves going, so this is why we took especial care.

We camped right with the Oglalas of Crazy Horse and we camped the farthest up the Tongue River of all of them. We lived in tipis made of duck at this time, because we got our tipi cloth at Fort Robinson while we were there. They told us to move camp so we moved right close to my uncle,

Iron Crow. Men hunted every day and there was plenty of meat now. Small parties went out on scouting expeditions during the four nights we stayed here.

About the fourth day after joining Crazy Horse's band the scouting party reported that they had seen an enemy, the Absolokas [Crows]. When herding the horses, we were warned to take good watch over the horses for there were enemies in the vicinity. Nothing happened but everyone was excited nevertheless. The next night there were still rumors about the enemies. There were guards stationed all over the camp to watch. The fifth night I went to bed, but was quite restless, and I thought the Crows were coming and I dozed off, but didn't sleep very well. I looked through the hole of the tipi looking at the stars. Just as I was thinking this way I heard a shot and afterwhile another shot occurred. Then I heard voices. Someone hollered that a village visitor had been killed (Crow horse thief) so I got up with some others and we ran toward where the Crow had gotten killed. When we reached there, what I saw was horrible. The Crow's arms and legs were off and he was scalped. As we arrived someone said: "Take the coup stick and hit him." So everyone carried sticks to touch the enemy. After couping the enemy, you could see a big pile of sticks there beside the Crow's scattered body.

(Counting coup—whenever a man shoots an enemy and kills him, it is a great thing for him to do and it is one point toward his being a great chief. It gives them distinction.)

They built a fire right near the body and they were going to have a kill dance, rejoicing about the killing of an enemy. Men, women and children danced right in the middle of the night. This is the song they sang in the honor of the man who had counted the first coup. (Yellow Shirt struck first coup.) Everyone brought their bow and arrows and they put the body up and shot it full of bullets. The song:

Yellow Shirt, he whose heart for greatness is known.

Crow Nose was the man who shot the Crow thief. He was the guard at the opening of the tipi at this time. Blue Horse was visiting Crow Nose this night in the guard tipi. Crow Nose's son-in-law was Yellow Shirt. There was a tipi on each side of the corral. Yellow Shirt was on the right side of the corral. The visitor [Blue Horse] went to bed. There were holes in the tipis so that they could peep through into the corral. Crow Nose peeped out of the holes in the tipi (snow was on the ground) and he felt that there was an enemy coming. Finally Crow Nose got sleepy and he woke his wife up and told her that he was going to sleep and he said: "You'd better stay up and guard for I have a queer feeling now and must have a rest." Crow Nose went to sleep just as he was. This woman soon saw a man among the horses and he had caught a horse. She said: "Old man, you'd better get up, I see a man in there among the horses." So Crow Nose got up and peeped out of the hole and saw a man looking for the best horse. He had the rope around the horse's neck and then he was sure that this was a Crow. He was going to go out but then he thought he would just look through the hole and watch him a little longer. He had his gun ready, pointing at the doorway. Crow Nose looked at the other camp and then you could hear nothing but the bars of the opening of the corral coming off. Crow Nose just stood at the door and watched and he told his wife to make a motion when the Crow went out of the corral. The horse jumped over the big bar and as Crow Nose turned around his wife gave a signal and Crow Nose just lay down by the horse on the other side of the Crow. Just as the Crow jumped up to get on, Crow Nose killed the Crow. Crow Nose went and told his son-in-law to come and coup the first kill. As he started out he fell down and got up again and shot the enemy twice with a pistol. Then he took a stick and couped the Crow. If a person kills an enemy he should not touch him, because you have had the honor of killing him. Another person is required to coup the enemy and then still another is required to scalp him.

Everyone went back to the camp when they had finished the celebration and it was morning at this time. Early this morning the crier came around saying that they were going to break camp and camp where Root of the Tail had died. Crow Nose painted his face black and rode the horse that the enemy had tried to steal. He wore bear claws on him and he was all dressed up in war regalia. When the men blacken their faces the women all rejoice. Crow Nose sang this song about his son-in-law to represent the act he had done:

> Yellow Shirt, come forth, I have got him.
> All you have to do is coup him.

Everyone was breaking camp, loading the horses. The day before this a war party had gone out. When the party was half way back their crier was saying: "Yeah-hey." They said: "The Loafers who went to the war party, it has been reported that they have been slain." All the women in this village sent up the tremolo and at this time a big whirlwind came in the camp and knocked some of the trees down and took some tipis down, and stampeded the horses. There was one party who had not gotten killed and came back alive. The Crows had killed these Loafers of Red Cloud's. The Crows at this time were supposed to attack us but were afraid of our power; this is why they wanted to steal our horses. Just before this the war party had gone out and had seen the tracks of the Crows. They went to bed and the Crows surrounded them and killed them all but the scout who had gone out scouting. One of the Loafers was trying to fix his gun and one of them had evidently gone out to get some wood for a fire and the Crows had killed them in the acts. This Crow party who killed these Loafers were starting over to steal horses. So the Sioux were satisfied because they had gotten some revenge by killing one of the Crows who had stolen the horses.

BLACK ELK'S FATHER'S STORY OF THE
1875 BLACK HILLS COUNCIL

Now we were camping at the Root of the Tail death place. I was now twelve years old; after this we broke camp and started back for Fort Robinson again [February 1876]. Crazy Horse stayed, and only a small band returned. We stayed at the fort that spring and then the treaty of 1876 was made up.[6] At Fort Robinson there was a big tree under which the treaty was made. On the other side of the tree there were soldiers standing with their guns and on the north side there were Indians sitting. There were officers sitting all around and someone fooled me by telling me that they were going to fight. We found out that Grandfather in Washington was going to explore the country as far as the pines extend. Red Cloud was having Red Dog speak for him in his place. He was willing to lease it out all right, but [he said] that seven generations should receive pay for the

6. Black Elk incorrectly places the signing of the Black Hills agreement in spring instead of September 1876. Black Elk's band left Red Cloud Agency after the first Black Hills council in September 1875 and joined Crazy Horse's people on Tongue River. That winter, messengers arrived at the camp announcing that white soldiers were coming in the spring and that any Sioux who did not return to the agencies by January 31, 1876, would be considered hostile (Hyde, *Red Cloud's Folk*, pp. 250–51). Black Elk's band evidently complied with this order and returned to Red Cloud Agency in February 1876 (*Black Elk Speaks*, p. 90). There all the talk was about the proposed sale of the Black Hills. But at this point in his narrative, Black Elk describes the Black Hills council of the previous year, September 1875.

use of the hills. The officer asked him what he meant by seven generations. And he said that he meant that seven sons from his generation should receive the leasing money.

Black Elk's father told him the following. Red Cloud said that the Sioux nation in the form of seven generations should get pension out of it in the form of clothing and rations and this would include farm implements that Uncle Sam should give to the Indians. They wanted to buy it outright, but Red Dog said to Red Cloud: "Cousin, they claim that if we don't lease it to them that it will be like snow in your hand melting away, so let us just lease it for seven generations and it will still be ours after that." Then next Spotted Tail got up and pointed his forefinger at Red Cloud and said: "Cousin, you are a cheap man," and they all said "How!"—that is, agreement. Then turning to the officers he said: "I, myself, Spotted Tail, it is I who am speaking. I speak not for my sake but for the sake of my people of the future I speak. What I will say is this. In the future so long as there is an Indian or even the Indian may vanish, and perhaps there may be only a dog belonging to the Indian still living, and [then] the Great Grandfather shall provide even that dog with food and clothing." Then One Horn of the Minneconjous got up and everyone said: "How, hetchetu." He said (pointing to the Indians that were there): "You selfish people, we are not the only ones in the Sioux nation. Raise your heads up and look to the north and the west. There are Sioux still out. [*My people are out yet.*] According to that, we should not be selfish. We shall wait and when this Sioux nation gets together we shall decide on this." Everyone said: "How, How!"

This is all my father told me about this treaty of 1876 [1875]. In the night soldiers went from camp to camp, getting every chief to sign the treaty by filling them up with liquor (minnie wakan [*mni wakan*]).[7] Two or three days after this we broke camp and started out for Crazy Horse's camp [May 1876].[8] Red Cloud was blamed for this treaty and they said that he

7. The rumor that the chiefs were given whiskey to induce them to sign the agreement is a persistent theme in Lakota oral tradition. Cf. Vestal, *Warpath*, p. 269. However, there is no documentary support for this accusation.

8. There is further confusion here, again stemming from Black Elk's merger of the two Black Hills councils and his incorrect memory that the signing of the Black Hills agreement took place in spring 1876. According to *Black Elk Speaks*, p. 92, Black Elk's band left Red Cloud Agency again in May 1876 to rejoin Crazy Horse, but this could not have been "two or three days after" the council; here Black Elk must be remembering once again the council of September 1875.

was a cheap man and that they would have to go out and make up for it. I thought now that the time had probably come for me to do my duty and this was the time to try my power.

BLACK ELK TELLS ABOUT ATTACKING
A WAGON TRAIN NEAR WAR BONNET CREEK

We camped at War Bonnet Creek and we broke this camp and we saw some immigrants coming up the Bozeman Trail toward the Black Hills.[9] There were two riders who came up here to scout. One of the immigrants took a shot at the scouts. Then they formed a circle and put their oxen inside the circle. When the scouts returned, we decided that we were to attack the wagon train. As small as I was, I made up my mind that I might as well die there and I'd be known probably if I'd die here. I told a friend that I was going with the war party. I went and this boy, my cousin, Jumping Horse, followed me with some other boys also. We began to attack and we rode around in a circle around the wagon train. We fired from our horses at the wagons. I had a six-shooter that my sister had given me at the fort.[10] [Little] Big Man, who held Crazy Horse when he was killed, came up to me and told us to ride and attack them. We followed him and rode around and around the circle. I did not shoot but I just went around once to see what it was like. Just then I began to recall my vision again while looking under my pony's neck. I was only twelve years old and all I could do was to hang on to my horse barely and the bullets would just whiz over me. We went round in a circle twice. They were pumping bullets at us, but they didn't even hit our horses. It probably was my power that kept us from being hurt. Not a soul was killed, not even a horse or an ox. I was afraid to attack at first but when I looked I was ready to fight all right. Coming back I noticed that I was the youngest boy there. Jumping Horse and I were the youngest ones, I guess. I overheard the Cheyennes saying that we were brave boys and they made a motion that we had to fight from now on. This is the first time that I was on the warpath. Crab was the only boy who got close to the wagons, [*and*] without getting shot.

9. Again, this is not the Bozeman Trail, but one of the trails into the Black Hills.

10. According to the stenographic record, the six-shooter was a present from Black Elk's sister, but *Black Elk Speaks* has "aunt" (pp. 92, 109).

We camped next at the Den of the Bears [Devil's Tower, Wyoming].[11] Some more scouts claimed that they saw some soldiers in the Black Hills. Warriors went out and I did not go this time. They had a fight there and the boy, Crab, went with them and was the hero over there. They came back and had killed only three soldiers. None of us were killed. We were moving fast now because we wanted to get back to chief Crazy Horse and we were in danger. As we got on top of the ridge on this side of the Rosebud River, we could see the six bands of the Sioux gathering there with many ponies and a multitude of people—Oglalas, Hunkpapas, Minneconjous, Santees, Black [Feet, Two] Kettles,[12] Brulés. The scouts came out to meet us and escorted us to the camp. Everyone rejoiced to have us back there. The band I was with was selected with all kinds of bands mixed in it [that is, it was comprised of individuals from many different bands]. Red Cloud's oldest son was with us, but Red Cloud himself was not there. We went back to chief Crazy Horse's now.

IRON HAWK TELLS ABOUT THE 1875 BLACK HILLS COUNCIL

We were on the Missouri with Sitting Bull (Hunkpapa). There was a runner there by the name of One Horn who went over there and reported there was a treaty. This runner wanted to see Sitting Bull himself. One Horn said: "Brother, Sitting Bull, this is the way I talked at the treaty so I am now going to tell you. Listen, Sitting Bull, my brother, I will not tell a lie, but the truth I will tell you. I have said this to the white faces in the treaty. I have said: 'Red Cloud, Spotted Tail and you people, you are doing the act of thieves. Don't you know there are more people out than here? We should depend on them and when they gather together we must decide on this, but you are very cheap.' This is what I said to them." Sitting Bull said: "How! Brother, it is well that you have said that; these hills are a treasure to us Indians. That is the food pack of the people and when the poor have nothing to eat we can all go there and have something

---

11. Called by the Lakotas *mato tipila,* bear lodge.

12. Black Elk evidently considered the No Bows (Sans Arcs), Blackfeet, and Two Kettles as a single group. The English rendering "Black Kettles" is a meaningless confusion of two of these names. See p. 140, n. 27.

to eat, and it is well that you have said this." The people gathered around
to hear the conversation between Sitting Bull and One Horn.[13]

STANDING BEAR TELLS ABOUT THE
1875 BLACK HILLS COUNCIL

At this time of the treaty we were camped at the Tongue River. My
brother came all the way from Fort Robinson to us people, the Minneconjous. Next day, chief Crazy Horse and his band came to [from?] the
Black Hills to camp with us on Tongue River. There I heard [about] the
treaty of 1876 [1875]. This uncle of mine came there to my place and here's
how he heard it. (All chiefs were here to listen; Crazy Horse wasn't here
yet.)

"I've heard all that they said. This I will tell and you people shall hear.
The officer said: 'Your Grandfather over to where the White House is has
sent me to see about the Black Hills and also to see you.' As the officer said
this, Red Dog got up and evidently was supposed to talk for Red Cloud.
The officer wanted Red Cloud to speak for himself. Red Cloud got up and
said: 'I will lease just the surface of the Black Hills, not under nor below,
for seven generations.' The officer asked Red Cloud what he meant by the
seven generations and Red Cloud's son was standing [*near*] him and he
pointed to him and said: 'My son is the first generation and his son and his
son's son will have pay for this Black Hills and after that seven generations
are up, we'll decide what to do further with it.' Then Spotted Tail got up
and said to Red Cloud: 'Cousin, you are a cheap man and so thus I will
speak. I will not speak for myself [but] for the good of the people that
Grandfather should pay as long as the Great Spirit doesn't make the Black
Hills over.' Then One Horn got up and pointed at chief Red Cloud,
Spotted Tail, and the people and said: 'You are not the only Sioux. Raise
your heads up and look over to the north and to the west. There are people
of ours roaming the country and killing buffalo. We should wait until they
are all here together.'"

This is just what I heard from my uncle when he came directly from the
camp. The next morning we moved camp. The next morning the crier

13. One Horn or Lone Horn (*He Wanjila*) was the leading chief of the Minneconjous. He died in winter 1875–76, of grief over the Black Hills, the Lakotas say. See
Sandoz, *Crazy Horse*, p. 294.

announced that we should break camp and we were to go forth to the Rosebud River. (There were now four bands—Minneconjous, Crazy Horse's [Oglalas], Sitting Bull's [Hunkpapas], Shahila [*Šahiyela,* Cheyennes]).[14] We had plenty of meat now, and I wish we had that much right now.

STANDING BEAR TELLS ABOUT THE SUN DANCE ON THE ROSEBUD, JUNE 1876

We broke camp and went up the Rosebud for the sun dance.[15] We camped so that the Rosebud flowed through the center of the great oval camp. We selected a place in the center of the oval for the sun dance. (This was about the middle of the Moon of Fatness.) Next morning early the announcer [camp crier, *eyapaha*] cried out saying: "Brave men, be ready, for your time has come. It is your time to do your duty now to send voices up to the Great Spirit. The religion we have now at will [sic] and we shall go forth and pray and repent."

The chief Sitting Bull was the leader of the sun dance. From every band some came to dance. There were very many dancing here. Most of the Sioux nation was there except ones around the agency and forts. They danced two days. The chiefs sent out scouts all over guarding the sacred place so that we should not be disturbed. We were ready if anything should come up.

We boys chewed up elm leaves and threw them at each other here. Then we got out in pairs and collected some spear grass and had three or four in a bunch. When we would pass by a man with no shirt on we would stick him with them. The next endurance test we had there was using pop guns; we'd take ash boughs and make pop guns out of them. We'd pop these guns on the women's faces and on the men. It was like a Fourth of

---

14. Touch the Clouds, son of One Horn, was leader of the Minneconjous in this camp (see Sandoz, *Crazy Horse,* pp. 293–94). The leader of the Cheyenne fighting men was Ice (White Bull), although Two Moons and several of the Northern Cheyenne council chiefs were also present. See Powell, *People of the Sacred Mountain,* 2:1019.

15. In *Black Elk Speaks,* pp. 95–99, Neihardt attributes this section to Black Elk. The details concerning the sun dance ritual in *Black Elk Speaks* were apparently taken from published sources. During this very important sun dance, Sitting Bull had a vision of soldiers falling into the Indian camp, which prophesied the victory over Custer's troops. See Vestal, *Sitting Bull,* pp. 148–51, and Powell, *People of the Sacred Mountain,* 2:947–53.

July celebration. Some women had babies (holy little ones)[16] and they had water bags to carry water with for the little ones. We made some short bows and arrows and hid them and if we saw a bladder bag, we would shoot this arrow into them and the water would run out. The next thing boys would do was to wound dogs with the arrows. We had a good time here and many men took lots of endurance.

When the sun dance was over there was a rumor that the white men were coming from the south. We sent out scouts and after they went out, the announcer announced for us to break camp. From Rosebud we went south toward Greasy Grass Creek. The next day we moved slowly toward the Little Big Horn. We camped at the head of Spring Creek which flows into the Big Horn. The scouts reported that soldiers were coming, so the war party got ready and met the soldiers on the Rosebud. The announcer said: "The scouts have returned and they have reported that the soldiers are now camping on the Rosebud River, so young warriors, take courage and get ready to go meet them." At the same time before the announcer announced, there was a war party going out and I was going with them. I had an uncle who thought lots of me and he said, "Nephew, you must not go. Stay and look at the helpless; stay here and fight." So the warriors went on ahead.

IRON HAWK TELLS ABOUT THE ROSEBUD BATTLE

Battle of the Rosebud [June 17, 1876].[17] I got on my horse and went forth. Two parties went, one from the south and one from the north. I joined the northern party and there were only thirty or forty men in this party. The south was a very large party. The soldiers were at the forks of the Rosebud Creek. The northern party was a little late and the southern party got there a little ahead. [Brigadier General George] Crook had some Crows with

16. This is a folk etymology of the Lakota word for baby, *wakanheja* or *wakanyeja*.

17. For an overview of the Rosebud battle see J. W. Vaughn, *With Crook at the Rosebud* (Harrisburg, Pa.: Stackpole, 1956). Also see John S. Gray, *Centennial Campaign: The Sioux War of 1876* (Fort Collins, Colo.: Old Army Press, 1976), pp. 110–24. The best summary from Indian perspectives is Powell, *People of the Sacred Mountain*, 2:954–1002. The best Lakota eyewitness account is White Bull in Vestal, *Warpath*, pp. 185–90, and in Howard, *The Warrior Who Killed Custer*, pp. 48–50.

him.[18] Then the battle proceeded. The fight began with the Crows. Then the soldiers began to advance. We were on one side and when the soldiers attacked we had to retreat and they were upon us. Then we headed to join the larger party, but they pursued us and, as we retreated, the Crows began to fight harder, seeing the soldiers coming. When we got to the bend, the Crows were among us and fighting. There was a Sioux Indian by the name of Without a Tipi who was pulled off his horse by a Crow. Of course, me, I ran for my life. It was all mixed-up fighting. There was a brave Cheyenne with me and a man by the name of Sitting Eagle. I was about fourteen years old at this time. This was a pitiful long stretched-out battle.

As we charged the Crows back, we were going south. Then all at once we began to retreat, and as we were running we saw ahead about thirty cavalrymen approaching us, who were probably returning from a scouting trip. Then we heard voices crying: "Take courage, it is a good day to die. Think of the children and helpless at home." Then we charged on the thirty cavalrymen. Then, before we knew it, the whole other band was in front of us and we began shooting the cavalrymen off their horses. We were still between the Crows and the thirty cavalrymen. The cavalrymen were retreating southward and meeting the big party. I could see that they were fighting over there from a distance. We turned around and charged back on the Crows now and in order to get away we had to charge on one or the other. We charged on the Crows but when we approached them we saw that the soldiers were behind them so (saying "Yeah-hey") we turned and ran from them.

I ran for my dear life and came to a rocky place and my pony stepped in between two stones and tore his hoof off. Then I got off and I could see a Crow come up this hill just then. My friend, the Cheyenne, saw what happened to me and he turned around and went to meet that Crow. Then it was a hand to hand fight and he fought the Crow down. He made a whoop and went over and couped him. Another man went over and couped him. I wish I had stuck with the Cheyenne because I would have had a chance to coup one of them. My horse had lost his hoof and I had to run very fast for my dear life on foot leading my horse.

18. Crook had 262 Crow and Shoshone allies with his troops (Gray, *Centennial Campaign,* p. 120).

Just as I got even with the soldiers, I saw smoke coming out at the creek. I went over and there were three men there who had killed a buffalo and were having a feast. They invited me so I sat there and ate. We had to watch out at the same time. A fellow put some blood in the hide of buffalo and tied it on the hoof of my horse and it made it easier for him to go. So I went on horseback. We were watching all the time we were feasting and a Sioux came over and said:"We're fighting. What are you doing here? Why don't you think about the poor people at home? All you think of is to eat. Make haste, come on, we have got to stand our ground!"

So I started off on my horse. We got on a ridge and I could see down the valley of the Rosebud the fighting going on. It looked like they were getting the best of the Sioux. The Crows began to chase us and a fellow came up by the name of Acts Low. I was young and I was scared, but as we looked I could see the Crows charging at the Sioux and I could see a rider coming and then a Sioux running for his dear life. A Crow came up and said: "Uh, uh, hey," meaning he was going to coup him. Another rider came up and leaned over and grabbed the Sioux's gun. The Sioux hung on tight. My horse stopped right here and I started out very quickly and fled for dear life.

Another time, as I got on my horse again, I noticed this Crow start pursuing the Sioux and I noticed that this Sioux had a sacred ornament on him that made him bullet-proof. The first Crow couped him and didn't hurt him. There was another Crow on him with a feather on his head riding a buckskin. He came right up and fired at him and missed him. This showed that the sacred ornament was bullet-proof. I looked at them. The Crow was pursuing the Sioux and probably the Crows knew he had a sacred ornament. He, in turn, turned around and chased the Crows. [*Met his Crow and missed him also.*] There was another Sioux behind him and the Crow got off his horse and began prancing around. The second Sioux got up to him but missed him again. Both the Crow and the Sioux were bullet-proof.

It was a day like this and they announced they should quit and go back and take care of their women. There was no finish fight here. We were afraid that Crook's army was too much for us so we decided it was better to go back. [*Standing Bear says they thought the soldiers were too much for them and they were going home to defend their women and children.*] When my horse got hurt I had to retreat and when I got back I did nothing but eat and I had no chance to see any more of it.

STANDING BEAR TELLS ABOUT THE DEAD SOLDIERS

The fighters came back in the night and everyone was excited that night and no one slept. Next morning about twenty young fellows started out and I joined them. We were going toward where the Rosebud fight was held. The first thing we saw was a dead horse. The next thing we saw was a horse with shoes on (cavalry horse). The next place we went was where the horses were standing when they fought. Here and there were horses all over dead and rocks were all over. Where the cavalry horse was lying there was a man lying near him who was full of arrows.

We got to where General Crook camped and there was a place where the dirt was fresh and they had built a fire up there and this is where they buried the dead. One of us got on it and started to dig it thinking that there was something hidden in here. We all got down on our hands and knees and dug into the ground. We got down to where the dirt started down and we noticed that it had been dug by spades of the white men. We had now dug about two feet. We dug further on and the first thing we saw was a blanket. The blanket was wrapped around a soldier and it was tied around his legs and waist and neck. We got ahold of him and pulled him out. After we had done this one of the men said: "This is my blanket. I have been looking for this blanket. I shall have this blanket," and he took it. We pulled another blanket and each time we pulled them out they each took blankets from the dead men. The fourth blanket we took out was wrapped around a Negro. Next we pulled out another one and I said: "I want this blanket myself," and I took this blanket myself. (Buried soldiers one on top of the other.) It was a young man I had gotten my blanket from. He must have been from a wealthy family because I noticed he had a diamond ring on his finger. Someone had cut the man's finger to take the diamond ring off of it. After I took another look at him I found he was an officer (probably a lieutenant). He had only a shirt on, without coat. One of the men scalped a white man and started home with it on a stick.

After that we got on top of the ridge and we could see from a distance General Crook retreating. There was dust flying and of course we did not want to go there, as it was just a small bunch of us. We went home.

We stopped here at Spring River two days; then we broke camp and started for Greasy Grass [the Little Big Horn River]. We followed Spring Creek over the hill to Greasy Grass.

BLACK ELK TELLS ABOUT THE BEAR MEDICINE CEREMONY

We camped there before noon the day before the battle right on the place where the battle was held. We took our horses out on the prairie beyond to graze them. We had about ten thousand ponies—so many you couldn't count them. So many tipis we couldn't count them also. We were guarding our horses. The women were out hunting turnips and the men were out hunting also. We had guards all around. The boys and the old men were taking a bath in the [Little] Big Horn River which was flowing pretty full from the June rise. I was so young yet and I wasn't very dependable, but in a case like this some of the boys asked me to go swimming.

As I got ready I noticed that there was someone wounded in a tipi and bear medicine men were treating him.[19] This medicine man's name was Hairy Chin and he had about six [five?] sons with him and they had to take part in the ceremony. I was to take part too. They had to have four [six?] young bears [that is, boys to play the role of bears] to help the medicine man. They asked me to sit down beside the four bears and I knew I was to be used as a young bear to help this man to be cured. Then I thought about my vision and it seemed to raise me off the ground. Maybe this medicine man knew that I had this power, so this is why he brought me over.

I knew then that something terrible was going to happen within a day. I thought about the bow and arrows that the spirits had given me. I thought lots of things in a short time there that couldn't be imagined.

The five sons of the medicine man were painted red. There were bear skins tied on their [*wrists*] and ankles. The sixth one had a bear robe on him. They told me to take my clothes off and the medicine man stared at me and you could tell that he knew something about my power. He came forward and began to paint my body yellow and all over my face too. Then

19. The Lakotas believed that their knowledge of healing wounds had been taught by the grizzly bear, and those men who shared in this knowledge formed the bear society. See George Sword and Thomas Tyon in Walker, *Lakota Belief and Ritual,* pp. 91–93, 157–59. Also see Clark Wissler, "Societies and Ceremonial Associations in the Oglala Division of the Teton-Dakota," American Museum of Natural History, *Anthropological Papers* II, pt. I (1912), pp. 88–90, and Densmore, *Teton Sioux Music,* pp. 195–97.

they put some black lines on either side of my nose from the eyes down. Then they tied my hair like a bear's ears. They then put some eagle plumes on our heads. The five red boys had some real bears' ears put on their heads. The main bear (medicine man) had a robe which had the bear head on it. In the middle of the back of the big bear they put an eagle outstretched. Then the medicine man sang:

> At the doorway the sacred herbs are rejoicing.

The wounded man, Rattling Hawk, was shot through the hips and was wounded in the Rosebud fight. It seemed to be an impossibility to heal him. They gave him a holy stick painted red. There were two women with the man on either side. One of them had a cup of water and the other girl had an herb. After this song they presented me with the red stick and the cup of water and I looked into the cup expecting to see something in it like a blue man. It was impossible for the wounded [man] to get up and the chief bear told the girls to give the water and herb to the man and then it came to my mind that someday I will have to perform this myself. Then when they gave the wounded the stick, he stood up. The two girls led [him] out of the tipi and faced the south. Then all the six bears began to groan like bears and you could see flames coming out—all kinds of colors—and feathers coming out. They did this toward the wounded man. Then after this the man began to walk with this sacred red cane.

When I saw all this happen I thought this was part of the vision and that some day I'd be doing this only it would be greater. This bear medicine man came forward and pulled me toward him. He began to chew an herb and blew it into my mouth and then he threw me down and before I knew it I was standing up on my four haunches like a bear. I made a cry and it was a genuine bear sound and I felt like a bear and wanted to grab someone. We all went out of the tipi then acting like bears. After this the medicine man came out and he looked like a real bear to me—a big bear—and he was fierce too.

This man was not strong enough to fight the next day, but he got well. This all took place four days after he was wounded. The bears ate a dog raw at this ceremony. Then we had to take a swim to take the paint off. When we returned people began to have kill talks and dances all over the camp. Everyone began to bring in the horses now, as it was getting sundown. The dances were still going on after dark all over the camp. We were camped close to the Hunkpapas.[20] We went from one dance to another and I got tired and so I went home to bed.

BLACK ELK TELLS ABOUT THE CUSTER BATTLE

At daybreak my father woke me up and told me to go with him to take the horses out to graze. A cousin of mine and I were getting ready to take several tipis' horses out to graze. Then as I started my father told me to be careful and I ought to have one horse with a long rope on it, easy to catch, and we should keep our eyes on the camp and look around us always. He said, "If anything happens bring horses back to camp right away as soon as you can." We took the horses out and herded them as the sun was coming out. We stood out there until the sun came up higher. We just let the horses go and I tied a long rope to one of them and turned them all loose. We went back to the camp. It was getting warm now and so the people were all swimming in the river. Some men went out hunting and women were out digging turnips and it was about eight or nine o'clock. We had no breakfast and had to go back to get it. Everyone took his horses to water.[21]

20. According to Standing Bear's rough sketch map in the Neihardt Collection, the order of the six tipi circles of the camp from south to north was: Hunkpapas, Oglalas, Minneconjous, No Bows—Blackfeet—Two Kettles, Cheyennes, Santees. Each camp circle is shown near the west bank of the Little Big Horn except the Oglalas', which is depicted farther from the river, considerably west of the others. See *Black Elk Speaks,* p. 106. Indian accounts vary as to the exact number of camp circles that comprised this great village. Wooden Leg, a Cheyenne, said that only six of them were important (i.e., formal camp circles); the others comprised stragglers from various bands. See Thomas B. Marquis, *A Warrior Who Fought Custer* (Minneapolis: Midwest, 1931), p. 208. Bad Heart Bull depicts only five camps (omitting the Santees). See Amos Bad Heart Bull, *A Pictographic History of the Oglala Sioux,* text by Helen H. Blish (Lincoln: University of Nebraska Press, 1967), p. 215. By careful analysis of all available data, Gray, *Centennial Campaign,* pp. 346–57, estimates the size of the whole village at "no more than a thousand lodges."

21. For a modern overview of this battle, see Gray, *Centennial Campaign.* For an excellent summary from Indian perspectives, and a bibliographic guide to Indian sources, see Powell, *People of the Sacred Mountain,* 2:1009–1030, 1138. For Lakota eyewitness accounts see Red Horse in Garrick Mallery, *Picture-Writing of the American Indians,* Smithsonian Institution, Bureau of American Ethnology, Annual Report 10 (1893), pp. 563–66 and pl. 39–48; W. A. Graham, *The Custer Myth: A Source Book of Custeriana* (Harrisburg, Pa.: Stackpole, 1953), pp. 45–100; Kenneth Hammer, ed.,

I did not feel right—I had a funny feeling all this time, because I thought that in an hour or so something terrible might happen. The boys were all swimming and I did not go down because I did not feel very good. I made up my mind I would go swimming anyway, so I greased up my body. At the Hunkpapas I heard the crier saying: "They are charging, the chargers are coming. Where the tipi is they say the chargers are coming." (The tipi where they had put their dead before when they came down to the Greasy Grass.) Then the crier at the Oglalas announced it and then each village announced it one after the other. We heard the cry going from village to village.[22]

Just about this time my cousin had taken the horses to water and they were then just coming from the water. I had a buckskin mare and got her. Everyone was catching their horses at this time. We were lucky to get our horses—most of the peoples' horses were out grazing yet and they were running after them. My older brother had a sorrel which he bridled and saddled. My father said: "Your brother has gone to the Hunkpapas. You had better take this gun over to him." I got on my horse and as I went I could see the dust flying as I took the buckskin to my brother. When the dust parted, I could see the soldiers. These men looked big and husky and tall. Just then they began to shoot. The Hunkpapas began to retreat on foot and at this time there were lots of people swimming. I could see the little ones all naked running from the river. As I saw this all I wanted was to find my brother. Just then I saw him. The announcer cried that there was a boy who had gotten killed out there somewhere.[23]

My brother came up and took hold of his horse and told me to go on back, but I had a six-shooter with me, which my sister had given me; and I

Custer in '76: Walter Camp's Notes on the Custer Fight (Provo, Utah: Brigham Young University Press, 1976), pp. 195–215; White Bull in Vestal, *Warpath*, pp. 191–205 and in Howard, *The Warrior Who Killed Custer*, pp. 51–62, 69–70; and Bad Heart Bull, *A Pictographic History of the Oglala Sioux*, pp. 212–72.

22. The detachment of Custer's forces under Maj. Marcus A. Reno was the first to charge the village, at about 3:10 P.M., striking the southern end where the Hunkpapas were camped. The tipi mentioned here was the burial lodge of a warrior killed in the Rosebud battle. See He Dog in Hammer, *Custer in '76*, p. 205; also Gray, *Centennial Campaign*, pp. 173, 175.

23. Two boys found a pack full of hard bread that had been dropped by the soldiers. As they sat eating it, the soldiers returned and fired at them. One boy, named Deeds, was killed, and the other escaped to bring the news to the Hunkpapa camp (Vestal, *Sitting Bull*, p. 160).

had given my brother his gun. There was a woods on the other side of the Hunkpapas. All the men got together and gathered in front of the woods. My brother hit for the brush. He told me to turn back, but I took after him. When I got to the timber the soldiers were shooting above us and you could see the leaves falling down off the trees where the bullets struck. I went in there and after that I did not know what happened back of me. We got under the brush little by little and we crossed the flat and the soldiers began to shoot at us and all we heard was: "Take courage, don't be like a woman." Some of them said: "Take courage, the helpless are out of their breath."

The women were running to the hills. Little bunches at a time began to cross the flat. I was underneath in the brush and I did not quite notice what happened above me. I stood there under the trees and recalled my vision there again and it made me feel stronger. Then I thought that my people in my vision had been Thunder-beings, but I didn't see why the soldiers should be doing this. I thought then that perhaps the people had used some of my power because I knew that we were going to wipe out the soldiers.

Close after the crying about courage we heard that Crazy Horse was coming. He was riding a white-faced horse. Everyone hollered: "Crazy Horse is coming!" Just then I heard the bunch on the hillside to the west crying: "Hokahey!" and making the tremolo. We heard also the eagle bone whistles. I knew from this shouting that the Indians were coming for I could hear the thunder of the ponies charging. A little above us I could hear the hoofs of the soldiers' horses that went down into the brush. Then after a little while they [the soldiers] went back up again and I followed after them. It was a bad mixture then—soldiers, then Indians, etc. I could see nothing much but I heard shots and voices. We all hollered at each other: "Hurry, hurry!"

The soldiers were running by this time up the stream—soldiers and Indians mixed up. Just then I could see a Sioux charge at one of the soldiers and try to get ahold of his horse and the soldier shot the Sioux off his horse with a revolver he had. Then I saw that this white man had shot two of the Indians at that time. (This white man was named Captain [Thomas H.] French.)[24] Before we knew it, the soldiers were firing on us

24. Red Horse said that one of the soldiers was the bravest man the Indians had ever fought; from his description, Dr. Charles E. McChesney, an army surgeon and later an

and the women and children were fleeing for their lives. Then the Indians were mad and it was hard to check them—they were plum crazy.

We followed [Maj. Marcus A.] Reno's retreat. Then when we got up the creek a little ways we went into the river—three of us boys about the same age together. I noticed a six-shooter so I got off and picked it up. Everyone was weaving in and out—that was really all I could see. I was very small and I had no chance to shoot anyone. There were a lot of Indians ahead of me. We stopped on a flat and everyone would get a soldier and strip him and put on his clothes for himself. We took everything they had—pistols, guns, ammunition, etc. We went to the river and turned back from there. As we turned from the river we saw a kicking soldier and a man came up and said: "Boy, get off and scalp him." So I got off and began to take my knife. Of course the soldier had short hair so I started to cut it off. Probably it hurt him because he began to grind his teeth. After I did this I took my pistol out and shot him in the forehead. This was down by the river where we jumped in.

We three boys turned back from here and downstream I could hear the battle going on. By this time I could see the soldiers [Lt. Col. George A. Custer's troops] upon the hill in a bunch—about three miles away. Indians were below just like a bunch of swallows flying all around. I returned to where my mother was standing on top of the hill with the others. (Before the battle was on I saw a valley burning from a camp).[25] I brought home an enemy's scalp so my mother gave a shrill tremolo for me. The women could see the battle and they had given tremolos all over in encouragement for their men and they were also singing. I heard a very pretty single woman singing among the fighters where they were gathered under the brush. She was singing:

> Brothers-in-law, now your friends have come.
> Take courage.
> Would you see me taken captive?

acting Indian agent, identified the man as Captain French. See Mallery, *Picture-Writing of the American Indians,* p. 564, and Graham, *The Custer Myth,* pp. 61, 341.

25. Black Elk probably saw the column of smoke in the valley south of the main village where Custer's Indian scouts set fire to a Sioux lodge. See O. G. Libby, ed., *The Arikara Narrative of the Campaign against the Hostile Dakotas, June, 1876,* North Dakota Historical Society Collections 6 (Bismarck, 1920), p. 31.

When I got back to my mother, men were bringing soldiers' horses and scalps. As I came back home I saw this wounded man whom we had cured, and he had a gun and was watching the fight. He was singing a Fox song in the Oglala village.[26] [*He had a Fox lance in front of him and*] he was singing a song of regret that he was not able to fight. The song was like this:

> Friends, what you are doing, I cannot do.

I heard this man singing this as I passed by going to my mother. I stood there awhile and watched the fight.

Pahuska Gasot(h)ah [*Pehin Hanska kasota*], "Rubbing out of Custer [Long Hair]" [the Lakota name for the battle of the Little Big Horn].

STANDING BEAR TELLS ABOUT THE CUSTER BATTLE

That morning when we got up, most of the women went out to dig turnips and my uncles were out hunting. My grandmother who was very old and feeble, my uncle and I all stayed in a tipi. I went down in the river to take a swim. My hair was braided and all I had on was a shirt when I came back from the swim. My grandmother began frying some meat on the ashes of the fire. Then she fed us all. As we were eating, my uncle said: "After you are through eating you had better go and get the horses, because something might happen all at once, we never can tell." An older brother of mine and another man were out herding horses in two bunches on the Muskrat Creek downstream. Before I finished eating there seemed to be quite a lot of excitement outside.[27] Then I heard a crier announce that the chargers were coming and there were two men who went out to look for horses and one of them got killed.[28] When we heard this, my uncle said: "I told you before, that this would happen. You'd better go right away and get the horses."

The horses were across the Little Big Horn and so I ran for the horses

26. This refers to a song of the Kit Fox warrior society. See Densmore, *Teton Sioux Music,* pp. 314–17, and Wissler, "Societies and Ceremonial Associations," in the Oglala Division of the Teton-Dakota," pp. 14–23.

27. In 1910 Standing Bear had given a brief account of the Custer battle to Walter Camp. See Hammer, *Custer in '76,* pp 214–15.

28. Probably a reference to the boy named Deeds.

and waded through about breast deep. I got on top the Black Butte and looked upstream. I saw soldiers beginning to charge and they were all spread out, going down a hill. They crossed the Little Big Horn and were coming up the flat (Reno's men). At this time Custer was coming around, probably. There was a bed of cactus here and it was hard to go down the hill, so I stopped and saw the troops coming down the river. I tried to find my way through this cactus in my bare feet and I could see the dust flying. Soon the dust was coming closer and closer and over on a hill in the south there I could see Custer coming the other way. Custer stopped on top of a big hill. Then I turned back to the camp without getting the horses.

As they proceeded downhill I noticed that the Oglalas and Hunkpapas were fleeing and everyone was excited. I waded across the Little Big Horn again and got into the camp. We waited for the horses thinking they might bring them back. Then we could see the Indians charging close to the soldiers. There was nothing but Indians at the place. There were voices all over and everyone was saying something. It seemed that all the people's voices were on top of the village. Just then our horses were brought back and I had a gray horse and I went and caught him. One of my uncles said: "Hurry up, we shall go forth."

We got ready and started and this was before the women got back. We proceeded toward Custer and we crossed at the mouth of Muskrat Creek. We were north of the Santees at this time. When we crossed the Little Big Horn you could see nothing but Indians swarming on Custer and you could hear guns going repeatedly. There was a Sioux coming back with his mouth full of blood and his horse was wounded, with blood all over him. This was a brave warrior by the name of Long Elk. This is the first thing I saw as were going up there. My party was on the west side of Custer at this time. There were some Indians ahead of us (the fronters— all the braves are in the front), but where I was we called it the rear end (those not as brave). I caught a horse and tied it up. As we went on I saw another Sioux with blood in his mouth. He was very dizzy. He stood up and then began to come down again—he was wounded. I went on further and saw a soldier lying dead, and there were Indians lying among them on this hill. I don't know how they got killed together, because I wasn't down there.

When I got far enough over to see well, I noticed that the men were off their horses holding them by the bridles. They were ready for us, of course, and then they began to shoot and the bullets were just raining.

The Indians were creeping up to them and the bullets went over us. All of us yelled "Hokahey!" and started charging up the hill. The next thing I saw was soldiers sitting with their hats off on this hill. Then the soldiers immediately started to shoot at us. Custer was now on a ridge and we followed the ridge there and I saw one Indian go up and shoot at the soldier and in answer the soldier began firing again. As I got up there was a Sioux on horseback behind me. He asked me who it was who had gotten shot and I told him that it was Bear Horn.

I started down [*hill*] again and just about this time there was a man by the name of Burst Thunder who came up to us and told us to go down a little ways that there was a dead man here whom we should scalp (a Ree). So we went and just as they scalped him there were two Cheyennes that came up to us. Burst Thunder asked him if this was a Ree or a Cheyenne that we had scalped. One of the Cheyennes got off and turned the body over and found out it was a Cheyenne that they had scalped. This shows how crazy everyone was at this time.[29]

Three riders appeared and they had a dead Cheyenne with them carrying him by riding abreast. As these riders went down I peeped out to where the soldiers were and they fired once more. The first time I looked there were many there and after the Indians shot at them some more, I noticed there were very few of them left on the hill (Custer's). I heard some of the men say: "They have gone!" I looked over there then and I noticed there were the cavalrymen's horses running away after breaking loose. On the north side the boys took the horses after they had stampeded. I looked out again and I saw that there were very few of them left this time. Every time I looked there were less soldiers living. There were Indians all around the hill here. Right after the stampede of the horses I heard them say: "They are gone!" and the soldiers were retreating downhill toward the Little Big Horn. Then we hollered: "Hokahey! Hurry, hurry!" Then we all went up.

I could see Indians charging all around me. Then I could see the soldiers and Indians all mixed up and there were so many guns going off that I couldn't hear them. The voices seemed to be on top of the cloud. After the soldiers went toward the Little Big Horn they went into the side of a hill into a draw and there was tall grass in here. We were right on top

29. This man was identified as Lame White Man, the Northern Cheyenne Elk society chief. See Powell, *People of the Sacred Mountain*, 2:1028.

of the soldiers and there was no use in their hiding from us. Then I saw an Indian rush at the men and then the Indians killed every soldier including some of our own Indians who had gone ahead of the rest. When we killed the last man, we could hear the women coming over and it was just a sight with men and horses mixed up together—horses on top of men and men on top of horses.

After we wiped Custer out we started back in formation downhill, ten or fifteen riders abreast. At the mouth of the Muskrat Creek there was a little divide and before we crossed this creek we could see another band of soldiers here ([Lt. Edward S.] Godfrey's men) [*that had come back*] to help Custer.[30] They began to fire on us then and everyone said: "Hurry!" and began to charge on them. Then they began to get on their horses as I looked out again. They retreated and I noticed two spades on the hill. When we got up there we shot at the soldiers but only got one of them. Then we all got on our horses and pursued the soldiers. After we shot one of the men we all got off and couped him.

The soldiers fled and went back on Reno's Hill where they had their pack mules. Then the Indians surrounded them again and Reno's men were digging in the hill and we hollered: "Hokahey!" and began firing on them once more. After a while I could see some of them going toward the creek to get water. Then we kept shooting at them and the others turned back from the creek. On the east side there was an Indian rider going up close to the whites showing how brave he was. He was shot here and it was impossible for us to get the body.[31]

By this time it was nearly sundown. I smelled blood all over and I did not feel very hungry at first, but now I began to get hungry. The soldiers were still on the hill surrounding the pack mules. The bravest of braves got together and talked over what they were to do tonight. They decided that some would stay while the others went to get something to eat, and we did stay here all night. We couldn't get at the soldiers, so we decided we would starve or dry the soldiers out. We started back to the camp to eat and some of them stayed there. We got back at about sundown. I was still barefooted and had been all day. The weapons I had were bow and arrows and a revolver.

30. This is the so-called Weir advance. See Gray, *Centennial Campaign*, p. 180.
31. White Bull identified this man as Long Road, a Sans Arc. Vestal, *Warpath*, p. 203.

(Standing Bear was asked: "Did you kill anyone?") Of course it is embarrassing to tell all of it, but I will tell some. Probably every person doesn't know quite what he is doing during this kind of a time. We would shoot at soldiers but we did not know whether or not we had hit them. We had to lie down every time we would shoot, for they would fight back. It was hand-to-hand fighting and bullets would come back at us each time we shot. As we charged up the hill, when Custer was retreating, I took my pistol and hit a soldier on the head and knocked him down and then I killed him. There were about four or five Indians to every white man here. As I did this I turned around to retreat. I knew that the Indians killed lots of their own men so I began to retreat and as I went I saw a Sioux coming up and there was a soldier coming along and the former grabbed at the latter's bridle. The soldier jumped off his horse in a great fear, and there were several Indians who camp up and killed this man. The Indians couped him and went off.

I was dressed thus: I was barefooted and I had on only a shirt. Before the battle I had shot a redbird and had skinned it. Indians should have a sacred ornament, and I took this bird along on my head and I vowed that I would make an offering if this bird should help me in the battle to keep from getting wounded.

After the battle I heard a lot about Crazy Horse. It has been proven that it was Crazy Horse who broke Reno's left wing. Crazy Horse went through once and cut them off.[32] After the battle I went over the battlefield. Where Reno had charged I noticed there was a Ree who had gotten killed there. (Down in the brush of the creek there was another Ree killed by the name of Bloody Knife.) They had retreated up a little cutoff; there was another Ree killed.[33]

Going back, I thought they had broken camp, but they hadn't. I was hungry and I ate heartily when I got back to camp. The camp pulled

32. The Indian pressure on Reno's left flank forced him to withdraw his skirmish line into the timber along the river; that Crazy Horse was responsible for leading this maneuver is debatable. See Gray, *Centennial Campaign*, p. 175; Sandoz, *Crazy Horse*, pp. 326–27; and Powell, *People of the Sacred Mountain*, 2:1011.

33. Custer had thirty-five Indian scouts with him, most of them Arikaras (Rees), the rest Crows. Two of the Arikaras (including Bloody Knife, Custer's favorite scout, who was half Arikara and half Sioux) were killed in the battle, and two others died later of their wounds (Gray, *Centennial Campaign*, p. 287).

together in one solid mass. There was quite a lot of excitement yet, so we did not have any war dances this night. We built fires all over the camp. Then, before the next morning, I couldn't sleep, because I kept recalling the horrible things I had seen. It seemed that everyone was excited and moving around and the whole village did not sleep a wink. Next morning the criers said: "The remainder of the soldiers shall perish today." Then everyone got on their horses ready to finish the soldiers. I got on my horse and went with them.

This time I was well dressed and I had my moccasins and leggings on. This time I had my saddle too—I was prepared for the fight. This was early in the morning and when we got there the watching party of Sioux went home. We surrounded the soldiers and we hollered: "Hokahey!" and [*raised up and*] fired at the soldiers. Some of us were on one side and others were on another side—we were scattered all around. By this time the soldiers were getting thirsty and they would crawl to the creek and try to get water. We would shoot some of them and then the followers would turn back to their trench. We were pretty well hidden from the enemy and we hid our horses so that they couldn't get hurt. They sent shots at us again and I heard one of our horses get hit. Then beside me there was an old man and this was his horse. We told him that his horse had gotten shot and this old man went over and got his horse and said that he was shot all right but that he was bullet-proof. They happened to hit the buffalo skin blanket of the saddle and the bullet bounced off of it. We looked for the bullet and found it right near the horse. We lay down back where we were. We heard someone say: "Hey, hey" meaning that one of the Indians had gotten shot. So we crawled around to this man. He had gotten shot above the eyebrow and he had been killed instantly.[34] We kept on shooting at them but we couldn't do any harm for they were entrenched. Just about this time we heard the crier announcing that it is reported that some soldiers are coming. "We will leave this and let it go" (meaning that they would move camp). Everyone started to go back to the camp, so I joined them. If [Gen. Alfred H.] Terry hadn't come along all the soldiers would have perished that day.

34. This may have been Dog's Backbone, a Minneconjou, although White Bull stated that he had been killed during the seige of Reno's men the previous afternoon. See Vestal, *Warpath,* p. 203, and *Sitting Bull,* pp. 173–74.

IRON HAWK TELLS ABOUT THE CUSTER BATTLE

A boy was out with the party that went hunting and when they were coming back they stopped at Spring Creek. After they got there his horse played out and he was riding home double with someone. Then when he returned, his father told him and another boy to go and get his horse, and this was the last of the boy.

The morning of the fight I was eating and I heard someone say: "Chargers are coming!" When I heard this I jumped up and rushed out to get my horse. I roped one and just then the horses stampeded. They all got away from me. As they got away from me an older brother of mine headed them off. I got on my horse with a rope around his nose and just then Reno was charging. Everyone left their children and they all tried to catch their horses which were stampeding. The children came out of the creek where they were swimming. I put on my bridle and got my horse and chased the other horses. I fled with the horses among the Minneconjous. That is, I tried to get them out of the danger zone. I headed them off and brought them back. Just about that time there was brush there and the Hunkpapa men on foot were running toward this brush. I heard Sitting Bull announcing: "Boys, take courage, would you see these little children be taken away from me as dogs?"[35] I had only bow and arrows. I got dressed for war as quickly as I could, but it took me a long time to put an eagle feather on my head! I painted my face a dark red. About the time I got through dressing for the war the Reno troop was through fighting so I did not get to fight any. I braided the feather through my hair. I started out downstream toward where Custer was going. I saw Custer riding up there and the Indians were surrounding him.

(The girl who was singing alone in battle before [p. 183] was Iron Hawk's aunt.)

The Hunkpapas gathered at the foot of the gulch on the east side of the Little [Big] Horn that leads up to the Custer hill. When they gathered there someone said: "He is going." We all looked and it was a Cheyenne. He had on a bonnet and a shawl made out of the skin of an animal of some

35. In *Black Elk Speaks*, p. 122, Neihardt identifies the speaker only as "a very old man."

kind. This bonnet was a spotted war bonnet. I was going up the hill toward Custer now. My horse stopped all at once and then he started out again. The Cheyenne went right in front of the soldiers in a circle and finally came around to where we were. Then he came to the Hunkpapas and then he started back around again. The soldiers would shoot at him but did not hit him. He had a hairy belt around his waist to hold the hide on. He was a good-looking fellow. Little Bear was standing with me and asked: "Cheyenne friend, what is the matter?" The Cheyenne said: "Ah, ah." He began to undo the belt and you could see all the bullets dropping out of the belt. The Cheyenne are very sacred and thus he was bullet-proof.[36]

We stood here a long time and right after this I heard a voice say: "Now they are going, they are going." We looked up and saw the cavalry horses stampeding. They were all gray horses. Little Bear began to get ready. He put on his pretty saddle blanket. He was riding a pinto gray horse. Little Bear said: "Take courage, the earth is all that lasts." Then Little Bear's horse reared up and started out. He began to charge at Custer and when he got right near him his horse was shot out from under him. Little Bear jumped off and decided to run back and got shot. He got up again after being shot in the leg and started back. His friend, Elk Nation, started out to save him. As he went up there the soldiers shot at him and Little Bear got on with Elk Nation. The soldiers kept pumping shots at them both. Just as the two got back everyone hollered: "Now they have gone." We looked up and the soldiers all were running toward the Hunkpapas on foot. I had nothing but bow and arrows. Someone on the right side began charging first—his name was Red Horn Buffalo. The Hunkpapas said: "Hokahey!" and charged at them. The soldiers were running downhill and the Hunkpapas were charging. When they saw us, the soldiers swung down and Red Horn Buffalo rode right into the soldiers. This was the last we saw of this man. The Hunkpapas ran right up to the soldiers and encircled them from all sides. I noticed that Red Horn Buffalo's horse was going alone, empty saddled.

By this time I was up among the soldiers. Of course they came to fight us and we had to fight. I was there to fight. I went among them and met the soldiers, so I just took my bow and arrow and shot one of them

---

36. The identity of this Cheyenne warrior has not been determined. See Powell, *People of the Sacred Mountain*, 2:1024.

straight through under the ribs and I heard him scream. Just about this time I looked over there and I saw two soldiers fleeing alone and Indians on top of them. Then I went after them. There was a little creek going up there and one of the soldiers got killed by Brings Plenty. There are headstones all over there and the furthest headstone shows where the second man that I killed lies. These white man wanted it, they called for it and I let them have it. The first time I did not kill this man, as I hit him crosswise over the back of the shoulders. Then I let him have it with the bow over the head until I killed him. Because they wanted it and called for it, I was very mad because the women and children had run away scared and I was thinking about this when I did this killing. I said: "Hownh!"[37] three times while hitting the man. After the man fell off the horse I got off and was still beating him because I was so mad. Probably this was the last of Custer's men to be killed and I killed him.

As I looked around I saw a rider coming down along the creek. Just then there was another Indian on top riding above it and he was hollering, warning that there was a soldier sneaking along in the gulch, so he called out "Hey!" and charged on him. The Indian had something shiny in his hand and the Indian charged at him and cut him up in pieces after knocking the soldier off his horse. Then we began to go toward the river and we could see the women and children coming up. The women stripped the soldiers. The women and all were hollering in fun and I rode over there and there was a dead soldier there (pretending). They were stripping him and found out he was alive. The white man was naked and he got up and fought with the Indian woman. Behind this man there was another woman who was trying to stab him. The man was swinging the two women around while they were trying to stab him. Another woman stabbed this man and killed him. After they stabbed him I left this place, anxious to go to another place.

We saw that the Indians were charging again on some soldiers of Godfrey's coming over from Reno's Hill. I took after the soldiers and they began to retreat.[38] They got back to the pack mules and entrenched. Then I found that there was a Hunkpapa that was shot here by the name of Powder Side. Again the Indians said: "Hey, hey!" We looked and saw a

---

37. The sound of an angry grizzly bear, used by Lakota warriors in battle.
38. Again a reference to the Weir advance.

soldier going down to the water with a pail to get some water. When we got over there where the soldiers were, there were some young fellows down by the water. The only weapon the soldiers had was a bucket. The boys took dirt and threw it in their faces and also threw rocks. Finally they drove them into the water. Just about this time it looked as though the Indians were charging back up the hill so I went back up the hill with the others who were charging. We did not kill anyone here for they were lying dug-in. About this time it began to become sundown. Some of the men stayed, but the ones who were very hungry went back, for we hadn't eaten all day. I went back to camp and just as I was eating someone reported that there were some more soldiers coming from downstream.

BLACK ELK TELLS ABOUT THE DEAD SOLDIERS
AND THE SIEGE OF RENO'S MEN

While on top of the hill with my mother I could see the battle going on across the Little [Big] Horn. We could not see much because of the dust and the buzzing of the bullets and shots. At the same time the women were singing and sending tremolos out. At about this time about six boys asked me to go with them and we started down on ponies. Up a little further there was a ravine and we crossed through this. As we went down the hill we could see the gray horses coming toward the water on their stampede. Then we crossed the Little Big Horn and were nearly up and we could hear them hollering more and we could see the soldiers coming down the hill. They were making their arms go as though they were running, but they were only walking. We could see some Indians right on top of them whirling around all over the place. It seems as though the Indians could have just trampled them down even if we had not had weapons. Before we got there, the whites were all wiped out. When we got there some of them were still alive, kicking. Then many more boys came. And we got our arrows out and put arrows into the men and pushed some of the arrows that were sticking out in further.

There was one man there who was alive. I was going to take his coat and then another man came and pushed me away and took the coat. I saw something bright hanging on this soldier's belt and I took out something yellow on either side on a chain—it was beautiful. I did not know what it was—it looked like an ornament. It was engraved. When I brought it home, I used it for a necklace for I did not realize it was a watch. Every time I took this watch to look at it I felt like taking it away from something [sic].

The women were here at this time. We went up on top and saw gray horses lying around where Custer was on top of the hill. You could see only a few Indians here by that time because most of the Indians' bodies had been taken away before this. I shot quite a few with my arrows and we got to one who was still alive. [*This all happened up on the hill.*] I had only one blunt arrow. The man was raising his arms and hands and groaning. I took this blunt arrow out and hit him right in the forehead and it seemed as though I stunned him, for his arms and legs began to quiver.

From here I saw some men holding up a man and when we went over there I found it was Chase in the Morning's brother called Black Wasichu. A few feet from here there were several soldiers wounded. Black Wasichu was still living and they were giving him some medicine. He was shot through the right shoulder, downward, and the ball lodged in the left hip, because he was leaning on the side of his horse when he was shot. My father and Black Wasichu's father got so mad about the latter's son getting wounded that they went and butchered a white man and cut him open. They said the meat looked so good that they felt like eating it. That man was surely fat! We rode around all over the battlefield. There was an eleven-year-old boy there with me who asked me to scalp a man. I did and gave it to the boy to take home.

About this time the Indians began to gather the dead. There were two Sioux who got killed and their relatives came and got them and wrapped them in a blanket to take back. Then I got tired of looking around here. I could smell nothing but blood and gunpowder, so I got sick of it pretty soon. I was a very happy boy. I wasn't a bit sorry. I knew beforehand that this was going to happen. When Reno charged I thought about the people as my nation and that they were relative-like to Thunder and that the soldiers were very foolish to do this, so I knew they were going to get wiped out. On top the hill we gathered just the way we were and from here we went after our tipis. That night nobody slept—everyone was up.

While we were going among the corpses, the Indians were surrounding Reno. We stayed here still and the next day the war party went out after the Reno men, and I went along with them. Even the women went. They were dug-in lying [that is, Reno's men had dug in and thrown up breastworks]. Right below Reno's hill near the water on the west side of the creek there were some bullberry bushes. Around here there was a man, Round Fool's Impersonation, who was the largest boy there.[39] We boys asked him what they were chasing around that bush for and he said: "There is a white man there in the bush," and this man was there all night but he shouldn't have stayed there. That is just like chasing rabbits. We took our blunt arrows and shot at him and the man would crawl from one side to the other with those Indian boys chasing him. One of the Indians hit him and stung him evidently and you could hear him say: "Ow!" We set the bush on fire because we couldn't get him.

Round Fool's Impersonation came and coaxed the boys to come over on the other side to fight and so they went. He took us to the safety place and we advanced up on the hill. We did not realize quite how far it was until we had gotten there. We got about three hundred yards from Reno's camp. We could see the heads of the men and they began to shoot at us so we ran down the hill. We got back to a safe place. This man tried to coax us up there again but we refused to go this time. As we got back to a safe place it looked as though the Indians were again charging on Reno. They were quite a distance from us from now on and we were afraid to get close to them. We could see the soldiers trying to go after water and the Indians would shoot at them and they would go back into their dug-ins.

They were signaling from the camp with looking glasses when the sun was getting low in the afternoon, to the warriors. My mother was riding a mare with a colt and she tied it so that it would run right beside its mother and they would shoot at us while crossing this stream, but they did not hit us. Mother and I started back on the gallop to the camp. When we got back it was nearly sundown and at the same time there was another war party that came in from somewhere. They reported that there were soldiers coming upstream so we began to break camp.

39. In *Black Elk Speaks*, p. 132, Neihardt shortened the name to Round Fool. The name refers to a personification of *heyoka* in the Thunder-beings dreamer ceremony.

[5]

The Scattering of
the People (1876–81)

THE CELEBRATION OF CUSTER'S DEFEAT

At about dark [June 26, 1876] we were all ready so we went upstream on the Little Big Horn. When we broke camp, my two younger brothers and I had to travel in a travois and my mother put the pups in with my brothers. I had a job all night putting the pups back in the travois if they started to crawl out. We were heading for the Wood Louse Creek (Little Fat Creek, [the] Crows called it) in the Big Horn Mountains. We fled all night, following the Greasy Grass Creek. By morning we reached a little dry creek and stopped here, making camp at once. We roasted some of our meat here and had a big feast. It was spotted with fat here and there. I wish I could have some now.

Then the crier said: "Get ready, we are going." It is broad daylight now, as we broke camp, and when the sun was a little higher we made camp again at Wood Louse Creek. We had a wounded man with us at this time and he died shortly after we reached there. This man would get fits and when he did he would say: "Geneny," so they called him this name. This camp was called the camp where Geneny died. His real name was Three Bears. We broke camp here at about noon and started to follow the creek up. We camped at the foot of the Big Horn Mountains on Wood Louse Creek.

Everyone got all excited again that evening and they said: "The soldiers are coming!" And they looked over and sure enough soldiers were coming riding abreast. We found that these men were all Indians dressed in the soldiers' clothes just to fool us. It was reported that Terry was not following us and everything was safe. They were having kill dances all over the camp. These are some of the kill songs I heard:

1

When you came attacking, why did not
      you have more men?
Why didn't you bring more men so that
      you would be a little stronger?

2

Long Hair has never returned yet, so his wife
      is crying all around.
Looking over, she cries.

3

Long Hair, guns I hadn't any.
You brought me some.
I thank you.
You make me laugh!

4

Long Hair, horses I hadn't any.
You brought me some.
I thank you.
You make me laugh!

5

Long Hair, where he lies nobody knows.
Crying they seek him.
He lies over here.

6

Let go your holy irons [guns].
You're not manly enough to do any harm.

7

An attacker, I drew him.
Before he did harm, I wiped him out.

We danced all night and of course we were sleepy and tired from traveling all the other night. I got tired dancing finally and I went to bed and dozed off.

Standing Bear's favorite kill talk [*song*]:

> A charger, he is coming.
> I made him come.
> When he came, I wiped him out.
> He did not like my ways; that is why.

FLEEING FROM THE SOLDIERS

Black Wasichu died here and the next day we all went out hunting buffalo. As the hunters were hunting they got some horses from a small body of soldiers.[1] We camped here for three days on Wood Louse Creek. Then we broke camp and went across to the Greasy Grass Creek where we camped. Then we crossed over to the Rosebud where we camped again. Then the next day we moved down the Rosebud to the place where the Rosebud goes through high bluffs where we camped. We moved then downstream again as far as where we had had the sun dance and we wanted to see what the remains of the sun dance looked like. This was nothing but dirt all stirred up—the horses had just ruined everything. Reno had scouted through there and defiled it with the band of horses. Next we stopped at a sacred place where a big rock bluff was. The Indians claim that before the Custer fight the whole thing was pictured on it. No man could possibly get up to where the picture is. Things are foretold here always. When there was a man hanging down headfirst, why something will probably happen that year. And a year before [the] Custer fight there was a bunch of soldiers with their heads hanging down pictured on this bluff. Anything important that will happen that year will be pictured on this bluff. This rock is called Rock Writing Bluff. This rock stands right next to the water on the Rosebud. Here we camped and the drawing of the Custer fight was still there and the other people also saw it.[2]

1. These horses were abandoned by a detachment of soldiers led by Lt. Frederick W. Sibley after a skirmish with the Indians on July 7. See Powell, *People of the Sacred Mountain*, 2:1044–1045, 1374; Gray, *Centennial Campaign*, pp. 340–41.

2. This sacred place is known to the Cheyennes as Deer Rocks or Painted Rocks and is located in Rosebud County, Mont., above the Northern Cheyenne Reservation. Its archaeological designation is site number 24RB401 (personal communication from Stuart W. Conner, Billings, Mont., June 29, 1982). See Marquis, *A Warrior Who Fought Custer*, pp. 191–92, and Beverly Badhorse, "Petroglyphs: Possible Religious Significance of Some," *Wyoming Archaeologist*, 23(2) (September 1979):18–30.

We sent scouts out all around the camp. The next day we broke camp and went downstream. I did not know where we were headed, but we were just moving around. From here we broke camp and went nearer to where the Rosebud was; then we crossed the divide to Tongue River from here. Then we went on to Powder River where we camped. Some scouts returned and reported that there was a steamboat which had come up here with a load of corn for the horses. These Indians went over there and helped themselves to the corn. Some of the Indians swam across to see the corn. They were out of luck—naked without weapons—and the steamboat was just coming up. They had a fight there with the soldiers of the steamboat.[3] Yellow Shirt got killed here. Some of our relatives brought home lots of corn, which we parched and had a feast on. It was very good.

The next day the scattering of the people began. Crazy Horse's band started up Powder River to the Rocky Mountains. The Cheyennes moved westward toward the foot of the Big Horns. Crazy Horse's band encamped on Tongue River that fall. He had a fight with some Crows and brought back a lot of scalps. The Minneconjous came from Slim Buttes and stayed with Crazy Horse's band that winter. All this fall we moved around the vicinity of Tongue River and Powder River. Then we finally got back to Tongue River. At this time [Gen. Nelson A.] Miles had his camp at the mouth of Tongue River [site of Fort Keogh]. We sent out scouts [*at the*] beginning of the winter to see how everything was. The scouts came back reporting that the soldiers were still there at the mouth of the Tongue River.

As I remember, the Minneconjous and Crazy Horse's band got together and tried to make peace with the whites. We sent some delegates to the soldiers to make peace with them. Quite a bunch of Indians went with these delegates. There were fellows by the names of Drum on His Back, Gets Fat with Beef, Red Skirt and Hollow Horn, who were the delegates sent. Just as they neared the camp the bodyguards stayed behind and the four delegates went ahead. The Crows were camped near the soldiers' camp. They went into the Crow camp and they had come as friends but the Crows surrounded them and seized them. Just before this Crazy

3. On August 2, 1876, a party of Sioux attacked the steamer *Far West* at a temporary supply depot on the Yellowstone below the mouth of Powder River. See Joseph Mills Hanson, *The Conquest of the Missouri: Being the Story of the Life and Exploits of Captain Grant Marsh* (Chicago: A.C. McClurg, 1909), pp. 325–27.

Horse had whipped the Crows and killed one of the Crow women. This husband of the woman was there and he took out his pistol and killed Gets Fat with Beef as a revenge. There was a hand-to-hand fight here. The three [remaining] delegates tried to get away to the soldiers' camp, but they were all killed while fighting.[4]

Drum on His Back had made friends of the soldiers before this and this is why they sent him as one of the delegates. The soldiers had given him a gun with an inscription that he was a peacemaker between the Indians and whites. Then when the uprising came the soldiers began to run over there and they saw this gun and knew that their friend was shot. The soldiers were going to seize the Crows who killed these delegates and arrest them. The Crows found this out and all broke camp and fled before the soldiers could get there. They fled toward the Missouri. There was ice on the river, but the Crows swam across anyway. The bodyguards saw this and fled bringing the news back to Crazy Horse. Crazy Horse was on a warpath against the Crows and was going to get revenge. Crazy Horse started to the camp to see if there wasn't someone there, but he found that there was no one there. Crazy Horse thought the soldiers had helped the Crows to do this so they were mighty sore over this. They stole cattle and butchered them from the soldiers and this was what started the battle. Butchering of the soldiers' cattle was what started General Miles to coming down to fight them.[5]

We broke camp and fled toward Powder River. Then we went on up to Otter Creek which flows into the Powder. From here we moved up to Forest Creek on Powder. The Cheyennes were camping on Willow Creek up in the Big Horn Mountains and it was very cold with deep snow. The soldiers attacked them at night, burned their tipis and drove their women

4. This event occurred on December 16, 1876, as the leaders came under a flag of truce to the cantonment at the mouth of Tongue River to talk with Miles. Drum on His Back was an Oglala, also known as Sitting Bull (the Good). In 1875 President Grant had presented him with an engraved rifle in recognition of his friendship to the United States. See Powell, *People of the Sacred Mountain*, 2:1072–1073, and Harry H. Anderson, "Nelson A. Miles and the Sioux War of 1876–77," *The Westerners Brand Book* (Chicago) 16(4) (June 1959):27.

5. The Indians drove 250 head of cattle from Miles's cantonment on the Tongue River in December 1876 after the killing of the friendly Sioux leaders by the army's Crow scouts. See Powell, *People of the Sacred Mountain*, 2:1074.

and children into the snow and the men fought naked in the snow.[6] Then the Cheyennes fled and came to Crazy Horse's village on Forest Creek and together we went over on to the Tongue River. Some men went from camp to camp to collect clothes and tipis for the Cheyennes before they moved.

As we moved back to Tongue River to set up our tipis the scouts that we had sent out returned just then and reported the soldiers were coming. Then we moved camp up the river a little ways off the Tongue River. The Tongue flows through a gap here and we moved through the gap to a high place just about a mile from the Tongue River. This was a good place to stay.

Then we had a council and we checked the ones who wanted to go out to meet the soldiers. Before going to war, the Cheyennes had a sacred arrow, and they would point [their own arrows] upwards standing in a circle. There was a medicine man to perform this ceremony so that they would have power. The sacred arrow the medicine man shot up flew right over the warriors and came back to the owner. As the arrow circled around them, they pointed their arrows at it, as it passed them. I recalled my vision as the arrow passed me. Probably this was the arrow that was given to me and probably someone was going to get power from it.[7]

Then we proceeded and went on the warpath. It began to snow now. All this time we had scouts sent out. The war party got to the big gap, and just then the scouts returned. Crazy Horse and Dull Knife were leaders of

6. Black Elk mentions this event out of historical sequence. Troops under Col. Ranald S. Mackenzie surprised the Cheyennes in the Big Horns on November 25, 1876, destroyed their entire village, and captured their pony herd. The Cheyenne refugees fled to Crazy Horse's camp. See Powell, *People of the Sacred Mountain,* 2:1056–71.

7. In 1915, Sitting Elk and Little Killer, both Oglalas, dictated very similar accounts of what seems to be the same event. They are printed, in Lakota only, in Eugene Beuchel, S.J., *Lakota Tales and Texts,* ed. Paul Manhart, S.J. (Pine Ridge, S.D.: Red Cloud Indian School, 1978), pp. 202–4, 261–62. Walter Hamilton, Cheyenne Sacred Arrow Priest, told John H. Moore (personal communication, October 4, 1983) that Louis Littleman, a former Arrow Priest, had described this sacred arrow ceremony to him. It was not the Sacred Arrows themselves that were shot, but rather votive arrows made especially for the occasion. Hamilton said that a person who wished to hunt buffalo could bring two of these special arrows to the Arrow Keeper. After appropriate ritual, the hunter shot them into the air; by interpreting the behavior of the arrows in flight, the priest could determine where buffalo were to be found.

this war party. Some of the warriors slipped out before the rest knew it and had a fight out there with them [the soldiers]. The scouts returned and reported it. This spoiled the plan. The war party went on to meet the soldiers. We made camp and we young fellows stayed at home. That night some of the party went out. Next morning early the warriors came back with one of the comrades being carried home. They had had just a little skirmish here.

Then we went out to meet the soldiers again. The soldiers used cannon balls on us but they did not explode. General Miles had captured some of the Cheyennes. Of course I was young and I stayed away from the fight and just looked on. I stayed with some boys about my age and we saw a cannon ball coming and we threw ourselves down and the ball went right above us and one of the boys went out and picked it up and brought it home. We got hungry and we came back home. Then we broke camp and went up the Tongue River again. About this time there was a bad famine. Finally, we got to the mouth of the Rosebud Creek.[8]

THE RETURN TO FORT ROBINSON AND
THE KILLING OF CRAZY HORSE

Most of the time Crazy Horse was not in camp. On the road to Fort Robinson we found Crazy Horse all alone on a creek with just his wife. He was a queer man. He had been queer all of this winter. Crazy Horse said to my father: "Uncle, you might have noticed me, how I act, but it is for the good of my people that I am out alone. Out there I am making plans—nothing but good plans—for the good of my people. I don't care where the people go. They can go where they wish. There are lots of caves and this shows that I cannot be harmed." (There were things that he had to figure out and he was wanting the spirits to guide him. He would then go back to his people and tell them what he had learned.) "This country is ours, therefore I am doing this," said Crazy Horse.

8. Miles's troops left their cantonment at the end of December 1876, taking two cannons with them. They skirmished with small parties of Indians during the first week of January 1877, and on January 7 they captured a small group of Cheyenne women and children. The fight described by Black Elk took place on January 8 and was an attempt by the Cheyennes and Lakotas to rescue the captives. See Powell, *People of the Sacred Mountain*, 2:1075–77; Olson, *Red Cloud and the Sioux Problem*, p. 236; and Anderson, "Nelson A. Miles and the Sioux War of 1876–77," p. 27.

We got back to Fort Robinson in about May. When we had stayed a few days, we heard that Crazy Horse and his band were coming. Red Cloud sent out men to escort him home. They met him at the buttes called Sits with Young One [Pumpkin Buttes]. There was a big council on and it was attended for chief Crazy Horse. They thought that Crazy Horse would have lots to say to them because he had been out meditating in the wilderness. He had only about ten words to say. (The custom when going to war—the warrior ties up his horse's tail.) Crazy Horse said: "This day I have untied my horse's tail and layed my gun aside and I have sat down." This is all he said and he sat down. They wanted Crazy Horse to go back. He said: "Not until I rest, then I will be willing to go. But before I go, give lots of ammunition to my people. I have set a place for my people that will be the reservation. The Black Hills belongs to my people. I wish for my people to go there when I am gone." Crazy Horse was killed in September of this year [at Fort Robinson, September 5, 1877].[9]

CRAZY HORSE

Never was excited. Sociable in the tipi, but at war he was not at all sociable. He never had a good horse in his life. Horses couldn't go far with him for some reason. He was small and slender. Warriors think that the stone he carried with him had something to do with this. They think he had a vision about a rock and that he was as heavy as a rock. That's why no horse could pack him. He got wounded once when he was fourteen or fifteen years old, but ever since that time he was never wounded and was

9. During the winter, messengers had come to Crazy Horse's village from General Crook at Fort Robinson, promising amnesty if the Sioux world surrender and live on their reservation. Black Elk's party arrived in advance of the main village, probably about the first of May. Crazy Horse and nine hundred of his followers surrendered at Robinson on May 6, 1877. There on September 5, 1877, while resisting arrest, his arms pinioned by Little Big Man (an Oglala scout for the army), Crazy Horse was killed in a scuffle with the soldiers. He was only about thirty-five years old. See Olson, *Red Cloud and the Sioux Problem*, pp. 237–46, and Sandoz, *Crazy Horse*, pp. 360–413. There are several eyewitness accounts of the killing of Crazy Horse. See E. A. Brininstool, *Crazy Horse: The Invincible Ogalalla Sioux Chief* (Los Angeles: Wentzel, 1949), and Caroll Friswald, *The Killing of Crazy Horse* (Glendale, Calif.: Arthur H. Clark, 1976). For contemporary perspectives on Crazy Horse and speculation on his burial place, see Edward and Mabell Kadlecek, *To Kill an Eagle: Indian Views on the Last Days of Crazy Horse* (Boulder: Johnson Books, 1981).

in a great many battles too. At Crazy Horse's deathbed he said nothing except, "Hey, hey, hey" (regret). He had killed nothing and he was going to die. He was wounded by his own tribe.

(Question: Where was Crazy Horse buried? [*For the details of this story Black Elk says that Neihardt may say "I was too young to know this, but—."*] Response: Two hunters on Pepper Creek saw the parents of Crazy Horse carrying the body of him to Pepper Creek. A short while afterward they saw the old folks on Horse Creek further down and they had not the body with them at that time, so the two hunters believed that Crazy Horse was buried on Pepper Creek south and a little west of where Black Elk now lives. What makes Black Elk believe that the two hunters were telling the truth is this: Black Elk saw the old folks going away with the body from Fort Robinson. He remembers that the horse that pulled the travois on which the body of Crazy Horse lay was a buckskin and that Crazy Horse's father rode a white-faced bay with white hind legs. The two hunters described these horses perfectly to Black Elk which makes him believe that they had actually seen what they said they had. There has been a great deal of gossip about the matter and many believe that the body was taken up into the badlands, some say on Bear Creek. The mother was riding a brown mare with a bay colt.)

THE ESCAPE TO CANADA AND FIGHTING
WITH THE CROWS

I recalled my vision now and then and wondered when my duty was to come. This winter we moved up to Canada with Sitting Bull and Gall.[10] We stayed over here all winter and then it came spring. We were on Clay

10. Sitting Bull and the Hunkpapas had escaped to Canada in May 1877 to avoid further confrontations with Miles's troops. After the death of Crazy Horse, the government forced the Sioux at the Red Cloud and Spotted Tail agencies to move to temporary agencies on the Missouri River. During this trip, in autumn 1877, Crazy Horse's Oglalas and the Northern Sioux who had surrendered with them fled north to join Sitting Bull. Black Elk's family evidently went with this group. In autumn 1878 the Oglalas and Brulés moved again, this time to their permanent homes on the Great Sioux Reservation, and their agencies were renamed Pine Ridge and Rosebud. Most of the Lakotas eventually left Canada, and Sitting Bull returned to surrender to the military in 1881. See Vestal, *Sitting Bull*, pp. 206, 232; Olson, *Red Cloud and the Sioux Problem*, pp. 254–63; and Hyde, *Red Cloud's Folk*, pp. 299–303.

Creek [White Mud or Frenchman River] here in Canada. In the spring while here the scouts came in and announced there were some buffalo and we were getting ready to go hunting. As I was saddling my pony up I heard a voice up above me that said: "Be ready, something in the morning you shall see." About this time I was out among the hunters for I could kill deer and buffalo now. I had my uncle, Running Horse, with me and I had a roan pony which was pretty fast. I led my roan and rode my bay. Running Horse was riding a roan and leading a brown horse for a spare.

We came to Little River Creek and crossed it and everyone was hunting, because there was an abundance of buffalo here. As we were going I felt queer and I told my uncle: "I have a queer feeling that something is going to happen today. It has been told to me that it will happen, so, uncle, you shall chase the buffalo alone and I'll not hunt. You just get one and we must make everything quick work." When we got to a ridge there were some buffalo and I stood there and watched my uncle get a buffalo. I went down there and helped him butcher it. I hung on to my horses, for I thought something was going to happen. While butchering and when nearly through, I heard a voice: "Raise your head." My uncle said: "Hownh, hownh." This meant that he suspected something. He said: "Nephew, get on your horse and get up on that hill and look. I feel something."

As I got on the hill I saw a valley below and there were two hunters chasing buffalo toward the bluff. As the riders went beyond the bluffs, my horse began to look around, meaning that he smelled something. Just then I heard three shots close together and I could hear some horsebacks galloping and heard some more shots. Of course my uncle was watching me, so I went right back to my uncle and he also got on his horse. We took part of the meat and we heard another two shots again. Just as we got on another ridge we could hear the enemy saying "Unhhey!" meaning that they had killed probably two. On top the bluff we could see about sixty riders. These men had killed and scalped these two Crows. This is the first time that I had used my prophetic power. We got away because we saw them in time and we warned the other hunters. All the hunters left meat and we picked up some of the meat along the way and ate lots of meat when we returned. We got back to the village all right.

I am now fifteen years old. We were still in Canada yet. That June [1878], Sitting Bull and Gall had a sun dance at the Forest Butte [Wood Mountain] in Canada.[11] After this sun dance we went out hunting again and camped at Muddy Creek. We stayed here three days and we all dried our meat. My uncle said, "Go out and get another buffalo and bring just the fat back." So we went out and we chased the buffalo while they were breaking camp. I got a big fat buffalo. As we were butchering, all at once a thunderstorm came and it poured down. I heard a voice say: "Make haste; before the day is out something will happen." Of course when I heard this I got excited, and I told this Iron Tail who was with me that I heard something amongst the clouds and that we should hurry up and go. We left everything but the fat of the buffalo and fled.

Everyone was breaking camp and when we got back there was a meal ready for us. We got on our horses and broke camp at once. I told them to hurry and get out of here, that I had heard something and so we made haste. We came in the winter to Muddy Creek and had great difficulty to get through. Some of the horses sunk in. We went down below and got through easily. Just as we crossed the creek we saw the enemies (Crows) were upon us and they were attacking the people at the ford. We fled anyway and did not dare go back. The others at the ford fled up Muddy Creek. We were fighting at them, but were also fleeing at the same time. There was a brave hero called Brave Wolf who had done a great deed [*while the enemy was upon those at the ford*]. There was an old man and woman there and a beautiful girl on foot and when he [Brave Wolf] saw the enemy upon them, he turned around and made a charge at the enemy and flung the enemy back and put the pretty girl on his horse and stood his ground on foot and defended the old woman. There were so many Crows there that they were all killed but the beautiful girl who had gotten away with his horse. The old folks' travois was stuck in the ford. My cousin, Hard to Hit, turned back to fight the enemy then. He made a charge at a Crow who was preying on a Sioux in the brush. This cousin and the Crow shot at each other at the same time and they were both killed.

This was evidently what was supposed to happen. This showed that my power was growing.

Then I had to stay with Hard to Hit's wife and protect her. This little band of ours got on top of a big hill and I got off my pony there and sat down and went to sleep. When I woke up there was no one there—they

11. Vestal, *Sitting Bull,* p. 210, mentions that Sitting Bull's people had held a sun dance at Wood Mountain the previous June (1877).

had all gone off. I heard somebody cry and just over the hill I heard my cousin-in-law crying about the death of her husband. We got our horses and left. I was afraid that some enemy would hear her crying and so she stopped crying and just then she said, "There are some men coming." I went before her and began to look. Just then a flash of lightning occurred and I could see about ten men coming on horses. I said to her: "You'd better hang on the side of your horse and I will stand right here off my horse." I had a rifle and a six-shooter. I cocked the rifle and said for her to keep still, and if it was the enemy I'd shoot and hurry. I shot fast so they would think there were a lot of warriors here. Just as they came up there about the time I was going to pull the trigger I recognized them as tokas [*toka,* "enemy"], but they were [in fact] friends. They were a bunch of Cut-noses (Nez Percés).[12] One of them could speak Sioux, and he said, "How!" They asked me what I was doing here. They all hollered not to shoot that they were friends. I told them that I thought they were enemies and I was ready to kill them. They asked me where we were going and we rode back with them to the band.

When we got back to camp, everyone put their arms around the shoulders of the people and began to wail. I cried all day there. It was hard work crying all day, but this was the custom. This is the way I had to cry: "Hownh, hownh—My cousin, he thought lots of me and I thought lots of him." I did not feel like crying, but I had to do it all day.

BLACK ELK FINDS BUFFALO DURING THE FAMINE

The whole year following I forgot all about my vision. We were camping in Canada still. My father and I went out hunting from Clay Creek to Little River Creek where we camped. We had nothing to eat now because it was in the winter and we did not see any game of any sort. That night we

---

12. The Nez Percés had long been enemies of the Sioux. But when Chief Joseph finally surrendered to Miles near the Bear Paw Mountains of Montana on September 30, 1877, after leading his people on a long flight from their homeland in Oregon, some one hundred Nez Percé families continued to flee north and found refuge in Sitting Bull's camp. They stayed there two years or longer before returning to the United States. See Stanley Vestal, *New Sources of Indian History, 1850–1891: The Ghost Dance — The Prairie Sioux, A Miscellany* (Norman: University of Oklahoma Press, 1934), pp. 240–45.

got very hungry and it was in cold weather. We fixed up a little place so that we could build a fire in it. We went out looking for rabbits. I saw a rabbit get into the hollow of a tree. I got my axe and stuffed up both ends of the thing and I got four rabbits out of this stump and we had a feed. We ate two of them up before going to bed. As we were getting into bed we heard a coyote howling and then I heard a voice say: "Two-legged man, on this ridge west of you over there are buffalo. Beforehand you shall see two two-legged people." I told my father: "Father, you heard that coyote howl—that coyote said there are buffalo on that ridge west of us, but before you shall see two two-leggeds. So father, let us rise early."

It was very cold and it was snowing. Early that morning we got up before the dawn and had a bite and started toward the ridge. The two riders had evidently gone that way the night before and you could still see their tracks. As we neared the ridge we saw a little creek and the snow was blowing. When the snow blew away you could see two horses and snow blowing over them. After I noticed closer, there were other horses there. There were only two men sitting there however. One man was old and the other was young. They were Sioux Indians and were glad to see us. They had been out hunting two days and had gotten nothing. They were in camp here. We camped here with them in their camp in the brush. We all got on top the ridge and looked all around. We could see miles and miles but no sign of buffalo. So we sat there in the shelter from the wind. There was lots of timber over there. I could see all of a sudden a buffalo appearing out of the snow haze. Then seven appeared. There was quite a famine at home so we were all downhearted. Just while talking about the conditions these buffalo appeared. We all stood up and gave thanks to the four quarters of the earth, saying: "Haho, haho."

The buffalo came down the draw and we were all proceeding toward them. We got together and stood in a gap waiting for the buffalo to come. We caught up the speedy horses. I had on a gray flannel soldier's shirt and some leggings and a robe tied up at the neck. I had on a scarf made out of wool. They were coming closer now. The two older ones crept up and began to shoot. Then we younger ones were going to take after them after they had shot. They were so anxious for them that they couldn't hit them. But just as they shot one they said "Hoka!" and this meant for us to follow, so we ran after them. They had only one buffalo and we pursued the rest. The snow was blowing all the while and the buffalo just turned around and took back track and the snow being broken, it was much easier for the horses to follow them back. As I neared the buffalo I could see the snow flying out and I knew that the buffalo had gone into a snow-filled gulch. It was too late and the horse had fallen down in the gulch with the buffalo and neither one could get out. The snow crust was hard and I got off my horse and took my gun and shot four of the buffalo and my hands got numb and I couldn't do a thing after the fifth shot. The other young man got three buffalo. The gun froze on my hand in no time and the other fellow tried to help me get the gun loose from my hand. After the gun was off I took the snow and began to rub my hands with it. I had my horse tied to my belt so it couldn't stampede. He tried to break loose, but couldn't.

When we have too much meat to carry home, we usually cache it. We put the meat together after butchering and [piled] the snow over it. My hands were frozen, so I did not help butcher—I just looked on. By the time we had four buffalo butchered it was about sundown. Right below here there was a fine shelter behind a big rock with brush around it. We erected a camp here and built a fire. We put our little tipis up as one, so that it would be larger. We put the blankets over our horses. We fed the horses on cottonwood trees. While the old men were cooking, I fed the horses cottonwood bark. We had some cooking utensils with us. We melted snow and cooked the meat. We had plenty to eat. I was very hungry and took a piece of liver and cooked it halfway and ate it before the men were through cooking the main dinner. Oh gee, it was good! I wish I had that now.

They had to keep a fire all that night and outside we could hear a whimpering sound. It was a mob of porcupines which had come to get warm in our camp—they were cold. Next day we went back and butchered the other four buffalo, which took us all day. Then we came back to camp again and stayed all night. My father and I stayed at camp today and the boy and his father did the butchering. They brought back meat and we feasted a long time again. I wish I had some of that meat now! We divided the meat up evenly. The meat was not frozen but when it was put on the horses it began to freeze. Only three of the buffalo were fat that we killed. The other young man, older than I, took the lead and we started out. We camped once that day and the next day we kept on going, and at about sundown we got back to the village. When we returned, I took the horses out to the feed. Next day I went out to look for them and five of them had died.

THE RETURN TO THE UNITED STATES

Nothing of much importance happened here. We broke camp in the spring [1880]. All of our horses had died and most of us had to travel on foot. There were six women and two men in this party besides myself. We started back to the U.S. because we were tired of being in Canada. There was a medicine man named Chased by Spiders who was with us. We came to All Gone Tree Creek. There was timber there but the soldiers cut it away; that is why it was called that name. This was right close to Poplar, Montana. In the two families we had there were only five horses. We camped here at this All Gone Tree Creek and while camping here, I got the horses ready to take out to the grass, and just then I heard some voice say: "Be careful and watch. You shall see." I felt queer and did not understand this very much. I studied this a little and did not take the horses very far away.

There were two bluffs away from the camp a little piece. I got on top of the highest point and lay down among the rocks. I was out scouting now and I looked all over watching. I couldn't see anything and I just wondered about it. I looked this way and I thought I'd seen something. Right below the other point on the bluff I thought I saw something move. Then noticing again, I saw it was two men climbing up the other point. I knew they were enemies so I kept on watching. One of them lay there and the other peeped over to where the camp was. They were very close to me. The other man peeped over and saw our tipis. The other one began to crawl up with him after he made a motion to him. I heard them talking and they went up again, so I knew they were making plans as to how they would attack us. I thought if I had my rifle now I could have fixed them, but I knew very well that I should lie there and watch them. Then they went down the hill running as they went. As I came down the hill I sat down and wondered about my vision and I began to pray to the spirits: "Grandfathers, something may happen to me. They will come. But I will depend on the power you have bestowed upon me. Hear me!"

I came back to camp and reported what I'd seen and said, "We'll move at once, for I've seen two enemies spying on us." We all broke camp again. The creek was small, but as it had rained the day before, the thing was bank to bank, so we had to swim across it. We two younger fellows swam across with some ropes. In this way we towed the old women across. We were wet but anyway we had to flee. This was the time when the grasses were showing their tender faces. About the time we proceeded there was a cloud appearing and I knew that this thunder was coming to protect me. It did not rain much, but you could see the lightning once in awhile. It was very dark. I could hear the Thunder-beings saying, "Hey, hey!" In fleeing I was the leader and all the time we were fleeing the cloud was over us as though it were protecting us. We were fleeing east and the cloud was coming from the west. It seemed to others that the time was long but it seemed very short to me. Of course we were so anxious to get out in a hurry that we had left our tipis. When that cloud appeared we could hear gun shots out there and the enemies were probably shooting into the camp after surrounding it, thinking that we were in there. All at once the cloud cleared off and it was daybreak. The enemy did not find us.

Now I realized that I really had power, because my prayer was answered for the first time. In the first place when I started up on that hill I wasn't thinking about anything like an enemy. As we came along we saw a big village and I went ahead and noticed it was a Sioux village so we came up to it—Minneconjous on Poplar River. That evening this enemy had killed a band of Crow Indians that was right near to our camp after we had fled. These pursuing Indians were the Blackfeet. We started off, leaving Chased by Spiders and Red Eagle behind us. We made camp near a band of Assiniboines. The latter came over with their guns and pointed them at us. At about this time these two men, Chased by Spiders and Red Eagle, came along. Just at this time a small man with a red blanket on came and said for them to let us go, that we were Oglalas and instead for these men to get something for us to eat.

Right after the two Sioux got killed, an Assiniboine blackened his face indicating that he had scalped somebody. And when he came back to the camp of the Sioux they asked him why his face was blackened up and he said he had met some enemies and had killed them. These two men who had gotten killed were Hunkpapas and they told him to take the black paint off. Then they stabbed him because of his doing this deed to friends. As he was dying, he sang this song (song of the Brave society):

> Friends, difficulties I seek.
> Difficulties I have now.

Then he said, staggering: "Friends, I was an Indian too. You should not have done this to me." Then he fell over and died. (This is the winter count: "The Year When the Assiniboine got stabbed.") The Assiniboines heard this and surrounded us and tried to kill us. Then the man with the red robe on said this to the men to the effect that they should feed us rather than kill us.[13]

The two fellows behind got in at about this time. The Assiniboines started home now and brought us many presents and lots of things to eat. The next day we went back to the Assiniboines' agency where the Indians gave us plenty more to eat. From the fort [Fort Peck agency, at Poplar River, Montana] we headed down [up] the stream (Poplar). We saw a horseback following us on a white horse and he went right by us. We could see that he was an Assiniboine. Afterwhile we saw him again after he came around us. As he passed by it looked as though he was getting ready to shoot us. But he did not, because he was afraid. Chased by Spiders knew what he was going to do. As we neared the gap in the timber this fellow was coming behind us again. Then Chased by Spiders said: "You are nothing but a boy; I know what this man is going to do. He is either going to shoot me or that young man. You get ready and I'll get ready and whenever you see him get ready to shoot, you let him have it." About the time we were getting into the gap, I saw him coming up on us on the gallop. Just as we neared the opening, this fellow got right behind us and we found a big war party here in the gap and this fellow saw the war party and he galloped on. If it hadn't been for that war party this fellow would have killed us. They gave us some of the meat they had there (the war party).

We came back to the Missouri River and crossed it on a steamboat. We met a fellow by the name of Running Hawk here. We camped here and went out hunting—Red Eagle, Chased by Spiders and Running Hawk—all that day. We got deer and buffalo. Early the next morning we got up at daybreak and started back with our meat. There was a little band on the creek here at the opening between two bluffs. We stopped here and put our horses in here. We stopped here and had a big feed. I got on top of one of the hills here and I looked all over with my spy glasses. I noticed just then there were six riders coming up this creek. This was pretty close. I hurried away down the hill and told the other party that some men were

13. The Braves or Brave Hearts (*Cante T'inza*), was an important warrior society among both the Lakotas and Assiniboines. See Wissler, "Societies and Ceremonial Associations in the Oglala Division of the Teton-Dakota," pp. 25–31. I am unable to locate any winter count that records this event.

coming. Then Running Hawk said, "Take courage, there are only six of them and if we try we will probably get all of them."

We started after our horses to get them ready and one of the men went over the hill to see what these six riders were doing. He made a motion at us to hurry up, so we proceeded up there. We were told to watch the horses and when we heard the shots we were to hurry toward a certain direction. They told us to flee, but I wanted to see them so I crawled up to where the warriors were. I could see by this time they were ready to fire at the six men. I thought that I was old enough to get my first coup, so I made up my mind that I was going to coup the first one [even] if I got killed doing it. I thought it would be a great honor and I really wanted an honor very much. So I got on my horse and stayed up close to the warriors. Then we fired and I started up on the hill and so I went up there and couped two men. When I got over there I found out I had couped some Sioux!

LIVING IN FEAR OF THE THUNDER-BEINGS

We started back to Tongue River and camped here at the fort [Fort Keogh]. We had a sun dance here. It was now June in the summer. As we came across here the soldiers took our guns and horses away from us and all the horses we got back were two head apiece and a tipi. After the sun dance I recalled my vision again and I was very much in fear and it seemed as though I hated to see a cloud. I could hear the Thunder-beings calling. I could understand the birds whenever they sang. When a cloud appeared with the birds it seemed that they would say: "Behold your grandfathers; make haste." From here on I couldn't get along with men—I had to get out and think about this and I knew all the time I had something to do but I couldn't figure out what it was that I was to do that I didn't do. I was always afraid of the spirits. I was sixteen years old now (1880). All this summer I thought that every time it lightninged and thunderstormed I was afraid. Several days I heard voices toward the east just before the break of day. The morning star of my vision seemed to be singing this song:

> In a sacred manner I am walking
> Thy nation has beheld me.

It seemed as though when coyotes or crows would cry they would say: "It is time." Some of them would say "Behold him!" or "Behold them!" I just pondered and wondered and thought and it seemed that I just held back, but I did not want to tell mother and father, for they would think I was getting queer again. I would take my horse and go out by myself and compare everything on earth with the things in my vision. I was glad that it was getting fall because the Thunder-beings would quit coming, because I feared the Thunder-beings so bad. When they would appear, I would cry every time and pray to them to save me.

This winter I was seventeen years old. During this winter I heard a voice saying: "Your grandfather told you to do these things. It is time for you to do them." I knew it was my time and they told me to do it and then by this time it was fall. We were at this fort [Fort Keogh] at the mouth of Tongue River near the soldiers all this winter. When the grasses showed the tenderness of their faces I was seventeen years old. My parents had noticed me all the summer before. Just about this time there was a cloud came up and I could hear voices saying, "Oo! Oohey!" meaning that they were charging. The voices said then, "It is time; it is time." I got so scared that I would run out of my bed and run into another tipi and I would keep doing this all night long just as though I were crazy. Mother and father knew I was doing this and they felt bad about it. They invited a medicine man to come over by the name of Black Road and he came over. My father asked him to ask me if I had a vision and if he could help me out so that I would not be in great fear. So he asked me if I had had a vision and I told him it briefly. He said, "Ahh!" meaning that he was astonished. He said: "Nephew, I have been there for a vision but you have not seen my tracks. There I have been and I have seen a boy in a council tipi and I knew that it was you, I now recognize you. The main thing for you to do, and it is your duty to do as the bay horse that you have seen told you, that you should perform that duty on this earth." (I was to dance the horse dance first.)

[6]

Walking the Red Road
(1881–85)

Black Road and a real old man by the name of Bear Sings went to a tipi and the next morning the crier announced that the camp should camp in a circle around the council tipi. They drew pictures on the tipi—buffalos, elks, etc., representing the four quarters, and also the herbs and all that I had gotten, and a rainbow on the door. It took them all day to paint this up and I was to put on all my regalia. Everything was ready and in the evening they told me to come over to this tipi. They asked me if I had heard any songs connected with my vision. I was asked to sing these songs. I was not to sing them in the performance, but I was to teach them my songs to sing for me while I had this horse dance. They spread fresh sage all over the floor of the sweat house. I had to fast before doing this. As I was teaching these songs the Thunder-beings occurred and we could hear thunder all over the camp. We stayed here all night. I did not eat anything all this time.

Early in the morning we went into the sweat house to purify ourselves. We sang while in the sweat house. I was very young and my father and mother got the material I had to use and brought it to me. They brought me four black horses, representing the four quarters, four sorrels, four buckskins, four white horses. I rode a bay mare. I had looked for this bay all year. We got the four prettiest maidens in the village. The flowering stick was carried by one of the virgins; one of them had the pipe with the spotted eagle on it; another one had a bow and arrow and a cup of water; the other girl had the herb from the north. It was announced that everyone was there. They had twelve riders dressed as in the vision and everyone had whistles made out of eagle bone. They each had a black mask over their faces and they were all naked. They each had eagle feathers [*like horns*] standing on their heads. They were all facing the tipi, representing the four quarters. Then we sang this song and as we sang it all the horses neighed, even the ones in the camp, and they pawed the earth. (You must perform this duty on earth just as you have seen it in the vision and if you do not, there will be a disaster come to you.)

> Father, paint the earth on me. (three times)
> A nation I will make over.
> A two-legged nation I will make over.
> Father, paint the earth on me.

The four riders from the west were painted black, then we put lightning on the legs and arms and hail spots on their hips. At the base of the spine on the riders they painted a star representing the morning star.[1]

The four riders from the north (white). The men painted their bodies white and they had red streaks of lightning on their limbs and the horses were painted with red streaks of lightning on their limbs. The riders had white plumes hanging down on the back of their heads which looked like geese.

The sorrels of the east. The men were painted red and there were streaks of black straight lightning on their limbs and across their breasts. The sorrels were red already and they had straight black lightning streaks on their limbs and around across the chest from the shoulder.

The buckskins of the south. The men were painted yellow and they had black streaks of lightning in the same places as the others. The horses were painted with black lightning. They [*horses*] were [*painted*] black from the knee down.

The maidens braided their hair and they had red dresses on. Their faces were painted red. They had a wreath of sage around their heads and an eagle feather in the wreath in front. (Sage is used because it is the most fragrant of the plants and it is used for medicine in various ways. It is very

---

1. According to the description in *Black Elk Speaks,* p. 168, the lightning painted on the western riders and horses was blue, the hail spots white. The published version does not mention the morning star design.

soft too and our lives should be likened unto this sage. It is used to purify everything. It is used in the sweatbath to wipe their bodies with.)

My bay horse had bright red streaks of lightning on her limbs clear to the hoofs. Right on the back of the bay horse was painted a spotted eagle and I was to ride right on the eagle. I was painted red all over and I had no horns. I had a black mask with only one feather diagonally downward across my forehead.

These horses looked beautiful, but still they looked fearful.

These virgins and I were in the rainbow tipi now. There were six old men who were representing the six grandfathers. They all sang for me. The riders were in here also painting themselves up. Right in the middle of the tipi we made a circle with a little trench and put two roads across— the red running north and south, the black running east and west. Then they made a [*morning star out of a*] buffalo hide and put it on the east side of the circle. We put a cup full of water on the west side and we made a bow and arrow and laid it across the cup of water. The maiden of the north carried the herb[2]; the one of the east carried the pipe; the one of the south carried the flowering stick; the one of the west carried the nation's hoop, thus holding the destinies of the people in their hands.

Everyone is waiting to see who it is that has the power and probably some of them will not get to see who it is. We were about three miles above the fort on Tongue River. I was still in the tipi and nobody had seen me yet. I painted my forearms black. The only thing I had was a stick painted red and this was to represent the sacred arrow I had. The people are to appear just the way they did in the vision now. The six old men sang this song announcing the appearance of the riders of the west—the black riders:

> They will appear, may you behold them. (twice)
> A horse nation will appear, may you behold them.
> A Thunder-being nation will appear, may you behold them.
> They will appear, may you behold them. (twice)

The black riders came out and got on their horses and faced the west. The next song they sang was:

---

2. According to *Black Elk Speaks*, p. 169, the north maiden also carried a white goose wing.

They will appear, may you behold them.
A horse nation will appear, may you behold them.
A geese nation will appear, may you behold them.

Now after this song the riders of the white horses come out and get on their horses and face the north.
The next song:

Where the sun shines continually they will appear, a buffalo nation.
They will appear, may you behold them.
A horse nation, they will appear, may you behold them.

These riders of the east came out and got on their horses and faced the east.
Then they sang this song:

Where you are always facing, an elk nation will appear.
May you behold them.
A horse nation will appear.
May you behold them.

The buckskin riders came out and got on their horses and faced the south. Then the virgins came out and faced the south where the flowering stick was. Black Elk was still in the tipi and where he was with the six grandfathers. Black Elk sang this song then:

He will appear. May you behold him.
An eagle representing the eagle nation will appear.
May you behold him.

Just before I came out my horse began to snort and raise her ears, and then I went out and got on her and we faced the west. Then the six grandfathers sang this song. (This was a lively, rapid air. Black Elk composed it himself.)

Wachipee kta. Ha na wani ung. Ah oo way.
[*Wacipi kte. Hena wani on. Au we.*]
[They will dance. Those make me live. They are coming.]

They are dancing. They are coming to behold you.
To the north the horse nation is dancing. They are coming
        to behold them.

(This song was repeated to the different sides.)

The bay I was riding began to dance. The west riders proceeded to where the white riders were and the white riders proceeded to the west [east?] riders' places and the west [east?] riders proceeded to the north [south?] riders'places.³ [*All the horses began to prance.*] There was an opening at the west and the four virgins led and they were going around through the crowd. Black Elk followed immediately after the virgins. They had moved over one [quarter] in a clockwise motion. The virgins started out in front of the tipis and Black Elk started out following them. They started west through an opening in the horses; then came the six grandfathers following Black Elk; then came the black horses, white horses, sorrels and buckskins following. We all stood facing the west. As the west virgin passed [those who were] sick, they made little offerings to her and she would accept the offerings and heal them. Before this the men got off their horses and stood beside them while they danced to the next song that the grandfathers sang:

> A horse nation all over the universe, neighing as they come,
> Prancing as they come. May you behold them.

After singing this song the virgins started to the right toward the north and east and went around the circle, the horses milling around them and dancing as they went. The whole village was [on] horseback and it too circled around the inner circle where the dancers were. Then they started over in order toward the west and as they stood out there, there was a thunderstorm that came up from the west and stood close and watched the dance. This was the Thunder-beings that came to see them. You could see the hail falling, the great sheets of rain descending and the lightning flashing in the clouds and you could hear the thunder roaring. The people on horseback thought surely that a storm was about to break in the village so that they all went to their tipis to fix them against the wind. But after the black horse riders sang this song the storm which by this time was very close, stood still, but it continued to hail, rain and thunder a little ways from the village. The Thunder-beings had come to behold this. The song that the black riders sang was this:

> I, myself, made them fear.
> Myself I wore an eagle relic.

3. This sentence is confusing. Evidently each group of riders moved over one quarter in a clockwise direction around the circle, as indicated later in the paragraph.

I, myself, made them fear.
I, myself, made them fear.
Myself a lightning power I wore.
I, myself, made them fear.
I myself, made them fear.
Myself, hail-like powers I wore.
I, myself, made them fear.
I, myself, made them fear.
Behold me!

And all the while the storm was raging near the village but did not approach any closer. Then the old men sang again the song about the horses prancing and neighing. Then the people made offerings to the virgin [representing the west] in red—scarlet relics.[4] Then the four virgins offered their relics to the west. (Black Elk explains [below] why they did this.)

They did this to show the spirit (outer) world that they have given me power to cure the people and to prove that I have really done this on earth. I had to perform my duty according to my vision. Of course you know what I have told you and I did it to show the people that I had this vision and to show the people what I would be among them. And as we stood there facing the west, when I looked in the cloud [*I could see what I've seen again in the cloud*], only [the] grandfathers were beholding me and I could see the flaming rainbow there and the tipi and the whole vision I could see again. I looked at what I was doing and saw that I was making just exactly what I saw in the cloud. This on earth was like a shadow of that in the cloud. And then on behalf of my people I sent my voice to the spirits in the cloud like this, "Hey-a-a-hey" (four times).

Now the six grandfathers sang for me (I could see myself too on the cloud as in the vision, but I was on earth really):

At the center of the earth may you behold a four-legged.
They have said this to me, etc. (see vision[5])

4. "Scarlet relics" refers to small bundles of kinnikinnick wrapped in red cloth, a traditional offering to the spirits.

5. This song, however, was not recorded as part of Black Elk's great vision, although the imagery is integral to the vision.

Then a strange thing happened; when they sang this song my horse
began to paw and stick her tail up and point her head toward where the
sun goes down, neighing and snorting. Even the horses out grazing on
the plains neighed at her. The four black horses neighed also. Then the
bay horse turned toward the north and neighed. The horse would start
and stop suddenly and neigh. Again all the grazing horses neighed from
that direction. The same happened from all directions. Some of the people in order to show their respect got off their horses and began to dance.
When the bay was through neighing to the four quarters she was facing
the west again and I could see my vision in the cloud still—the rainbow
tipi and the six grandfathers in it, with their hands out to me and even
myself sitting there on the bay horse. All raised their hands toward me and
the horses. And so I prayed to them:

> Grandfathers, behold me.
> What you have said unto me, I have thus performed.
> Hear me.

(As they started to go around the circle clockwise beginning at the west
where they were standing, the white horses led moving to the quarter of
the north and the white [black] horses fell into the rear, and so around the
circle the red horses led as they approached the east, and the white horses
following in the rear, and the buckskins leading as they approached the
south, the red horses falling in the rear, and now the black horses were
leading again as they approached the west. At every quarter they stopped
in formation facing that quarter with the horses of that quarter in the lead
behind the grandfathers and at each quarter an appropriate song was sung
and a prayer made.)

(Only the sick people offered the relics to the virgin who bore the
sacred hoop; they were cured and this was in fulfillment of the promise of
the vision that he should make over his people (nation).)

Now as the procession started clockwise around the circle to the north,
the grandfathers sang this song:

> From all four quarters they are coming to behold you. (twice)
> The four-legged nation of nations is coming to behold you. (twice)
> From all the quarters the wings of the air are coming to behold
>   you. (twice)

Then there appeared black swallows which swarmed all over the village, and among them you could hear the shrill cry of the spotted eagle.

Now they are facing where the giant lives. The grandfathers sang this song:

> All these things my grandfathers have said to me.
> Where the giant lives a sacred herb, the sacred wing.
> Behold them. This my grandfathers have said to me.

Then I recalled my vision and as I looked to the north I saw a two-legged with body painted white as I have seen in my vision, and he was holding his right hand toward me. Then I prayed to the man where the giant lives: "Grandfather, behold me. What you have presented to me has been presented to the people—your power in the herb and in the wind. I thus make my people over. Hear me!"

Then we proceeded toward the east and sang a song again. Then the sorrel horse riders faced the east and sang this song, holding their hands out:

> My horse neighing as he ran, prancing as he ran.
> In a sacred manner he ran.
> Behold me!

Then I looked toward the east and said: "Hey-a-a Hey!" (four times). Then as I said this I saw the morning star in the east and a buffalo facing the north. Then the buffalo snorted and his breath was visible.

The prayer to the east:

> Grandfather, behold me.
> My people, with difficulty they walk.
> May you behold them and guide them. Hear me.

Then we proceeded to the south and between east and south they sang this song about "the horse nation is coming [p. 133]." This is sung between each quarter while they are on the march. At the south they sang this song:

> A good nation thus I have made over.
> Where the sun goes down the grandfather has said this to me.
> Thus I made a nation over.

At each quarter the sick made their offerings to the virgin representing the west or the nation's hoop. She represents all womanhood and the woman's part in the world and is there in behalf of the women. The sick offer this virgin anything that is sacred—for example a piece of red cloth with kinnikinnick wrapped in it with a stick wrapped in with it.

Then I prayed again saying: "Hey-a-a hey!" (four times). "Grandfather, I have presented your sacred stick to my nation and the sacred hoop. Hear me, Grandfather, you have power to guide this sacred stick that I have presented to the people. Guide the people that they may bloom on your sacred stick. Your sacred stick may be the center of your sacred hoop. Hear me!"

Just then I looked over to the south and I saw the vision that they had shown me in the vision. [*There shall be four chiefs in the camp and*] there were four [*old*] men over there dressed in warbonnets and in full regalia and I could also see the flowering stick. Right in front of these four men there was the sacred hoop. This is the nation and on this flowering stick in the middle the nation was to bloom. But just then the stick budded out as I saw it. I could see little birds on top of it. It did not bloom, it just budded out. While seeing this I prayed that it might bloom. We started toward the west dancing, the drums beating faster and singing a more lively tune. Then as the second circuit began my horse danced now and before she had walked in a sacred manner. All the riders then said: "Hey-a-a-hey!" (four times). I could hear the voices in the air. No one was allowed to go into the rainbow tipi for the sacred pipe was there. The star was inside the tipi on the east side and in the west was the sacred cup and the bow and arrows. Just before we had gone out we had strewn fresh earth all over the floor of the tipi and there were no tracks in here. Then we faced the west again as we started around the circle again.[6] The horses began to rear up and somehow they wanted to go. All this time the hail storm was standing over there. I could hear the voices over there cheering and rejoicing that my work was nearing completion. The horses and the people here were all rejoicing. You could see a flashing of lightning; even the horses outside the camp were rearing.

We stopped in formation in the west, virgins first, I came next, the

6. According to *Black Elk Speaks*, p. 178, the dance consisted of four complete circuits around the village.

singers next, and eight riders on either side of the grandfathers—the south and the east on the left side and the north and west on the right side.[7] Then one of the old grandfathers said: "You people be ready. He shall send a voice four times and at the last voice you shall go forth." (Meaning that they were going to coup the tipi and whoever couped the tipi first would be given great honor. So they were all eager, the horses even knew it and were eager.) Then I said: "Hey-a-a-hey!" (four times). At the last call they were all ready. Then they all turned and rushed for the tipi. Then the horses knew just what they were going to do. And at the fourth cry they all said: "Hokahey!" The horses just went in a hurry and my horse just turned around and I couldn't hold him. Because of the power going on in the tipi the horses all rushed to it. My horse neighed right at the door and it stopped then and I got off. I did not get there first for some of them were closer to the tipi than I was. We had some orderlies which took the horses and we all went into the tipi. Everyone was eager to see the place, too. On the fresh dirt we could see small horse tracks all over the tipi floor. The spirit horses had been dancing around the circle of the tipi. When we went in there we all sat there and Black Road, the medicine man who helped me perform this ceremony, lit the peace pipe and offered it to the four quarters, above, and to mother earth, and we smoked for the good of the people. There was quite a lot of sage there and we rubbed it on our bodies and the horses were also rubbed with sage to purify us. They offered the pipe we had carried around the circle in this manner: "Grandfather, to where the sun goes down, the wings of the air and also to the four-leggeds of the four quarters and also to the sacred wind of where the giant lives and to the day that appears where the sun shines continually and to where you are always facing, a generation appears. I, myself, and my horse nation have thus finished the performance that I was to do on earth. To all these I offer this pipe, that my nation may live." Then they all said "How!" Then the pipe outside was lit and all the people of the village smoked it. This pipe which should have lasted only for a few men burned long enough for all to smoke at least a puff. One of these pipes belonged to me and one belonged to the people.[8]

7. In *Black Elk Speaks*, p. 178, this formation faces east; the stenographic record indicates that the formation first faced west, then turned to face east. Thus the south and east riders were on the south side of the grandfathers, the north and west riders on the north side.

8. *Black Elk Speaks*, p. 179, mentions only a single pipe.

After this ceremony was completed, it seemed that I was above the earth and I did not touch the earth. I felt very happy and I was also happy to see my people, as it looked like they were renewed and happy. They all greeted me and were very generous to me, telling me that their relatives here and there were sick and were cured in a mysterious way and congratulated me, giving me gifts. Especially the sick people had given me gifts. I was now recognized as a medicine man at the age of seventeen. Everyone had respect for me.

(Every time the six grandfathers were singing, the virgins were singing with them. After we started singing this song, the horses all paced around:

> All over the universe a horse nation pacing they come,
> dancing they come.
> May you behold them.

As the song started the horses would jump up and then they started to pace.)

[*Pony dances held. Pony dance held first time at the mouth of Tongue River. Second time two dances held on the big flat at Oglala* (Pine Ridge). *Thirty-five years ago the last dance was performed* (1896).]

After this my people were cured all over for their sicknesses. It seemed that even the horses were healthier after the dance. Before this I was unable to be friendly with the medicine men but after this they were all very friendly with me and wanted to talk to me all the time. The fear that I had had now all disappeared and when the Thunder-beings came I was always glad to see them come, as they came as relatives, and even the four-legged animals seemed to have respect for me.

The next morning after this horse dance I felt that I was very different from the other men and it seemed that I could pity my people when I looked at them and I found that this little blue man was in my body and I could feel that I was to have power from him. The little cocoons in my right and left forearms are the power from the sacred wind of the north. I should have this power so that I could give a good wind to the sick. These cocoons were little whirlwinds. When I looked around the hills I could see a bush standing someplace right near and I would walk over there and find it was a sacred herb, or I could see a coyote come and it would be an herb.

I was this way right among the people. It has been proven to me that my people should have the power through the animals through the Great Spirit. I usually get up about the time the morning star rises and my people were to have knowledge from this star and people seemed to all know this. They were eager to see it come out and by the time the daybreak star came out the people would be saying, "Behold the star of wisdom."

THE MOVE TO PINE RIDGE

After the pony dance, we were put on a fire-boat [steamboat] and we floated down the Missouri River to Fort Yates and there were unloaded. Then I came back all the way on foot to Oglala, because we had no ponies, as the government had taken our ponies from us at the mouth of the Tongue River. I came back here [to Pine Ridge] because I was an Oglala and I was coming back to my people. This was the year count When We Floated Down the Missouri (1881).[9] Another reason why I came back was that my duty was to be performed with the Oglalas and also that some of the powers in the medicine that I used would be found here the year around. I knew this would be my future home. We arrived at Fort Yates in July. I started for Oglala in about September after staying at the fort for about three or four months. September, the Moon When the Plums Were Scarlet, I came to Pine Ridge. At this time they were building an agency and during this winter it was just like a long dreary night. It seemed the night was so long and I longed to see the day. The whole winter was like a night and the springtime was like the day coming. This was because I was homesick for the Thunder-beings. I was then supposed to perform another ceremony here on earth.

In coming from Fort Yates to Oglala we camped about seven times. There were four of us. We first went to the Brulés on the Rosebud. Then I came to Pine Ridge. As we crossed the Grand River coming toward the Brulés from Fort Yates, it was a nice quiet evening and there were no clouds in the sky and it was warmer in the evening though the days were cold. All the weapons we had were bows and arrows and all we had to eat was a bushel of plums and we filled up on them. As we got to camp from the plum bushes, there was a little hill there and I got on top of it and took

9. I have not located a winter count with this exact entry for 1881, although several of them refer to the return of many Lakotas by steamboat from Tongue River (Fort Keogh) to Standing Rock (Fort Yates) (e.g., White Bull in Vestal, *Warpath*, p. 270).

a seat facing the west and it seemed as though I wanted to see somebody. I arose and began to sing the first song that the two spirits sang to me in my vision. As I sang this song I looked toward the west and I saw the two men coming again and they were pointing at me with their bows and arrows and as I sang they raised the bows above their heads and stood with their hands toward me. They said nothing but I knew that they wanted me to perform that duty, the power that I had gotten from them. I knew this was time now. When I stood and looked at them, they turned back. These people at camp saw me sing the song and they wanted to know what I'd seen. They knew I had power. I told them that I only heard that in the other world they were singing and that I was helping them. The party I was with, two of them are still alive today. At the time I was at Pine Ridge, at Manderson; the Oglalas were there.

THE VISION OF THE THUNDER-BEINGS

When I performed the horse dance there weren't any people hardly here who had seen my horse dance. They knew nothing about my power. They were heavy people in comparison to the ones I had left in back of me. On account of this I looked for the spring to come and I longed for spring as it would come like a day for me. In this year when the tender faces of the grass appeared I could hear the Thunder-beings coming again under the earth. I had not yet completed the duties assigned me by my vision to be a medicine man. I could hear the Thunder-beings say: "It is time to fulfill what your grandfathers have assigned you."

I had to go out lamenting so I prepared myself. The people there did not know that I had power and they were a burden to me and I thought they just had to know it. This winter I was eighteen years old and this was to be the first lamenting I had ever done. So I prepared myself by going in to a sweat house to purify myself before my lamentation. Before a man goes out lamenting he should select a quiet and generous man to light and fill the pipe that he has to offer to the four quarters of the earth, the two-leggeds, the four-leggeds and the wings of the air. I took all my clothes off, [un]braided my hair and let it hang loose.[10] I had a robe to clothe myself on the cold night. The sun was nearly down and I had the pipe. This was

---

10. *Black Elk Speaks*, p. 185, mistakenly has: "He then braided my hair." Unbraided hair—like nakedness—was a sign of supplication, begging the spirits for their mercy.

all I carried with me. I had to make an offering so I fixed up some offerings of kinnikinnick and also some scarlet pieces of cloth and made bundles of it. A medicine man went along with me, of course.

Where I was to lament was quite a ways off, so I had to go on horseback. This was northwest of my place at Manderson about four or five miles. When we got up there we made the ground sacred by putting sage where I was to stand and we put offerings on the west, north, east and south. The flowering stick was put right in the middle of this place. I went out here to lament that it might be made clear to me what I should do. I was to advance from where I was standing to where the offerings were toward the west and I was then supposed to cry (mourn or wail). Then I was supposed to back up again and stand in the center and rest; then I was to go from here and face the north. Then I advanced again toward the north where the offering was. Then while standing toward the west I began to cry for clear understanding. While crying I had to say this: "O Great Spirit, accept my offerings. O make me understand!"

As I was crying, there appeared a spotted eagle from the west and it soared over me and I could hear the shrill whistle of it up in the air. Then the eagle began to light on a pine near me on the east side. Then I stepped backward to the middle and began to advance to the north. I was now facing the north and continuing lamenting my prayers saying: "O Great Spirit, accept my offerings. O make me understand that I may know." Then appeared to me a chicken hawk which hovered just over me and then flew toward the south and lit on a tree. Then I stepped back toward the center and faced the east and lamented on. Then there appeared to me a black swallow. It flew all around me and you could hear him sing. It flew toward the east and lit there. Then I stepped to the center again and faced the south. This time I really did cry hard and my tears began to just pour down on the ground. Here I recalled the days when all my close relatives had been living and now they were gone. I just cried myself to death nearly. I could hear the rustling of something from the south. I looked over and tried to make out what it was, but it was very far off and I couldn't find out what it was. So then the rustling sound came nearer and nearer and it seemed I could see dust flying. When they got nearer I saw it was beautiful butterflies of all kinds hovering over me. They were so thick when they flew around me that I could see nothing. Then I advanced back to the center where the flowering stick was and the spotted eagle spoke to me saying: "Behold them, these are your people." These little butterflies of all colors seemed to be crying. I could hear them whimpering here and there. The spotted eagle spoke again, saying: "These people shall be in great difficulty and you shall go there." These butterflies swarmed all over me and soon they started to fly back to the south and I knew what was going to happen. Then just as they disappeared, the chicken hawk said to me: "Behold your grandfathers shall come forth and you shall hear them."

I lifted up my head and there was a great storm coming. The Thunder-being nation was coming and I could hear the voices over there and the neighing of horses and the sending of voices and I knew they were coming in a sacred manner. It was a fearful sight but I just stood there. Of course it was pretty far into the night by this time. I looked over there and I beheld another vision. It was the two men that had come to me before in my first vision. They were coming down again from the clouds. These two men were coming down straight to the earth and from where they were going down I could see the dust flying and the head of a dog peeping out here and there in that dust. I noticed that under these men the dust was coming up and I saw it was the butterflies hovering over that dog and there were also dragonflies there. (Dog was showing through the butterfly bunch.)

As the men came down and neared the butterflies, I could hear voices in the thunder clouds cheering the two men. As they advanced with bow and arrow in the act of shooting (they were riding sorrel horses by now), the butterflies and dragonflies were now swallows. The men were coming now before the swallows and I knew they were attacking that dog now. The first man got his arrow pointed at the dog and as he swooped down on it, he glided upward and I noticed that the dog's head was taken upward in the air by the arrow. Then the people all cheered. Then the second man shot his arrow at the dog's head and brought it up into the air. As they glided upward they stood on the east side of their work (what they had done). The dog's head transformed into a man's head.[11] The heart of the dog turned into the heart of a man. You will remember that in the first vision I had they wanted me to kill a dog and in this I now knew what I was to do by getting the understanding of that power to be performed on this earth. Then I heard the voice of the eagle again. He said: "It is time to perform the duties of your grandfathers."

(Question. What did the dog's head represent? Answer: The dog is

---

11. In *Black Elk Speaks*, p. 189, the dog's head is said to be several dogs' heads, which turn into the heads of white men.

timid and at the same time people don't show them mercy. They kill them whenever they get hungry. The dog is used as the material for the performance of lots of ceremonials. The dogs are very useful among the Indians. It is their favorite food. Everyone enjoys dog soup. He is a domestic animal and is of more use to humans than any wild animal. You can depend on him. Just like my dog, Bob. They are the servant of man. We use the dog for material for medicine men. Bear medicine men use dogs too. They are at the same time regarded as animals. The dog is not allowed at the ceremonial nevertheless. The meat is to be eaten by the onlookers and performers, but the dog should not be around where the medicine men live. He must be cooked if he comes near there. When a dog is used for ceremonial purposes, it is called sacred eating and it will make clarity of understanding. Dog is a willing slave animal.)

(When I stood on Harney Peak they showed me good and bad and I was to do most of the good for the people.)

When the vision finished I proceeded again. I cried all the harder to break the storm and I thought I could break it aside. I was crying for fear now. I asked the great grandfathers to pity me and spare me—that I had the clearness of understanding now that I was willing to do it on earth. Now you could feel the wind of the hail storm and I could hear and see the falling of the big hail all around me. Then I did not care whether I got killed or not, that probably I would be better off in the other world anyway. I began to lie down then and offered this pipe. I covered myself with the robe and I could hear the growling of the thunder and the flashes of the lightning and I could hear voices saying this all over the heavens: "Hey-a-a-hey!" I looked for the hail to hit me, but not one of them touched me and I did not even get wet. It just fell all around me. Then the storm passed over and I raised my robe up and I could hear the streams flowing from this rain down the canyons. It had been a big rain and there was hail all around the sacred place. Within the circle of the offering it was dry and no hail fell. I looked toward the east and here I could see clouds.

Then as the clouds passed eastward, I could hear the spirits in them say: "Hey-a-a-a-hey!" This was late in the night so I was beginning to get sleepy. There I had to have a clear understanding to get my powers. Then I dozed off to sleep and saw my people sitting all around a tipi all sad and weary. They were all worried and some of them were sick. Everyone was troubled. This side close to the camp I saw a beautiful thing. It had flames of all colors sparkling and when this was gone, I found that it was an herb.

A voice said: "Your people are in difficulty. Make haste. They need you."
Just then this voice woke me up as I was noticing the herb. The east was
just getting light. I faced the east and began to lament and cry again. As
the morning star appeared of course that represented the wisdom and
knowledge of my people. I looked over there and it was beautiful. It
seemed there were many little faces all around the star. These faces were all
smiling at me. These were the faces of children yet to be born and I
thought perhaps they would be my grandchildren. The color of the star
seemed to be all colors—more beautiful than ever. Right underneath the
star I could see the heads of men and women moving around and even the
birds singing and the mooing of buffalo and the whistling of the deer and
the neighing and snorting of the horses. I could hear what I did not see.
Everything was moving around.

It was now daybreak and the sun was coming out. I was still crying. I
did not sleep all night. I was waiting for the medicine man to come after
me. Then it was hard to believe what had occurred during that night. I
was lying down thinking about it and resting and I knew what to do now
because I had clarity of understanding, and I was to be a medicine man.
When the sun was a little higher I dozed off again. I had seen so much that
night that I should have been scared, but I was not in fear.

All of a sudden someone said, "Get up, I came after you." Then I was
very scared. It was the medicine man, Few Tails, who had come after me.
He said, "Wake up, I've come after you." It was a man that I should fear
and it frightened me. When the medicine man called me he was standing
right above me. He had come to awaken me.

[*The dog in this vision was a symbol of any enemy and all enemies should be
killed without pity like dogs.*]

We brought the pipe back home and went into the sweat house. There
were old men who wanted to know what had happened. As we started
into the sweat house they made me smoke the pipe to the four quarters,
above, mother earth and all. I was asked by the old men to tell them exactly
what I'd seen without telling any story about it. Of course I had to tell the
truth after puffing from the peace pipe because if you lie something will
happen to you. I related it all to the old men. Then they all said that it was
time and that they did not know but what I would be a great man and they
told me that it was now time to do these things on earth to help mankind.
They also said that this appointment was not for everybody and that very
few had ever had such appointments. Many are called but few are chosen.

After twenty days I had to perform this duty. Most of the people were at Pine Ridge now on the flat and I was eighteen years old now. I proceeded over here intending to perform this where most of the people were at the time.

(Pine Ridge—the Seat of Red Cloud. Some called it "Where they distribute everything" [*Wakpamni*].[12])

THE *heyoka* CEREMONY

The manner of performing this duty is what is called in the ethnological reports a fool's impersonation. The actors in this ceremony are what the Sioux call heyoka—that is to say sacred fool or rather sacred comedian. Only those who have had visions of the west, that is to say of the Thunder-beings, can act as heyokas. The heyoka presents the truth of his vision through comic actions, the idea being that the people should be put in a happy, jolly frame of mind before the great truth is presented. When the vision comes from the west, it comes in terror like a thunderstorm, but when the storm of [the] vision has passed the whole world is green and happy as a result. In the ceremony of the heyoka this order is reversed, the creation of the happy frame of mind in the people preceding the presentation of the truth.

This is the way the ceremony was performed: The people gather around in a circle and in the center there is a pot. The dog must be choked first because when you kill one he is mutilated and he must not be mutilated. No scars should be on him. They have helpers who do the choking—[and] an intercessor. The intercessor's name was Wachpannee [*Wahpanica*, Poor]. The sacred comedian has the power of the west which is the power of lightning so the dog is killed immediately without pain. Before killing the dog they make an offering of incense of sweetgrass to the west. They hold the rope with which they are going to choke the dog over the incense of the sweetgrass. Then they tie a slipnoose and put it over the dog's neck and two men pull four times and on the fourth pull they jerk with all their might and it kills him quickly. Then they take everything off but the head, spine and tail of the dog. The hair is singed off

12. Stemming from an error in the stenographic transcript, Neihardt wrote in *Black Elk Speaks*, p. 183, "the Place Where Everything is Disputed" instead of "Distributed." The Lakotas call Pine Ridge *Wakpamni*, Distribution, referring to it as the place from which government annuities were distributed.

the dog first and washed off well. Then the intercessor comes and takes the head, spine and tail and walks about six steps away from the pot—one step for each grandfather. And turning toward the west he offers the dog to the Thunder-beings. Then to the north, then to the east, then to the south, then to the spirit above, and then to mother earth. Then the intercessor sings a sacred heyoka song and then he faces the pot and says: "In a sacred manner I thus boil this dog." Then he acts as if throwing the dog three times. Then the fourth time he throws it and it lands in the pot. The same thing is done with the heart of the dog. In the meanwhile thirty heyokas, who have been dressed in a clownish manner, are performing funny tricks among the people to make the people happy.

Then Black Elk himself and One Side, his fellow comedian, had the whole right side of the hair shaved off their heads, the left side hanging loose and long. They had their bodies painted red all over and streaks of black lightning all over them. They each carried a very long crooked bow and crooked arrows. The herb that Black Elk had seen come out of the multicolored flames in his dream was in his hair for an ornament. They were riding sorrels which were painted with streaks of black lightning all over their body, thus simulating the figures of the vision of the night. Then Wachpannee sang a heyoka song:

> These are sacred, (meaning the heyokas)
> They have said. (repeated about twelve times)

While the pot was boiling, Black Elk and One Side got on their horses and sang this song facing the west:

> In a sacred manner they have sent voices to you. (twice)
> Half of the universe send their voices in a sacred manner.
> In a sacred manner they have sent voices to you.

(Half the universe meaning the west, for it is the power of the west only that is now being used and this is half the universe. This is why the hair was cut on the right side, because when you are looking to the south the right side is to the west. The right side was cut off for humility to the west. All this is being done in front of a sacred tipi. The intercessor, Wachpannee, was sitting in the tipi.)

(A characteristic bit of clowning by the heyokas who are walking among the people making them jolly before the sacred act was performed by Black Elk who is chief of all the heyokas at this ceremony. For instance two heyokas with long bows and long crooked arrows painted in a funny manner come to a little shallow pool of water. They act as though they thought it were a wide river and they want to get across it; they think it best first to determine how deep it is. So taking their long arrows, instead of thrusting them downward to determine the depth they push them straight out parallel to the water until the whole arrow is wet. Then setting it up on the ground they show that it is far over their heads. So they get ready to swim. One of them plunges into this shallow muddy pond head first, getting his face in the mud and fighting the water wildly as though he were drowning. Then the other one plunges in to save him and their antics in the water made the people laugh. Another had an arrow with a point on it that looked like steel and they supposed it a dangerous arrow. They shot this up in the air and the people were afraid of it and ran and when it came down it was nothing but a piece of rawhide and it did not hurt anyone.)

Black Elk and One Side sang this song to the four quarters. In the meantime the intercessor was singing a song and everyone came around to dance to it. The heyokas fought over the head just pretending to be trying to take it out. Each one of them must get a piece of this dog and they throw some of this hot water on everyone who passes, but of course it does not burn. After Black Elk and One Side got through singing they proceeded to the west. They had some sharp pointed arrows. They charged on horseback back on the pot. Black Elk lowered his arrow and caught the head on it. The other one caught the heart on his arrow. Heyokas would run after the meat and tried to get some of it, playing funny antics as they went. They plunged their hands in the water and got pieces of the meat without getting burned.[13] Where they dropped the meat, the other horsebacks charged to get it. Then the meat was divided up among the people and this was like giving them medicine. Even the smallest piece of meat was enough. After the heyokas got away with the meat, the pot was all dry, nothing was left in it. While doing this the Thunder-beings were coming again in a thunderstorm with full force and the hail was coming from the west and before it came to the gathering it

13. The *heyoka* dancers rubbed their hands and arms with a paste made by chewing red false mallow (*Malvastrum coccineum* [Pursh]), which prevented them from being scalded. See Tyon's account in Walker, *Lakota Belief and Ritual*, pp. 155–57, and Gilmore, *Uses of Plants by the Indians of the Missouri River Region*, p. 103.

spread and went on both sides, but once in a while you could see a few hail pieces falling near.

[From] this ceremony that I have performed the people had seen with their own eyes that I had a certain power. Some of them had already seen me do the horse dance. Everybody was glad and they regarded this as a medicine to make them happier all around.

BLACK ELK'S FIRST CURE

One Sides's original name was Kills the Enemy, but when I saw him in the vision he had the name of One Side. After this he was always called One Side, because of his hair being cut on one side.

After the heyoka dance we settled down at Manderson in little log cabins and One Side came also and settled down near us. Nobody was living around Grass Creek at this time.

One day I invited One Side to come over and eat with me. I told him I had seen an herb in my dream and we should go out and look for it.[14] Of course I did not tell him that I had dreamed about him, but I needed an herb for my medicine acts. That morning we got on our horses and went out in search of this herb. We got on top of a big hill and saw a place and knew this was in the vicinity of the place that I had seen in my vision. We sat down and began to sing some of the heyoka songs on this hill. Pretty soon I began to sing the song I had sung in the first vision: "In a sacred manner they are sending voices to you," etc. When we finished singing this song, down toward the west I could see magpies, crows, chicken hawks and eagles swarming around a certain place. I looked over to One Side and said: "Friend, right there is the herb." And it seemed as though One Side knew it. So we said: "We will go forth and see."

We went down to the Grass Creek and followed it down a little ways where there was another dry creek and we followed this up. As we neared the place, the birds all disappeared. At this place there were three or four dry gulches together and we saw the herb right there on the side of the

14. This is the daybreak star herb that Black Elk saw in the great vision when he was taken to the center of the world; it is apparently different from the herb that he wore in his hair earlier during the *heyoka* ceremony. The latter was the herb he had seen in the Thunder-being vision. However, in *Black Elk Speaks,* p. 200, Neihardt identifies these two herbs as one.

bank and I'd never seen one like it in my life. It had two stems and had all the colors of the four quarters. This was in the month of June. Everything was blooming at this time. The colors were blue, red, yellow and white. (The heyoka ceremony had been held in May.) This place is about eight miles from Black Elk's present home. We got off our horses and proceeded up toward where the herb was. I offered some kinnikinnick to the four sides of the earth. I offered a prayer to the herb saying: "Now, we shall go forth," (meaning the herb and I) "to the two-leggeds, but only to the weakest ones. Take courage, for there will be happy days among the weak." The herb has just one long deep root and at the top it is about one inch in diameter. It has only two stems upon which it bears the flowers of the colors of the four quarters. About a foot of the herb is all I ever used. It was at the edge of the bank and was easy to dig. Then after getting this herb, we started back. When we got to Grass Creek again we got some good sage in which we wrapped the herb. We got back to where we were staying now.

That evening was to be my first performance in medicine. While eating supper a man by the name of Cuts to Pieces came over and was saying: "Hey, hey, hey! I have a boy of mine and he is very sick and I don't expect him to live, and I thought since you had so much power in the horse dance, heyoka, etc. that you might have the power to cure my son." I did not know how to go at it, but I had seen other medicine men so I thought I'd follow their way. So I sent him back and told him that if he wanted me to go there and do a little curing that he should bring me a pipe with an eagle feather on it, which would mean that I was really wanted. The fellow went back and brought me the pipe back with him. I told him to come around the left side as he came in, and to put the pipe with the eagle feather on it facing me, and then he should walk out on the right side. I took the pipe and lit it and offered it to the four quarters, Great Spirit, and mother earth. I recalled the vision and asked for power. Then I began to smoke. My father, my mother and a man were there so I had to pass it around to them also. I just figured out how to go at this. When the power of the west comes to the four-leggeds it is a rumbling and when it passes it leaves the world green and fresh. Everyone lifts his head up in expectation and everyone is left happier as a result. And so now I used the drum to make the rumbling sound which represented the power of the west. Of course I had never received any instructions from anyone, but I just fixed a way for my curing.

(The drum arouses one's mind enough to make you feel the actions of this world and think about them and after you have thought about this you are happy. This has been used for a long time with the Indians and it is also used for enjoyment. The voice of the drum is an offering to the spirit.)

Then I went to get One Side and brought him to my tipi. We went out now to the sick boy and when we got there Standing Bear was there too. Medicine men usually use several medicines but I only had the one herb now.

(Question: Why in following around the quarters do they go from left to right? Answer: The flowering stick, the source of all life, comes from the south for the sun lives there. And as men and things grow older they move with the sun toward the setting sun where all things pass, and as they get still older they approach the north where the white hairs are and completing the circle with the sun they come back again to the place from whence they sprung—dust to dust. The west is the greatest source of power probably, because as men get older they get wisdom.)

We went into the tipi, left to right, and sat ourselves on the west side. The patient was on the northeast. The boy was about four years old and was very sick. The child seemed to be just skin and bones. He had been sick a long time. The parents presented me with a horse first, because the horse is about the only property that we had and we were to stay here until the child had been cured. This was my first experience so I had to borrow the drum, the eagle bone whistle, and a wooden cup which I told them to put some water in. They set the cup right in front of me with water in it. From here on I had to think awhile, because I had a little bit of doubt about whether or not I could do this. I gave the eagle bone whistle to One Side and told him how to use this. I filled my pipe with kinnikinnick and there was a pretty girl here too and I gave the pipe to her and told her to hold it just as in the vision. Then everything was in readiness and I sent up a voice. The power I had to use was in the pipe, cup, drum, and the chief power was in the herb. The eagle bone whistle represented what the eagle had told me in the vision.

Everything was now ready so now I beat the drum in time while sending up this cry: "Hey-a-a-hey" four times. It seemed that while I was doing this a feeling was coming over me from my feet up. I was still beating this drum in time while sending a voice saying:

"My grandfather, the Great Spirit, you are the only one and to no other can anyone send voices. They have said you have made everything.

The four quarters crossing each other you have made, and you have set a power where the sun goes down. [*You have set the six grandfathers where the sun goes down.*] The two-leggeds on earth are in despair. In their behalf I thus send a voice. On this earth the two-leggeds will not perish. You have said this to me. The weak shall walk. Thus you have given me power. The two-leggeds right here on earth, raising their heads they shall walk. The little blue man from whom I shall have the power, you have presented to me. In my vision you have taken me to the peak and there you have shown me the power to make over my nation. The water in the cup that you have given me—through this power shall we live. All beings that are not able will thus walk through your herb you have given me. Through the offering of my pipe to all the quarters, above and to mother earth, may you all hear me. From where we always face, there shall appear a virgin with scarlet relics and [she] shall walk the good road offering her pipe as she walks. The virgin shall thus depend on the sacred stick" (meaning the tree) "that you have presented to me. Through the power of this stick she shall face mankind. All this you have said to me. From where the giant lives you have given me a sacred wind. It is said to me that through this wind I shall draw power. The sacred wind, as he passes, the weak shall have strength. Through this wind I will breathe the power on the weak that they may see a happy day."

And then I prayed to the powers of all the other quarters as I had been taught in my vision. One power might have been enough, but I was so eager to cure the child that I used all the powers of my vision.

(The power vision cannot be used until the duty we got with the part of the vision has been performed upon the earth. After that the power may be used.)

I was of course facing the west, standing, and then I went to the right and stopped at the south, showing that I should walk the good road with my people [*healing as I walked*]. The song I sang:

> In a sacred manner I have made them walk.
> A sacred nation lies low.
> In a sacred manner I have made them walk.
> A sacred two-legged, he lies low.
> In a sacred manner I have made him walk.

When I sang this I could feel something queer in my body and I wanted to cry. At first I was in doubt but I was in earnest now. After singing this song I walked toward the west where the cup of water was and I saw the little sick boy looking up and smiling at me. Then I knew that I had the power and that I would cure him. The next thing I made an offering and took a whiff at the pipe. Then I drank part of the water and started toward where the sick boy was and I could feel something moving in my chest and I was sure that it was that little blue man and it made a different sound from anything else. Then I stamped the earth four times standing in front of the boy. Then I put my mouth on the pit of the boy's stomach and drew the north wind through him. At the same time the little blue man was also in my mouth, for I could feel him there. I put a piece of white cloth on my mouth and I saw there was blood on it, showing that I had drawn something out of his body. Then I washed my mouth with some of the water of the cup. And I was now sure that I had power.

This was the first time that I had ever conjured. I took some of the herb, powdered it, and put it all over the top of the hot water in the cup. I mixed it up and put some of it in my mouth and blew it over the boy to the four quarters and gave the rest of it to the boy to drink. I did not give this to the boy, but I let the virgin carry it to him. We ordered the virgin to help the boy stand up. We made him walk from the south to the four quarters. Of course, the boy was very poor and it would take some time for him to get perfectly well again, but he was cured and grew to be a young man and died before the age of thirty. I was not there, and if I had been I would probably have cured him again, for he was sick another time after this.

Always when I was doctoring I could tell whether or not I could cure the patient, for if I could cure him, I would always see him smiling in the cup of water.

The horse gift is not supposed to be accepted before four days are over, because by that time it will be known as to whether or not the person can be cured. When the people heard about my curing this boy, it got to be my business. I was very well-known by this time. The people all knew of me. Once, along toward the middle of one of my ceremonies, a Black Robe [Roman Catholic priest] came into the ceremony and took all my sacred relics around and stopped the ceremony. Not long after this, the Black Robe fell off his horse and died. The patient of this ceremony was cured anyway.

I was now nineteen years old and I had performed my first medicine man act. For three years now I kept up my practice and I cured tuberculosis and all sorts of diseases. It is too bad that they did not give me money! They gave me only horses. Right soon after my first cure, I performed the buffalo ceremony of my first vision. I was now about twenty years old. Then after this performance I had to do the act of the elk again.

THE BUFFALO CEREMONY

I put up another tipi and went after Fox Belly (Red Dog), an old medicine man, because he had had the same vision. He came to help us. He asked me about what I had to do concerning my dream. I told him about the good road from the south to the north on which they were to walk. One of the counselors was a buffalo and I was to resemble a buffalo. I was to go to the center of the nation's hoop and there my people would live. He asked me in what manner the buffalo was dressed. I told him he had an herb on one side of his horn and on the left side of his body was an eagle feather. This feather represented the people hung on the side of the buffalo, feeding on it. (It is the duty of the four quarters to nourish and strengthen the flowering tree at the center which represents the growth of the people in all its generations. The east gives the sunlight and peace, the south brings the warmth, the west brings the rain to nourish, the north gives it a strong wind so that it may have strength and endurance, and all these so that the tree may grow and flower.)

Red Dog said: "Boy, you had a great vision, and I know that it is your place to see that the people might walk the good road in a manner satisfactory to all its powers. It is the duty for you to see that the people will lead and walk the right road, because if it is not done, in the future our relatives-like will disappear." Then Red Dog made the sacred place like the buffalo wallow on the east side by the entrance. Red Dog also made the red road north and south across the circle and made buffalo tracks on either side of this red road, meaning that people would walk buffalo-like and as a result would be tough. Then he took the wooden cup full of water and put it on the north side, the tracks of the buffalo going toward the north side from the south side over the good road to the water of life. I had buffalo horns on and was painted red all over my body and One Side followed me painted red with a drum and a pipe filled with kinnikinnick. Red Dog sings this buffalo song:

Revealing this they walk
A sacred herb, revealing it, they walk.
Revealing this they walk.
The sacred life of the buffalo,
         revealing it they walk. (four times)
Revealing a sacred eagle feather. Revealing it they walk.
The eagle and buffalo, relative-like they walk.

After singing this song, Red Dog made a snorting sound of a buffalo and from his breath was visible red flames. I could tell from this that he must have had a great vision about the buffalo, and he was a very sacred man. (All this took place inside the tipi in the sacred place.)

I went outside the tipi. Then the sick made scarlet offerings in the same way, as they gathered around. The people were all eager to see me. In this act I represented the relationship between the people and the buffalo. From the buffalo, people had reared their children up. I went around acting like [a] buffalo and behind me followed One Side, representing [the] people. Everyone saw that my power was great. There were several wichamogahs [*wicaḣmunǵa*, wizards] in the crowd and none of them undertook to use his power on me because he knew my power was very great.[15]

After going around among the people, I returned to the tipi. Then the people brought some of their children over there to be cured. I gave the water to the little ones to lead them on on the good road to happiness. Before this I felt rather wild and when the Thunder-beings came I felt scared; but now the power was in me and I felt like a man.

We are here on earth and at the same time we go—we are born and die. When there is a newcomer, there is always another one that goes and I always think that if that patient isn't too far gone, I can cure him.

[*Up to this time we had been living in accordance with the old religion and we had plenty and things were good for us. When we wanted to perform a ceremony there was no interference with the whites and so we were still fortunate.*]

---

15. Wizards employed the power of evil spirits (Walker, *Lakota Belief and Ritual*, p. 94). However, their activities were apparently not entirely antisocial, for in an instance such as this they served to test the legitimacy and power of the man enacting his vision.

THE ELK CEREMONY

I was now twenty-one years old when I performed this act.[16] I had performed everything now by this time except the elk performance [*impersonation*]. At this time I was in full swing as a medicine man. I had to depend on my power and by the way I used this prayer the people recognized that I did have the power. This elk impersonation took place three or four miles south of Pine Ridge on the flats. I performed this here because I wanted to be where the biggest crowd of people was. I was now a success with the Great Spirit and I had to try to induce the people in the line that the spirits had predicted [along the good red road], so that the people would be prosperous. I tried my best to do my duty. This act was done during the time when the ponies were shedding. I went to Running Elk (Standing Bear's uncle) and offered the pipe to him, meaning that I wanted to have him for my intercessor in this Elk performance.

We had to have another tipi erected, so Running Elk came over. I had to use six elks [and] four virgins. Running Elk suggested this. Two of the elks were chosen by Running Elk and four should be chosen by me. We had to have elk hide that was just dried stiff without being tanned. We cut the rawhide in the shape of an elk's head and we had some eagle feathers for horns. The virgins had scarlet dresses on and braided hair with one feather in their hair. Their faces were painted yellow. One of the virgins had a red star on her forehead. Another virgin had a crescent in blue on her forehead. Another one had a red disc (sun) painted on her forehead. Another one had a circle of blue around her mouth and eyebrows— representing the sacred hoop. The men were painted black from the knees and elbows down and the rest of their bodies were painted yellow. There was a large heart-shaped figure enclosing the neck and coming down over the chest. On the backs of these men there was the sacred hoop in black. In the center of the sacred hoop on their backs they sewed to the skin an eagle feather. Running Elk was one of the six men, as he was taking part in it.

In the tipi in the same arrangement as the buffalo act they made a sacred place in the center of it where they put the roads from north to south and from east to west. The men wore masks of painted yellow rawhide. There were eye-holes in the mask, large feathers for horns and smaller feathers for the ears. Some of them had to carry flowering sticks. They cut the bark off of cottonwoods and left the leaves growing at the

16. This probably occurred in spring 1885. *Black Elk Speaks*, p. 212, places it in 1883.

tops of them. They painted the stick red. One of the virgins had this flowering stick and one carried the pipe with the eagle on it. One of them carried the herb and one of them carried the sacred hoop. Everything was in readiness now—we had finished painting and everything. Then before we performed the ceremony, we all had to go through the sweat house to purify ourselves. The intercessor sang:

> Advance to the four quarters. (twice)
> They are coming to behold you. (once)
> (Repeat above once more.)

After singing these songs they [the dancers] made the elk sound, *unh, unh.*

> Singing a voice as I walk. (twice)
> A sacred hoop I wear as I walk. (once)
> (Repeat above once more.)

After singing these songs, they [the participants] went out of the tipi; the virgins first—the one with the pipe first, the one with the sacred stick next, the one with the herb [next], the [one with] the sacred hoop last. All of the virgins faced the west now, standing together. Then we six men came out snorting and acting like elks, stamping out feet. We all carried an eagle feather and some sage with us. One of the six elks carried a drum. The four virgins offered the relics to the west and then proceeded on to the north. As the virgins went the men danced around them like elks. (The five men I was with were all bewitched, but I wasn't for they knew I had more power, evidently.[17]) The virgins then faced the north, the elks dancing around them all the while. The virgins offered their relics to the north this time. Then the virgins proceeded to the east and offered all the relics again to the east. There was a big crowd around us now. Then the virgins went on to the south and offered all their relics again. Then they went straight north back to the tipi by way of the red road. The virgin with the sacred hoop went in first, then she with the stick, then she with the herb, and then the virgin with the pipe came in last. Then the six elk men

17. According to Bushotter, "Lakota Texts," no. 88, the elk dancers carried hoops with mirrors attached at the center, which they flashed at onlookers to bewitch them. They used this method to seduce women, as well as to protect themselves from becoming bewitched by similar mirror flashes of other men with supernatural power. Bushotter says that the elk ceremony itself was considered a test of the dreamer's power.

went into the tipi. After we got into this sacred place we could see tracks of all kinds of animals in there—spirit tracks.

(In the tipi the [cup of] water was to the west, the same as in the buffalo act [sic].[18] All six elk men partook of this water when they returned into the tipi. They also smoked the peace pipe, but only among themselves this time—it was not passed on.)

18. Black Elk's account of the buffalo ceremony placed the cup of water on the north side of the circle.

[7]

Seeing the World of
the *Wasichus* (1886–89)

BUFFALO BILL'S WILD WEST SHOW

At that time the people began to settle down and some of them were living in square houses and some of them were living in tipis, wherever they wanted to live. And in the fall of the year I heard that a show (Buffalo Bill's) was going to go out and I heard rumors that he was going to go across the great water.[1] I wanted to see the great water, the great world and the ways of the white men; this is why I wanted to go. So far I looked back on the past and recalled the people's ways. They had a way of living, but it was not the way we had been living. I got disgusted with the wrong road that my people were doing now and I was trying to get them to go back on the good road; but it seemed as though I couldn't induce them, so I made up my mind I was going away from them to see the white man's ways. If the white man's ways were better, why I would like to see my people live that way.

Some of my close friends were going with the show so they got me to go, and it was their thought that made me go. I was not yet married at this time. We bought all the material we needed. I had some moccasins, buckskin clothes, war bonnet and everything. The show outfit sent some

---

1. For Indians and the Buffalo Bill Wild West show, see Don Russell, *The Lives and Legends of Buffalo Bill* (Norman: University of Oklahoma Press, 1960), and Henry Blackman Sell and Victor Weybright, *Buffalo Bill and the Wild West* (New York: Oxford University Press, 1955). A good account of personal experiences with the show is Luther Standing Bear, *My People the Sioux* (Boston: Houghton Mifflin, 1928), pp. 245–69.

wagons from Rushville [Nebraska] to get us. There were over ten of my friends in there and quite a few whom I did not know. In all there were about one hundred women and men. There were about eight or more wagons that came after us. My relatives told me to stay and keep up my practice in medicine, but I insisted on going anyway. They all followed us up to Rushville. Our friends all wished us luck when we left for Rushville. When we got in the wagons we were giving whoops of joy and we left our relatives crying behind us. We stopped half-way at noon and had our meal there on a hill. Then we started out again and got to Rushville before sundown. That evening we had a big dance there.

The trains were awaiting our arrival and we had everything ready to leave. We got on the train and I began to think about my people and I felt very bad—I was almost sick—I felt like turning back but I went anyway. The train hooked on to our car and started off. We ran all that night and had breakfast at Long Pine and arrived at Omaha that evening. Right there I could compare my people with the whites' ways and right there I felt bad again and was sorry that I had left my people behind. I thought that something would happen to them while I was gone.

The train proceeded eastward now from Omaha. We arrived at Chicago next morning and stayed all day and all that night here. Then we went on eastward and we arrived in New York soon. Then we got off the train and walked to Madison Square Garden. We carried our clothes and sacks. I was surprised to see those skyscrapers there in New York. We ate in the center of the Hippodrome and we heard the Pawnee Indians whooping at us. They couped us in a friendly way and we just had to hurry out of there. These Indians were also going with the show. I enjoyed the Indian part of the shows that we put on here at Madison Square Garden, but I did not care much about the white people's parts.

We stayed here at Madison Square Garden about six months.[2] While I was there, I felt that my people were just altogether lost, because I was a long ways from home. I wondered about their future and about the vision and I thought I had just lost my people. Everything that I was doing here on earth I left alone and was among other men just as a common man. At

2. The Buffalo Bill show opened at Madison Square Garden on November 24, 1886, and closed on February 22, 1887. See Nellie Snyder Yost, *Buffalo Bill: His Family, Friends, Fame, Failures, and Fortunes* (Chicago: Swallow, 1979), pp. 179–82; Sell and Weybright, *Buffalo Bill and the Wild West*, pp. 155–56.

the end of six months I heard some of them were going to cross the great water, and all my friends decided that they would go. I wanted to come back from there but my friends induced me to go. The chief we had was Rocky Bear and he returned so we got Red Shirt to take his place.

THE TRIP ACROSS THE GREAT WATER

One day we got up early to load on to the ship. This was a very large fire-boat.[3] Then just as we started out there was another big fire-boat that came along and when I first heard them [the steamboats] make [a] big voice I got scared, but I got used to them after while. Of course when I saw those great lights they made, I soon learned that it was the light of the thunders [electricity]. There was something here at the prisoners' house that made me feel very bad. Men pointed guns at them and ordered them around and I thought that maybe my people would probably be treated this way some day (Blackwell's Island [the New York City penitentiary on an island in the East River]).

As we left New York I could see nothing but water, water, water. It looked as though there would be an end where we would drop off somewhere. It looked as though the sky and the water met and that when we got to this we would not be able to go on. Then when I looked back I could not see New York—there was nothing but mist behind. Everyone was in despair and some of them got sick, some of them were singing their death songs. We were sleeping in hammocks hung from the ceiling, but we did not like it, so we took them down. There were about sixteen of us in here (steerage). It was evening now and time to go to bed. We did not understand about these hammocks, so we put them on the floor. They would keep going back and forth on the floor with the sway of the ship. Afterwards I learned that there was a big storm and everyone was in despair. The women were crying and some of the men were crying, singing their death songs. The white people laughed at us at first, but they soon were in despair themselves. Everyone was running all around, as they were excited. Somehow the white men began to realize that they were in danger and they began to hand out life belts, but I did not put on a

3. The Buffalo Bill show, including 133 Indians, left New York on the steamship *State of Nebraska* on March 31, 1887, bound for England ("Buffalo Bill's Good-Bye," *New York Times,* April 1, 1887). See Sell and Weybright, *Buffalo Bill and the Wild West,* p. 159.

life belt but I dressed for death and began to sing. We sang in order to cheer up our women and to take courage, as we were out there for adventure. We wanted to know this and now we were learning it. I was sorry that I went out there now. The storm lasted all night, so nobody slept.

At about daybreak the storm quieted down and we were traveling evenly. It seemed that the boat was traveling eastward and that the sun was coming up in the west. The water looked like big mountains. Then we'd see another fire-boat come up and we didn't see it for a while and then it would come up again. It looked as though the sun came up on the water and then it came down into the water again. We couldn't drink the water, as it was salty. It had been about five or six days now. Some of us got pretty sick. The next day all of them were sick and I was also very sick. Everything I'd eat would come right back—I couldn't keep anything in my stomach. In the middle of the way we saw a big black thing—his body was in the middle and his tail and head were way on either end of him. It seemed as though it would go up and down, yet the water was still. Some of the buffalo and elk that we were taking with us were dead, so we took their carcasses out and dumped them in the ocean. When I saw the poor buffalo thrown overboard I felt very sad, because right there it looked as though they were throwing part of the power of the Indian overboard.

We could see lots of houses and when we neared there, we saw lots of fire-boats (nearing harbor). We thought then that we would land in a very short time, but we traveled all night and the next morning and then we began to see land. As we neared the gate of the great water there was another fire-boat smaller than ours that had come through the gate and stopped alongside of us. They looked all over our ship and everything before we could land (quarantine boat). From here we traveled very slowly nearly all day, and finally we got to a place where there were lots of houses. They took us to London where the fire-boat stops. These houses were altogether different from the others. We stayed all night on the boat and the next day they unloaded us. It seemed that the men here were all different than the others. They took us to a place that they called the Show. We were on land, but we still felt dizzy as though we were on water still. We stayed here six months. I was over twenty-two years old by now.[4]

4. The show disembarked at Gravesend on April 16, 1887, then took the train to Earl's Court, London. Buffalo Bill held a special preview performance for the Prince of

GRANDMOTHER ENGLAND'S JUBILEE

We traveled all over England that summer. They took us to a place called Her Majesty (this was Queen Victoria). One morning we heard that the old Grandmother England was coming. When we heard this, we selected the best looking types of the Indians and the best dancers.[5] I was one of the five men selected. Onlookers were not permitted to come on this day to the show. The soldiers came in and were stationed all around. The three who came were Grandmother England and two women and one boy. I noticed that there were soldiers on both sides of Grandmother England as she came. About fifty chariots came that day. There were soldiers and officials along with Mother England. In the show we had to shoot at times, but this time we were not allowed to shoot. We danced the Omaha grass dance then. I was one of the five dancers at this dance. We stood right in front of Grandmother England. I was a boy now and so I was a pretty good dancer. We danced the best we knew how. I was limber at this time and I could dance many ways.

After the show was over they put all of us Indians in a row according to size. I was next to the youngest boys and girls. Then Grandmother England came out and shook hands with us. She made a speech, saying that she was seventy-five years old.[6] She said: "All over the world I have seen all kinds of people, and I have seen all kinds of countries too and I've heard about America as being a great country. Also I have heard about some people that were in America and I heard that they called them American Indians. Now I have seen them today. America is a good country and I have seen all kinds of people, but today I have seen the best looking people—the Indians. I am very glad to see them. If I owned you Indians, you good-looking people, I would never take you around in a show like this. You have a Grandfather over there who takes care of you over there, but he shouldn't allow this, for he owns you, for the white people to take

Wales on May 5. The show opened officially in London on May 9 and closed on October 31 (Russell, *The Lives and Legends of Buffalo Bill,* pp. 327–29; Yost, *Buffalo Bill,* pp. 186–203; Sell and Weybright, *Buffalo Bill and the Wild West,* pp. 159–76.)

  5. This command performance for Queen Victoria was held on May 11, 1887. See Russell, *The Lives and Legends of Buffalo Bill,* p. 330; Sell and Weybright, *Buffalo Bill and the Wild West,* pp. 169–71; Yost, *Buffalo Bill,* p. 192.

  6. In *Black Elk Speaks,* p. 225, Neihardt altered this to sixty-seven, the queen's actual age.

you around as beasts to show to the people. There is something that I want to tell you and perhaps this thing that I'll tell you will happen while you are alive (pointing to Black Elk) or sometime one of them will know (pointing to the others) this thing that will happen. There will be a big war in the future and I wish that I had owned you people, for I would not carry you around as beasts to show to the people." [*Black Elk's description of Grandmother England, Queen Victoria. She was short and heavy-set, medium-sized woman.*]

When she finished her speech to us, she raised her hand and we all hollered and gave cheers. She did not care much about seeing the white men in the show. She only shook hands with the Indians. Then about fifty chariots came in and we did not see which one she got into, but she got into one and left. Just before she went home she said: "It's up to you to come and see me now." About two weeks afterward the show boss told us to put on the best dress we had, so we dressed up and they put us in some chariots and took us to Windsor Castle.[7] It was a beautiful place. There were soldiers with guns all around there and where she was coming from there were soldiers all over. I noticed that it was a great big house with sharp pointed towers on it. The people all around there pounded their heels on the ground and said: "Jubilee, jubilee, jubilee!" There was a large grandstand there and there was a big amphitheater of seats. There appeared a beautiful black wagon with two black horses and it came in and went around the show place. I heard that this was her grandson, a small boy, probably King George when he was a boy. Next appeared a beautiful black wagon with four gray horses hitched to it. On this wagon there was a rider on each of the right-hand horses and a man walked holding the bridle of the front left-hand horse. Some relatives of the King were in this wagon. Next appeared eight buckskin horses drawing a black wagon— two by two. There were riders on each of the right-hand horses and a man afoot led the left-hand horse. There were soldiers with bayonets facing outward all over the wagon. The white men were all making a big noise and tramping on the floor. All I could hear was "Victoria!" and "Jubilee!" The Queen was sitting in this wagon and was well-dressed. Two women

7. This command performance took place on June 20, 1887, for the Jubilee guests celebrating the fiftieth anniversary of Victoria's reign. See Russell, *The Lives and Legends of Buffalo Bill*, p. 329; Sell and Weybright, *Buffalo Bill and the Wild West*, p. 172.

were sitting in the front facing her and the Queen was sitting in the back facing the women. The Queen had a shiny hat with shiny stones on it. Her dress was shiny. Later I heard that there was yellow and white metal [gold and silver] all over the harnesses and the wagon. She looked like a fire coming.

(We went to London for six months. Then we went to Manchester and gave the show.[8] Then we went to the Queen's place to give her the show. [*This was the Queen's Jubilee.*])

As the Queen passed us, she stopped and stood up back to where the Indians were sitting. All her people bowed to her, but she bowed to us Indians. We sent out the women's and the men's tremolo then. Some people got so excited that some of the people suffocated from the great crowd of people in there. Then we all sang her a song. This was the most happy time!

WANDERING IN EUROPE

This was all over now and we started back. After the Jubilee three other young men and myself got lost in Manchester and the show was leaving the next morning. We roamed around there and we found a resting place and stayed all night in a rooming house. That night the fire-boat pulled out leaving us here by ourselves. We could not speak English. We found two other men besides ourselves who had gotten lost and one of them could speak English, so we got to London where we roamed around for about three days.[9] We made up our minds we would try to make some money to go home on by giving shows. The third day a policeman came to us and took us back to the courthouse and asked us where we were that night before. We did not know but what we were arrested. We told them where we had stayed, which was at this English speaker's place. They questioned us about everything. This party told the police where we had been all this time and what we had been doing. The police questioned us

8. Black Elk apparently confused the chronology of these events. After closing in London on October 31, the show moved first to Birmingham, then to Manchester, where it opened on December 17 and closed on April 30, 1888 (Russell, *The Lives and Legends of Buffalo Bill*, pp. 204–8).

9. Buffalo Bill sailed from London for New York on May 6, 1888; Black Elk and his companions must have narrowly missed him (Russell, *The Lives and Legends of Buffalo Bill*, p. 341).

and let us go. They had probably blamed us with something that had happened.

This English interpreter came back one day and told us about a show-man called Mexican Joe who wanted us.[10] We got there and found there was nothing there but Omahas. We got better pay here. They would give us thirty dollars a month if we would join them. This was a small show. We gave a show at London and then later we went over to Paris. From Paris we went into Germany. Then we went to the place where the earth was on fire—there was a butte here in a cone shape (Naples) and I learned that some people had disappeared in the earth a long time ago (Pompeii). Of course I did not feel right and I thought the best thing to do was to stick with this show so I could get money to go home with. I felt so sad that I got sick. It had been over two years now since I had left my people. We went back to Paris again and I was very sick and couldn't go on with this show. They advised me to go back there, for I had lots of white friends there. I came back to Paris. I was all by myself now and I had saved all my money and I came back to where I had a girl friend there. All I wanted was to go back to my country. I rested up here and got well again.

SPIRIT JOURNEY HOME

One morning I had on a white man's clothes and the only difference was that I had long hair. I had good clothes on and shoes and everything. It wasn't braided, just hanging back. I was all slicked up one morning and I was sitting down to breakfast. This girl friend of mine sat by me and her father and mother and two other sisters were sitting there. As we sat there I looked up at the roof and it seemed to be moving. The house was going around up at the top and I saw a cloud appear as the ceiling was rising—the cloud was coming down and it seemed that they all began to rise to the clouds and the cloud took me on up with it and then the rest of the people descended alone.

After the cloud caught me I hung on top of it and I could see the houses

10. Captain Mexican Joe Shelley, encouraged by Buffalo Bill's success in England, organized a rival wild west show that was reported to have sailed from Baltimore in July 1887. See John M. Burke, London, to Secretary of the Interior, July 12, 1887, and attached memo (Letters Received by the Commissioner of Indian Affairs, 1887–18450, Record Group 75, National Archives and Records Service).

and towns below me and soon I was right above the ocean. Then soon I began to see the houses in America again. I was happy now, because I had been wanting to come home for a long time. I could see the rivers and towns below me and as I was coming back I could recognize the country. I could see the Black Hills and Harney Peak. I was coming right over Pine Ridge and was going to descend. The people were all gathered here and there was quite an excitement. I could see my mother in her tipi too. The cloud just stood up there and I could see down. I just figured I would jump off the cloud but I was afraid I might get killed if I did. It seemed as though I could see everything ahead of time. I wanted to get off very badly. Then the cloud rose again and started east. I saw that my mother looked up to me and it seemed that she saw me. They were eating and I could see them cooking outside clearly. I knew some of the men in that camp and knew just what they were doing. Now it was dark and I was traveling eastward. I could see the towns and the cities below me. Soon I couldn't see any lights so I knew then that I was right over the big water again. Pretty soon the light began to appear in the east—it was day—and now I was near England. The cloud stood right over where I had been eating breakfast. Then when the cloud stood over the house, it [the house] began to come up and touch the cloud. I was caught on the house again and then the house began to descend. Just as the house hit the ground again I heard someone say, "He's alive." Bells rung in my ears before I heard this.

When I came to the first thing I noticed was that I was lying flat on my back and there was a doctor there. I saw a coffin there. All this day since breakfast and all that night I had been on my vision. The next morning I came to. I had actually dropped over and died. They had announced me dead and had a coffin ready to put me in. When I got up I was well again. They took the coffin back. When I got up people got scared and ran into the other room. From the looks of the coffin it was very expensive. I wish I'd died there, as I would have had a good coffin, but as it is, I won't have a good one. They told me that when I sat down to eat I smiled and then keeled over backwards and they were going to catch me but they couldn't. They sent for the doctor and he came and my body was still warm. Once in a while my heart would beat a little bit. Several doctors came and they all thought that there wasn't enough life in me to bring me to. I did not tell them about my vision. The people took good care of me during this time.

RETURN TO PINE RIDGE

A few days after, these people heard that Buffalo Bill was here somewhere.[11] I had a little money and hung on to it as much as I could. I told
the folks that I was going over there and I told my girl that I would go first
and she could come afterward. I got on a fire-boat and went across the
English channel. Then I took a train and started for Paris and got over
there at about eleven o'clock that morning.[12] The show was right near the
station, so I got off and went over there. I guess my parents were grieving
for me, because I had written to them once in a while. I met some of my
friends there and while I was talking to them I heard that Buffalo Bill
wanted to see me so I went to see him. When I got there Buffalo Bill had
gathered all the people together there and they gave me four big cheers.
Buffalo Bill asked me if I was going to stay or go home. I told him that I
was going home. He bought me a ticket and gave me ninety dollars. We
then had a big dinner on my account. That day I was kind of a spectator.

In the evening a policeman came and told me to get my luggage and
the police showed me where to get my ticket. I started from Paris at about
eight o'clock. I came to a seaport next and stopped here at a rooming
house. Next morning at about nine I got on the fire-boat and we started
out again. The first boat I came on took fourteen days and this one took
only eight days. This was on the White Star Line. I got back to New York
then and I was there all day. That same evening I left for home. I traveled
from there to Chicago all that night and all the next day. From there I
caught another train and got to Omaha early the next morning. I started
from Omaha the same morning and got to Rushville at about five o'clock
in the morning. No Sioux were there at all. There was a covered wagon of
mules starting out for Pine Ridge, which I came back on.

When I got back, everything was just as I saw in my vision abroad. All
the Sioux were there. This was in the year of the treaty (1889).[13] My

11. The Buffalo Bill show opened in Paris at the Exposition Universelle on May 19,
1889 (Yost, *Buffalo Bill*, p. 221; Russell, *The Lives and Legends of Buffalo Bill*, p. 350).

12. There is confusion here. Earlier Black Elk had indicated that the family he stayed
with lived in Paris, but here it would appear that he was living in England because he
had to cross the channel to meet Buffalo Bill in Paris.

13. The agreement of 1889 reduced the Great Sioux Reservation by about half
(eleven million acres) and created five smaller reservations out of the remainder: Standing Rock, Cheyenne River, Pine Ridge, Rosebud, and Lower Brulé. See Olson, *Red*

mother's tipi was right where I saw it, and when I got back to our tipi I saw all the people just exactly where they were in my vision. I had lots to tell. My mother [was] overjoyed to see me back, and I was crying for joy. I was supposed to be a man, but my tears came out anyway. During the time of my vision, my mother had dreamed during her sleep that I had come back on a cloud.

Cloud and the Sioux Problem, pp. 312–19; James Mooney, *The Ghost-Dance Religion and the Sioux Outbreak of 1890,* Smithsonian Institution, Bureau of American Ethonology, Annual Report 14, pt. 2 (1896), p. 826.

[8]

The Ghost Dance and
Wounded Knee (1889–91)

THE MESSIAH'S DANCE

When I came back my people seemed to be in poverty. Before I went some of my people were looking well, but when I got back they all looked pitiful. There had been quite a famine. I returned in 1889.[1] While I was gone I had lost my power, but as soon as I returned I was called out to cure a sick person and just then my power returned.

At this time people were all talking about the land they had sold to Three Stars [General Crook] as a result of a treaty.[2] This fall I had another brother who went out on a show which went all over the world. He started out on this show.

This fall I heard that there were some men named Good Thunder, Brave Bear, and Yellow Breast who had gone and seen the Messiah.[3] It was toward the west right around Idaho somewhere. There was a sacred man there. These three men had gone to see this sacred man and they came

1. Conditions had worsened significantly during the years Black Elk was away. The beef rations had been steadily decreased, and in 1889 they were again cut by more than half. There was famine at Pine Ridge, coupled with disease and drought. See Olson, *Red Cloud and the Sioux Problem*, pp. 320–21; Mooney, *The Ghost-Dance Religion*, pp. 826–42.

2. General George Crook headed the 1889 commission that secured the Indians' consent to the reduction and division of the Great Sioux Reservation.

3. The Messiah, a Paiute Indian called Jack Wilson (Wovoka), lived in Mason Valley, Nev., forty miles northwest of the Walker Lake reservation. Sword also mentioned this first delegation to the Messiah in 1889; see Mooney, *The Ghost-Dance Religion*, pp. 767, 797.

back that following fall [1889] and reported that they had seen the Messiah and actually talked to him and that he had given them some sacred relics. They had had the meeting at the head of White Clay [Creek] and the people gathered together there to hear what these men had to say about it. I did not go over there, I just heard of it, that's all. These three men had brought some sacred red and white paint that the sacred man had given them. This paint was broken up into little pieces and distributed among the people.

These people told me that these men had actually seen the Messiah and that he had given them these things. They should put this paint on and have a ghost dance, and in doing this they would save themselves, that there is another world coming—a world just for the Indians, that in time the world would come and crush out all the whites. But if you want to get into this other world, you would have to have this paint on. It should be put all over the face and head [*show them this ceremony to be performed*], and that this ghost dance would draw them to this other world and that the whites would have no power to get on so that it would crush them. In this other world there was plenty of meat—just like olden times—every dead person was alive again and all the buffalo that had been killed would be over there again roaming around. This world was to come like a cloud. This painting and ghost dance would make everyone get on the red road again. Everyone was eager to get back to the red road again.

This sacred man had presented two eagle feathers to Good Thunder, one of these three men. The sacred man had said to him: "Receive these eagle feathers and behold them, for my father will cause these two eagle feathers to bring your people back to him." This is all that was heard this whole winter. At first when I heard this I was bothered, because my vision was nearly like it and it looked as though my vision were really coming true and that if I helped, probably with my power that I had I could make the tree bloom and that I would get my people back into that sacred hoop again where they would prosper. This was in my mind but I still worked on as clerk in the store.[4] I wanted to see this man personally and find out and it was setting firmer in my mind every day.

It was now the spring of 1890. The winter of 1889–90 I heard that they wanted to find out more about that man. So Kicking Bear, Short Bull, Bear Comes Out and [Mash the] Kettle and a party started out to find out

4. Probably the store at Manderson.

more about this sacred man and see him if possible.[5] These fellows came home in the spring of 1890. I did not hear of the news that they had. But I heard that at the head of Cheyenne Creek, north of Pine Ridge, Kicking Bear had held the first ghost dance. From the rumors and gossips I heard that this Messiah was the son of the Great Spirit that had come out there. Then the next thing I heard was that they were dancing below Manderson on Wounded Knee.[6] I wanted to find out things, because it was setting strongly in my heart and something seemed to tell me to go and I resisted it for a while but then I could no longer resist, so I got on my horse and went to this ghost dance near Manderson and watched them dance.

They had a sacred pole in the center. It was a circle in which they were dancing and I could clearly see that this was my sacred hoop and in the center they had an exact duplicate of my tree that never blooms and it came to my mind that perhaps with this power the tree would bloom and the people would get into the sacred hoop again. It seemed that I could recall all my vision in it. The more I thought about it, the stronger it got in my mind. Furthermore, the sacred articles that had been presented were scarlet relics and their faces were painted red. Furthermore, they had that pipe and the eagle feathers. It was all from my vision. So I sat there and felt sad. Then happiness overcame me all at once and it got ahold of me right there. I was to be intercessor for my people and yet I was not doing my duty. Perhaps it was this Messiah that had pointed me out and he might have set this to remind me to get to work again to bring my people back into the hoop and the old religion.

Again I recalled Harney Peak in the Black Hills [*the center of the earth*]. And I remembered my vision that the spirits had said to me: "Boy, take courage, they shall take you to the center of the earth." When they took me here, they said: "Behold all the universe, the good things of the earth.

---

5. These delegates represented the Pine Ridge, Rosebud, and Cheyenne River reservations. They were chosen at the autumn 1889 council mentioned above by Black Elk and were sent to learn more about the Messiah. See Mooney, *The Ghost-Dance Religion*, pp. 797, 820; Robert M. Utley, *The Last Days of the Sioux Nation* (New Haven: Yale University Press, 1963), p. 61.

6. Kicking Bear probably initiated the first ghost dance at Pine Ridge in August 1890; Good Thunder organized the dance on Wounded Knee Creek that Black Elk attended. See Utley, *The Last Days of the Sioux Nation*, pp. 84–85.

1. Black Elk and Elk (an Oglala Lakota) in London, England, 1887. Taken while the Oglalas were on tour with Buffalo Bill's Wild West show, this photograph is a good representation of Lakota men's grass dance costumes of the time, which included sheep and sleigh bells; otter fur waist and neck pieces; pheasant feather bustles at the waist; dentalium shell necklaces; and bone hairpipes with colored glass beads. These costume items, more decorative than symbolic, flourished as art forms during the Wild West show period. Photograph collected on Pine Ridge Reservation in 1891 by James Mooney. Courtesy National Anthropological Archives, Smithsonian Institution.

NICK BLACK ELK AND FAMILY
CATHOLIC CATECHIST.

2, 3. Nicholas Black Elk, Anna Brings White, and Lucy Black Elk at the Black Elks' home in Manderson, South Dakota, circa 1910, 1930. In both photographs Black Elk wears his catechist's dress, a Western-style suit. Brings White wears traditional Sioux women's cloth dresses decorated with elk teeth and ribbon-

work, and in the earlier photo she wears a woman's hairpipe breastplate. Lucy's traditional dress in the earlier photo—a miniature of her mother's—gives way to modern dress in the later one. Photographs by Eugene Buechel, S.J. Courtesy Buechel Memorial Lakota Museum, St. Francis, South Dakota.

4, 5, 6. These three photographs show the development of an image of Black Elk as a catechist that was fostered by Catholic missionaries and used in fund raising. In the first one, taken about 1910, Black Elk's daughter, Lucy, in her cotton dress and braids represents the new generation of Catholic Indians. This photograph was the basis for the Fall 1926 cover illustration of *The Indian Sentinel,* the fund-raising magazine of the Bureau of Catholic Indian Missions. The artist has redrawn Black Elk in stereotypical Indian costume to emphasize the passing of the old Indian way of life and the acceptance of Christianity in its place. The third photograph, taken about 1935, was reproduced on Holy Rosary Mission fund-raising literature during the 1940s. First and third photographs by Eugene Buechel, S.J.; courtesy Buechel Memorial Lakota Museum, St. Francis, South Dakota.

NICK BLACK ELK & LUCY.

The Indian Sentinel

FALL 1926

PUBLISHED QUARTERLY AT WASHINGTON, D.C.
BY THE BUREAU OF CATHOLIC INDIAN MISSIONS
VOL·VI   NO·IV

7. John G. Neihardt, Nicholas Black Elk, and Standing Bear during the interview sessions for *Black Elk Speaks* in Manderson, South Dakota, May 1931. Photograph by Hilda Neihardt Petri, from the scrapbook of Enid Neihardt Fink. Courtesy John G. Neihardt Trust.

8. Black Elk praying to the six grandfathers on Harney Peak, May 30, 1931. Black Elk lifts his right hand in prayer and with his left hand offers his catlinite pipe—decorated with colored ribbons symbolizing the directions and a single eagle tail feather representing *Wakan Tanka*—to the grandfathers. He wears long red underwear in lieu of the red body paint of his vision, and over it the traditional breechcloth along with stockings and beaded moccasins. His buffalo-hide turban is decorated with eagle tail feathers. Photograph by John G. Neihardt. Courtesy John G. Neihardt Trust.

Black Elk", Medicine Man - Duhamel's Sioux Indian Pageant in the Black Hills

9, 10. Black Elk at Duhamel's Sioux Indian Pageant in the Black Hills. These photographs by Canedy's Camera Shop, Rapid City, South Dakota, were published as postcards and sold at the pageant. At left, circa 1935, Black Elk poses in his healer's regalia: headdress ornamented with sacred herbs and eagle feathers, and sacred ornaments around the neck; lightning streaks painted on the face and body; and a square drum representing the sound of thunder, beat-

en with a Pet Milk can rattle representing the sound of rain falling, to invoke the power of the west. Courtesy South Dakota State Historical Society, Pierre.

At right, circa 1940, Black Elk in the role of ceremonial elder wears a magnificent headdress with real buffalo horns and a trailer of eagle tail feathers and holds a lance symbolizing leadership; the elk teeth on his vest represent long life. Courtesy Patricia Albers, Salt Lake City, Utah.

11. Black Elk at Manderson, South Dakota, 1947, at the time of the interviews for *The Sacred Pipe*. Photograph by Joseph Epes Brown. Courtesy National Anthropological Archives, Smithsonian Institution.

All this behold it, because they shall be your own." Then I saw people prospering all over. And I recalled my six grandfathers. They told me through their power I would be intercessor on earth for my people. They had told me that I should know everything so therefore I made up my mind to join them. What I went there first for was to find out what they had heard, but now I changed my mind and was going there to use my own power to bring the people together. The dance was [all] done that day, but the next day there was to be another dance, so I stayed all night for another one.

The fall before [1889], I regret to say that I lost my father and I was fatherless on this earth and I was supporting my mother at that time; and while sitting there I could recall my father watching that dance and I made up my mind to communicate with my father about the other world. So that night I had it deeply in my heart that I was to be in there to make the tree bloom. So I dressed up in the sacred clothes. I told no one that I was going to join them but I got ready for the next day. (After dancing this ghost dance, they fall over and faint and see visions.)

Before the dance was on the next morning I got among them around the sacred pole. Good Thunder, an uncle of mine (Good Thunder later married Black Elk's mother), took me in his arms and took me to the sacred stick, offering a prayer for me here. He prayed thus: "Father, behold me, this boy your ways he shall see, and the people shall know him." (Then Good Thunder began to cry.) Just then I happened to think of my father and my sister and brothers which I had lost the year before. I couldn't keep the tears from running out of my eyes and so I put my head up to keep the tears from running out. I was really sorry and cried with my whole heart. The more I cried, the more I could think about my people. They were in despair. I thought about my vision and that my people should have a place in this earth where they would be happy every day and that their nation might live, but they had gone on the wrong road and they had gone into poverty but they would be brought back into the hoop. Under the tree that never bloomed I stood and cried because it faded away. I cried and asked the Great Spirit to help me to [make it] bloom again. I could not stop crying no matter how much I tried.

Then I had a funny feeling of shivering over my body and this showed that it really was the real thing. Everyone knew my power and with my own will to make that tree bloom, I joined the people there. Kicking Bear

held one of my arms on one side and Good Thunder held the other arm
and I was ready for the dance now. The song we sang next was:

> Ha-t(h)oo-wa-cha-oo-ga-cha-nee-who-wo. (two times)
> [*He tuweca* (*he u huwo*) *u ecanni huwo*.[7]]
> Who do you think he is that comes?

> It is he who seeks his mother.
> Father has said this.

(To be said in the other world to someone coming there from here.)

At the first dance I had no vision, but my body seemed to be raised off
the ground while I danced and I had a queer feeling. We danced all day.
When I went back after the dance, I thought about the other world and
that the Messiah himself was with my people over there, and perhaps my
tree was actually blooming over there and my dream was really coming
true. I thought to myself that I would try my best to know more about
this. While I was thinking this, it occurred to me that in my vision I had
seen beautiful things and in the center of the earth I had seen everything
and perhaps this land of my vision was where the people were going and
that we would disappoint the white race and only my people would live.

BLACK ELK'S GHOST DANCE VISIONS

The next morning we danced again. As we started out to dance Kicking
Bear offered a prayer saying: "Father, behold me, these people shall go
forth today. They shall see their relatives that they may be happy over
there day after day and there will be no end to that happiness." Then all
the dancers around began to wail and cry. As we started to dance again
some of the people would be laughing and some would be crying. Some
of them would lie down for a vision and we just kept on dancing. I could
see more of them staggering around panting and then they would fall
down for visions. The people were crying for the old ways of living and
[that] their religion would be with them again.[8]

7. This song, as written in Lakota by Lizzie Black Fox, a Lakota woman, was
published in George Sword, "The Story of the Ghost Dance," *The Folk-Lorist* 1(1) (July
1892): 34.

8. By this time all the traditional public rituals of the Lakota religion, including the
sun dance, the soul-keeping ritual, and the give-aways (of material goods after a relative's death) were prohibited by the government.

It took quite a while for me to get in this condition. They sang all sorts of songs. Then I began to fear that my breath was coming up while we were dancing. The first feeling I had was that my legs seemed to be full of ants. We always danced with our eyes closed. Then we heard wailing of women and people were lying around all over as though they were having visions. It seemed as though I were swaying off the ground without touching it. This queer feeling came up [*farther*] and it was in my heart now and I was panting. It was not a fear. It seemed that I would glide forward like a swing and swing back again. Of course it took me quite a while. I was panting hard and I must have fallen down, for they let me go.

All I saw was an eagle feather in front of my eyes at first. I felt as though I had fallen off a swing and gone out into the air. My arms were out-stretched and right before me above I could see a spotted eagle dancing toward me with his wings fluttering and the shrill whistle he made. I could see a ridge right in front of me and I thought I was going to hit that ridge, but I went right over it. I did not move at all, I just looked ahead. After I reached the other side of the ridge I could see a beautiful land over there and people were camping there in circle[s] all over. I noticed that they had plenty, and I saw dried meat all over. I glided over the tipi. Then I went down feet first and lighted on the ground. As I was going down to the center of the hoop I could see a tree in full bloom with flowers on it. I could see two men coming toward me. They were dressed with ghost shirts like I was dressed. They came and said to me: "It is not yet time to see your Father, but we shall present to you something that you will carry home to your people and with this they shall come forth to see their loved ones." I could see fat horses all over and the wild animals ranging out over the country and hunters were returning with their meat. I was very happy to see that and I'm hungry for some of that meat right now. They told me to return at once and I was out in the air again and I glided the same as before back.

When I got right above the dance place, they were still dancing the ghost dance. I hoped to see that tree blooming [*but the day following it was not blooming*] and it was just seemingly faded. I went down to my body then and I could hear the voices. Then I got up from my vision. Whenever a man comes to, they ask you what you have seen. So most of the people came over there to see what I had dreamed. I told them the exact vision I had had. What I brought back was the memory of what they had shown me and I was to make an exact copy of it. This ghost shirt was to be used always in the ghost dances. So I started the ghost shirt.[9]

That evening we got together at Big Road's tipi; the chief dancers came. They decided there to use my ghost shirts. So the next day I made ghost shirts all day and they had to be painted by me. The first two shirts I made were made according to the Messiah vision. In this vision I saw everything old-fashioned and the only things that spoke to me were the two men in the vision and I was told to take the way they were dressed home to my people. So when I came back to earth I made these shirts accordingly. When I saw the tree in the vision it was in full bloom, but when I came back the tree was wilted and dead. If this world would only do as it is told by this vision, the tree would bloom. I made the first two shirts according to what I saw in the vision. The first one I made was for Afraid of Hawk. I made another one for the son of Big Road. I got a stick to resemble the one I had seen in my vision and painted it red with the sacred paint of the Messiah. I put one spotted eagle feather on top of the stick. I worked all day making shirts. I spent the evening making the sacred stick. I wanted all the people to know the facts of this vision.

I decided to go to the dance. Every time we danced Kicking Bear and Good Thunder were on either side of me. As we proceeded to the place where we were to dance, we stood in a straight line facing the west. I was to perform the ceremony. They all looked forward for me to take part, because they all knew I had had a better vision than they had. We began to pray: "Father, behold me! The nation that you have and the nation that I have, they are in difficulty. The new earth you promised, I want my nation to behold it!" After the prayer we stood with out right hands raised to the west and we all began to weep. Right there as they cried some of them fainted before they had danced. They all began to pant and fall down before they had danced. The ones who did not faint got into a circle and started to dance. We sang this song:

> Over here they have said, over here they have said.
> Father, in tears I have said. The Wasichu have said.

9. A reservation schoolteacher, Mrs. Z. A. Parker, wrote an excellent description of a ghost dance she had witnessed on White Clay Creek in October 1890. She was told that the ghost shirts, which she understood that the Indians were wearing for the first time, had been seen in a vision by a woman, the wife of Return from Scout. See Mooney, *The Ghost-Dance Religion,* pp. 916–17. It seems likely that several of the ghost dancers had had visions relating to sacred regalia for the ceremony.

As we danced around I felt the same feeling that I had before—as though I had my feet off the earth and was swinging. I just hung on to the men, for I was in fear. They let go and again I glided forth. The same thing happened; I ascended into the air again and there was a spotted eagle in front of my eyes and I could hear the shrill whistle and scream of the eagle. I was gliding again prone through the air with my arms out. I was right on a ridge again and as I neared it I could hear strange noises, [a] rumbling sound. Right below that ridge there was flame coming up. As it began to flame up, I glided right over it. I glided over the fifth circle village and glided over the sixth circle village. I landed on the south side of this sixth village.

As I landed there, I saw twelve men coming toward me and they stood before me and said: "Our Father, the two-legged chief, you shall see." Then I went to the center of the circle with these men and there again I saw the tree in full bloom. Against the tree I saw a man standing with outstretched arms. As we stood close to him these twelve men said: "Behold him!" The man with outstretched arms looked at me and I didn't know whether he was a white or an Indian. He did not resemble Christ. He looked like an Indian, but I was not sure of it. He had long hair which was hanging down loose. On the left side of his head was an eagle feather. His body was painted red. (At that time I had never had anything to do with white men's religion and I had never seen any picture of Christ.[10])

This man said to me: "My life is such that all earthly beings that grow belong to me. My Father has said this. You must say this." I stood there gazing at him and tried to recognize him. I could not make him out. He was a nice-looking man. As I looked at him, his body began to transform. His body changed into all colors and it was very beautiful. All around him there was light. Then he disappeared all at once. It seemed as though there were wounds in the palms of his hands.

Then those twelve men said to me: "Turn around and behold your nation, your nation's life is such." The day was beautiful—the heavens were all yellow and the earth was green. You could see the greenward of the earth [the plains]. The men that I saw were all beautiful and it seemed

10. This statement is not strictly true, in that Black Elk was clearly familiar with Christianity while he was in Europe. He probably meant to indicate that at this time he had not yet accepted it. Later, however, Black Elk commented to Neihardt (p. 266) that he thought he had truly seen the son of the Great Spirit in this vision; the account he gives here rings of the imagery of the Transfiguration.

there were no old men in there. They were all young. There were no children either, all were about the same age. Then twelve women came and stood in front of me. They said: "Behold them, your nation's life is such. Their ways of life you shall take back to the earth." The women were dressed beautifully with ornaments of all kinds. As they finished speaking to me I heard singing in the west (where the sun goes down). When I heard this song I learned it. I prepared myself to come back and before I started the twelve men took two sticks and pounded them into the ground and they said: "Take these, you shall depend upon them." One of the sticks was painted white and the other was painted red. They were about a yard high.

Then these men said: "Make haste!" As I advanced it seemed as though the wind went under me and picked me up. I could see plenty of meat there—buffalo all over. I was hungry and they should have fed me then. The wind went under me and took me up there. I was up in the air then with outstretched hands. I had to go over a big river now and the village in circles was on the other side of the river. This was a very fearful, dark river, rushing with foam in it. On this side nobody was living. As I looked down there were men and women. They were trying to cross this river, but they couldn't do it so they were crying about it. They looked up to me and said: "Help us!" I came on and glided over them. Of course when I came over the river I heard the strange rustling and rumbling sounds and the flames also, but I just glided over them. I saw my people again and I just figured that I had brought something good for them. When I came down I came back to my body again. This was the vision I had. All the people there were eager to hear of what I had to say and they all gathered around me. Lots of these people are still alive. These visions that I have told to the people they still remember.

At this time there was quite a great famine among the people and some of them really believed in this Messiah business and were hoping that this land of promise would come soon so that they would be through with the poverty. Many of them wanted to know more about this. I told my vision through songs. As I sang one song, there were older men [*than I*] there to tell what they meant to the others. Before I told this everyone took out his pipe filled with kinnikinnick to make offer[ing]s to the sacred man that I had seen. Then I told my vision in song and I sang this song three times. I sang a song the words of which were the same as the one the man on [beside] the tree had said, and the melody of it was that which I heard above the sixth village in my vision. [*I sang this song three times and*] the fourth time I sang it the people all began to cry, because the white man had taken our world from us and we were like prisoners of war.

I went to the sixth village in the vision because in the flaming rainbow of the first vision I had seen six grandfathers. The sixth one was myself. And this was to represent six grandfathers—the powers that the earth got from these six powers. I saw two men first in the vision and now I saw two men in the Messiah vision also. Here on earth I had six children; three have died. In my first vision I had seen twelve riders and again I saw twelve men in this vision. It represents the twelve moons in the year. This village might represent six generations from the first and perhaps in the sixth generation the tree will bloom as in my vision.

At this time I think my nephew, Mr. Neihardt, would have cried too, because they had nothing—they were starving and had no guns. They had this hard time because the whites were killing off all their relatives-like [the game animals]. Just to look at the people would make anyone lonesome. Some of them just fell over as they were lean and poor and all this because of the white man's treachery. Everyone who was there when they heard the translation of the song, everyone cried. I realize now that I had prophesied. The Big Foot massacre occurred and I saw them wailing. They were shedding tears for the old ways and old religion. When the people had this they were never feeling bad. They were always happy. Through the four-leggeds, Indians reared their children.

I noticed how the twelve men in the vision were dressed and I made six sacred shirts according to what these twelve men wore. I took six copies of the fashion of the twelve women that I'd seen in my vision. The Brulés were camped here too. We invited them over. I made six more of these outfits for the Brulés after making them for the Oglalas. The Brulés were camping at this time at Cutmeat Creek.

At this time every once in a while I would get dizzy as a result of this vision. Every time I danced I never fainted again, but the dizziness would affect me. I would think I was going to but I did not. Later I had a vision again, but not much. The last vision I had was in a ghost dance again. I was back here again. The only thing I saw was toward the west I saw a flaming rainbow that I had seen in the first vision. On either side of this rainbow was a cloud and right above me there was an eagle soaring, and he said to me: "Behold them, the Thunder-being nation, you are relative-like to them. Hence, remember this." During the war I was supposed to use this rainbow and the Thunder-beings but I did not do it. I only depended on the two sticks that I had gotten from the vision. I used the red stick.

It seems to me on thinking it over that I have seen the son of the Great Spirit himself. All through this I depended on my Messiah vision whereas perhaps I should have depended on my first great vision which had more power and this might have been where I made my great mistake.

(Black Elk was considered the chief ghost dancer. [One] might hear that Black Elk had made [created] it, but he did not, only he had so much power that he became the most important ghost dancer.)

I was the leader in every dance. Soon I had developed so much power that even if I would stand in the center of the circle and wave this red stick, the people would fall into swoons without dancing and see their visions. The Brulés had wanted me to come because they thought they might get some power from me. I took a special trip over there for this purpose. I made six shirts and six dresses for them. I was over there four days and we were dancing every day. I told the Brulés what I had seen in my vision of the Promised Land. I told them everything that I had told the Oglalas. In the center was the sacred tree and on either side were the six dressed in sacred clothes. Everyone raised their right hand toward the west and I recited that prayer and waved the sacred [*red*] stick. Then they all began to cry and some of them began to have their visions before the beginning of the dance even. After the dance I stood right in the middle by the tree and talked to the people making this speech concerning the Messiah (Wanekia [*Wanikiya*] — "Make Live"), son of the Great Spirit. In olden times way back the sacred men would make an offering to the Great Spirit saying: "Great Spirit, our grandfather, mercy may you have on us and make us live."[11]

TROUBLE WITH THE SOLDIERS

I returned from the Brulés to the Oglalas with lots of things to bring home with me. Before I left I heard that there were soldiers here at Pine Ridge

11. Although published histories make no mention of Black Elk's participation in the ghost dance, it is interesting to note the great similarity of the images Black Elk used to speak of the ghost dance and those used by Short Bull, the Brulé ghost dance leader. See Mooney, *The Ghost-Dance Religion*, pp. 788–89.

already.[12] When I left, the Brulés all followed me. It seemed that I just drew them along with me. I knew that they were depending on me, so they just followed me.[13] Still my people were dancing right below Manderson on the Wounded Knee [Creek]. There was a big camp here. Next morning it was reported that the soldiers were coming over here, so we broke camp and started west across the country to Grass Creek. We broke camp there and moved from here to White Clay [Creek] where we set up camp. Over at Medicine Root Creek the largest part of the Brulés were camping. Some chiefs came over from Pine Ridge to White Clay Creek north of Pine Ridge— Fire Thunder, Little Wound[14] and Young American Horse. These men brought a message in behalf of the soldiers that this matter of the ghost dance should be looked into, that there should be rulings over it, but they did not mean to take the dance away from us. We moved camp from White Clay Creek and we moved nearer to Pine Ridge and camped here. We had a meeting over this ghost dance, but I did not attend it. I knew that Good Thunder and Kicking Bear were at the meeting. There were many soldiers there now. We were dancing nearly every day and I heard that this is what the agent said to the people. He had made a ruling that we should dance three days every month and during the rest of the time we should go out and make a living of some kind for ourselves. This was all he said to them.[15]

When these men brought the news back, we were all satisfied with it and we agreed to do it. While I was sitting in a tipi with Good Thunder a

---

12. Troops commanded by Gen. John R. Brooke began to arrive at Pine Ridge on November 19, 1890 (Mooney, *The Ghost-Dance Religion*, p. 850).

13. Short Bull led the Brulé ghost dancers to Pine Ridge, evidently around the beginning of October 1890. In a talk recorded by a newspaper reporter, he told his followers that the sacred tree was sprouting at Pass Creek, on Pine Ridge Reservation, and that they should go there to dance and meet their dead relations who were returning with the millennium. See Mooney, *The Ghost-Dance Religion*, pp. 788, 849.

14. Following an error in the typewritten transcript of the stenographic record, *Black Elk Speaks*, p. 254, has "Red Wound."

15. The stenographic record adds: "(McLaughlin)." But the Pine Ridge Indian agent at this time was D. F. Royer; James McLaughlin was agent at Standing Rock. On November 8, 1890, Royer called a council of the chiefs in a vain attempt to convince them to give up the ghost dancing, which had been officially banned by the Office of Indian Affairs. See Olson, *Red Cloud and the Sioux Problem*, p. 325. Historical records make no mention of a promise to allow the Oglalas to perform the ghost dance three days a month.

policeman came over from Pine Ridge. He said: "I was not ordered to come, but I came over anyway just for an errand for the good of you and Good Thunder." He said, "I have heard that you two will be arrested and also Kicking Bear."[16] Of course I did not want to flee and I was going to take it as it came. If it was the will of the Great Spirit it was all right with me. The Brulés were coming and Good Thunder suggested that we go out and meet them. So we saddled up that evening and started out. We came through White Horse Creek and followed it down to the mouth of [that is, at] Wounded Knee [Creek]. We followed this creek down about six miles below Manderson. There was a big camp of Brulés here.

Early in the morning the crier announced that we would have a meeting with the Brulés. When the people got together this is what I told them: "My relatives, there is a certain thing that we have done. From that certain sacred thing we have done, we have had visions. In our visions we have seen and we have also heard that our relatives that have gone before us are actually in the Promised Land and that we are also going there. They are with the Wanekia. So therefore the Wasichu if they want to, they may fight us, and if they fight us, if we are going to we will win; so have in your minds a strong desire and take courage. We must depend upon the departed ones who are in the Promised Land that is coming and who are with the Wanekia. We should remember this. Because in the first place our grandfather has set the two-leggeds on earth with the power of where the sun goes down" (meaning that the two-leggeds have the Thunder-beings' power).

Some more Brulés came over soon after this time from the Porcupine and Medicine Root Creeks. From Wounded Knee camp we followed the Wounded Knee down toward White River. That same evening of the day that I had talked, my mother was over there at the camp. We moved camp again to Red Hawk's place. When we camped here, some of the Oglalas

16. Agent Royer, in a letter to the Acting Commissioner of Indian Affairs, November 25, 1890, recommended that the leaders of the ghost dance be arrested and confined for a time in a prison off the reservation. He listed the names of sixty-six men on Pine Ridge who were "considered by the [Indian] police the prime leaders." Kicking Bear is number one on the list, Good Thunder is number sixty-four, and Black Elk is number sixty-five (Letters Received by the Commissioner of Indian Affairs, Ghost Dance Special Case 188, Doc. No. 1890–37076, Record Group 75, National Archives and Records Service).

turned back. A Black Robe [*Catholic*] priest came here and some of them turned back with him. Later this priest was stabbed at the Big Foot massacre.[17] From here we moved camp to a place called High Pocket's place southwest of Cuny Table in the Badlands. (Cuny Table is called by the Sioux the Top of the Badlands.) Then again some chiefs came from Pine Ridge with many people.[18]

American Horse and Fast Thunder came over to where I was and asked me to put this ghost dance aside quietly (in other words, stop it). Just then Kicking Bear and Good Thunder and Big Road came in. I knew there was trouble now, so I consented to do this. Then we moved camp, as the chiefs had come after us. The Brulés interfered and kept us from moving, as they did not want us to go. The soldiers band [*akicita*] of the Brulés tried to stop us and we tried to go anyway and they hit many of us. We had quite a little struggle here and Good Thunder, Kicking Bear and others were trying to quiet them down. Somehow they induced Kicking Bear to go back to the Brulés, although he was going to go with us. Then we left them peaceably. Then we camped on White River. We started and moved north of Oglala to White Clay Creek.[19] Some of the Brulés went with some of the Oglalas, but more of them stayed in the camp at Cuny Table. Later, the Brulés and Oglalas who stayed back went to the Onagazhee [*onajince*], "Place of Shelter," on top of the Badlands.[20]

THE WOUNDED KNEE MASSACRE

We moved camp to the Cheyenne River north of Pine Ridge. Most of the Oglalas were camping around Pine Ridge. I was out looking for horses

17. Bundled in an army cap and overcoat, Father Francis M. J. Craft was mistaken for a soldier and stabbed by an Indian during the Wounded Knee fight. See Mooney, *The Ghost-Dance Religion*, p. 872, and Utley, *The Last Days of the Sioux Nation*, p. 215.

18. The Indians began to gather in the badlands in late November 1890 as troops arrived at Pine Ridge (Mooney, *The Ghost-Dance Religion*, p. 850).

19. On December 18 some one thousand Indians under Two Strike and Crow Dog left the badlands for Pine Ridge and went to the agency. By December 29 Kicking Bear and Short Bull's people were also moving toward the agency. No Indians were left in the badlands. See Mooney, *The Ghost-Dance Religion*, pp. 861, 867–68.

20. Known in English as the stronghold, this was a natural fortress on the northeastern edge of Cuny Table. See Utley, *The Last Days of the Sioux Nation*, p. 122.

and when I returned I learned that two policemen had come after me to be on their side as a scout.[21] Two days later I learned that the soldiers were marching toward Wounded Knee. This was in the Month of the Popping Trees—December. I heard that Big Foot was coming from a young man who had come there.[22] Rough Feather I heard was going to get Big Foot, who was coming from his camp near the mouth of Medicine Root Creek on White River. At that time there were some soldiers camping somewhere around there on the other side of the river. Rough Feather went over there in order to get Big Foot. He wanted them to come in a southeasterly direction, but they did not do it. They wanted to follow up Medicine Root. They followed it to the head and then scouts for the soldiers saw them here at the head of Medicine Root. The scouts represented this to the soldiers and from here it was represented to Pine Ridge. On this same evening the soldiers went toward where Big Foot was camped at the head of Medicine Root. Big Foot's camp came to the creek of Porcupine Butte where the soldiers met them and they nearly had a fight here. The soldiers brought Big Foot back to Wounded Knee.[23] That evening the soldiers gathered around where they had camped. The soldiers had them well guarded all night.

It was December 29, 1890, the next morning. They carried Big Foot over to the officers, for he was sick. They told the rest of Big Foot's people to bring their guns over there. Everyone stacked their guns and even their knives up in the office [at the officers' headquarters]. The soldiers were searching all the tipis for weapons. There were two men near Big Foot's tipi who wore blankets made out of white sheets, with just their eyes showing. Some of them had probably hidden their knives. The officer who was taking the guns from them went up to these men and pulled their

21. Although Black Elk himself apparently never joined the Indian scouts, another Oglala with the same name—probably Black Elk's brother—did enlist as a scout. A photograph of this man, in uniform, is in the Nebraska State Historical Society, Lincoln.

22. Big Foot and his band of some three hundred Minneconjous had fled from the Cheyenne River Reservation on December 23. They were alarmed by the news of Sitting Bull's death on Standing Rock Reservation, December 15, and feared the soldiers on their own reservation. See Mooney, *The Ghost-Dance Religion*, p. 865.

23. Big Foot surrendered to Major Samuel M. Whitside on December 28, and together the Indians and soldiers camped for the night on Wounded Knee Creek, twenty miles northeast of Pine Ridge agency (Mooney, *The Ghost-Dance Religion*, p. 867).

white blankets apart and one of them had his gun concealed inside the sheet. He proceeded to the other one and opened it and just as he was going to get his gun, this man shot him. This man's name was Yellow Bird. This fellow did not want to give up his gun, and did not intend to shoot the white man at all—the gun just went off. Of course the soldiers were all around there already with their [wagon] guns on the hill north, across the flat east, and across the creek. The Indian scouts were behind the soldiers on the south. Yellow Bird and the white officer were wrestling with this gun and they had rolled down together on the ground and were wrestling with it. Dog Chief was right there where they took the guns and was standing right by these men while wrestling. This man was a friend of mine and he saw the whole thing.

Big Foot was the first Indian that was killed by an officer before the [wagon] guns began [to shoot]. They had carried Big Foot over to where the guns were being given up and immediately after the shot of Yellow Bird the officer shot Big Foot. Yellow Bird went into a tipi nearby and killed lots of them probably before he died. The Indians all ran to the stacks of guns and got their guns during a lull while the soldiers were loading again. A soldier ran up to tear the tipi away to get at Yellow Bird, but the latter shot at them as they came up and killed them. They fired at the tipi and the soldiers' guns set it afire and he died in there.[24]

The night before this I was over in the camp at Pine Ridge and I couldn't sleep. When I saw the soldiers going out it seemed that I knew there would be trouble. I was walking around all night until daylight. After my meal early that morning I got my horse and while I was out I heard shooting over to the east—I heard wagon guns going off.[25] This was a little distance from the camp and when I heard this gun I felt it right in my body, so I went out and drove the horses back to the camp for I knew there was trouble. Just as I got back with the horses there was a man who returned from Pine Ridge and had come back because he had heard

24. For other Indian eyewitness accounts of the Wounded Knee massacre see Beard in Walker, *Lakota Society*, pp. 157–68; James H. McGregor, *The Wounded Knee Massacre from Viewpoint of the Sioux* (Baltimore: Wirth Brothers, 1940); and Donald F. Danker, ed., "The Wounded Knee Interviews of Eli S. Ricker," *Nebraska History* 62 (2) (Summer 1981): 151–243.

25. The troops had four Hotchkiss machine guns, which they used against the Lakotas at Wounded Knee. See Utley, *The Last Days of the Sioux Nation*, pp. 201–202, 215–16, and Mooney, *The Ghost-Dance Religion*, p. 868.

this. He said: "Hey, hey son, the people that are coming are fired upon, I know it."

I took my buckskin and saddled up. I had no gun. The only thing I had was the sacred red stick. I put on my sacred shirt. This was a shirt I had made to be worn by no one but myself, which had a spotted eagle outstretched on the back of it, a star on the left shoulder, the rainbow diagonally across the breast from the left shoulder downward toward the hip. I made another rainbow around the neck, like a necklace with a star at the bottom. At the shoulder, elbows, and wrists were eagle feathers. And over the whole shirt I had red streaks of lightning. This was a bullet-proof shirt. I painted my face red. I had another eagle feather thrust through my hair at the top of my head. Of course I was going out by myself, and I could see that there were some young men following me. The first two men who followed me were Loves War and Iron White Man. I asked them where they were going and they said they were just going over to see where the firing was. I told them that I was going there to fight for my people's rights and if they wanted to, they could come along. So they went with me and about this time some more older men came.

I just thought it over and I thought I should not fight. I doubted about this Messiah business and therefore it seemed that I should not fight for it, but anyway I was going because I had already decided to. If [I] turned back the people would think it funny, so I just decided to go anyway. There were now over twenty of us going. As we neared there was a horseback coming toward us. He said: "Hey, hey, hey, they have murdered them!" Just then right before us I could see a troop of soldiers coming down a canyon. They stopped their horses and asked me what to do, so we decided we'd first see what we could do and then we'd do it. We started out and at the head of the gulch we went along the creek and got on top of the hill at the head of the gulch now called Battle Creek.

In the morning when the battle started, I could hear the shooting from Pine Ridge.[26] With about twenty other young men, I started out to

26. The following section of the stenographic notes was recorded while Black Elk took Neihardt around the Wounded Knee battlefield, pointing out various locations. The monument referred to marks the common grave of the Lakotas killed at Wounded Knee; situated on the hill overlooking the battlefield, it was erected in 1902 by Joseph Horn Cloud, a survivor of the massacre.

defend my people. When we got on the hill at the head of the draw about two and one-half miles west of the monument, we could see some Indians being captured by two small troops of soldiers. This was at the head of the draw. I could hear the cannons and rifles going off down there and I could see soldiers all over the hills on each side of the draw. I then depended on my Messiah vision. As we faced them we sang a sacred song which went like this:

> A Thunder-being nation I am I have said. (twice)
> You shall live. (four times)

Then I said to the men whom I had led here: "Take courage, these are our relatives. We shall try to take the captives back. Furthermore, our women and children are lying dead. Think about this and take courage."

I had good eyes at this time and I could see cavalrymen scattered all over the hills. After I had said this to my young men I proceeded down on horseback and they followed me. Right by the yellow pine in the head of the gulch there was an Indian wounded through the legs by the name of Little Finger. Another man was following me, Iron White Man, and we put this wounded man behind [him on] his horse. At the very end of the gulch this wounded fellow fell off. Then another Indian came along and we asked him to take him over to a safe place. We took him across the hills northwest to safety. At the head of the gulch I saw a baby all alone. It was adopted by my wife's father. Its name was Blue Whirlwind. I was going to pick her up but I left her for she was in a safe place.

We started north toward where the horses are and we stopped right this side of the horses. We started out straight north under the first white clay spot a little ways up the hill. To the north was a troop of cavalry and about one hundred yards to the east was another troop of soldiers (by the pine trees). Two of my men went to where the captives were and there was another Indian riding a black horse standing right this side of the captives. Just as the two men got to where the soldiers were and got to where the black horse rider was standing, the farthest troop over there fired on us first and shot right across the draw as we retreated. Then after a little bit the main body of the men said: "Take courage, it is time to fight!" As the cavalrymen fired, the horses stampeded across the hills here.

Then the body of Indians charged down this draw toward the captives. I could feel the bullets hitting me but I was bullet proof. I had to hang on to my horse to keep the bullets from knocking me off. I had the sacred bow with me and all I had to do was to hold the bow toward the soldiers and you should have seen the soldiers run! They saw they couldn't hit me so they ran eastward toward the monument. The other boys were not bullet-proof so they had to get behind the hill back there. I was alone. Every time I pointed the bow at the soldiers they couldn't run fast. If I had had a gun I could have killed a lot of them. When they got over the hill they peeped out ready to shoot. Just as I got up to them about twenty yards away, they shot at me and missed me. The soldiers on the other side came down the creek and lay down ready to shoot and they pumped away at me but they didn't hurt me. I proceeded back to where my men were. I had to hold my bow in front of me in the air to be bullet-proof but just as I had gotten over the hill after completing my charge, I let my bow down and I could feel some bullets passing through my ghost dance shirt near my hip. You could see the marks of the bullets on the shirt. I got shot but not much. I could only feel a bullet graze my body, was all. Then I made another charge, as the soldiers had crept over by this time. (After I had made the charge the other young men came and got the captives while I had the soldiers chased away.) Then as I charged again you could hear the bullets whizzing by me.

In this draw there was another Indian. Then right in here I was surprised to see two boys about fifteen years old who had repeaters and who had evidently done quite a lot of damage. They killed lots of soldiers lying around. These two boys followed after the soldiers and had lots of ammunition. After this we made the soldiers retreat. As I charged they all fell back and they all gathered together in a little bunch over the hill there. These two boys were the bravest of all of us, for they were not bullet-proof but they did not get a scratch—they were lucky. One of my men was shot and two got wounded—one broke his leg and the other broke his arm. They retreated so fast that we just pulled up and went along after them. The battle started at about ten o'clock and we fought all day here. We went back to Pine Ridge just after dark. It was about fifteen miles by the old road. When the soldiers gathered on the hill they began to go back on that ridge over there. After the soldiers did their dirty work over there they began to march up Wounded Knee. The soldiers wanted to fight yet, but we did not care so much about charging at them. I wanted to see the place where Big Foot and his people got killed and as I followed down the draw I could see men and women lying dead all along there. Soldiers and Indians afterwards were here and there. [*Then as I got nearer there were more of them lying there.*] Right at the beginning of the draw there were many Indians and there were more soldiers further down.

This was a good day—the sun was shining. In the evening it began to snow. It was a very bad snow. The day was cold even though it was sunny. That night the snow covered us and we all died from the cold. As I went down toward the village, I could see children dying all over—it was just a sight. I did not get as far as Big Foot's body though. Somehow I did not feel sorry about these women and children. There was a time that I did not use my first vision, but I used the power of the vision about the Messiah. I was not sorry, I was not feeling bad about it, but I thought there will be a day. I was not sorry about the women and children because I was figuring on dying and then I would join them somewhere. I just thought I would probably die before this thing was over and I just figured that there would be a day when I could either take revenge or die. I did not recall the vision that I should have recalled at this time.

There was a big stronghold between Manderson and Oglala where all the people gathered and after I gathered them there, I recalled the first vision and therefore I gathered them here and then I prayed and sent voices to the spirits above and I said:

Yeah hey! (four times)
Grandfathers, behold me and send me a power for revenge.

(While fighting here the women were in the stronghold.) Just as I said that (it was a clear day with no clouds; January—snow on the ground), in the west there appeared clouds and there was a thunderstorm in the winter. After this the people all depended on me. The people and chiefs got together and made me commander of all the Sioux there in the stronghold. When they made me commander, I made some sacred herbs. They brought all their guns to me and had me make them holy. When I got through blessing the guns, the next day there was a treaty and there was peace. Chief [Young Man] Afraid Of His Horses came back from the agency and said there was peace. He was the big chief then and next was Red Cloud.

(At this time I had no children and maybe if I had been killed then I would have been better off.)

BLACK ELK IS WOUNDED

After the battle [December 29, 1890] we went back on the north side of Pine Ridge [agency] where the hospital now is and as we were standing here the soldiers at Pine Ridge shot at us. We went back because we thought there was peace back home. The Indians fled from our camp at Pine Ridge and there was no one at home. The camp we left in the morning had been deserted. We were pretty hungry so we peeked in from tipi to tipi and we saw something cooked to eat, and so we had something real to eat. This was Red Crow and myself alone. As we were feasting there about three feet apart we heard some shots and just then the bullet went right between us and threw dust over our plates. We kept on eating anyway and had our fill and we got on our horses and went the way the people had fled. Probably if I had been killed there I would have had papa [dried meat] in my mouth.

The people fled downstream (White Clay) and we followed them down. It was now dark. We followed them up all night and finally we found their camp below the stream which is east of Oglala.[27] The people had no tipis, they were just sitting by their fires. They had fled without their tipis. I went among them and I heard my mother singing a death song for me. I followed the voice and found her in a little log house which they had found and moved into. Mother was very glad to see me, as she thought I had died over there. Of course, I did not sleep the night before and I had fought all day and then there was a war party that went out, but I did not go as I was very tired and wanted to sleep that night. Some of the Brulés and Oglalas were gathered here now.

I got up at daybreak the next morning. This morning more war parties went out to Pine Ridge to fight. A man by the name of He Crow and I went east of the White Clay Creek staying as far from it as possible, because we could see all over the country from here and we could see just where the trouble was all the time. This war party had met the soldiers

27. As the sound of the firing of the Hotchkiss guns at Wounded Knee was heard at Pine Ridge, the Indians began to flee toward the northwest, down White Clay Creek, where they met Short Bull and Kicking Bear's people, who had been on the way to the agency. They joined together—a total of some four thousand people—and established their camp near the site of No Water's village, fifteen miles north of the agency. See Utley, *The Last Days of the Sioux Nation*, p. 251, and Mooney, *The Ghost-Dance Religion*, p. 873. Evidently part of this large camp fled the next day to the stronghold.

right where the [Holy Rosary] Mission is today and we could hear the cannon go off here.[28] We proceeded toward this. We went to the White Clay Creek and crossed it, following the creek up on the west side and we could now hear the gunshots plainly. We then proceeded west following the ridge to where the fight was going on. Right from the ridge we could see that the Indians were on either side of the creek and were pumping at the soldiers who were coming down the creek between the Indians. As we looked down we saw a little ravine and across this was a big hill and we went down the ravine and got on the big hill. The men were fighting right here. They sent a voice to me saying: "Black Elk, this day is the kind in which to do something great!" so I said, "How!" [Yes!] I got off my horse and started putting dirt all over myself. I had a rifle and I proceeded up the hill and right below here the soldiers were firing and they told me not to go up, that they were pretty good riflemen there. I got on up the hill anyway and I was in very close range of the enemy. Then I recalled my vision, the north where the geese were; then I outstretched my hands [*and my rifle*] and then made the goose sound. They pumped away at me from the creek then, but not a single bullet came near me—they couldn't hit me.

As I went back down the hill again I heard them say: "They are gone!" So I got on my horse and started down the north side of the hill and right there a buckskin rider went past me; his name was Protector. He went past me to look at them and just then they fired so he came back again. I did not expect them to be so close and I went up there right away and they were about one hundred yards from me and they began to shoot at me. I proceeded toward them anyway. If I had kept on I would not have gotten hit, probably; some of them started to flee toward the creek and I turned around and as I fled toward the hill I could hear the bullets hitting my clothes. Then something hit me on the belt on the right side. I reeled on my horse and rode on over the hill. I was riding my buckskin then. I should have kept on coming like that with my hands up. I was in fear and had forgotten my power. I had forgotten to make the goose sound there and to keep my hands up. I doubted my power right there and I should have gone right on imitating the goose with my power and I would have

28. The fight at Drexel Mission (Holy Rosary), about four miles north of Pine Ridge agency, occurred on December 30, 1890. See Utley, *The Last Days of the Sioux Nation,* pp. 237–40, and Mooney, *The Ghost-Dance Religion,* p. 875.

been bullet-proof. My doubt and my fear for the moment killed my power and during that moment I was shot.

Protector ran up to me and grabbed me for I was falling off my horse. I said: "Let me go, I'll go over there. It is a good day to die so I'll go over there." He said: "No, nephew." Protector tore his blanket up and wrapped it around my wound. This kept my insides from falling out. Then Protector told me to go home and said: "You must not die today, you must live, for the people depend upon you."

THE CAMP IN THE STRONGHOLD

The soldiers were now retreating and the Indians were fighting harder. The Mission was there then and there were lots of Indian children in there. The priests and sisters were all over there praying. That building now has many shots in it. A man by the name of Little Soldier brought me back to the camp near the stronghold. When I got back the people were on top of the stronghold. Old Hollow Horn was a bear medicine man and he came over to heal my wound. Of course he was a powerful medicine man and my wound began to heal and I was able to walk in about three days.

I heard that soldiers were coming now and I caught up my buckskin. My mother asked me not to go, but I went anyway. About sixty men of us started out on a warpath east. We heard that the soldiers from the battlefield were marching through Wounded Knee to White River and were coming to the stronghold. The soldiers were now at Black Feather's place. We Indians followed Little Grass Creek down and got on the west side of the river on a hill and saw the soldiers down on White River. We got off our horses and we saw some Indians coming on the other side on the north. The soldiers began to corral the wagons and were preparing themselves to fight. We proceeded down toward the Indians on the other side. They saw us and they fired on the soldiers because they took courage by seeing us coming. As we neared the Little Grass Creek, flowing into White River on the south side, right above was a little knoll. The soldiers [were] across the creek. As we looked over the bank of the creek we saw some soldiers' horses coming to the water with harnesses on. I said: "Fire at them and I will go and get the horses." The Indians fired at the soldiers and I got the soldiers' horses and drove them southward. Then they saw me and began to pump on me. I got back with five horses and they killed two of their own horses. There was a little gulch there and I got away with five of their horses. When I got out of bullet range with the horses I caught the best horse—a bay horse with a bald face. I turned mine loose and from there I drove the rest of them back.[29]

About this time there was a whole detachment of cavalry coming up the river. I knew there were a lot of them, so I hurried with the horses. Just then I met a man running on foot without a horse. The Indians on the north side had retreated up the river. About that time they had come up to where I was. This man on foot was Red Willow. His horse had played out. He said: "Cousin, I am on foot." So I caught him a roan horse with a halter on dragging a rope—a soldier's horse. About that time the soldiers were very near us and you could see the bullets coming and the dust kicking up. Then there was another man whose horse played out, so I caught him a brown horse and gave it to him. I was a Wanekia just then, saving these two men by giving them horses. There was hard fighting now since the cavalry came up. The soldiers had come around and stopped the men in front. The soldiers were not crack shots so several fellows got away. Two of the men got wounded but they got home alive even though they were badly wounded. One of them was Long Bear, but I don't remember the other one's name.

After we got into the badlands the soldiers let us go so we came back to the stronghold that night. The next morning I got up early and myself, One Side, Poor Buffalo, and Brave Heart, we all started out east again and we came to where Manderson is at present. When we were there we could see the soldiers coming up the creek toward Manderson. They were cavalrymen coming back after that fight. On either side of them there were scouts and we had gone on the other side of the hill on the west side of the store and hid there. I wanted to shoot, but the other three men didn't allow me to. I said: "Let's stay here and kill at least one." They said they would kill us if we did. We had quite an argument. So the three men led me away on my horse to stop me.

We came past this sacred butte [near Black Elk's home] up through this little cut and went over to Grass Creek. There were a lot of cattle there, so we butchered three of them and took the meat back to the stronghold on White Clay.[30] As we were on top the stronghold we could see Sioux

29. This was the attack on Capt. John B. Kerr's detachment on Little Grass Creek, January 3, 1891 (Mooney, *The Ghost-Dance Religion,* p. 882).

30. The Indians had captured the government beef herd, and they depended on it for food during the fighting (Mooney, *The Ghost-Dance Religion,* p. 881).

hiding along the rocks, guarding the stronghold all night. They were
guarding all around the camp. They asked us if the soldiers were coming
and we told them that everything was all right now. That day that we had
butchered there was a soldier lieutenant and some scouts that came over
there and they surrounded him and killed him.[31] We thought that the
scouts would probably report this and there would be a surprise attack so
we were on guard all night and did not sleep any.

The next day I went on the highest point and asked the people to
gather there. The announcer announced it and the crowd came. This day I
remembered my six grandfathers, although I had completely forgotten
my vision for a spell before this. I had some white paint with me, so I told
them to bring their weapons that I might make them sacred [*to do their
great damage*]. I put a little bit of white paint on every gun that they
brought and when that was done everyone stood facing the west, pointing their weapons toward the west.

Then I thus sent a voice: "Hey-a-a-a-a (four times). Grandfathers, the
six grandfathers that I thus will recall to you today, behold me! And also
to the four quarters of the earth and its powers. Thus you have said if an
enemy I should meet that I should recall you. This you have said to me.
Thus you have set me in the center of the earth and have said that my
people will be relative-like with the Thunder-beings. Today my people are
in despair, so, six grandfathers, help me."

About this time we could see a storm coming up (in January, in the
middle of winter), but the Thunder-beings appeared with lightning and
thunder. The people all raised their hands toward the Thunder-beings
and cried. The Thunder-beings followed the White Clay up and went
toward Pine Ridge.

We were well prepared now and were going out again for revenge.
Revenge is sweet. We got ready and just then [Young Man] Afraid of His
Horses came over to make peace with Red Cloud who was in our bunch
then. [General] Miles had told [Young Man] Afraid of His Horses to
come over and make peace.[32] We had gathered there at this time. Red

31. On January 7, 1891, Plenty Horses, an Oglala graduate of Carlisle Indian School,
killed Lt. Edward W. Casey, commander of a troop of Cheyenne Indian scouts. See
Mooney, *The Ghost-Dance Religion*, pp. 888–89; Utley, *The Last Days of the Sioux Nation*,
pp. 256–58; and Marquis, *A Warrior Who Fought Custer*, pp. 335–36.

32. Young Man Afraid of His Horses had been absent from Pine Ridge for two
months, visiting on the Crow reservation. General Miles, who commanded the cam-

Cloud got up and made this speech: "Boys, this is a hard winter. If it were in the summer we would keep on fighting; but, boys, we cannot go on fighting because winter is hard on us, so we should make peace and I'll see that nobody will be hurt."

After that meeting [Young Man] Afraid of His Horses wanted to talk to me, Good Thunder, Kicking Bear, and Short Bull. We went over to a tipi and [Young Man] Afraid of His Horses began to speak: "Relatives, if this were in summertime it would not be so hard. If this were [not] winter, my people at Pine Ridge would have joined you and we would have had to fight to a finish, and I don't want my and your people to make us kill each other among ourselves. I don't care how many the soldiers are, without the Indian scouts they cannot fight and the army will be helpless. So, relatives, if this were in the summer I would have joined you and had it to a finish. But this is winter and it is hard on our children especially, so let us go back and make peace."

THE END OF THE FIGHTING

We all agreed. I wanted revenge anyway. I knew that when those clouds had appeared the Thunder-beings had talked to me. I did not want to have peace, but the people insisted so we broke camp the next day and went down from the stronghold and camped several places and got to Pine Ridge where we camped on the northwest side. That day we were going to camp right in Pine Ridge. People gathered here—hundreds on horseback. Then Kicking Bear and High Hawk (Brulé) were among these young men who were going around among the young men. They came to me and made me stand at a certain place. They put another man by my side—his name was Lick His Lips. Another one was brought here named Red Willow and another man whom I do not know. These were supposed to be the great warriors and they told the people that we were commanders of the Indian army and we were to take the lead. The men on foot were first, then the horsebacks followed. Then the wagons followed the horsebacks. We had started toward the office at Pine Ridge. We were now

---

paign, sent word for him to return. He arrived back at Pine Ridge agency on January 8 and went out to talk to the Indians in the hostile camp. Red Cloud himself left the camp on January 7 and returned to the agency. See Utley, *The Last Days of the Sioux Nation*, pp. 258–59.

inside where the guards were and we could see soldiers all around. As we went down there, the soldiers that were coming stood in two bodies on either side of us and were ordered to present arms. We went right through the middle of them. There were many soldiers there. We went through Pine Ridge and went in front of the office; the officers saluted us. We went to a place on White Clay Creek and camped.[33] The next day we were supposed to make peace. We made a law that anyone who should make trouble in the fort [agency] should be arrested and tried and if found guilty he would be punished.

Two years later I was married.

33. The Indians from the hostile camp arrived at Pine Ridge on January 15, 1891, and surrendered the following day. They pitched their camp of 742 tipis along White Clay Creek, just west of the agency. See Mooney, *The Ghost-Dance Religion,* pp. 887–88.

[9]

Teaching Flaming Rainbow (1931)

The Indians were in camp and they had a meeting to send scouts out to kill buffalo. They were on top of a hill and as they looked to the north in the distance something was appearing. They were going on, but they wanted to find out what it was and they kept looking and finally it came closer; then they found out it was a woman. Then one of the men said, "That is a woman coming." One of them had bad thoughts of her and one of them said, "This is a sacred woman; throw all bad thoughts aside." She came up the hill where they were. She was very beautiful, her long hair hanging down, and she had on a beautiful buckskin coat. She put down what she was carrying and covered it up with sage. She knew what they had in their minds. She said, "Probably you do not know me, but if you want to do as you think, come." So the one said to the other, "That is what I told you, but you wouldn't listen to me." So the man went and just as he faced her there was a cloud that came and covered them. The beautiful woman walked out of the cloud and stood there. Then the cloud blew off and the man was nothing but a skeleton with worms eating on it. That is what happened to him for being bad.

She turned to the other one and said, "You shall go home and tell your nation that I am coming. Therefore in the center of your nation, they shall build a big tipi and there I will come." So this man left at once and he was very scared, for his friend was a skeleton. He told the tribe what had happened and they all got excited and right away they prepared a place for her to come. They built a tipi right in the center and she was now in it. She put what she was carrying facing the east. All the people gathered right there. She sang a song as she entered the tipi.

> With visible breath I am walking.
> A voice I am sending as I walk.
> In a sacred manner I am walking.
> With visible tracks I am walking
> In a sacred manner I am walking.

Then she presented the pipe to the chief. It was an ordinary pipe but there was a calf carved in one side and there were twelve eagle feathers tied on with a grass that never breaks. She said, "Behold this, for you shall multiply with this and a good nation you shall be. You shall get nothing but good from this pipe, so I want it to be in the hands of a good man, and the good shall have the privilege of seeing it, but the bad shall not have the privilege of seeing it." This pipe is still in the possession of the Sioux.[1] The first man who kept it was a man by the name of High Hollow Horn. The pipe is handed down from son to son. [*Pipe was filled with red willow bark.*][2]

She taught them to "keep spirits" and if a man's son dies, the father keeps a piece of his son's hair.[3] This woman was really a white buffalo. Thus the respect for the white buffalo. She told them that when there was no food they should offer this pipe to the Great Spirit. And they would

1. The stenographic record notes that the pipe was brought by the White Buffalo Woman "800 years ago way back east." The event is depicted in Battiste Good's Brulé winter count (Mallery, *Picture-Writing of the American Indians,* p. 290) and in the copy made by High Hawk (Curtis, *The North American Indian,* 3: 159). Mallery (p. 31) figured the date at about A.D. 900, but Curtis argues persuasively that the count should be interpreted to date this event at 1540. Other important recordings of the story of the gift of the pipe include Percy Phillips in George A. Dorsey, "Legend of the Teton Sioux Medicine Pipe," *Journal of American Folk-Lore* 19 (1906): 326–29; Lone Man in Densmore, *Teton Sioux Music,* pp. 63–67; Finger in Walker, *Lakota Belief and Ritual,* pp. 109–12, and Tyon pp. 148–50; and Black Elk in Brown, *The Sacred Pipe,* pp. 3–9.

2. The sacred pipe bundle is still in the keeping of the Sans Arc Lakotas. The bundle is rarely opened, but on one such occasion the contents were described and photographed. The bowl was found to be of smooth catlinite, lacking any signs of a carving of a buffalo calf. See Sidney J. Thomas, "A Sioux Medicine Bundle," *American Anthropologist* 43 (1941): 605–9, and John L. Smith, "A Short History of the Sacred Calf Pipe of the Teton Dakota," *South Dakota University Museum News* 28 (1967): 1–37.

3. For Black Elk's description of the spirit-keeping ritual see Brown, *The Sacred Pipe,* pp. 10–30.

know from this pipe when they were going to have trouble. The pipe gets long at certain times and this means hard times. When it gets short the times are good.[4] After she went back she sang another song. As she went out of the tipi everyone saw a white buffalo kicking up her hind legs and leaving in a hurry, snorting as she went.

Some hunters went out and got [killed] a buffalo and it was in the spring of the year when the calves are in the womb yet. They got the insides out and found a calf in it and cut the womb open and to their surprise it was a human in there. It looked more like an old woman. The hair was pure white. All the men gathered there and saw it. This actually happened about eighty years ago.[5] It was too long ago for any white man to have been here and so it was a real miracle.

(Black Elk thinks the Indian has been an animal changed into a human. He says, if Indians were animals, the fact that the white men are killing off animals [means that] perhaps when the wild animals are all gone the Indians will also be all gone.)

PRAYER TO GO WITH THE VISION

The Indians put everything aside and pray with body and soul.

Standing Bear talks. When I was twenty years old I heard this prayer. This prayer has been used before Black Elk was ever born. They call upon the Great Spirit (hold[ing] pipe with the stem toward the heavens). In the old history of our people there are seven tipis (seven stars—seven tipis)[6] and from this time these prayers have originated. We had this prayer from the seven tipis of our people from whence our wisdom comes (as far back

4. Some contemporary Lakotas reverse this interpretation and say that the pipe is now getting shorter, meaning that the Indians are becoming fewer. See Ernest L. Schusky, *The Forgotten Sioux: An Ethnohistory of the Lower Brule Reservation* (Chicago: Nelson-Hall, 1975), p. xiii.

5. This event is recorded on several winter counts. Lone Dog gives it for 1850–51 (Mallery, *Picture-Writing of the American Indians*, p. 282). See also W. P. Clark, *The Indian Sign Language* (Philadelphia: L. R. Hamersly, 1885), p. 88.

6. The Lakotas frequently speak of their nation as comprised of "seven council fires" (*oceti śakowin*). This conceptual organization by sevens is an alternative to Black Elk's organization by sixes. It can be argued that the two schemes have the same basis—the four directions plus the heavens and earth; the seventh is completed by considering the other six as one (in offering the pipe, e.g., the person making the offering draws toward himself the powers from the six directions, and he thus forms the center of the cosmic circle of the universe). Compare Black Elk's 1944 account, below, pp. 307, 313.

as we can remember). The first thing to do in making an offering is this: "A voice we will send to the Great Spirits."

The prayer

He he he hey (four times). Grandfather, the Great Spirit, you have been always, and before you no one has been. There is no other one to pray to but you. You, yourself, everything that you see, everything has been made by you. The star nations all over the universe you have finished. The four quarters of the earth you have finished. The day, and in that day everything you have made. On earth, everything you have done. Grandfather, Great Spirit, lean close to the earth so you may hear the voice I send. A nation we shall make; without difficulties we shall make it.

Toward where the sun goes down, behold me. The Thunder-beings, behold me.

Where the giant lives there is power with the buffalo, so I heard, behold me.

To where the sun shines continually with the elks, behold me.

To where you always face, a man with power, behold me.

Each time the pipe is pointed to the direction about which they are speaking.

To the depths of the heavens, so I heard, an eagle with power, behold me.

To mother earth, it is said (pointing with pipe) you are the only mother that has shown mercy to your children.

Now, the prayer to all these places. One must make a vow that he will make an offering to the Great Spirit and that he is going to talk to the Great Spirit through this hole in the pipe. Holds the pipe up and makes offering.

Behold me, the four quarters of the earth, relative-like I am. Give me power to see and the strength to walk the soft earth, relative-like I have been. Give me the eyes of power and the strength of knowledge so I may be like unto you. With your strength I may face the winds.[7] In facing the winds, may you behold me. May I have the power of the winds.

7. The winds symbolize life.

Oh Great Spirit, Great Spirit, my Grandfather, may my people
be likened unto the flowering stick. Your stick of sticks, tree of trees,
forest of forests, tree of trees of the earth, trees of all kinds of the
earth. Oh, flowering tree, here on earth trees are like unto you; your
trees of all kinds are like unto you, but yet they have chosen you. Oh
tree, you are mild, you are likened unto the one above. My nation
shall depend on you. My nation on you shall bloom.

The cottonwood is mild, and like other trees, it has beauty and it could
grow anywhere and bloom, even in the badlands. This tree is used for sun
dances, the sacred pole, and they use this form of prayer in these sun
dances.

When they get so far in the prayer, they burn sweetgrass, which has a
beautiful fragrance.

Offering
To the Great Spirit's day; to the center of that day I will
go and make an offering. (Songs at the offering:)

This I burn as an offering; behold it.
A sacred praise I will make. (Repeat this verse twice.)
The nation, may you behold it.

The path of the night moon will be my robe.
The day of the sun promised me a robe.[8]

Meaning that everything works in the daytime and that when it gets dark
it is like a robe coming down over the heavens in the path of the moon. At
night men lie down and in that robe of night most of the Indians get their
power.

Sun talking as it comes up.

With visible face I am appearing.
In a sacred manner I am appearing.
For the greening earth a pleasantness I make.
With a visible face I am appearing.
Your center of the nation's hoop a pleasantness I make.

8. The Lakotas use the single word *wi* to designate both moon and sun; they
differentiate between the two by referring to *hanhepi wi* (night moon) and *anpetu wi*
(day sun—here mistranslated as day of the sun).

With visible face I am appearing
Your earth on it the four-leggeds, I have made them walk.

With visible face I am appearing.
My day, I have made it sacred.

All over the earth faces of all living things are alike. Mother earth has
turned these faces out of the earth with tenderness. Oh Great Spirit, behold them, all these faces with children in their hands. Without
difficulty they shall walk facing the wind, walking on the good road
towards the day of quiet (winter). Great Spirit, mercy may you
have on us that without difficulty may we walk the good road. Great
Spirit, this is my prayer, hear me. The voice I have sent may be
unworthy; yet with earnestness I have sent the voice. With final
words once again I say, hear me. It is finished.

THE PIPE

[You] should smoke this pipe every morning, offering it to the six grandfathers of the west, asking them to guide you, and also to the north, south,
and east, and to the Great Spirit above and to mother earth.[9] Ask all these
powers to please guide you. Then smoke this pipe and it will help you.

THE INDIANS AND THE WHITE PEOPLE

At that time I was young, but I began to realize the facts that were going
on and sometimes I think about it.[10] The four-leggeds and the wings of
the air and the mother earth were supposed to be relative-like and all three
of us lived together on mother earth [*we all had a teamwork at that time*].
Because of living together like relatives, we were just doing fine. We
roamed the wild countries and in them there was plenty and we were
never in want. Of course at that time we did not know what money was
and we got along just fine. We would get out just a little ways to bring
home plenty of meat. At the same time we were outside in the fresh air,
because it was this way that the Great Spirit wanted us to live. He had also
given us a way of religion. According to the four quarters and the four-

9. Black Elk presented Neihardt with a pipe and these instructions for its use.
10. Black Elk recorded this section just before telling about his trip with Buffalo Bill.

legged animals—through them we send up our voices and get help from the Great Spirit. It was his intention at that time to put us together so that we would be relatives-like. We got powers from the four-leggeds and the wings of the air.

But from time to time the white man would come on us just like floods of water, covering every bit of land we had and probably someplace there is a little island where we were free to try to save our nation, but we couldn't do it. We were always leaving our lands and the flood devours the four-leggeds as they flee. When we get to the island the water is all around us and today I feel very sorry—I could just cry—to see my people in a muddy water, dirty with the bad acts of the white people.

Here we are today; also, our wild animals have fled to another little island. Our relatives-like with the four-leggeds will vanish first because where they are there is no feed. The water just closes in on us continually. All of our religion of the old times that the early Indians had was left behind them as they fled and the water covered the region. Now, when I look ahead, we are nothing but prisoners of war, but the Great Spirit has protected us so far, and this Great Spirit takes care of us.

We are here and have been here for many years and all this time we have never had any harm done to us by the Thunder-beings, but the white people have been wiped out in places. I figure that this is a punishment and I think there will be a great punishment for the whites in the future as a result of this. White men have a way of living and also we have our way of living and we had plenty before we had money and now it is hard for us to get money and live that way. But it is up to the Great Spirit to look upon the white man and they will be sorry and this great thing that happens might be just among themselves.

The whites think we have the power from the devil, but I'll say that they probably have that themselves. They have done this, but I have hopes in the future that it will be different altogether and it is because they have overpowered us that they went first and slaughtered all the relatives-like we had. From them we had our power and when we lost them we lost our power. Right today, they [the whites] get their power from the Thunder-beings [electricity] and we have no more power today that we can fall back on. They take everything we have just gradually until we won't have anything left.

The first thing an Indian learns is to love each other and that they should be relative-like to the four-leggeds. The next thing is telling the truth. Whatever they say, they stand by it. Here's where the Indians made their mistake. We should treat our fellowmen all alike—the Great Spirit made men all alike. Therefore, we made a mistake when we tried to get along with the whites. We tried to love them as we did ourselves. On account of this we are now in misery. They were men like us in all but color and therefore we wanted to like them and get along with them. Because we Indians were relatives to the four-leggeds, we wanted to get along with them. But now we see that the white race has done great wrong to the Indians.

A long time ago (about seventy years) there was an Indian medicine man, Drinks Water, a Lakota, who foretold in a vision that the four-leggeds were going back into the earth. And he said in the future all over the universe there shall be a spider's web woven all around the Sioux and then when it shall happen you shall live in gray houses (meaning these dirt-roof houses in which we are living now), but that will not be the way of your life and religion and so when this happens, alongside of those gray houses you shall starve to death. He said: "You people have made me regret, so I will go back to mother earth," and shortly afterward he died. The people believed in this forecast of Drinks Water. What he said we are now into. The Long Knives [Americans] have woven the gray blanket over us and we are now prisoners of war. Drinks Water had the ability to make everything nearly—[he] made sugar, tobacco, matches and other things just by his words alone. This is probably the only man who had the power direct from the Great Spirit and this is why he was so powerful.[11]

THE SACRED HOOP

You realize that in the sacred hoop we will multiply. You will notice that everything the Indian does is in a circle.[12] Everything that they do is the power from the sacred hoop, but you see today that this house is not in a circle. It is a square. It is not the way we should live. The Great Spirit

11. Drinks Water's Lakota name was probably *Wiyatke,* Drinking Cup, which Neihardt translated Wooden Cup in the 1944 interviews, when Black Elk told about this medicine man and his prophecies in more detail (see December 7). The stenographic transcript has: "You people have made me regular"; but "regret" seems a more plausible reading.

12. A good discussion of the symbol of the circle is given by Tyon in Walker, "The Sun Dance and Other Ceremonies of the Oglala Division of the Teton Dakota," p. 160.

assigned us a certain religion and etc. The power won't work in anything but circles. Everything is now too square. The sacred hoop is vanishing among the people. We get even tents that are square and live in them. Even the birds and their nests are round. You take the bird's eggs and put them in a square nest and the mother bird just won't stay there. We Indians are relative-like to the birds. Everything tries to be round—the world is round. We Indians have been put here [*to be*] like the wilds and we cooperate with them. Their eggs of generations are in the sacred hoop to hatch out. Now the white man has taken away our nest and put us in a box and here they ask us to hatch our children, but we cannot do it. We are vanishing in this box.

When we were living in our natural state, boys became men at twelve and thirteen years old because they were in a natural state. But now boys don't mature nearly as early as because they are in unnatural conditions.

ORIGIN OF THE NAMES OGLALA AND BRULÉ

Oglala. Two brothers eating together saying that each other are women because they couldn't do something.[13] One got up and threw dirt into the other's face. Then they called them "Oglala," because this means "throwing something on each other."

Brulé. There was a war party went out and built a fire and somehow or other he stumbled and fell into the fire and burned his thigh. [In Lakota the Brulés are called *Sicaŋġu,* Burned Thighs.]

MOON, SUN, AND STARS

Months of the year.
The Moon of Frost in the Tipi—January
The Moon of the Dark Red Calf—February
The Moon of the Snowblind—March
The Moon of Red Grass Appearing—April

13. Lakotas tell many different stories to explain the origins of their various tribal and band names, but most have no basis in historical fact. Many of these names are very old and function as nicknames to differentiate social units one from another, but as a classification the names do not reflect a single developed system of symbolic connotations.

The Moon When the Ponies Shed—May
The Moon of the Blooming Turnip, or,
    the Moon of Making Fat—June
The Moon of Red Cherries—July
The Moon of Black Cherries—August
The Moon of the Black Calf, or,
    the Moon When the Calf Grows Hair—September
The Moon of the Changing Seasons—October
The Moon of the Falling Leaves—November
The Moon of Popping Trees—December

Phases of the moon.
The appearing of the moon—new moon
The round moon—full moon
When the bitten moon is delayed
The time of the moon bitten off
The little left of the moon—nearly dark
    (most storms come at this time)
The time when the moon is dark

Weather. Sun dogs—sun making himself fires. In the wintertime the sun gets cold and makes them start fires. According to these phases the Indians know what type of storm is coming (blizzards, etc.)

Stars. The first star noticed is the morning star (daybreak star). In traveling by night they go by the seven stars (the big dipper—the man carrying). The star right west of the big dipper is "comes against" (coming toward the man carrier).

North star is called "sitting with the little one" (there used to be a little star beside it, but it is gone now, apparently).

Wagon travelers when asked about the distance say it is one camp, etc., from where they are to a certain place (by the stars). If you go horseback, they call it one bedding.

Traveling by night they go by the big dipper (man carrier). Handle is in the west in the evening and when they are going out they figure so much from the handle toward the south and they allow so much space. A long time ago a big chief got wounded and so someone carried him home and everyone went to meet him and that is why they called the one next "comes against."

All Indians know what the meanings of the stars are and they study these stars carefully.[14]

BUFFALO NAMES

Buffalo bull—ta tunka [*tatanka*]
Buffalo cow—pte
Fat cow—pte chepa [*pte cepa*]
Calf—pte zheela [*ptejincala*],
  "blonde calf"
Calves in the fall—hen sapa
  [*hin sapa*] [black hair]
Yearling bull—hebola [*hepola*],
  "horns swell"
Heifer (yearling)—pte hayuktala
  [*pte heyuktanla*], "horns begin to bend"
Two year old bull—heychoghaycha
  [*hehloǧeca*], "hollow horn"
Two year old cow—pte chikala
  [*pte cik'ala*] [small cow]
All three year old buffalo—
  heshlooshloodah [*he šlušluta*]
  [slippery horn]

MAKING THE TREE BLOOM

You have heard what I have said about my people. I had been appointed by my vision to be an intercessor of my people with the spirit powers and concerning that I had decided that sometime in the future I'd bring my people out of the black road into the red road. From my experience and from what I know, and in recalling the past from where I was at that time, I could see that it was next to impossible, but there was nothing like trying. Of course probably the spirit world will help me and I thought I'd

14. See further discussion of stars, p. 406.

just figure on a scheme to have the people be all as one and if I had done this probably we would have been as we were before.

At that time I could see that the hoop was broken and all scattered out and I thought, "I am going to try my best to get my people back into the hoop again." At this time, when I had these things in my mind, I was abroad with strange people. They were not like my people and I couldn't have any clearness of understanding and somehow I had in mind that I was in a strange country and a strange land and that it was not the place nor the habits or religion that the spirits had assigned me, but then I had often wished that someday I might see a day for [*me and*] my people. At that time the wilds were vanishing and it seemed the spirits altogether forgot me and I felt almost like a dead man going around—I was actually dead at this time, that's all. In my vision they had predicted that I was chosen to be intercessor for my people so it was up to me to do my utmost for my people and everything that I did not do for my people, it would be my fault—if my people should perish it seemed that it would be my fault. If I were in poverty my people would also be in poverty, and if I were helpless or died, my people would die also. But it was up to me to scheme a certain way for myself to prosper for the people. If I prosper, my people would also prosper.

I am just telling you this, Mr. Neihardt. You know how I felt and what I really wanted to do is for us to make that tree bloom. On this tree we shall prosper. Therefore my children and yours are relative-like and therefore we shall go back into the hoop and here we'll cooperate and stand as one. This is why I want to go to Harney Peak, because here I will send the voices to the six grandfathers. And you remember I saw many happy faces behind those six grandfathers and maybe it will be that Mr. Neihardt['s] and my family will be the happy faces. Our families will multiply and prosper after we get this tree to blooming.

CEREMONY ON HARNEY PEAK

Black Elk gave four "Hey-a-a-hey!"

Grandfather, the Great Spirit, behold me on earth. It is said that you lived first. You are older than all the prayers that are sent to you. All things on earth, the four-leggeds, the wings of the air, belong to you. It is said that you have made all things. Also, you have set the powers of the four quarters to cross each other. Also day after day everything lives day in and day out through your power. Everything you made and gave power to. I thus will send up a voice in behalf of everything that you have made. The Indians, you have made their ways to live. They are in despair right now. Therefore I will send a voice to you, Great Spirit, my grandfather. All the universe, the stars and the heavens and the earth and the four quarters you have set. Day in and day out all the wings of the air live and the morning star and all beings that walk the earth. Thus I send a voice in behalf of my people and also my relatives-like, the four-leggeds and the wings of the air, of the four quarters and the powers you have set. But the most powerful is where the sun goes down. You have set the six grandfathers over to that power where the sun goes down and thus you have taken me over there. Thus you have said to me if in great difficulties that I should send a voice four times representing the four quarters of the earth.

[*My*] Grandfathers, the six, may you behold me. You have made me intercessor of my people and you have given a way of living to my people. Where the sun goes down you have presented [*to*] me a pipe, that through this pipe I should make my offerings. This all you have said and also you have sent me to the center of the earth with your stick to bloom. And you have presented to me a sacred wind from where the giant lives that my people, with this wind, should be stronger. Also you presented to me from where the sun goes down a cup of water—the living water that makes the two-leggeds live. And thus you have said that my people will be saved. From the south you have presented me with the sacred hoop of my nation and the tree that was to bloom, but with tears running, I shall say now that the tree has never bloomed. Thus I will recall my vision when they have given me all the powers and made me intercessor and then sent me to the center of the earth.

And here at the center of the earth I am now [at] the same place that you have taken me and showed me all the good things of the earth that were to be my people's. The four-leggeds and the wings of the air, through them, relative-like we should be, and through them we should send up our voices to you, O Great Spirit! In setting me at the center of the earth and showing me all the good things that were to be my people's and now my people are in despair and I will thus send a voice again. You have set me here and made me behold all things, the good things, and at this very place, the center of the earth, you have promised to set the tree that was to bloom. But I have fallen away thus causing the tree never to bloom again; but there may be a root that is still alive, and give this root strength and moisture of your good things that you have given to us people and through all the powers of the four quarters, the mother earth and the four-leggeds of the earth and the wings of the air through whom we should send up our sighs and voices. May you behold them and also behold me and trust me and hear me, O Great Spirit, my Grandfather!

In sending up my voice I prayed that you may set the tree to bloom again so that my people will see many happy days. The six grandfathers, my grandfathers, through your power you have sent me to the center of the earth and showed me all the good things that were to be mine. Hear me, that my people will live, and find a way that my people will prosper. Again, and the last time, probably, I will recall my vision and call on you again for help, six grandfathers, representing the Great Spirit and the two-leggeds on earth and the four quarters of the earth and also all the beings of the earth. May I send a voice once again so that you may hear me and bring my people back into the hoop and at the center there should be the tree that was to bloom and help us and have mercy on us. Hear me, O Great Spirit, that my people will get back into the sacred hoop and that the tree may bloom and that my people will live the ways you have set for them, and if they live, they may see the happy days and the happy land that you have promised.

(Raising his voice to a wail, he sang) In sorrow I am sending a voice, O six powers of the earth, hear me in sorrow. With tears I am sending a voice. May you behold me and hear me that my people may live again.

(Before reaching the top of the peak, Black Elk told his son, Ben, that if he still had power with the spirits that it would rain a little sprinkle when he gave this ceremony. It did rain out of a perfectly bright sky and then it cleared up immediately afterward.)

Grandfathers, behold this pipe. In behalf of my children and also my nephew's children, I offer this pipe, that we may see many happy days.

PART THREE

The 1944
Interviews

The teachings that Black Elk gave to Neihardt in 1944 were of a very different nature from the earlier teachings. They can be characterized as a historical summary of Lakota culture told through a series of anecdotes, each a distinct story, from the large body of tribal oral literature. By arranging these tales in a roughly chronological sequence, Black Elk attempted to give Neihardt some understanding of his own perspective on the development of Lakota culture.

At the beginning of these interviews, as Black Elk struggled to provide Neihardt with a sense of the earliest times remembered by the Lakotas, he commented: "It is very hard for me to go way back to that time," a time beyond tribal memory, outside the knowledge passed down through stories from father to son. Only glimpses remained. Yet for Black Elk it was important that even these fragmentary memories be recorded to memorialize the history of his people. Black Elk's historical teachings provide explanations for and justifications of the old Lakota way of life, much as the Old Testament provides the historical foundations for Christianity.

No one remembers how human beings came to be, Black Elk said. There were seven original people—four women and three men. (Black Elk probably considered them to be human embodiments of the stars of the Big Dipper, which he calls "The seven stars," although he does not make this explicit.) From them the Indian people developed. In the very early days men were strong, living without fire, hunting only small animals and birds with slingshots, using sharp shells, stones, or bone to butcher their kills. Then Red Thunder, a culture hero, had a vision in which all the animals of the universe held a great race around the Black Hills. The four-leggeds raced against the wingeds, who represented mankind in the contest. The outcome was to decide whether the four-leggeds or the humans would have mastery of the world. The wingeds won, and since then mankind has been able to kill all kinds of animals and make his living from their flesh. In the same vision Red Thunder was taught how to make bows and arrows for more effective hunting. Later, another culture hero named Moves Walking had a vision from Sun through which he learned the art of fire making. From then on the people cooked their meat, usually by boiling it in water through the use of heated rocks. The people had chiefs to lead them, headmen (*wicaśa yatapika,* called "candidates" for chief in these interviews) to guide them, and warrior societies (*akicita*) to police them.

All the people lived together, Black Elk thought, on the shores of a great sea in the south. Then Slow Buffalo, a third culture hero, had a vision that the people had become so numerous that they should disperse throughout the land. He called a council and divided the people into seven bands, appointing a chief for each band, and divided the common fire among them (symbolizing their autonomy). Slow Buffalo prophesied that in the future seven important events would occur. It was from this point that tribal history began.

Black Elk recalled only three of the band chiefs appointed at the council. High Hollow Horn led his people east, but Black Elk apparently knew nothing about this group. Slow Buffalo apparently led his people west; they were given the Sacred Arrows, and eventually they found an important new four-legged, the horse. They developed into the Cheyennes, Kiowas, and other tribes. Moves Walking led his people north; they domesticated the dog and were given the Sacred Pipe. They became the Sioux (and apparently the Arapahoes as well, because they also had a tribal pipe).

At the time of the council, nothing had yet been named. Slow Buffalo named the directions and created relationship by naming the kin relations that would ever after be the standard for living in harmony and peace. Rather than start from biological relations as exemplified by human kinship, in Black Elk's story relationship is cosmic, reflecting first and foremost man's relations to the universe at large; these universal relations were then extended analogically to relationships among human beings.[1] The act of invoking relationship, *wacekiye,* means equally to pray or to address someone by a kinship term. Thus the creation of relationship in Black Elk's history ties man through an intricate web of reciprocal obligations and privileges to all the universe. As the bands dispersed, they created names for everything they met along the way. Through this means their languages came to be different; and out of this, warfare developed. Black Elk thought the Sioux had managed to stay out of the fighting until the Cheyennes discovered the horse, but after that, warfare among the tribes became general.

Beyond this story of how Lakota culture developed, Black Elk taught Neihardt about the system of chiefs, the council, the *akicita,* and war leaders. He discussed the individual's life cycle and most aspects of Lakota culture in general. He also told of the prophecies of Wooden Cup (Drinks Water), who long before Black Elk's time foresaw in visions the coming of the white man, the subsequent disappearance of the animals back into the earth, and the destruction of the Indians' lifeways. Such prophecies taught that events as they progressed were inevitable, making the outward defeat of Lakota culture part of a cosmic plan rather than the result of individual failings. It lifted the burden of responsibility from all, Indians and whites alike.

To illustrate historic Lakota culture, Black Elk told stories that demonstrate the interaction of the sacred in daily life: the war party saved by the skull, Red Hail and the two suitors, the woman four times widowed, and the Santee Owl wizard, to name a few. He also told of war expeditions, like the story of the killing of sixty-six Flatheads and the tale of how Crow Butte was named. Many of these stories reflect Black Elk's travels. Some were learned from the Cheyennes and Arapahoes, others came from the Sissetons, and yet others could probably be traced to the Crows or Winnebagos. What is certain is that Black Elk's stock of oral tradition was unusually rich, integrating elements from many plains tribes. Clearly, although Black Elk proselytized for Catholicism on various reservations, he also spoke there of traditional matters; and he learned stories from far

1. See Brown, *The Sacred Pipe,* p. 15, n. 5: "For the Sioux, all relationships on earth are symbolic of the true and great relationship which always exists between man and the Great Spirit, or between man and Earth understood in its principle."

and wide. They all bear the marks of his own telling, of course, which gives each story a special explicit message, lightened by a generous dose of humor. Black Elk's final story, the first part of his version of Falling Star, reveals his genius for weaving elements from various sources into a single tale. Folktales of this sort, called *ohunkakan* by the Lakotas, were designed to entertain children through the long winter nights, to keep them interested in the story and guessing what would happen next.

Black Elk's teachings in 1944, when he was eighty-one, reveal the extent to which he had reflected on Lakota history and culture from the perspective of changing times. This was no random collection of stories, but a developed attempt to make sense of the past. Black Elk emphasized to Neihardt that all Lakota history had been handed down from one generation to the next as oral tradition by certain men who specialized in remembering and passing down these stories. Black Elk himself was such a man, and there were many others among the Sioux. Only a few of them recorded their stories and knowledge in such a way that they could be preserved in books for future generations. Among those who did, we can see strong parallels with Black Elk's teachings.

The work that is closest to Black Elk in its conception is the winter count of Battiste Good (Brown Hat), a Brulé. The winter count is an annual calendar depicting a significant event for each "winter" (the Lakota year, measured from first snow to first snow), beginning in 1700–1701. To supplement this annual count, Good also drew a series of "cycles" depicting symbolically the Lakota camp circle and a significant event that summarizes a period of years. The first cycle shows the camp circle before tipis were invented; as the sequence progresses, the introduction of fire, stone boiling, tipis, the bow and arrows, the coming of the White Buffalo Woman, and the discovery of the horse are all noted in their proper places. Concerned to make his history complete, Battiste Good even added a pictograph to memorialize Columbus' discovery of America. Thus the cycles lay the foundations of Lakota culture and serve to introduce the winter count. Good made many copies of the cycles and the winter count, as did his son-in-law, High Hawk, and in this sense they served as chroniclers of the Sioux people. By recording this developmental sequence of the features of Lakota culture, these pictographic histories accomplish the same goal as does Black Elk's narrative. Another pictographic history of the Lakotas by Bad Heart Bull has a similar aim, but it is less developmental, focusing largely on more conventional battle scenes and depictions of the regalia and activities of mid-nineteenth-century Lakota culture.[2]

Left Heron, an Oglala known for his story-telling abilities, recorded the accounts that are most similar in style to Black Elk's. He also told of the times long past when the people lived near the ocean, of the first fire, and of the discovery of horses. Left Heron, who specialized in telling stories throughout his long life, was, like Black Elk, especially skillful in taking the old pantribal myths of the plains and combining them into stories with particular reference to Lakota culture. Stories told by Left Heron were recorded as early as the turn of the century and as late as 1939. He also owned a winter count with historical cycles that took the history of the Lakotas back to earliest times, apparently similar to (or perhaps a copy of) Battiste Good's.[3]

Eagle Hawk, another Oglala, likewise recorded a variety of historical material on the Lakotas. Of special interest is a long tale about a hero named *Wicowicaja*, Generation, a mythical personification of the Lakota people. Eagle Hawk told the story to Martha W. Beckwith in 1926, illustrating it as he talked by drawing sketches on a blackboard. He had learned the story from his uncle, who in turn had learned it from his grandfather, so it was part of the oral tradition in the same way as were Black Elk's tales. Eagle Hawk's story tells of the seven camps of the Sioux and, through the course of a young man's adventures, describes many of the salient features of Lakota culture.[4]

Many other Sioux left similar records of the past. Most of their material is in the form of connected narratives modeled after the white man's

2. Battiste Good's winter count is published in Mallery, *Picture-Writing of the American Indians*, pp. 287–328. One of High Hawk's copies is published in Curtis, *The North American Indian*, 3: 159–82. Amos Bad Heart Bull, *A Pictographic History of the Oglala Sioux*, reproduces the entire collection of Bad Heart Bull's drawings.

3. See Walker, "The Sun Dance and Other Ceremonies of the Oglala Division of the Teton Dakota," pp. 183–91, 203–10, 219–21; Martha Warren Beckwith, "Mythology of the Oglala Dakota," *Journal of American Folk-Lore* 43(170) (October–December 1930), pp. 377–98; James R. Walker, *Lakota Myth*, ed. Elaine A. Jahner (Lincoln: University of Nebraska Press, 1983, pp. 101–33); and H. Scudder Mekeel, "Field Notes Summer of 1931, White Clay District, Pine Ridge Reservation, South Dakota" (Department of Anthropology Archives, American Museum of Natural History, New York), pp. 48–53.

4. Beckwith, "Mythology of the Oglala Dakota," pp. 368–77.

literature, rather than in preserved traditional oral forms. The autobiographical and historical writings of Charles A. Eastman (Santee),
William J. Bordeaux (Brulé), and Luther Standing Bear (Oglala) represent this body of literature.[5] To some extent, each of these authors made
use of written sources as well as oral tradition in recording his own version
of the Sioux past.

It is no exaggeration to assert that among the Indian peoples of North
America, the Sioux have been foremost in recording their accounts of
traditional life. By reading these materials it is possible to restore the
human dimension to a reconstruction of historic Sioux lifeways.

Neihardt utilized Black Elk's 1944 teachings as the basis for much of *When
the Tree Flowered,* but he did not include the material in its entirety. Nor
did he preserve Black Elk's developmental sequence for Lakota culture,
but recast the material instead to fit his literary purposes. Because he was
writing a novel, he used the interviews in a freer manner than those from
which *Black Elk Speaks* was written. For example, the stories of Crow
Butte and of the Shoshones' killing of thirty Lakotas are combined in
When the Tree Flowered (chap. 20). Many of Black Elk's other tales are told
in the book only in abbreviated form; and the stories of the war party
saved by the skull, the killing of sixty-six Flatheads, the war party that met
a Crazy Buffalo, and Little Powder's rescue of his family from the
Shoshones are not included. Appendix A of this book is a concordance of
the interview notes and *When the Tree Flowered.* A significant portion of
the material in the book came from Neihardt's interviews with Eagle Elk,
also recorded in 1944. This includes many biographical details of the
fictional narrator Eagle Voice, information about Crazy Horse, the war
expeditions with Kicking Bear, the sun dance, and the Custer battle.
Other material, including the story of High Horse's courting, fights with
the army, and the trip abroad with Buffalo Bill's Wild West show, was
reworked from *Black Elk Speaks.*

Publication in full of this later set of Black Elk's teachings provides new
insights into Black Elk and his perceptions of his people. Much of the

5. Charles Alexander Eastman, *Indian Boyhood* (New York: McClure, Phillips, 1902),
The Soul of the Indian (Boston: Houghton Mifflin, 1911), and *From the Deep Woods to
Civilization: Chapters in the Autobiography of An Indian* (Boston: Little, Brown, 1916);
also W. J. Bordeaux, *Conquering the Mighty Sioux* (Sioux Falls, S.D., 1929); and
Standing Bear, *My People the Sioux* and *Land of the Spotted Eagle.*

information recorded here has not been previously available, so that few readers have understood the extent to which *When the Tree Flowered* incorporated material directly from Black Elk. We can be grateful that Neihardt preserved Black Elk's 1944 teachings intact, allowing us to follow Black Elk step by step as he reflected on the Lakota past and as he explained Lakota culture in order to preserve a record for future generations.

[10]

December 5

A long time ago before we have a history, as far as the Sioux could remember back, it used to be they had the seven bands and in these seven bands there was a chief by the name of Slow Buffalo.[1] I figure they were living way out toward where you always face (south) along the edge of the ocean. One day the seven bands got together and they were going to scatter all over the universe. This Slow Buffalo was a chief of the whole seven, but before that this tribe of Indians might have [been] two tribes or one. They expanded and grew to have seven bands. The chief thought he should call a council of the seven bands. Slow Buffalo, probably his great grandfather, was a chief of one band, but as they grew up and expanded it was getting so it was quite a tribe, so he called all the men and they had a council. He said: "We are seven bands and from now on we will scatter over the world, so we will appoint one chief for each band."

At that time there was no fire existing, so the people lived by raw meat and vegetation, fruits, and all that.[2] The only weapon they had was a slingshot and a blunt instrument (tomahawk) thrown with the sling. At that time men were powerful, so they could [here there is a blank in the

1. The seven bands can be considered as symbolic analogues of the seven stars. See above, p. 285.

2. "At that time" refers to the time long past, before the council. Black Elk states below that the people had both fire and the bow and arrow at the time of the council.

manuscript]. They lived on rabbits and birds killed with slingshots. What they used for knives was rocks and oyster shells and pieces of bone.[3]

At this council Slow Buffalo appointed a chief for each band. After appointing the seven chiefs he appointed a chief by the name of High Hollow Horn. He was to go to where the sun comes toward the daybreak. He appointed one chief by the name of Moves Walking; he was to go north with his band. Toward where the sun goes down, Slow Buffalo was to take his band. At this council it seemed there was no name for anything at that time. So at this meeting they named the four corners [quarters] of the universe: where the sun goes down, toward where there is always snow, where the sun comes from, where you are always facing. When they named the corners, the chief told the other chiefs and himself to go to the three corners of the earth, but not to the south. It seemed he did that because he did not want anyone to go south, because he thought [other] people would come from that direction. They were down by the ocean, so they could not go south. At this council they named the animals and things. He told the chiefs: "The Mysterious One [*Wakan Tanka*] has given us this place, and now it is up to us to try to expand ourselves. We will name every person and every thing."

At the time of the council we had bows and arrows, slingshots, stone knives, and fire.

According to my estimation the origination of the peace pipe was about eight hundred years ago. This was beyond that, so it is close to a thousand years. It is hard for me to go way back to that time. Of course we know not exactly, but how many years have gone by since the Sioux tribe have got the peace pipe, but the other way it is difficult. The reason I said that is because when the peace pipe was presented to the people, there was at that time a square stick and some of the wise chiefs have that and they put a notch on the stick for each year. By that we know approximately how many years it has been since the peace pipe.[4] But the council was beyond that.

Before I go on I would like to get it straightened out how the bow and arrow originated and how they got fire.

---

3. High Hawk mentioned the Lakotas' use of large blue shells, "obtained from the Great Water beside which they lived," for knives in early times (Curtis, *The North American Indian,* 3: 159).

4. Battiste Good also mentioned the use of notched sticks to record time (Mallery, *Picture-Writing of the American Indians,* p. 291).

THE GREAT RACE AND THE ORIGIN
OF THE BOW AND ARROW

I shall proceed with how the early nation got the bow and arrow. It was originated by a chief named Red Thunder. He had a vision. This Red Thunder was out hunting one day. He roamed the woods and he got lost. So he roamed quite a long time and it seems he got exhausted. A big thunderstorm came up, and while seeking shelter it seemed that it did not rain. He heard voices, and the voices said: "Red Thunder, arise, we came after you, and we are taking you back to a place where they will have a big decision which will decide the destiny of your tribe." So he found himself at a certain place. It was one of the most beautiful lands he ever saw; everything was green. There were a lot of four-legged animals and the birds of the universe were all gathered there. The Thunder-beings said to him: "Red Thunder, the destiny of your people lies here; we are going to decide it. So we're going to have a race, and on the race will depend your destiny. The two-leggeds of the universe are considered with the wings of the air, and the four-leggeds are on one side. They are going to race. Now, Red Thunder, you will notice, if the two-leggeds win, your people will live and spread themselves and not be in want. But if the four-leggeds win, they will eat you, the people, and the birds."

So Red Thunder was very much surprised at the gathering of all kinds of four-leggeds; there were some ferocious animals there. It was the same with the two-leggeds. They started. They had a big race track; there were trees all around, but not on the track. The race track was the circle of the earth. Everything was ready, and the race started. The race started, the four-leggeds and the two-leggeds. It seemed that the magpie knew everything; so he got on a buffalo's ear and just sat there, because the race lasted quite awhile. Sometimes a big wind came in, and the birds could not fly; the big animals could stand it, so they could keep on going. Another day a hot day came, and the buffalo could not run. The wings of the air were ahead. A big rain came and killed some of the birds. Still the magpie was sitting on the buffalo's ear. I guess that took quite a while; it was a long race track. When nearing the goal, it seemed that the buffalo was in the lead, so all the four-leggeds made the noises they knew. They were cheering. As they neared the goal, the buffalo was in the lead, but suddenly the magpie took off in the air, just as high as he could, then he came down. The magpie was pretty weak, because he had not eaten; as he came down he beat the buffalo right at the goal and then just fell over.

The wings and two-leggeds won the race, so they took Red Thunder and the magpie in front of the Thunder-being, who told the magpie that he won the race, and so he was to wear the rainbow. If you kill the magpie now, you will see that the end of the tail is the rainbow. Another power given to the magpie was that it could go as it pleased the year around, whether it was winter, spring, or summer. Red Thunder the Thunder-being presented with a bow and arrow. The Thunder-being told Red Thunder: "With this weapon the tribe shall expand and be mighty. So you go back to your people and teach them to make these bows. Hereafter you can shoot the buffalo." (Red Thunder: Wakina Luta [*Wakinyan Luta*].) They further told him that at the place where they had the race was the heart of the earth. He said, "Someday your tribe will be in this land." It was the promised land. "This land is a being. Remember in the future you are to look for this land." I think at the present time we found it and it is the Black Hills.[5]

At the same time the people were out hunting, and they came on to Red Thunder. He had not eaten and was pretty weak. So they carried him back. Red Thunder was asleep or in a trance when he had the vision. When Red Thunder got his strength back, he thought about his vision. So he took a knife and went out into the woods and made a bow and arrow. He made a string out of the elm tree bark by twisting it. He tried the bow and arrow, and it went a little way but was not so accurate. So they put feathers on. A couple of other Indians were with him, so they came to a creek and saw a beaver. The first arrow was just wood, and they killed a beaver with it. Pretty soon he got to thinking about it. In the vision he had seen the arrow with a point on it, but he did not know what to do. He kept looking around and quite awhile afterwards he found this sharp piece of flint. He took it and put it on the arrow. After he found the flint, he improved the bow. After it was used they always put it in the water, so it would get tighter. Red Thunder later got his first deer with a bow and arrow. They cleaned the deer and dried it by the sun and ate it

---

5. The "race track" (*okiinyanke*) for the Great Race surrounds the Black Hills. See Thomas E. Odell, *Mato Paha: The Story of Bear Butte* (Spearfish, S.D., 1942), p. 5. A graphic depiction of the race track appears in Bad Heart Bull, *A Pictographic History of the Oglala Sioux*, pp. 289–90. The fullest versions of the story of the race are recorded from Cheyenne sources. See Peter J. Powell, *Sweet Medicine: The Continuing Role of the Sacred Arrows, the Sun Dance, and the Sacred Buffalo Hat in Northern Cheyenne History*, 2 vols. (Norman: University of Oklahoma Press, 1969), 2: 472–77.

without cooking it. The four-leggeds were not wild at that time. They did not have much trouble killing. That is the origination of the bow and arrow.[6]

THE ORIGIN OF FIRE MAKING

In one of the seven bands was a chief named Moves Walking. He claimed that he had a vision of the sun, which is heat. He told them that he could make fire from the sun, somehow. Moves Walking took the soap weed, the bottom part which is like cotton (rotten). The root when dry is soft as hair and almost like cotton. He took a bunch of that and set it down. The stick coming from the soapweed is dry. He took that and made it into a square; at the point he made it sharp. Then he put the cotton on a piece of wood; he put the sharp stick down to the wood through the cotton. Then he spun the stick; it got hot and made fire.[7]

Moves Walking, in his vision, had been taught all this, so he taught the people. He had seen cooking with the fire in his vision. So he told the people to do this. He said, "Preserve this fire and never let it go out." So when they moved, each band carried its own fire in some rotten wood. They used the fire quite a lot. If one tent's fire died out, they went to the next tent to borrow fire. When they moved, the chief carried the fire in a rotten log.[8]

DISPERSAL OF THE PEOPLE AND
THE ORIGIN OF WARFARE

Now we go back to Slow Buffalo and his council. At that meeting they had the bow and arrow and the fire and the knife and the slingshot. The

6. Battiste Good also mentioned the use of the bow and stone-tipped arrows in the time before the coming of the White Buffalo Woman and the sacred pipe (Mallery, *Picture-Writing of the American Indians*, p. 291). The Lakotas commonly say that the stone arrow points were found on the prairies, and that they were made by the spiders (*iktomi*). See Curtis, *The North American Indian*, 3: 26.

7. Battiste Good's winter count depicts elm and yucca as fire-making materials; a dry yucca stalk was whirled in a hole made in a rotten elm root (Mallery, *Picture-Writing of the American Indians*, p. 291). Compare Left Heron's account of the origin of fire in Beckwith, "Mythology of the Oglala Dakota," p. 377.

8. The custom of carrying live coals from one campsite to the next was an important part of a formal camp movement, for the fire symbolized the unity and autonomy of the camp. See Walker, "The Sun Dance and Other Ceremonies of the Oglala Division of the Teton Dakota," pp. 73, 75; Walker, *Lakota Society*, p. 12; and Hassrick, *The Sioux*, pp. 152–53.

purpose of this council was to disperse the seven bands to all the corners of the universe except the south. Before that time they did not have the fire, so they stayed in the south where it was warm. With the fire they could go anyplace. One band was to go to the north. So the council was to appoint chiefs among the seven bands.

At this session Chief Slow Buffalo got up to talk to his people. At that time relationships were not known among the people. Slow Buffalo mentioned his father's father, great grandfather, and the mother, and brothers and sisters. He said: "All this, we are going to go on with these relations. Remember, they are the ones you are going to depend upon. Up in the heavens, the Mysterious One, that is your grandfather. In between the earth and the heavens, that is your father. This earth is your grandmother. The dirt is your grandmother. Whatever grows on the earth is your mother. It is just like a sucking baby on a mother. Remember that. The day sun comes out, and when it goes down, that is a day. Where it goes down, we shall call that where the sun goes down.

"You, some of the bands that are going to where the sun goes down, as you go along, you will meet the four-leggeds and the wings of the air. It is up to you to name every creature that you see. You will find the woods, the trees, and the smaller trees which bear fruit; you shall derive from them and also you shall name every plant, bush, and tree. Besides this vegetation, whatever you come to, you can name it as you go along. As you go along you people that are going to where the sun goes down, you will meet a four-legged that you will depend on very much in the future (horse).

"And you people that go where there is always snow, you people will do likewise as the people I have just told who are going where the sun goes down. You will meet something more important than the four-legged that you will depend upon—we shall all depend upon it [the peace pipe]. And you people going to where the day breaks and the star that comes out, the morning star, you shall have wisdom from this star, especially anyone who sees this star every morning shall have wisdom. Remember that. Toward the south, where you are always facing, that is where we came from.

"We have come on a good road of loving one another and sticking by one another. At this time we will disperse, so keep the good work and love one another. That is the road that we came from, the road of life, nothing but good, and have a strong will power to do all this. And all this, it will be so, and remember, seven things will happen to you. As you are now seven bands and seven chiefs, and you have seven fires, likewise seven things will happen. Remember all these words. Remember your grandfather, the Mysterious One, and your father in between the heavens and earth, your grandmother the earth, and your mother, the growing things. You shall grow up, multiply your tribe.

"Always remember, your grandmother is underneath your feet always. You are always on her, and your father is above." Then they all dispersed.[9]

At the adjournment of the council, chief Slow Buffalo gave a piece of fire to each band chief. He did likewise with the arrows. The seven bands went all over the universe. [For] the one that went toward where the sun goes down, the chief Slow Buffalo's words came true, for they met the horse. The ones that went toward where there is always snow came upon a peace pipe. The Indians used one language at that time, but at the dispersement of the bands, each band had named the creatures, the trees, etc., differently. That is how the different languages came. One band out of the seven grew a lot and they, too, disbanded. At that time they were all together, but the party that went toward where the sun goes down, they multiplied so fast, and somehow they got quarrelsome, and that is how the warpath originated.

I do believe that we belong to the people that went toward where there is always snow, and as Slow Buffalo said we would meet something, we met and received the peace pipe. The seven bands had grown up and dispersed some more, but the Sioux were going north and did not fight for a long time, until we had the pipe given to us by the Mysterious One. One day we found one of our tribe scalped, and we knew what band of other Indians did it, so we went to revenge that. I don't know what tribe it was. The ones we killed, we cut their necks off, believing we could stop the war by doing that. But it seems the heads grew back on, for we are still having war.[10]

9. Other Lakota accounts attribute the creation of the system of relationship (including under the term *wacekiye* both prayer and kinship) and the prophesy of the horse to the White Buffalo Woman. See High Hawk in Curtis, *The North American Indian,* 3: 159–60, and Lone Man in Densmore, *Teton Sioux Music,* pp. 63–66.

10. In the Plains Indian sign language the designation for Sioux connotes cutting the throat, said to have originated from the Sioux practice of severing heads from the bodies of dead enemies. See W. P. Clark, *Indian Sign Language,* pp. 326, 341; Walker, *Lakota Society,* p. 85.

Of course I know they were poor at that time and it took a long time to get any place. But they had a fire, they had a bow and arrow. After they had the bow and arrow, they got buffalo and deer; somehow they learned how to tan the hides and make tipis and clothes out of it, and the sinew they took for bowstrings. With the sinew the bows were pretty strong. Later on all the tribes named the things differently, and that is how the language has changed. Even among one band, they might have a little trouble, and then the bands dispersed. The Sioux all stuck together; the ones we did not understand we called "enemies" [*toka*]. The only ones we did not understand, and still we stuck together [with], were the Cheyennes and Arapahoes. That went along; instead of loving one another like Slow Buffalo said, we all grew to be enemies, and soon we scalped each other, [we] were [called] Cut Throats. We tried to be great warriors by killing an enemy. Soon a tradition came into the tribe [that] a youth could not be a warrior unless he had an enemy scalp or had the first coup. That is how we have been on the warpath ever since. So when we are on a warpath we go out and look for the enemy. We did not fight for our lands, but we merely looked for the man whose language we did not understand; he is our enemy.

DISCOVERY OF THE HORSE

The Cheyennes, the ones that went toward where the sun goes down, came as far as the Black Hills. There was another tribe that grew from this band, and they called them the Island Hill [*Witapaha*, Kiowas], by which I think they meant [that] the Sioux called the Black Hills at that time the Island Hills. Soon another tribe derived from the band and called themselves the Island Hills. They are the ones who traveled back to the south, and there they ran into the horse.[11]

The way this happened: When the Cheyennes went south, I don't know where and when, but with them was a medicine man and he had a vision about the four-legged horse; he had told his people they would meet a horse, but this medicine man had died before it happened. I don't

11. The translation "Island Hill" is probably a folk etymology. The Kiowas were living in the Black Hills area when the Lakotas first met them and drove them south. See James Mooney, *Calendar History of the Kiowa Indians,* Smithsonian Institution, Bureau of American Ethnology, Annual Report 17, pt. 1 (1898), pp. 156–57. Black Elk uses Island Hill as a designation for the Black Hills.

remember the medicine man's name. Two hunters went out. As they were going out they came upon a ravine or valley, and there was a spring down there. They saw some tracks they had never seen before. They followed the tracks. Later they went back with more men, and there they saw a four-legged with long hair on its neck and a long tail. They did not know what it was. They came back and told the chief. He said they should catch it. So they got some lariats of rawhide. The animal came to the water every day, so they fixed a snare and caught the animal. It was wild but it was tame.[12] They asked the medicine man to find out what it was. But nobody knew what it was. So they thought about the medicine man's vision. Some thought it was a big dog. They had a council and named the animal a holy dog [*śunka wakan*]. They got the horse and tied him up. They were afraid of him. They thought it was something holy. It had a colt, and it was amazing to the tribe, so they all came to look. Soon she made a funny noise (nickered) and another horse came there. It was a stallion. So they caught him, and he was gentle. Some of the younger warriors rode the horse, and after some time they found another horse. Soon they made a habit of hunting horses with this horse. This is how Indians got horses. From then on we had horses.[13]

We had never heard of white men at that time. The Cheyennes got the horses; the Sioux did not have any horses. So the Sioux met somewhere with the Cheyennes. So they made a swap for horses; the Sioux gave bows and arrows and other valuable things for the horses. While they were camping there together, they got into trouble and they fought. That is how the Cheyennes had to go back, and they are in Oklahoma now. If anyone wants to know the real facts, the Sioux have the peace pipe. When that was originated, they know what has happened since. The Cheyennes have the holy arrow, and they reckon what happened from that.[14] The Arapahoes have a pipe, too.[15] If anyone wants to go into detail, these are

12. Neihardt wrote on the manuscript: "Nobody owned it (wild) but it had been ridden by Spaniards and was 'tame.'"

13. Battiste Good's winter count depicts the finding of the first horses (Mallery, *Picture-Writing of the American Indians,* p. 292). According to High Hawk's copy of Good's winter count, the first horse was found in 1624, although the Indians did not begin to ride horses until 1680 (Curtis, *The North American Indian,* 3: 160–61).

14. For the Cheyenne Sacred Arrows see Powell, *Sweet Medicine,* 2: 481–610.

15. For the Arapahoe Flat Pipe see George A. Dorsey, *The Arapaho Sun Dance: The Ceremony of the Offerings Lodge,* Field Columbian Museum, Publication 75, Anthropological Series 4 (Chicago, 1903), pp. 191–212.

still in existence. After the Sioux and Cheyennes fought, the Sioux went back and met the Arapahoes. The Arapahoes also had horses; ever since there has been peace between the two tribes.

When the Arapahoes met the Sioux, the Arapahoe chief recalled the last words just before the dispersement of the seven bands. He recalled the words of Slow Buffalo. He mentioned that we were told to love one another and stick together, so we are going to live up to that. So the Arapahoes who had horses to spare gave them to the Sioux so they could get around, too. It seems that at that time they did not have war, but ever since discovering the horse they had war to get horses and fight.

THE WAR PARTY SAVED BY THE SKULL

I am going back to tell how they used the bows and arrows. At first the animals were gentle, and all you had to do was go out and get them. But later they got wild. A little incident happened when they used a bow and arrow to fight.

There was a little war party that went out—about twenty. They came down to a hill in the middle of the winter—there was [a] lot of snow. They came to a leaning tree, so they built a hut over the tree with grass. They pushed the snow off with their feet,and found a skull. They put it aside. They had a fire and meat. One of them took a piece of meat off and put it in the eye of the skull and painted it red. He asked the skull to give them any favor—that they should kill an enemy and scalp him.

The next morning they were going over the ridge and when they got down over the ridge they heard a woman crying, "Hurry up, they are going to kill them all!" They hurried along and two of the members went out to scout. They met three enemies and were about to be killed. The big party came just in the nick of time, and then killed the three enemies with bows and arrows. They cut their heads off and brought them back to where they were camping. They believed that when they fed the skull, that skull must be a woman, and it was her spirit that warned them when the scouts were about to be killed.

So that is a belief of the Indians that sometimes the spirit of a man [a dead person] still roams the country, so when they fed her [the skull], she helped them out. Of course this was way back and I could not tell very much about it. At that time the bow and arrow was not developed so that it did much harm. When the white man came, they used iron for the point, and it came to be very effective.

The party came back to the camp with the three enemies' heads. Coming back they met another party, and this party was a war party (enemy), but they had horses. So they schemed how to get their horses. So they waited until dark. They even hauled big rocks up on the bluff and by the time they were eating and resting, they shot at them and threw rocks on them. They went into the woods, and forgot about the horses. So the Sioux got their horses.

I was just telling you how the Sioux talked to spirits. They got what they wanted from the skull (spirit) that they fed. At that time they had a victory dance. I [would] like to know why they paint their faces black when they bring a scalp or stole some horses.[16] The relatives at home would paint their faces black and then dance. When we whip Germany, we will all black our faces.

THE INDIANS' RELATIONSHIP TO THE ANIMALS

The life of an Indian is just like the wings of the air. That is why you notice the hawk knows how to get his prey. The Indian is like that. The hawk swoops down on its prey; so does the Indian. In his lament he is like an animal. For instance, the coyote is sly; so is the Indian. The eagle is the same. That is why the Indian is always feathered up; he is a relative to the wings of the air. The horse according to the Indians came from the Thunder-beings; that is why in the ceremony the horse is always painted up.[17]

THE SEVEN IMPORTANT THINGS

The seven important happenings are still coming.[18] When they got to the peace pipe, that is where it comes in. I was just telling about the old times. The words of the chief just before the bands dispersed all came true.

16. According to Brown, *The Sacred Pipe*, p. 92, n. 4, Black Elk later said that the reason the Sioux blackened their faces after returning from war was that "by going on the warpath, we know that we have done something bad, and we wish to hide our faces from *Wakan Tanka*." Such a negative interpretation of the moral value of warfare apparently reflects Black Elk's Christian perspective on historic Lakota culture.

17. The horse is considered one of the *akicita* (soldiers or messengers) of *Wakinyan* (the Thunder-beings). See Walker, *Lakota Belief and Ritual*, p. 101, and Left Heron in Beckwith, "Mythology of the Oglala Dakota," p. 379.

18. That is, the seven important things prophesied by Slow Buffalo (p. 313), including the discovery of the horse and the gift of the pipe.

THE DOMESTICATION OF DOGS

The use of dogs was not from a vision, but Moves Walking and his band got some wolf pups and raised them. They got to be pretty gentle, so the chief thought the good-sized wolves could be fixed so they would pack something. Pretty soon they got two sticks and crossed them and tied them. They put the crossed part on the shoulders of the dogs and tied it under the neck. They then loaded the pack on the sticks, and the wolves dragged the travois. The dogs' hair turned a different color but still retained wolf ears.[19]

THE MINNESOTA SIOUX

The band of Sioux that roamed in Minnesota was called Cut Throats. I figure that some went into Canada and others turned into a different tribe.[20]

HOW MAN CAME TO THE EARTH

No man remembers but it seems this way: Suppose you went out of your mind. When you come to, you don't remember anything. There were three men and four women at first and they can trace back to where they had come to their senses.[21] That is all; they do not know where they came from.

The Indian, if we came from Asia, we should have iron, because Christ was nailed on the cross with iron nails. I just cannot believe we came from Asia.

19. See the discussion of the Sioux use of dogs in Hassrick, *The Sioux,* pp. 156–59.

20. All the Sioux were designated Cut Throats in the sign language. After the Minnesota uprising in 1862, many of the eastern Sioux fled to Canada, where some of their descendants still live. See Roy W. Meyer, *History of the Santee Sioux: United States Indian Policy on Trial* (Lincoln: University of Nebraska Press, 1967), pp. 102–32, 313, and Gotran Laviolette, *The Sioux Indians in Canada* (Regina, Sask.: Marian Press, 1944), pp. 124–31.

21. Again the number seven occurs in conjunction with Sioux origins.

December 6

LAKOTA GOVERNMENT

Next I want to go on about how they govern themselves.[1] I don't know, but they must have had at that council all this planned out. Perhaps it was improved later. In order to have law and order among themselves they had to have a certain way of keeping order in the bands. Each band was for itself. Maybe the seven camps had different rules, but it is all similar. They had a chief who was the head man. They already had the so-called "highest tipi" and "next to the highest tipi." The highest tipi is where the chief lives; the next one is where the laws for governing are made. This is called tipi iyokihe [*tipi iyokiheya,* council lodge[2]].

Any human being is the chief of everything. The people were first, and the next was where they made the laws—tipi iyokihe. It seems that the governing bodies of the seven camps were all similar but the people elected their chief. I don't know whether Slow Buffalo was elected by the

1. The best accounts of Lakota government are in Walker, *Lakota Society,* pp. 13–39, and Wissler, "Societies and Ceremonial Associations in the Oglala Division of the Teton-Dakota," pp. 36–41.

2. The term *iyokihe* means "next to," and it is this meaning that Black Elk selects to explain the council lodge as "next to" the chief's lodge. However, the council lodge is usually called *tipi iyokiheya,* literally, "lodge added to" or "lodge expanded," which is its etymologically correct meaning here, referring to the council lodge as composed of the poles and coverings or two or more lodges erected as one large shelter. Later Black Elk translates this as "tipi thrown over together." For further discussion of functions of the council lodge, see Riggs, *Dakota Grammar, Texts, and Ethnography,* pp. 195–96, 200–202.

people or not. But at that time you had to be a great warrior and a good man to attain the chieftainship. You had to prove yourself.

The chief ruled just like a president, but his actions had to be approved. If the chief had a son, he would be chief, if he could prove himself worthy of the honor. Otherwise, the councilors would choose someone. They went into the second tipi [council lodge] and whatever they decide is the law. The councilors would get together, and if they are going to elect anyone, they know all the people and know who is worthy.

The word akichita [*akicita*] is something that the seven bands had when at the dispersement it was up to them to name everything.[3] A certain medicine man had a vision of the Thunder-beings, and that is where the word akichita comes from. Akichita means you have made up your mind to do something and you are going to do it. Akichita means if I tell you to do anything, it has to be done. When the medicine man had a vision the Thunder-beings said they and akichita would be relatives and the Thunder-beings would give their power to the people. The akichita saw to it that the laws made by the sub-chiefs were enforced. Just like the Thunder-beings, the akichita could not be stopped.

There were chiefs in every band (tiospaya [*tiyośpaye*][4]). The chiefs of the bands are the ones that get together and elect the akichita. They sang a song to pick the men. As they went around singing they had a piece of charcoal and put a black spot [stripe] on the faces of the ones chosen. Then they brought them together and the people came and they had a dedicatory ceremony. Whenever you were elected for akichita you had a power almost like a chief, for they watched the chief. If the chief violated any rules he could be deposed. The chiefs had to watch over the akichita, and if one of them did not do the right thing, the chief could have him removed.

There was the governing body. The chief is the head man, and between him and the soldiers are six councilors (tipi iyokihe) who make the laws but were not chiefs. There used to be one chief in each band, but it changed sometime and they had as many as four chiefs. That is, a head chief and three sub-chiefs. Each band had its own chief, sub-chief, and akichita.

But when the bands got together there were higher laws. When they

3. For discussion of the *akicita*, see Walker, *Lakota Society*, pp. 28–29, 32–34, 76ff.
4. A good discussion of the *tiyośpaye* is in Deloria, *Speaking of Indians*, pp. 38–49.

were together and an important matter came up, then the third tipi came
into consideration. They built one big tipi out of three and all the chiefs
from all the bands, the akichita, the councilors, all got in there and decided
what the whole tribe should do. Akichita is singular or plural (like [the
English word] sheep). The tipi iyokihe from all the bands are taken together and made into one big tipi for the councils in which the whole tribe
takes place. This is called "tipi thrown over together."[5] When that happened, they took the tipi and put the poles in a way that it looked like a
corral. Then they spread the tipi hides all around. They did not cover the
top, for it was not permanent—maybe for just one day.

Ti (where we live) *ospaye* (apart but not separated completely).

Whatever the six councilors agree on is a law, and the akichita take care
of it. If anyone in the band breaks a law, the akichita go there and whip
him or knock him out. If he gets mad and tries to fight back, they kill him.
A lot of them were killed. Rules were made so the people would benefit.
For instance, in getting provision, everyone, especially the older ones,
were to get alike. Younger men killed for the older ones. They went
hunting at certain times, when the council said to go. When they said it
was permissible to go on a war party, then they could. If one or two went
on a warpath when the law says they could not go, when they got back the
akichita would go to the home and take down the tipi and chop up the
sticks [tipi poles] and cut up the hide [tipi cover]. If someone goes hunting when he should not, they knock him out and ruin his tipi. The akichita
were like the ash, which can be bent but not broken. When the men were
chosen for akichita, they were told, "You will resemble the ash. You have
noticed it can not be broken. It is up to you to look after the people and
take care of the laws." When there was to be a council meeting, the
akichita would go around and get coffee, meat, etc., for the meeting. The
people had to give what was asked for. If the councilors say you can't go on
a war party or hunting then the whole tribe moves. Everyone has to have a
fair share, and they could not let someone go out and scare the game away.

Another thing I forgot: besides the chiefs, sub-chiefs, councilors, and
akichita, there were those who were next in line for the chiefs. The warriors earned that. Whenever they had done so many brave deeds, then
they were eligible for next in line for the chieftains or councilors. You had

5. The same term is used for the council lodge of a single band and for that of a larger
encampment composed of several bands.

to kill an enemy, count coup first, second, and third, and then get a scalp. Then you had to bring in meat for old people, be kind to everybody and good. No one could say you were a bad man, so you had earned the right to be a candidate for chief, councilman, akichita. Wichasha yatapika [*wicaśa yatapika*].⁶ Whenever there is a chieftain to be made, the wichasha yatapika are the ones who elect the chief, or chiefs.

The wichasa yatapika get together and elect four big chiefs out of their own members from the whole tribe. They are over all the others, and they have equal power among themselves. If one chief is ousted by the akichita, then the akichita have the power to choose one man from the candidates to be the new chief. For example, the last big chiefs we had. Red Cloud was one, but he left for the white men, so they ousted him and Spotted Tail out. So they elected Crazy Horse, American Horse, [Young Man] Afraid of His Horse, and Knife [Sword].⁷ Crazy Horse was the only real chief, because the other three left for the white men and were ousted. Crazy Horse is the last big chief, and then it's all over.

The four chiefs had the power to care for the people, for the tribe as a whole. Next is the land; look after the land. Next is the helpless; see that they are taken care of. Remember you probably [will] have your graves in four different places; you probably will die on a plain or on a hill; it might be in a gulch; it might be the woods. They were elected to give their lives for the people, so they may have to die for the people.⁸ They are called nacha [*naca*], head man, [and] wichashitanacha [*wicaśa itancan*], principal man, higher than nacha.⁹

6. There is no satisfactory etymology for this term, which has been interpreted as "men they praise" or "men who own [the people]." See Hassrick, *The Sioux,* pp. 28–30. In the literature these men are frequently referred to as "shirt wearers" after the hair-trimmed shirts that were their badge of office, and they are sometimes spoken of as "head chiefs" of the Sioux. See Curtis, *The North American Indian,* 3: 12, and Wissler, "Societies and Ceremonial Associations in the Oglala Division of the Teton-Dakota," pp. 39–40.

7. Thunder Bear gave Wissler the same four names as the last leaders of the Oglala chiefs' society ("Societies and Ceremonial Associations in the Oglala Division of the Teton-Dakota," p. 39); Calico gave the same listing to Curtis (*The American Indian,* 3: 16).

8. Compare the very similar account given by White Bull in Vestal, *Warpath,* pp. 231–32.

9. According to Red Feather, an Oglala, the word *naca* is an older Lakota term for a chief (Buechel, *A Dictionary of the Teton Dakota Sioux Language,* p. 342). See Walker, *Lakota Society,* p. 35 and n. 42, p. 178.

Crazy Horse's grandfather and Black Elk's grandfather were two of five brothers. Great grandfather's name was Black Elk, grandfather, father, Nicholas Black Elk, Ben Black Elk [son], Henry Black Elk [grandson].

The biggest council consists of the candidates and the akichita and the chiefs and the councilors. They all take part in the council. Later on the akichita formed so-called societies. The chiefs also had a society called "Owns White" (Ska Yoha [*Ska Yuha*]), and the candidates and councilors belonged to this society too. The akichita formed five societies: the Brave Heart [*Cante T'inza*], the [Kit] Fox [*Tokala*], Packs White [*Wicinska*], Crowskin [*Kanǵi Yuha*, Crow Owners], [and] Eeyuptala [*Iyuptala*]—"Go Right on Through," Perseverance society. These societies are to build boys up to manhood. They guide the young and take care of the old people. There was a sort of rivalry among the societies as to which had produced more warriors than the others.[10]

GAMES AND THE EDUCATION OF CHILDREN

In order to make a boy to be a great warrior you have to teach him right from the start how to handle a bow and arrow. It is up to the parents and the societies to teach them various things. The Indians think it is an honor to die in battle; it is the greatest thing an Indian can do. So the little boys were taught to handle a bow. The first bird they shot with a bow, the parents would probably call over the neighbors and have a feast. There are three main things: knife, bow and arrow, and the rope. Boys were taught to use these things right from the start.

On the woman's side, the little girls were taught to play with marbles as soon as they were able. The round rock is similar to bowling, only there is only one stick. The stick is about two inches long and is set in a position, and the marble is rolled to it. Every time they knock that down, they mark it. That teaches them to have more patience. So if they have a life-target which they miss one time, they try it again. The game is called "rolling game." Later, when they are over ten, they are given a bag in which are knives, awls, sinews, needles, and other things women use. With that she could produce a good home and make clothes.

10. See Wissler, "Societies and Ceremonial Associations in the Oglala Division of the Teton-Dakota," pp. 7–74, and Walker, *Lakota Society*, pp. 32–39.

I think what was most important was when they were little they had their own little outfits and played moving camp. They used the little boys for pack horses and had travois tied to the little boys. Furthermore, the boys joined in with the tipis playing around. There might be another group camped around, so maybe a couple of scouts would come over and look around; then the little boys would come on a warpath on the camp. It would be all of a sudden. They used long weeds for clubs. They would charge, and the girls would pick up the tipis and run. The boys would stay to defend the camp. That is one way of playing. In other words they were taught how to live as they would live later.

There is one very important thing that I did not mention: the rope, knife, and bow and arrow for the boys, and the little bag for the girls. If a war party came, the men took those three things, and the girls the little kits. With those they could begin again and make another home.

There is another game to make warriors able to endure much. It is called the mud fight. They took a piece of clay and put it on a stick and it really stings. Some of the boys were pretty brave and could stand it. When they got closer together they used the sticks on each other. That made them brave and tough.

Another game is a kicking game. It is called a swing game because they swung their feet. They tried to trip each other and kick each other. Sometimes they would get into a real fight.

There is also a hoop game. They had hoops all different sizes which they roll and pierce with lances. Finally there is a very little one. They rolled the hoops, and the other side threw lances to pierce the hoops. If you miss a hoop, the other side has a right to pound you with hoops and sticks.

Another game is called "pull them off their horses." I remember they played this whenever they moved camp. One time we were moving camp, and we boys crossed the creek and there was another bunch of boys who were our rivals waiting for us. Just then they started charging and trying to pull us off. I met a good husky kid and he grabbed my wrist and pulled me off. I landed in a bunch of cactus. That was another war game. It is for the war, so that you learn how to fall off and not get hurt. After you had played all these games, you were pretty well toughened up and knew all the tricks.

They select a boy and give him a round cactus with a long stick tied to it. In the middle of the cactus is a target. The boy gets in the middle and moves the cactus around to keep the other boys from hitting the heart. If they hit the cactus, the boy starts chasing them with the cactus. If they hit the heart, the game is done. This is called the "cactus buffalo game."

Sometimes the boys got together and go down to the creek or some-place to have an endurance test. They all sat down by a fire. They took the inside of a weed (pith) and put it on their arms and lit them. They burned [it], and the others watched to see if they flinched. Some would push it off before it burned down; others would let it burn clear down. This endurance test was called "setting fire to your skin." The girls did that, too.

There is another game called "fox choking." They use a fox hide and strip the hide [cut it into strips]. They select one of a bunch of boys to choke all of them. They take grass and burn it, and when the smoke comes, they put the strip of fox hide over it, and then put the hide around the neck [of each boy in turn] and cross it loosely, and the fellow chokes. When he comes to, he makes funny motions, and they got a big kick out of it.

Another game for grown-ups too and teen-agers is the hoof game. They took a stake [sharp stick]. There was a boy and a girl on each side and a dozen sticks [counters] in the middle. The hoofs are made of deer hoofs [metatarsal bones]; there are four of them tied to a string on the stick. When you swing it, the hoof comes up and you string it [on the stick]. You hold the stick with the four hoofs swinging [from] it. Then you toss the hoofs up into the air and with the same stick try to catch one hoof on the end. There is one hole [in the hoof] (the mouth) that counts for one stick, and another, smaller hole in the middle. If you thread that hole you get all the sticks of the other side. If you don't get the stick in any hole, it goes to the next [player]; as long as you do not miss you have another try. If the other side calls for a certain hole, then if you don't hit *that* hole, it does not count.

The basket game. Six plum seeds—two black ones, white on the other side; two otherwise marked; and two more still differently marked. The seeds are thrown up or shaken and if there is a pair, something is won. Sticks are used for counters. It was a gambling game and anything might be gambled—horses, moccasins, etc.[11]

11. For descriptions of Sioux games, see James Owen Dorsey, "Games of Dakota Children," *American Anthropologist,* o.s. 4 (1891); 329–45; Louis L. Meeker, "Oglala Games," *Pennsylvania University Museum Bulletin* 3 (1901): 23–46; James R. Walker, "Oglala Games, I," *Journal of American Folk-Lore* 18 (1905): 277–90, "Oglala Games, II,"

MOVING CAMP

The next thing I want to tell is how they moved camps. I saw the fire
carried, and I don't think it ever went out. The councilmen decided when
to move, and a crier went around telling the camp. The first announcement was "Make moccasins for the children" or "Mend the children's
moccasins." The second morning the crier would say, "Loosen the tipi off
the ground." The third morning the six councilors were out in the middle
of the camp where a big fire was burning. The crier comes and tells the
people to pack. When they move, the people do not dare move until the
councilors move. The people did not know where they were going to
camp or when. It was up to the councilors. The councilors move on and
when they select the place to camp, they stop and build a fire. Then the
crier says, "Come in closer." That means they form a circle close to the fire.
When they got through from each tipi they would come down with a dry
piece of wood to get a fire. Of course in my time they had flint; this is the
way they did it before. The people put their tipis in a circle with the
opening to the east. The tipi faces east also.[12]

RED HAIL AND THE TWO SUITORS

I want to tell a story.[13] At one time the Indians found a good place to
camp and the councilors decided open season was on for war parties.
There was a warrior by the name of Good Voice Hawk. He was a nice-
looking warrior. The other was Brave Eagle; he was a sort of homely
fellow. Good Voice Hawk was very handsome. The two were after the
same girl, and the girl was pretty important because her father was a
candidate [*wicaśa yatapika*]. She was very pretty. Of course, Indian-style,
each one had a chance to see her and talk to her. The homely fellow went
there and talked to her and was going to see her quite often. Likewise

Journal of American Folk-Lore 19 (1906): 29–36, and "Sioux Games," *Collections of the
Historical Society of South Dakota* 9 (1918): 486–513; Hassrick, *The Sioux,* pp. 127–35;
Stewart Culin, *Games of the North American Indians,* Smithsonian Institution, Bureau
of American Ethnology, Annual Report 24 (1907).

    12. Compare the description in Hassrick, *The Sioux,* pp. 152–53.

    13. Neihardt first published this as "Red Hail and the Two Suitors," *Indians at Work*
13(1) (May–June 1945): 6–10. He also recorded a somewhat longer version of the same
story told by Andrew Knife, now in the Neihardt Collection.

Good Voice Hawk, every time he went to see the girl he talked about Brave Eagle and was knocking the other one. But Brave Eagle did not talk about anyone else.

One day the war party was getting ready to go and both were going. Good Voice Hawk was riding a good horse. The girl's tent was right by the path of the war party. She was standing there and Good Voice Hawk hesitated and smiled at her. He kept looking back as he went over the hill and stopped once in awhile. Just as he was going over the hill, he looked back once more. When he went over the hill, Brave Eagle came along riding a mule. He did not notice her at all and did not look back but just went on. She probably liked either one of them, but she felt bad that both had left. She came back in the tipi and was downhearted.

Soon her father came back so she said, "Father, I am going to where the war party went. I want to be with the boys. I want to go." Her father sat there for a while and finally let her go. He brought a couple of good horses and he decided to go with his daughter. So they both went. The war party was moving slowly and had camped for the night. The girl and her father caught up with them when they were making camp. They had relatives with the war party, so they went and camped with them. As they went along and camped several times, they all noticed that she was coming along. So the young warriors would make a killing and bring something to her, especially the one Good Voice Hawk. Brave Eagle never brought anything. Somehow the girl did not quite like it because Brave Eagle did not bring her anything to eat, so she decided to fix something for him and take it over to Brave Eagle.

I don't know what they did. The next day they were in enemy territory and made a camp and were very careful. I forgot to say that in such war parties there are leaders—blo-tan-hun-ka [*blotahunka*]—who are experts.[14] A few of them got together and decided they should put scouts out ahead. They decided to send Brave Eagle and Good Voice Hawk, the two rivals. They announced it and got both of them together. It was their responsibility to go out, and the commanders gave them instructions what to do.

Brave Eagle rode his mule. Good Voice Hawk rode his best horse. They started out that evening. They rode all night and toward daybreak

14. See Wissler, "Societies and Ceremonial Associations in the Oglala Division of the Teton-Dakota," pp. 54–61.

they came to a great bluff with pines. They tied their mounts below the hill and crawled carefully up the ridge. When they got on top they saw a camp down there with a lot of tipis. As they looked down on the camp it seemed the camp was not ready for enemies at all.

An enemy came along with some horses to put them out to feed during the day. Good Voice Hawk said "My friend, we had just as well get him, scalp him, and go home and take the horses." Brave Eagle said "No, I don't think it would be right to do that at all. We are sent out as scouts, and we could just as well tell them what we see, and it is up to the commanders to decide what to do. We are here as scouts." Good Voice Hawk insisted on killing the man and scalping [him], but Brave Eagle would not do it. So they had a little quarrel. Brave Eagle still insisted they should go back and report, as they were instructed to do.

Good Voice Hawk insisted, so Brave Eagle gave in. So they got their war bonnets on after they had gotten their horses. Good Voice Hawk made a charge and said "Hoka Hey!" The enemy had a bow and was going to shoot him, but he missed. Good Voice Hawk did not coup him—missed him. Brave Eagle came along and hit him and knocked him out and killed him with his tomahawk. Then he scalped him, and Good Voice Hawk couped the dead enemy. It happened so close to the camp, and they could not help noticing what happened. A lot of warriors from the camp came. Good Voice Hawk had the best horse and Brave Eagle had a mule; the warriors had nearly caught up. So Good Voice Hawk asked Brave Eagle for the scalp he had. Then Good Voice Hawk turned around and took his bow and hit Brave Eagle's bow and broke the string, and then he left.

There was no show for Brave Eagle, so Good Voice Hawk rode home as fast as his good horse would carry him. Good Voice Hawk, as he was fleeing, met his party. The war party and the others met and had quite a fight. After the fight was over and the party moved away from the territory, he made a report that he was the one that killed the Indian and scalped him. He thought that Brave Eagle was killed, so he took all the credit.

When they camped that night, the girl was crying. She stopped crying. Her father was out to look for her, but she was gone. They went out searching for her, but never found her. So they decided that she had gone on home. It seems the girl had her horse all ready, so she decided to go and at least see the body of Brave Eagle. She rode back toward the enemy. She rode all night, and the next day and the next night and went back to where they had the fight. She got to where he was supposed to have been killed, but the body was no place. She got on top of the ridge, and the camp had moved across the creek.

That evening after being on the ridge all day she went down to the creek and tied her horse in the willows. She started toward the camp. They were having a victory dance. She saw someone tied up to a stick in the middle and she thought it was Brave Eagle. She sat by the water and did not know what to do. She was fooling with some mud, and before she knew it she had made a mud doll. While making this out of dirt they were dancing. By doing this, singing a lullaby to the doll, she put the whole camp to sleep.

The drum died down, they quit dancing, and the people went home and went to sleep. Everyone was asleep; even the dogs were asleep. She said to the doll, "Here, baby, lie down here and sleep a long time." Then she started for the camp. No one noticed her, because they were all asleep, even the dogs. In the middle she found the pole but no one was there. She looked all around and pretty soon saw where a fire was burning pretty high in a tipi. She thought someone must be awake there, so she went right over without hesitating. She peeked in and there was Brave Eagle all tied up. There were two warriors sleeping in the doorway, and two more sleeping on the other side. There was also a good-looking girl asleep there.

The first thing she did was take all the weapons away from them. Brave Eagle was very glad to see her, and he smiled at her—the first time she had seen him smile. He cut the necks of the warriors and they were so asleep that they did not make a sound. They did not harm the girl, but she had a pretty good elk skin dress and [they] took that off of her. She did not wake up even when they took the dress off of her. She packed up some food and moccasins. They went out to where the horses were and Brave Eagle selected the very best horses—eight of them—and got some saddles too. They led them back to where she had her horse and then they started out. They thought the people would be after them, and they hurried. They changed horses every once in a while. There was no sign of anyone following, so they took their time the second day.

They stopped on the way and found some good, fat buffalo, so Brave Eagle got one of them, and they stopped a day or two to dry and pack the meat. The next day toward evening they struck the big camp. On top of a ridge they looked down and saw that they were having a big celebration.

Brave Eagle decided that she should stay out on the ridge. He said "I am going back alone. The first thing I am going to do is find your father and my father. I think it would be best for us to go in tomorrow in the daytime." So she stayed there and made camp, and he went on in.

In the olden times when anything happened to a warrior, the relatives at home would give everything away and cut their hair to mourn the loss of a son. Brave Eagle went back to camp and tied the horse in a certain place. He dressed up so they would not know who he was but only that he was a Sioux. He kept his blanket close to his face. Pretty soon he saw a little grass hut, near which he had tied his horse.

As he passed the hut, he heard his father's voice. He peeked in and there was his mother with her hair all cut off, and his dad with his hair cut off, and his sister, and they were poor instead of rich as they were before he had left. He walked in the hut, but his father did not raise his head, just sat with his head in his hands. His mother did the same. His father said "How. Whenever I see you young men, it makes me feel bad because of my son." The old woman gave him something to eat, but she did not look at him. The young sister saw him and went over and whispered in her mother's ear. So the woman came over and raised the blanket and said "Is that you, son?" She started to cry. He said "Yes, I am Brave Eagle. But do not cry, for I don't want the people to know." So they rejoiced.

Brave Eagle said, "Father, I suppose you heard about that girl that disappeared. I came back with her, and she is over here on the ridge camped. What I want you to do is go find her [father] and bring [him] here, so I can tell you just what happened." Before his father started out, he said: "Father I scalped these men and the girl killed the first one. I want you each to coup them before you go out. One scalp my sister will coup and you and mother can coup the other. I am saving this other scalp for my father-in-law to coup." They couped them, and the father went out to get the girl's father. He said: "Father, be sure to tell them not to cry, but bring him over here."

Pretty soon he brought the girl's mother, father, brothers, and sister. First they couped the two scalps. Brave Eagle said: "I want to tell you just what happened. When they sent me and Good Voice Hawk to scout, we went and soon we came upon a village camped. Just then an enemy came up with some horses, so Good Voice Hawk wanted to kill [him], but I myself would not do such a thing. I told him we should go back and report and let the leaders of the party do as they wanted to. It was our duty to scout. But he still insisted that we kill him, and we had a row, but I gave in. He had a fast horse, and in trying to get the enemy, the enemy had a bow and was going to shoot, but he missed. I was right behind him and got him with my tomahawk and then scalped him. The warriors were right on top of us, and my horse was slow, so the enemy caught up with me. Good Voice Hawk turned around and asked for the scalp; I handed it to him, and with his bow he broke my bowstring. He fled. I did not have a weapon and could not even draw my knife. They pulled me off my horse. A chief said something, so they tied me up and took me back alive.

"The next day I was tied up all night and they moved across the creek and had a victory dance. They had a live prisoner. They had me out in the middle and had a big time. One of them made signs to me that the next day I was to be killed at the stake. That night they had a dance. They took me back to a tipi and had me all tied up. Two men were at the door and one on each side. A girl was in the tipi too.

"They had a big powwow and then everyone went asleep. I heard a noise and looked and there was your daughter. She untied me and told me to cut two of the men's throats, which I did. We got eight good horses and some dried buffalo meat. I did not want the people to know I was back so I decided to let you know in secret. Your daughter is very much safe, and I would like to go on over there and come back with her in the morning.

"The girl told me like this. When they had that fight, Good Voice Hawk reported that I was killed and he is the one who killed the enemy. Somehow the girl did not believe it and decided that she would go and at least see where I was lying. When she got there, she found nothing, so she prayed to the Great Spirit. She decided to put the whole tribe to sleep, which she did. She sang a lullaby to the baby. She had so much faith in the Great Spirit that she went in there recklessly. She got me out. We got the stuff, and here I am, very much alive."

His dad and father-in-law told him that Good Voice Hawk had done a killing and got the first coup and that is why they were having a big celebration. He was in the middle and painted black. They were going to have a victory dance the next day too. Brave Eagle said, "I am going back to my wife. We are going to come in tomorrow. Just as soon as the sun comes up I want my father and father-in-law to black their faces and you can have a victory dance right here."

So he went back to his wife and told her everything. The next morning they came in. The next morning it seemed like a joke. They had been mourning, and everyone thought they must be crazy, because they were dancing when they had lost their son. Just then a couple was coming on horses. They recognized Brave Eagle and rushed back and told the people, and they came running toward him.

Then the crier announced that Brave Eagle and the girl who had been lost were coming back and were very much alive. So the candidates took blankets out there and carried them in the blankets. The candidates got a big tipi and put it in the middle and put them in there, and everyone was rejoicing. The chiefs and candidates all got together and they put the two there and gave them a peace pipe and told them to report. So they told what happened.

After that the chief gave orders for the akichita to go bring Good Voice Hawk. They said, "Don't bring him, kill him wherever you find him." They did not find him, but on the way coming back they met some boys who said that he had gone over the hill. They found him and he had stabbed himself and was already dead. After this was all over, the chiefs and candidates elected Brave Eagle to be a wichasha yatapika [a candidate].

The girl's name was Red Hail.

[12]

December 7

THE KILLING OF SIXTY-SIX FLATHEADS

I will go back now to the dispersion. At that time the tribe was getting along just fine, but after the dispersion every band was for itself, and probably the invention of the bow and arrow was the cause of the break in relationships. As they went out to different parts of the world, their language changed. Each band named the different things, and that made strangers of them. I believe the Sioux were the first Indians and that at that time everyone talked Sioux. The Sioux were hard to whip, and the most that ever got killed of them was at the Wounded Knee massacre. But in a war party the most killed was thirty when they had a fight with the Shoshones. In learning to be warriors and the way they governed themselves, I guess that had something to do with it.

Now I am going to tell you a story. Our history is handed down to us by our forefathers and we have to have it all in our heads. The story I am going to tell refers way back, after the dispersement. Of course events in the history of the people were handed down from generation to generation, and certain ones kept the stories and handed them down to their children and so on. Various people in each camp remember and are the ones who hand down the stories. One of these men was Standing Hollow Horn; he was quite a history teller. I heard the name of Elk Head.[1]

1. During the late nineteenth and early twentieth centuries, Elk Head, a Sans Arc, was keeper of the sacred Buffalo Calf Pipe brought to the Lakotas by White Buffalo Woman. Standing Hollow Horn was the name of the keeper before him. See Curtis, *The North American Indian,* 3: 55–56.

Mostly the history tellers were medicine men. They have the power and they know. The medicine man hands down everything to the younger ones. There are even some who seem to know things ahead of time. I know one medicine man I heard of whose name was Drinks Water [Wooden Cup]; he was known as a holy man. He foretold things that would happen later. The medicine men were the learned class, the scholars of the tribe. Later I will tell all about Drinks Water; that will be a long story.

Sometimes we do make mistakes, but when we tell anything it has to be what we heard from the spirits.

The story I am going to tell is about a chief who wanted to go on a war party. It was open season, so this chief made a feast and invited certain braves—about ten or more good fighters. He wanted a medicine man to be among the warriors, so he invited a certain one who was good. They invited the medicine man so they would have good luck, and they wanted him to offer up the peace pipe to the Mysterious One, as the peace pipe was the Bible to our tribe. By that pipe they know that what they ask for will come true. It is sacred. Whoever smokes that has to tell nothing but the truth. At that time all the people respected it very much. So they had the medicine man offer up the peace pipe to the Mysterious One. The pipe was so sacred that they filled it up with kinnikinnick but it was not lighted. It was sealed with fat. He offered that to the Mysterious One. They were to carry this and not smoke it until they had won the fight. Afterward they were to take the tallow out and smoke it as a thank-offering. As a rule a young man going on his first war party always had to carry that.[2]

It happened that there was a certain young man who was going for the first time, and he carried it on his back, all wrapped up. He was supposed to be [at] the head of the party; no one could go ahead of him; they were supposed to follow him. Of course the party was intended for just a few, but after the people saw there was going to be a war party, others volunteered, and it became quite a big party. When they had the ceremonial, the ten he invited were elected to be the leaders. The others joined in, and they went.

Something very important happened there. It was the first day out and they did not camp far away. While they were going they had the privilege of hunting any time. While they were going a few warriors went out and

2. See Walker, *Lakota Society,* p. 95.

got deer to provide the party with meat. When they brought these things, that is when the cooking of the meat originated. A medicine man had gotten a buffalo and fixed a paunch so it would not leak. He brought it back and told some others to heat some rocks. They fixed a place with four sticks and put the paunch on it. While doing that they built a big fire and heated some rocks. They were all watching to see what he was going to do. After he had everything ready they put water in it. A crier called out that all persons that wanted to eat meat done by water [should] bring pieces of meat to put in. They brought the meat and threw the hot rocks in the water and it started to boil. They had a big feast and they drank the soup. That is how they learned to cook with water in a paunch. Before that they used hollowed out rocks to cook.[3]

They camped several times before they got to enemy territory. Now they were in enemy territory and camped and were very careful. The leaders selected four warriors to go out scouting. They started out that evening to scout. They had to read signs on animals or anything to know things. The four traveled all night on foot. One of them ran into something and it was coyote droppings. They were black, so he called the others and said: "Friends, there are enemies pretty close, because the droppings indicate this fellow has been eating meat. That is a sign there are people around. We have to be careful. They must be camped near here."

So they went down and across the deep canyon and there was a big ridge beyond that. It was a climb, but they went on top of the ridge. As they looked down the sky was gray and it seemed there was a fire. One of them said: "There are camps over there." They could not see the smoke, but it was grayish. There was quite a flat before the next ridge. When they got there they were very careful. One of them saw a coyote running; he was running away from something. So the four crouched down and then looked over the ridge. Sure enough, there were three men coming, and the coyote had seen them. The men were going back to the camp. So they climbed on up the hill and from there they could see the camp.

The four scouts decided they should go back and report, so they started back. They used signals at that time, and the scouts had to use an animal [call] as a signal. The party was moving while the scouts were out. When

3. High Hawk mentions the use of heated stones as the oldest method known to the Lakotas for boiling meat (Curtis, *The North American Indian,* 3: 159).

they got to the appointed place, they could not find the party. One of them cried out like a coyote several times and pretty soon he got an answer and they knew where to go. They went a little way again and cried like a coyote; they got an answer from quite near and found the whole party. The party prepared to receive the scouts; it was quite a ceremonial to have them come back and they were all lined up to receive the scouts.

They sang the song that is sung whenever the scouts return. Each one had a pipe. The chief got out his pipe and filled it up and presented it to the scouts for each to smoke. That means they were swearing to tell the truth. The chief spoke: "Young men, don't fool me or try to deceive me. You grew up among the higher plateaus or down in the woods and on the flats and near the creeks and the forests; you grew up among these things. Whenever you stopped and if you have seen the actions of a dog or a coyote, tell it to me."

The leader of the scouts said: "We stopped at a certain place. The first sign that indicated enemies, the first thing we saw was the droppings of a coyote. The next thing we saw was a coyote running away, and we knew that he was running away from men. After we saw that coyote, we crawled up the hill, and there were three enemies going back. Quite a little way from there we knew there was a camp and the three men were going back there. We ran down the hill and got on top of another hill, and there was a big camp."

The chief said: "How far is it and how do we get there?" He said: "If we start toward evening, we can get to the camp by daybreak. It is that far." The crier went out to tell the warriors to get ready to start that evening. They traveled all night, and just at daybreak they were right at the camp. The leaders got together and decided what to do.

There was a bluff on each side of the camp, so they decided to split the party and lay on each side of the opening. They selected four good runners to go in the camp and make a killing and run back, so the enemy would run out between these two bluffs. The four selected went into the camp and the party split up and ambushed on each side. The four met an enemy and killed him and scalped him and hurried back. There were few horses at that time. The party was ready with bows and arrows and rocks. The enemy warriors came through the trap, and the party jumped on them with rocks, bows and arrows and everything. They had the advantage, and the enemy retreated.

When the fighting was over, they had killed sixty-six Flatheads.[4] That was the highest number the Sioux killed. That is how the Sioux fight; they are tricky and lead the enemy into a trap. They could have killed more at that time, but the enemy was so pitiful and cried to stop fighting. They had a lot of scalps and coups and so they started back. When they got back, they lit the sacred pipe and offered it as a thank-offering to the Mysterious One, and then it was smoked by the leaders of the war party.

One of the war songs, the wording is:

> Over toward where it always snows,
> That is where you turn,
> And that is where I feed the coyotes.

Better translation:

> Where it always snows,
> Where the road turns,
> That is where I fed the coyotes.

WOODEN CUP, THE PROPHET

This holy man made some caps and made kinnikinnick and powder and he made fire.[5] He would take certain kind of weeds and treat them somehow and then they would burn. He would take dirt from gopher holes.

Wooden Cup got married pretty young; he had a wife and one child. I was told the way he became a medicine man and foretold things was when he was out on a warpath. There was a fellow by the name of Good Thunder and he went out on a war party with Wooden Cup. When they camped someplace he told Good Thunder that he had a vision and knew things that would be of value to the people. When he got back from the war party he would tell them to the people.

In telling this to Good Thunder, Wooden Cup said: "This incident I have to tell, it seems I was in existence before I was ever born. It seems I

4. This fight is described in Vestal, *Sitting Bull,* pp. 118–24, and by White Bull in Vestal, *Warpath,* pp. 117–24. It occurred in 1871, and it permanently drove the Flatheads from the Lakota hunting grounds. White Bull says that only thirty Flatheads were killed. See also the Cheyenne account in Powell, *People of the Sacred Mountain,* pp. 389–90, which places the number of enemy dead at thirty-five.

5. See above, p. 290.

was in a marshy land. I don't know how many years I was there before I was born here. While I was there on the marsh I heard a voice underneath the marshy ground, and it was a woman's voice. She said: "You should tell my grandson things before he is ready to go back. You tell my grandson things because he is ready to go back." Then a voice from above said: "No, you are with him, so why don't you tell him something?"

The voice under the ground said: "Grandson, your Grandfather's place, try and see it, because in the future you will be there. In the future where you are standing the land will be altogether different. All the four-leggeds and the wings of the air that are with you are now going back. Over there where the sun goes down there is a person that you shall see. That person's name is Makes Horses. When you see this person you will see far ahead and see things that will happen far ahead. You are going back to your people now, and when you get back there you are supposed to do a certain thing and tell your people about these things and then you will see what I tell you. The few words you will hear now, you might think that is all. But these words fill the universe."

Wooden Cup just saw the marshy ground and did not see anyone. Then the woman's voice said: "This is the only thing you will take back." He looked down and saw a cap (white man's) on the ground and he picked it up. It was a black hat. "So you may go now," she said. There was nobody there.

Wooden Cup told Good Thunder that was his vision and he had told no one but had kept it to himself. When he got back from the war party, he said he would do the things and tell the people what he had seen and heard in the vision. This is a first-hand story, because Good Thunder told me this. Wooden Cup was singing, but it was different singing from the Indians' songs. Good Thunder asked what it was, and he said: "It is a white man's song." They went on a warpath and came back. Wooden Cup had told all this to Good Thunder but he had never told what power he had or from what animal he got it. He heard that Wooden Cup was going to do things, because he had a vision of the Mysterious One and that is where he got his power.

When my grandfather lived here, there was another old man, an old bachelor, and he was Wooden Cup's helper. His name was Tries to Be Chief. There were rumors at the camp that Wooden Cup had a vision and would do on earth as he had been told to do in the vision. Where he camped they put up a tipi. A crier came around and said they were going to help Wooden Cup make an offering. So they took tobacco and tied it in little bags and put it on sticks. Each one brought an offering or trinket, and they had a great pile of it. All the candidates and some chiefs and some akichita were invited and came over to Wooden Cup's camp, and the people all came.

Tries to Be Chief knew what to do, because Wooden Cup had told him what to do. He put up some sticks for a fire, but did not light it. Wooden Cup was dressed like a white man and he wore the black hat he had found. The people were waiting, and when he came out everything was in readiness. He raised his hands and turned toward where the sun goes down and sang this song four times, the words he had heard from above in his vision:

> Up above your Grandfather's place you shall see
> You shall see as you will be there.

While he was singing that, he stood where the pile of wood was and as he put his hands down toward the earth, you could see fire coming out of his hands, and he put his hands close to the pile of wood. You could see sparks coming out of his hands, and soon the wood was burning. "This is how I was taught to teach you people. So you people should take this fire home and build fires in your homes, because this fire will retain our four-leggeds and if we don't take care of this fire, the four-leggeds will be gone."

With this fire in order to retain the four leggeds he sang a sacred song:

> From the earth will come forth the yearling buffalo people
> Shall come from the earth, so try to see them, somebody
> told me.

Then he spoke: "You see me dressed this way in garments it is unusual for me to wear. When the voice told me I would see a person toward where the sun goes down, that person was dressed this way. He was a white man, but when I looked again it was a stallion. That person was Makes Horses. We will have plenty of horses." Then he sang a song:

> Friend, it's me. Behold me.
> The horse-maker, it's me. Behold me.

When he sang the song he said: "Horses I give you; there will be plenty among you. This land I can't give you, so you can't have any land. You people in the future remember all this land will be different. Likewise you people will be different from what you are today. The day will come, where I stand, you will stand. Then the people will never be in the hoop again. Remember this too: they shall entangle this universe (world) with iron and when you get to that time you shall live in different tipis. Then you will come upon great differences. From where you are always facing and where the day breaks different men are coming. They will fill this world. Those are the ones that will make this a different world. When you get there, there will be great wars. But, people, there is one thing. Remember your peace pipe; don't forget that, even when you come to the time I am telling about. Remember that. Maybe the Great Grandfather (Mysterious One) might send his voice to you. And maybe our Grandmother the earth might help us. When you get to where I am" (meaning the way he was dressed), "you see me dressed like this. The hat I am wearing was given to me by my grandfather the Thunder-beings. The power lies in this hat; the Thunder-beings have given me the power. So in the future there shall be a society created from this."

So he laid the hat on the ground and stood up; then he picked it up again, and when he did so, there was another hat. And so on. He selected some good young men and gave them twelve hats. They were the ones to form the society. That was the Owns White [*Ska Yuha*] society. The helper brought four pieces of bark of the cottonwood about a foot long. Wooden Cup took them and laid them on the ground and ran his hands over them. He had some sage, so he covered them with it. He said to Tries to Be Chief: "Go get the box you make our kinnikinnick in and make some kinnikinnick so the people can smoke and talk. He told him to take the bark out and when he did it had turned into pieces of plug tobacco. He gave one to Tries to Be Chief and told him to give the three pieces out to the people so they could make kinnikinnick.

He ordered Tries to Be Chief to get the dirt the gopher pushed out of the ground, and he brought some in a sack. Wooden Cup ran his fingers over it and handed it back to Tries to Be Chief and told him to give it out to the men that had guns. Tries to Be Chief looked in there and the dirt had turned into gunpowder. Next he wanted some little sticks. Tries to Be Chief brought him some in a blanket, and Wooden Cup ran his hands over them and they were matches. (Matches: "makes light" [*yuilepi*].)

Wooden Cup had a charm—an agate pebble about as big as a marble. He wore that, and whenever he wanted to do miracles he would rub his hands with the stone. When the old man died, his son had that stone and wore it. He formed the society and gave instructions to the twelve men he had given hats. They were all supposed to own white horses. The society was called Ska Yoha [*Ska Yuha*], "Owns White." The society is still going, but it does not function much. They had a horse dance after the ceremony and then the people dispersed. The hats were used mostly in war as a charm.

To prove this story you can go see Mr. Hat. Old man Hat died, but he has a son living at Oglala. This all happened before I was born; I never saw Wooden Cup. Tries to Be Chief was my wife's uncle. This happened about twenty years before I was born. It happened west of the Black Hills. They claim Wooden Cup died northwest of the Black Hills. His last days were spent when the Sioux were over there. He was pretty well, but one day he told his folks he was going back. That day he became very ill and they had all kinds of medicine men to cure him, but he died. His last wishes were that they build a big fire and burn up his body. But they did not do that; they buried him there. Where he was buried you could see a light for four days; it looked as if he were burning. They call [it] the place where the holy man lies (literally: "man holy he lies where"). He is about the greatest holy man of all; he is the only one I know of that had a vision about the Mysterious One.

Wichasha Wakan [*wicaśa wakan*], "man holy."

POUTING BUTTE

The warrior was a young man. His family was well to do; his father was a sub-chief. He belonged to the Cheyenne tribe. They were moving camp. The young man had two older sisters. The brothers and sisters respected each other so much that they did not even talk to each other. In the old times if you had cross words with your sister, either one would have to commit suicide. Usually the girl would take it so hard that she would commit suicide—or the man would, either way. In old times if a boy wanted to tell his sister anything, he would tell his mother, and she would tell her.[6]

6. This prohibition of speech between brother and sister, as a mark of respect, was rigidly observed among the Lakotas. See Gordon Macgregor, *Warriors without Weapons: A Study of the Society and Personality Development of the Pine Ridge Sioux*, (Chicago: University of Chicago Press, 1946), p. 55; Hassrick, *The Sioux*, p. 107; Jeannette Mirsky,

The young man was called Thunder Sounds. The family had lots of ponies and a good tipi. The boy had a couple of good sorrel spotted ponies, and they were just alike. He had good clothes. As they moved camp, his sisters jumped him about something he had done and scolded him. Thunder Sounds felt ashamed and took it to heart because they had scolded him. The next day he said nothing, but he took it pretty hard. He did not know what to do. After the tribe moved camp he just stayed at the old camping ground. He had his horses and bow and arrow and everything with him. When they moved, his sisters were sorry, so they told another young man to go back and get him, but Thunder Sounds would not go back. Several came after him, but he would not go back.

Instead of going south with his people he went out west and decided to roam and meet the enemy and fight and get killed. He was going to look for death or kill somebody. He left without provisions; he even did not want to eat. So he just kept on going because he felt very unhappy. But he got hungry and soon ran into some deer. He sneaked up to the deer and killed it with a bow and arrow. He butchered it and dried the meat. He stayed there a couple of days until the meat was dry and then he packed it on one of the horses.

Thunder Sounds was roaming around all over for quite awhile, but he did not meet any hardships at all. Finally he came to a butte. Down at the bottom of the butte was a forest and from there on the butte went straight up from the flat. He got into the woods and camped there. That is, he planned to camp someplace there, and before looking for a place he had something to eat. He was pretty well dressed. He had a shield of otter skin across his chest and good clothes. Even the blanket he had was quilled (porcupine). His quiver full of arrows was covered with porcupine quills. His whole outfit was good.

He found a good place to stake his horses. Then he went up the hill and found a nice place where he could get the horses right away. He decided to lie down and sleep. He had his blanket and knife and he found some flat rocks coming out making a kind of cave in two or three stories. He selected a good place under a shelving rock and lay down and went to sleep. He was tired, so he was pretty sound asleep and did not wake up.

When he did awake, it was nearly daybreak. He heard something

"The Dakota," in *Cooperation and Competition among Primitive Peoples,* ed. Margaret Mead, rev. ed. (Boston: Beacon Press, 1966 [original 1937]), pp. 398–99.

somewhere, so he listened. It seemed someone was snoring someplace, and it seemed to be right under him. He reached down, and right underneath on the rocks beneath him was a man, and when he reached down the man grabbed his arm. The fellow held his hand and made sign talk meaning: "Who are you?" So he replied in sign language: "Cheyenne," and asked: "Who are you?" The man was from a different tribe (two trees come together and rub each other), probably Chickasaw.[7] So one made a motion meaning: "Go to sleep. When the sun comes up we will see each other." He was so tired that he fell asleep again. He knew it was an enemy but he fell asleep anyway.

He woke up and the sun was coming up; he looked down and the other one was still sleeping. He waked him up and he jumped up. There was a fine young man, about his age—good looking and well dressed. So he sat down on a rock and began to motion to him in sign talk where he came from. Then Thunder Sounds told the Chickasaw where he came from. The Chickasaw asked Thunder Sounds why he was traveling alone. Thunder Sounds said he had two sisters at home. "As a rule I never said a cross word to them, but one day they said bad words to me and I made up my mind to look for death. I am going to roam around." The Chickasaw laughed. "Whatever you told me, in my case it was the same thing. I have two sisters and got in a row with them and I am just ashamed. I am out here just as you are—I am looking for death."

The Chickasaw was handsome just like the other one. He said: "I am looking for death, and you are too. So it is right here. But I have some good provisions. We shall eat first and then look for a good place and then fight to the death." So Thunder Sounds agreed. So they started to eat, and they had their fill. Then they dressed up the best they could, combed their hair, and got ready to fight. The Chickasaw had the ideas, and then Thunder Sounds agreed, but he did not have the ideas in the first place.

7. As a southeastern tribe, the Chickasaws probably did not use the sign language before their removal to present-day Oklahoma during the first part of the nineteenth century. Although it seems unlikely that this man was a Chickasaw, no definite identification seems possible on the basis of the sign language tribal designation. A similar story is recorded about two scouts, a Sioux and a Crow, who also met at night in a cave; in this story they killed each other the next morning, then the two war parties to which they belonged called a truce. See Ella Cara Deloria, *Dakota Texts,* Publications of the American Ethnological Society 14 (New York: G. E. Stechert, 1932), pp. 266–68.

The Chickasaw got to thinking and he said: "I don't think it is right for one of us to die here and one to go back alive. It is best for us to both live and go back alive. Your story is just like mine, so here is another proposition. We can have a hand game. I will bet all my clothes and my hair and my two good horses; I will bet all I have; you bet all you have, and we will play a hand game." (One sings a special hand game song without words except "hi-ye hi-ya." They use two sticks, one black and the other plain. They guess which hand has the stick: other sticks — twelve — are used for counters.)

Thunder Sounds agreed. They had the game. They went down in the brush and made twelve [counting] sticks and the [two] small sticks for the hand game. Thunder Sounds started to sing and the Chickasaw started to swing. Thunder Sounds was unlucky and missed every time. Every time he missed the Chickasaw took one stick. There was just one left — and then Thunder Sounds guessed correctly. He took the stick, and the Chickasaw sang. He missed four times, and the fifth time he guessed. Thunder Sounds had four sticks to the good, and there was no stick in the middle now. The Chickasaw got away with three sticks and then missed. Then it was Thunder Sounds' turn and the Chickasaw was unlucky. Pretty soon he had just one stick left. Thunder Sounds got that one, so he won. The Chickasaw took off all his clothes, moccasins, everything, and gave them to Thunder Sounds. Thunder Sounds danced and sang a victory song. When the Chickasaw gave his knife to Thunder Sounds, he said: "You can cut off my hair, because I lost." So Thunder Sounds gave a yell and touched him for the coup, and then he cut off the long hair of the Chickasaw.

Then he felt bad about it and he said: "Well, you have been propositioning me and I agreed so now it is my turn to make you an offer. I will make a proposition." So he took off his clothes and gave them to the Chickasaw and gave him his knife, and said he could coup him too. So the Chickasaw jumped up and yelled and then couped him, and cut off his hair. They both looked terrible and they laughed about it. Their clothes were right there on the ground. Thunder Sounds said: "I have two horses, and I am going to give them to you." The other said: "I have two, too, and you can have them." They did not dress, but went to get the horses naked. Thunder Sounds had two fine sorrel spotted horses, and the other had black and white spotted horses. They shook hands and said: "This is going to be the best and biggest thing we have ever done." They looked at each other's heads and they looked funny, so they both laughed. After they exchanged horses, each put on the other's clothes. Everything seemed to fit pretty well.

The Chickasaw said: "This will be a big thing. You go home, and I will go home. Before we leave we will select a day to meet here again. But your people and my people will meet here." They selected a day and time of year. This happened in the spring, and they selected a day as near as they could, When the Cherries Are Black [August] of the same year. They shook hands and parted.

Thunder Sounds went back, taking his time, and it took several days to find his people. It was the custom when you came back with a scalp and horses to make a charge. He tied the hair of the enemy on a stick and made a charge with the black spotted horses around the middle. He went and told everything as it had happened to his father. So they made a big celebration. The father got the candidates, chief and akichita together and made a proposition of going over there at a certain day. The council approved and one day When the Cherries Were Black the Cheyennes went all toward that place and arrived there. While they were moving camp, they gave orders for no one to go scouting.

When they got close to the place and could see the butte, they camped there. Early in the morning Thunder Sounds got on his horse and went out scouting. He met his friend up on the butte. Down there he saw the whole Chickasaw tribe coming. They made arrangements for all of them to coup each other with blunt instruments or a shawl. When you coup you say "An he." They also arranged to exchange everything when they couped. Their people were all dressed up the best they had. When the signal was given, they started for each other, and then couped each other as if they were fighting, but they were not fighting.

While they were couping each other, when they got through, the Chickasaw had two sisters. Everything they had they put together in the middle and gave to Thunder Sounds' father. Thunder Sounds' father took it and did the same. Each gave everything he had to the other family. The tribes did that all day; all the families exchanged things all day. There were too many Chickasaws, and some did not get to exchange anything. That is why the two tribes never did fight. They lived together and did not fight. They named the butte "Pouting Butte." The boys were brothers and so the sisters were their sisters too. Otherwise they might have married each other's sisters; but it was not possible.

THE STORY OF HIGH HORSE'S COURTING

Black Elk said High Horse's courting is absolutely true.[8] He knew High Horse and he told Black Elk that story. He knew his wife that he courted that way, too, and they lived to a ripe old age. High Horse was a Northern Cheyenne. It really happened. High Horse was an old man about thirty years ago, and that is when he told Black Elk the story. Black Elk visited him in his home about a week.

These are traditional stories and are not made up. They are handed down from parents to children. Any old man knows these stories.

THE YOUNG MAN WHO PRETENDED TO BE A GHOST

There was a party going back to camp someplace. There were four of them, three of them old men. They met a party—a man and his wife—going back to their camp. They ran out of smokes, had kinnikinnick but no tobacco. They asked the man if he had tobacco. He said: "No, but back here just yesterday my son died and he had a lot of it. He had three or four long plugs. I don't smoke so I left it there. We left my son on a couch (bier) in his tipi.[9] We stayed there last night and he just died yesterday. I put the tobacco at his feet. You can pick it up and go, if you want to." They decided when they got there they would light it and offer it to the spirit of the young man and then take the tobacco.

The young man was a hellish young man and decided to fool them. He said he was going for a horse he had seen. Instead, he went around and rode fast and went ahead of them and came to the tipi where the young man (dead) was lying. He left his horse and went down to the creek and took some black clay and used a bladder of a cow to cover his hair, and then put mud all over himself and sneaked into the tent where the dead man lay. He found the tobacco.

8. Black Elk had related the story of High Horse's courting to Neihardt in 1931, but stenographic notes for the story have not been located. It was originally published in *Black Elk Speaks*, pp. 67–76, and reprinted in Neihardt, "High Horse's Courting," *Indians at Work* 12(5) (January–February 1945): 19–22. The same story was reworded for *When the Tree Flowered*, pp. 77–83.

9. Sometimes a lodge was erected around the burial place of a distinguished warrior. See Hassrick, *The Sioux*, p. 297.

Pretty soon the other three came along. They said: "Well, our nephew should be coming back. It won't hurt if we go in there and get the tobacco. He will be along soon." The young man was in there and looked terrible. The three came in; the older one filled his pipe and said he would offer it to the spirit of the young man. So he did. "Young man, whoever you are and wherever your spirit is, here is the offering. We ask the favor of you that no evil will come to us for taking the tobacco. We will always remember when our days are ripe." About that time the young man peeked out and said, "How!" They threw down their blankets and ran away. The young fellow chased after them. One of the old men was slow running and the fellow grabbed him and he fainted. The other one the same. The third was pretty speedy so he chased him all around and then back to where the others lay. He grabbed him. The old man said, "Anhhh," and passed out. So the young fellow went to the creek and washed up and got his horse and went back and then came loping towards them as if he did not know anything.

When he came back their eyes were all popping out. He said: "What is the matter?"

"Well, nephew, the young man was a ghost and he chased us, and these two passed out, and I went all over the country and he chased me and when he caught me he touched me and I passed out." The young man said he would go in but they said: "No, he will chase you." But he went in and got the tobacco. They did not even want the tobacco. When he brought out their blankets, they did not even want to touch them.

[13]

December 8

I want to tell you about a fight between the Sioux and the Crows and how the Crows escaped. It was at Crow Butte.[1] The Lower Brulé band was camped at a creek east of what is now known as Crow Butte. There was another creek called Beaver Creek. The main body of the Sioux camped at Beaver Creek. The Lower Brulés were quite a distance from the main camp. It was in the winter time. Everything was quiet around the camp; nothing stirred. They were not afraid because no enemies were creeping around.

The Crows just ran into the camp. Of course the warriors were ready at any time. When the Crows saw the camp, they ran the other direction. There were about thirty-two Crows and they had one horse and two dogs. They fought on the way, but neither side did anything [counted coup]. The Brulés were on foot too. They came to the butte, and there is only one way to get up it. The Crows went up the butte and they had the advantage of the Sioux, so they killed two. They had guns. Of course when the enemy ran into the camp, it was toward evening. The Sioux had the Crows pocketed on the butte all night.

The next morning the other bunch at Beaver Creek heard of it, and a big war party was coming. That day the big party of Sioux came up; it was toward evening then. The Crows built a rock fence at the entrance to the butte and the Sioux could not go there. The Indians decided to wait until

1. Crow Butte is south of the White River, about eight miles east of Fort Robinson, Nebr. Cf. Bordeaux, *Conquering the Mighty Sioux,* pp. 40–45.

morning and then charge. They built fires all around the opening. They did not watch on the other side because it was very steep on the other side and no one could get down. The only way down was through that one pass, which they watched carefully. Right at the entrance a Sioux was killed and a Crow killed, but they could not get the bodies.

In the middle of the night one of the Crows was singing a death song, and soon he was moaning. That was in the middle of the night. After one of them was chanting the song, later they heard a dog howling. The Sioux knew they could not get out; it was just impossible. When dawn came, they were ready to charge. They selected leaders to go first and then they charged. When they went up, there was no one; not a soul was there. Even the horse was gone. They went around the bluff and saw ropes tied to a tree and they had crawled down. This must have happened early in the night because they traced them and they were far away. The Sioux knew that they got away and were pretty far ahead, so they decided not to follow them.

Later I went over there and I know a Crow who is a good friend of mine. He is old, but his oldest brother was in that fight; he was pretty young then. He told me just what happened. The one who was chanting a death song, after he got through singing he came over to cheer the boys up. "Cheer up. We are going to get out of here. I have a plan. But if we do get back alive, we are all going to offer a piece of our flesh to the Myste-rious One. We will all agree to do that. When we get home we will cut off the tip of our little finger and offer that as an offering." That was quite an offering. So he started to sing again and then sent a voice to the Great Spirit to guide him and keep him safe and said when they got home each one would offer up a piece of his body.

They selected two to go down to scout first. They were to go around the bluff and scout. They tied ropes together and each one had an extra one with him so if they did not get down, they could tie the ropes on the other end. They got down safely, and if they could get away, they were going to pull the rope twice; if there were enemies, they were going to jerk the rope three times and they would be pulled up. When they got to the ground they jerked it once and then went scouting. There was no one watching on that side at all. So they came back and jerked the rope twice. So the medicine man said they would send the horse down first. So they got all the ropes from the thirty men and got ready to send the horse down.

They let the horse down. First they tied his four legs together. Then they put ropes on him and sent him down. After the horse got down, the two men untied the horse and sent the ropes back up so that two at a time could get down. All the time the medicine man was singing to fool the Sioux and make them think they were up against it. Finally the medicine man went down—the last one, and that is when the singing stopped. It was full moon at that time, so the men all had to stop under the shade of the bluff so they would not be seen. Of course they had to sneak out, and they all stayed together as close as possible so they would not be seen. They got over a little hill and then started running. As they ran, there were two young boys in the bunch. One fellow would take one boy up, drop him, come back and get the other one who was having the harder time, then take him on up ahead and come back. They kept on doing that.

They had gone quite a way and remembered they had forgotten the dogs and had not let them down. When the Sioux went up the bluff, they did not find the dogs—they were not there. After they had gone quite a way, they took their time, for they were not pursued. One of the dogs got home four days before the men did, so the people at home thought they had all been wiped out. About two days later, the other dog got back. When they got back, they remembered their promised offering. They had a ceremony and a feast and then each one of the thirty cut off his little finger tip. That is how the thirty Crows got away and that is how the Crow Butte was named.

That is a [Crow] custom to offer a piece of flesh; even now if you go over there [Crow Reservation] you will find old men with the tips of their fingers gone.[2] A man is apt to do wrong, that is why in their life they should give something as a penance to reach the happy hunting ground.

The Crow's name was Arms around Bare.

THE SHOSHONES KILL THIRTY LAKOTAS

The story I am going to tell I got from a man who took part in it. To prove it, the old man who was in that fight died ten years after we settled down (1878) and lived to a ripe old age. His name was Bad Boy. (Ripe old age— gan-inhuni [*kan ihunni*]: "arrived old.") He was my grandfather in a way,

---

2. See Robert H. Lowie, *The Crow Indians* (New York: Farrar and Rinehart, 1935), p. 68.

and he was in that fight. This fight is pretty well known, so I cannot add on anything or tell it the wrong way. It is quite a story to the Sioux, because that was the greatest number of Sioux killed.

The Sioux were camping on the west side of the Black Hills, and the party went southwest. This happened along the Rocky Mountains. It was in the winter and they were all afoot. There was deep snow. It was a lot of warriors—over one hundred. The snow was deep, so they could not travel fast. They were at the foot of the Rockies in the deep snow. They stopped on a ridge, and down the ridge it was rolling and beyond was another ridge. Four volunteered to go scouting, and they went on ahead. They could see the four and it took quite a while to get over to the next ridge. When they got over there, it seemed something happened, for they heard shots. So the party got ready, for they thought the enemy was near. This happened in a way it could not be helped. When the four got on top of the ridge, two men on horseback came up the ridge. They shot one, and the other one got away. The two horsebacks were a boy and his father. They killed the father, but the little five-year-old boy got away. He was tied to the saddle, and when they shot the father, the horse stampeded and took the boy home. The scouts were on foot and could not catch the horses.

When they came back to report it it seemed one of the four was a smarty and he did not think trouble would come from his words. They had scalped the Indian and couped him, and each one had an honor from it. This fellow was not a good warrior, but he had a brother-in-law that was a good warrior. He said: "Brother-in-law, go see where your husband butchered."[3] At that time such words made a man mad. So the others told him to shut up. He said: "They will be coming, and we will fight." But the one man kept on nagging his brother-in-law about what he had done. So finally his brother-in-law said: "How. I will go see where you butchered. That is what I came for, I am a man to look for death." There were six brothers in the bunch, so when he went four of the five brothers went. All had friends, so they volunteered to go, for they knew there were enemies coming and the one man would have no show at all.

The warrior that went first to see where the brother-in-law butchered

3. In Lakota culture, kinship etiquette called for brothers-in-law to joke roughly with one another. In this case the joker has gone too far, calling his brother-in-law a woman. For the Lakotas, this was the greatest insult one man could give another.

was named He Crow. The one that caused the trouble was Last Dog. The thirty went and the others watched. The thirty were all fine young warriors. As the thirty went on top of the ridge where the man had been killed, the Shoshone war party came on horseback. The thirty were on foot. They were the very best warriors. The Shoshones had the advantage, because they were on horses. The big Sioux war party could do nothing, for they were on foot and could not get there in time. One of the thirty who was one of the brothers was the last one dead. He killed six Shoshones before they got him. The Sioux were really whipped there, because the Shoshones were on horseback. They fought for quite a time and even threw rocks down on the Shoshones. A blizzard saved the day, and the Sioux started to retreat. One man had left his blanket. It was pretty hard because [another] man had to share his blanket with this one.

When Last Dog taunted his brother-in-law, He Crow, who was a great warrior, he meant to insult his brother-in-law. Last Dog was not a great warrior, but just because he had killed the Shoshone, he kept bragging about it. So he was the cause of the thirty being killed. If He Crow had not gone, perhaps in the future Last Dog would have said "Hello, wife," or "How do you like what your husband did?" So He Crow had to go, for the other man had dared him to go. The trouble was all caused by a "mouthy" man. That was the only time the Sioux were ever whipped. On the way home they ran into some buffalo in a blizzard and they killed some. They ate and then used the hides to keep warm.

THE WOMAN FOUR TIMES WIDOWED

I am going to tell the story about how one woman became a widow four times and the fifth time she got killed. This is a story of the Sisseton. I forgot the name of the woman, so we will have to give her a name. This is quite a story and I want to get it as nearly correct as I can. The Sioux at Sisseton all know this story. I will give her the name of Sees White Cow. I got the story from a Sisseton; I was over there and got to talking with this old fellow who was gan inhuni. It seems that at certain times the tribe all got together and other times they all scattered. This happened when they were scattered.

This woman had a suitor named Turning Eagle. Turning Eagle had been courting her while the people were together. She and her folks were in a certain group going one direction and Turning Eagle belonged to a different band going a different direction. It was a hard parting, but Turning Eagle thought he would follow his girl and not go with his party. At that time there were few horses and he had a good horse, so he followed where Sees White Cow went. She was the only girl in the family and had four brothers. After arriving where the girl's band was, he went to her folks and made a bargain to buy her for the saddle horse he had. At that time horses were rare and it was quite a thing to have a horse. So they became man and wife. Of course this was long ago and there were not many guns, mostly bows and arrows. He had a bow and arrow. After he married her, he wanted to go back to his band with her. They got ready to go on foot. Sees White Cow packed their provisions for them.

Early the next morning they started out. On the second day they were coming down to a lake. There were trees around it. As they came down, Sees White Cow, who had keen eyes, said, "Look, there is someone peeking out of the brush by the lake." Turning Eagle said, "No that is not a man, that is an otter." She looked and saw another and several others. Still Turning Eagle would not believe it, because he [could not] see them. Sees White Cow [said,] "I am going, because there are enemies there." She ran and just as she got to the top of the hill there was a war party. They got her man and so she ran. They chased her and shot at her but they could not catch her. She got back to the camp and told about it. Some that had horses went out after the enemies. The enemy were Chippewas. The Sioux war party wiped out the Chippewas. Two of her brothers became famous there in that fight. Right there she had lost her first husband. If he had listened to her, he might have lived. This happened somewhere in eastern South Dakota or Minnesota.

Sees White Cow mourned for her man and cut her hair. Later another suitor came along and his name was Chasing Otter. I guess he bought her and married her. After she married him the Sisseton were camped near a lake and they had canoes. Across the lake was a bank with many trees and some plum brush. Someone said there were ripe plums. Her husband heard about the plums so he came back and told his wife. "Why don't we paddle over there and get some good ripe plums?" She said, "That would be nice." So they got in the canoe and crossed over. They found plums over there and while they were picking them, she saw some higher up on the bank that were very large and ripe. She crawled up and there was a ridge up there and beside it the plums. When she got up there, she looked over and saw a man on the other side. She ducked down and crawled back and told her husband, "An enemy peeked at us. Let's get out of here." But he would not believe her and said it was just someone picking plums. Sure enough, it was the enemy, and they started charging. She got in the canoe and paddled out. The man started running, but he was too late. They shot at her, but she got away in the canoe. She went back and told it, and a war party went out and killed a number of them. Again her two brothers became famous for killing, scalping, couping, etc. Twice she had been married and both times she sensed the trouble, but the men would not believe her.

The third husband was named Tall Horse. He bought the widow again and that was the third time she was sold. Tall Horse came from a distance and from a different band. After they got married, they stayed a while and then they started back to his people. There were few horses so they went on foot. They traveled all day, and in the night they came to a rugged country—hilly and wooded. They selected a good spot rather hidden and made camp there. They made a little hut with grass and brush and it was quite well concealed. Before they camped, her mind traveled back to how she had lost both of her husbands before, so she was on the alert all the time. She selected the place herself, and she thought it was pretty well concealed and safe. She lay awake all night worrying and toward morning she heard the call of an otter, but she sensed that it was a man whistling like an otter. Then she heard another otter call from a different direction. "Tall Horse, get up. I hear an otter calling but it is not an otter, it is a man. Then there was another one. You had better get up, because I think the enemy has surrounded us. We can go down the ravine and escape." But the man said, "No, that is just the otters calling to each other." She insisted they were men. He insisted they were otters. She said: "Man, I know. You had better come if you want to live. I am going and you had better come." He said: "They are just otters."

"I am going anyhow."

As she went out there was a little wash, and she crawled down it. When she got about one hundred yards there were men coming up. She lay still in the grass. A couple men nearly stepped on her. They went to the hut and pretty soon she heard shots. They had got her man again. Then she got up and started running and the men followed her. But it was late at night between midnight and morning. It was full moon. She followed the ravine to a flat place where there was a tree. She stopped in the shade. Two men ran past her, but did not see her. She crossed the ravine and went the other way as fast as she could and hid again in some brush. She went back traveling all night and all day. She told about it and where it was. The war party went out and her brothers with it. They came upon the enemy and her brothers were heroic again. It seemed in losing her man her brothers kept becoming more and more famous. They were up in the world and had proven themselves qualified to be candidates for chief. Every time she got married, it seemed her brothers were given a boost up. Now she was a widow again. By her becoming three times a widow, her brothers became famous. The three times she sensed the trouble and her husbands would not listen and got killed.

She did not want to get married; she never had luck, so she decided to stay single to save men. But she met a nice looking warrior, pretty nice fellow, and his name was Red Horse. He courted her for quite a while; but she did not want to marry him. She sensed she would lose him again. But Red Horse finally won her. Finally her brothers, who liked him, wanted her to marry him. His father was a chief. So she married him, all against her will. But she already sensed that there would be trouble. Of course Red Horse was from a different band and wanted to go back, but she would not go. She even forbid him to go on war parties. So they got along nicely for a little while.

At that time the enemy did not roam around much and they were enjoying themselves. But it was spring and everyone was out digging turnips. They had horses, so Red Horse went out to feed his horses. He came back and said: "There are a lot of turnips. Why don't we go out and get some?" She said, "All right, we'll go." So they went. She asked if it was far, but it was just near, so she decided to go. They decided to go on foot, for it was close. They crossed the creek, and found a lot of turnips. They dug all day long, for they had lunch with them. They did not intend to camp out there. But they had a lot of them and Red Horse decided they should peel them and braid them. He decided it was all right, and so he suggested that they sleep out and get up early and dig some more. He said they could go down in the ravine and build a good place with the two sticks they had to dig the turnips with and the little blanket they had. It was summer, and so they could just sleep there.

She went to sleep, and in the middle of the night she woke up and thought about the other husbands. Of course she had warned him before, but he would not listen. Lying there she heard an otter whistling again. The otters are usually in the lake, but she heard one whistle above and then from another direction. So she woke Red Horse and told him the enemy was surrounding them. "The otters are whistling, but it is men." He said: "No, that is otters. They are mating and are calling." She said, "I warned you before, and I am going." She crawled out and in creeping along she did not go far before she met two of them. She hid in the brush and saw the two men creeping toward their little camp. It was not long before she heard shots, so she got up and ran to the main camp. She got back and reported it, and again the war party went out. When the war party reached the little camp they found the enemies had butchered Red Horse like a hog and hung him on a tree. They had scalped him, too. So I guess the brothers became famous again, because they met the enemy and killed all of them.

When it was all over, she said she would never, never get married again. She stayed single quite awhile. Again a suitor named Flies Back came along. He was rich and wanted to marry her. He bought her for two horses, and she would not marry, but again her brothers insisted. They got along well. It was in the fall when the ducks were gathering to fly south. One day Flies Back decided they should go to one of the lakes and get some ducks. He thought it was safe to go out and camp out there and get some ducks early in the morning. She gave in, and they went and took a little dog with them. They went on foot and took a little tipi. They camped out there. He went out hunting to get ducks and she stayed alone in the tipi. She was looking around and in the trees she thought she saw something. It was a man behind a tree. He got out and dashed behind another tree. He just kept going from tree to tree and disappeared.

Just then her husband brought back some ducks. When Flies Back came, she told him: "I saw a man out in the woods. He went from tree to tree and then finally he disappeared. We had just as well go back." Flies Back said: "I don't think that is an enemy. It might be someone out hunting ducks." She gave in. But it bothered her. They cooked the ducks and ate and then went to bed. But she did not sleep. The little dog started to bark and she woke the man. "You had better get up. We are surrounded; there are men all around the camp." She warned him, and then she got up and ran. Her husband went the other way. She heard some shots. He got away and ran back, and when he got there, his wife was not there. So he told them, and a war party went out. At the kill her brothers became famous again. They looked for her and found her scalped and dead. Later on the story goes that she hid well but the dog followed her and the two enemies heard the dog bark. They found her and shot her and scalped her. That is how the woman got married and the men got killed four times and the fifth time she was killed and the man got away. After the war party got back, her brothers killed the husband, because he did not stay with her and defend her.[4]

THE DOG WHO SAVED THE PEOPLE

I am going to tell about how a dog saved a man. This fellow's name was Good Eagle and he was a good rustler [provider]; his family was well fed all the time. He was not noted for warfare, but he took good care of his family. He had two daughters, one about thirteen—a young woman—and the other two or three years old. They were out on a hunting party. Good Eagle went out for himself and took his family. There was no danger, for the scouts had been all over and reported no danger. The people had all gone out to hunt. They went a little distance and finally they came to a place with plenty of grass and water, so they camped there. He hunted and got several buffalo and deer. They felt safe and roamed at will. She dried lots of meat. They had a little dog with four pups. They enjoyed themselves camping there in their tipi. The man went out hunting and the family stayed home to dry meat.

One evening Good Eagle got tired and went to bed, but the others woke up. The little girl came asking for something to eat, and her mother gave her something; pretty soon she came back in asking for more, and she did that several times. Pretty soon the dog was sleeping in there with her pups. Meanwhile the enemies had crawled up to the tipi. There were about ten. I guess they had not eaten for so long that they were hungry. The little girl was giving the meat to the enemies—she did not know they were enemies. The taste of meat made them hungrier, so soon they went in the tipi uninvited. They did not know what to do. The man got up and told them to sit down. He told his wife to feed them. Then they lay down, for they were tired. The woman got some red paint. Whenever men came home tired, the woman would grease their feet to rest them. So the woman greased the enemies' feet and that made them more comfortable.

4. The theme of the woman who brings such bad luck to her husbands that each in turn is killed by enemies is repeated in "The Resuscitation of the Only Daughter," in Marie L. McLaughlin, *Myths and Legends of the Sioux* (Bismarck, N.D.: Bismarck Tribune Co., 1916), pp. 145–50.

Meanwhile the dog was yawning. The little girl thought the dog said something, so she listened. The dog was talking: "You take my little ones and run and you will be saved. If you don't, these men will kill you." So she told her mother the pup was talking. And the mother asked what the dog had said, and the girl told her. So she told the man. By that time the men had all gone to sleep. They could do nothing, so they went and got their horses, and the girl took the pups and put them inside her dress and started out. There was a fire in the middle and outside there was a big piece of tallow. So Good Eagle decided to do something to delay the enemies. He threw the tallow on the fire, and it made a big blaze. The grease flew all over and burned most of the men, and then he threw the burning tallow at them. The tipi was on fire and as Good Eagle rushed away he heard groans. The enemies were handicapped in chasing. That is how the family got away. The girl got to the camp and reported it and a big war party went out. They found the enemies and got them all—made a big kill. The enemies were on foot and were Blackfeet. They are noted for taking captives and were probably going to kidnap the little one.

THE DOG WHOSE WARNING WAS NOT HEEDED

This story is true, and the way I got it—this man's wife was pretty well known among the Sioux. Her name was Loud Woman. Her old man, I don't remember his name, but we will call him Good Buffalo. They had two sons and these sons had their wives. Good Buffalo had a sister and a young daughter. It was a family of eight. This happened about sixty years ago. They were out on a hunting party. It seemed everything was safe and they had the privilege of hunting in a small party. They were returning from the hunt. Good Buffalo told his wife and daughter and daughters-in-law to go to a certain place to camp so he and his sons could get some more game, which they did. They selected a good place and made a camp.

The men were out hunting and it was still early, but toward evening. They had a little dog and the dog was on a nearby hill barking. It barked and then howled. It was the girl's dog, and she listened, for she thought it was saying something. It said: "It is going to be terrible. We may as well go on. It is going to be terrible. We may as well go on." The girl told her mother what the dog seemed to be saying. The pup would come down and whine and wag its tail and seemed to be talking to everyone, but they did not understand. Then the dog went back up on the hill and started to bark and howl, and the girl understood again, "The ones from here are coming, and also they (enemy) are coming." The girl came running in and said, "Mother the dog is telling that my father and brothers are coming back and also someone else is coming—might be the enemy." Just then the dog said: "Let's go! Let's go!" So she told the mother that the dog said they should break camp. The mother said: "Yes, we should go, but we have to wait for the men. They should be here any time, and then we will know what to do." The dog went up and barked again, and said: "The men folks are coming. They are right here, but the others are here, too. We should go." It was just before dark.

The men folks came back. Good Buffalo's wife told him about the girl and what the dog had said. He did not believe it. "Sure, we are going, but we are camping now. We'll be going back." Then the dog went up on the hillock again. Again the girl understood: "They are here. You have no ears, so I am going," and the dog ran away. The girl told her father what the dog had said. Just then the old man called his sons and said, "Let's get together and see what happens." The dog barked far away and the girl said, "Mother, that dog is crying." Then they heard shots; the enemy had surrounded them.

After the dog barked and they heard shots, the old woman, Loud Mouth, got brave and made the sound they make when their men are doing something [the tremolo]. When she got out they shot her. So her man made a sound meaning he would be brave and face death. He went out, but he got shot. The sons went out and their wives made the tremolo, and they all went out but were shot. The daughter and the sister of Good Buffalo hid in the tipi under the blankets, but the sister was wounded in the leg. The enemy only took the horses and did not try to scalp. That is how these two lived to tell the story. The enemy were the Assiniboines. The Assiniboines are Sioux. The people figured they were Assiniboines because they did not talk. The two under the blankets lay there and thought the enemy would come back and scalp the others. They thought they might just as well die, too, so they lay there all night. But nothing happened. At daybreak the girl was unharmed and the aunt was wounded only in the flesh, not the bone. They went out and saw all their relatives killed, and they decided to drag them all back in the tipi, which they did. They thought they might just as well die with them if the enemy came back. They did stay there three days, but nothing happened.

The main camp was near there. Over there they had some near relatives and they usually camped together. One evening a dog was barking outside, and when they went out they saw the little dog, who barked and whined and started out, then came back, etc. So they thought the folks were coming back. The dog stayed three days there, and all the time barked and ran and howled and jumped up to the people and whined. One of the men noticed it and got to thinking about it. "This pup is trying to tell something. They might be in trouble; otherwise they would be back now. This dog knows something and is trying to tell us."

So this man told his son to get two or three warriors and get ready. "This dog is trying to tell us something. You should go out and hunt the folks." When the dog howled it seemed to be crying like a person. The warriors went out and the pup was full of joy and went with them. The dog was lame, so they carried it. Toward evening they were on top of a hill. The dog wanted to get off, so they put him down, and he went. They followed him and when they caught him he was sitting on the hill, barking. Down there they saw three tipis. Two had no smoke coming out; the third was smoking. The dog barked and went down to the tipi where his mistress was. The dog was full of joy. Just then the party of warriors arrived and the girl and her aunt came out crying. The warriors all cried, and when they were through crying, the girl told them all about it.

THE CHEYENNES RUN THE SHOSHONES OVER A BANK

I am going to tell about how the Shoshones were run up against the bank and all fell over the bank. The Shoshones were our worst enemies. Shooshooni [*Susuni*] is the way the Indians really say it. We called them Snake Men because that was the sign language name. This happened over toward the Rockies; the Cheyennes were camped there. One band was camped on top of the rock table and there was a creek or river bending below. The rest of the Cheyennes were camped down there. The Shoshones sent out some scouts and they came back and reported there was just one band of Cheyennes camped there, for they had not seen the other, larger camp. The Shoshones decided to attack with a big war party. As they came, they had plans to attack the next day; this was in the evening and dark. The leaders of the Shoshones said, "We will stay here, and you young warriors go to the Cheyenne camp and even if you get the horses one at a time, we will wait until morning." He planned to attack them afterward.

Among the Shoshones was a medicine man who objected to the plan. He said it would be a good thing to attack in the daytime instead of the night, because he said he saw clearly what would happen if they attacked at night. But the leader insisted they should attack that night after they had got the horses. The medicine man replied that in that case he was going to withdraw and would not participate. The warriors knew the medicine man and knew that he was right; as a sacred man they knew he saw things ahead. The medicine man stepped aside and said he was not going to take part and all those who wanted to should follow him. About half did go with him, but there were still a lot left. They started sneaking the horses out and all night long they did that. They did not know about the big camp below. It was just about dawn now.

Then they started to attack the village. They had guns. Little did they know what was in store for them; as they attacked they awoke the big village. The other Cheyenne warriors were soon there to fight the attackers. Some got killed on each side. It was quite dark. The Shoshones were going along a ravine and they chased them through there, and then there was a big bend and the Shoshones disappeared. It seemed they had disappeared into the ground. So the Cheyennes came back, and early the next morning they went out to where they had lost them and they saw a bend in the creek and a high bank. They had had the Shoshones cornered in there and they had fallen over in the dark. They had fallen on the rocks below and were all killed. That is how they chased the Shoshones over the bank. There was one Shoshone still hanging on the bank. He was caught on a rock and was alive. They selected a little ten or twelve year old boy and put a rope around him and he got the honor of couping him. Then they pushed him off the bank.

Lately we went over there because I wanted to find out the truth of the story. I met Washakie and he told me about this. Old man Fire Thunder that you knew was there and he saw the bodies.[5]

FLYING BY'S MOST DIFFICULT EXPERIENCE

I had an uncle and I asked him: "Uncle, what is the most difficult thing you ever encountered? Usually the Indians claim the most difficult things in an

---

5. This battle took place during late fall 1868. See Powell, *People of the Sacred Mountain*, pp. 771–73.

Indian's life [are]: food, losing the eldest child, losing your wife, a small war party meeting a big one." He said: "Nephew, that is nothing—those are not difficult. The most difficult thing I ever encountered was just a short time, but I never forgot it. We went on a warpath and stole some horses. I was with Crazy Horse. Gall was there, too. They were nice horses. We got back to the Missouri and had to cross it. It was high. I picked out a good bald-faced, white-stockinged horse out of the bunch for myself. We came to the river and had to swim through. We did and drove our horses across. The bald horse turned around in the middle of the stream and swam back. The others were on the other side, and I was also. So I told the fellows, "Wait for me, I will go back and get that horse." I left my clothes and everything and went across the river. I chased the horse and when I caught him, I heard something. All that time a steamship was coming down the river but they did not see it. The boat whistled, soldiers were on the boat, they fired on the Indians, and they ran. It was hot and I had no clothes or anything. The steamboat dropped anchor right there, and I could not very well cross. All night there were mosquitoes as big as my thumb. I went under the brush and all night long I fought mosquitoes. Next morning it was cool and moist. All the mosquito bites hurt. The boat had left and I swam across. The party had left, so I had to go back naked. It was the middle of the Moon of the Black Cherries and the sun was so hot that I got all blistered. That is the most difficult thing I ever encountered.

That was Flying By.

THE OLD BULL'S LAST FIGHT

Now I am going to tell about buffalo—how a buffalo eloped with a cow. This happened when we were in Canada. The people were moving and we went along on horseback. There were many buffalo, so we went out to hunt. We crossed the creek and over on the flat were a lot of buffalo. We were on top of the hill. We were looking over at the buffalo and saw two starting out away from the herd. Just then four others followed the two. There was an older man with us and he looked over and said: "There comes a buffalo with a cow. They are eloping. Whenever a buffalo elopes with a cow, that cow is fat. We will wait here."

As we watched, the two came down the creek and crossed it and then we could see them again. Then the other two came down the creek and were just below us on the level. The older fellow said to be very careful, because the buffalo would be mean. The couple stopped right below. We could see the cow was fat, and she stopped near the buffalo. The other four were stringing along. The buffalo stopped and the others stopped and looked at each other. The first of the four began to roll on the ground; they were bulls. Every time he hit the ground he threw a big chunk of dirt on himself. Then the buffalo that eloped with the cow did the same. The two bulls came pretty close together and then stopped and stared at each other. All at once they went for each other. When their foreheads hit they popped like a gun. They fought furiously and the dust covered them up. The dust cleared and it seemed one of the bulls flew up in the air and when he fell he staggered around.

After this fight the bull that won went over to the cow and then he wiped his horns on the ground. He was looking over at the three, and pretty soon one of the three began to roll, and then threw dirt on himself and bellowed. He came and then they charged on each other. They fought so furiously that the dust came in clouds. One went up in the air, and before he hit the ground the other one ran at him, hit him, and his guts came out. Then he went back to the cow and wiped his horns off again. The same thing happened again with the third buffalo. The one that eloped with the cow was the winner again. He went back and wiped his horns again. The fourth bull did the same. When he got up from rolling he had some kind of weed on his horns. This time they did not wait, but just went for each other. They fought a long time. We saw one go up in the air, and then the other one went up in the air. The bull who had killed three came back to the cow and stood there swaying. The other one fell over. The cow came over to the bull and bellowed and pushed him around, trying to make him come to. But it was just hopeless, the bull fell on his knees. Then one of the men shot the cow and we went down there.

I had never seen such a sight before. The first one killed was all broken, his ribs were all torn apart. The second one he had hooked right at the heart and he broke through the ribs and shoulder. The other one was stuck in the belly and torn down towards the hip and thigh. The fourth one was hooked between the ribs. Two of the ribs were torn and his shoulder was nearly torn off. The bull that eloped was stabbed in the ribs and down below the stomach. They all died. We got the cow and she was very fat. We did not butcher the bulls, because the older fellow said not to do it, since they had murdered each other. We divided the cow into four parts.

December 11

THE OGLALA WAR PARTY THAT MET A CRAZY BUFFALO

Just lately chief Red Cloud and White Hawk were the leaders of a war party. It was quite a bunch of warriors. They camped in the summer on the North Platte River. They went up the North Platte and camped several times before they got to enemy territory. Then they proceeded north. They came on a ridge and rested there for a while. As they looked down in the valley they saw a lot of buffalo. It seemed someone was hunting in the herd; the dust would fly up and when the dust would clear away, they could see something lying there but could see no person. That happened several times. One of the older men in the party said: "You men see something happening down there; that is a Crazy Buffalo. It is quite a distance, but a Crazy Buffalo has a sensitive smell. Pretty soon he will smell us, and he will be coming."

The hill where they were had no trees. The old man suggested they try to get down in the woods as fast as they could. They were all afoot, so they hurried to the woods. Just as they got on the edge of the woods, someone looked back and said, "Here he comes!" He was right on the ridge. He bellowed. Down he came, so the men all scattered for the woods. Luckily the first tree was a great big cottonwood. One of the limbs was down to the ground. They all ran for that big tree and climbed it. The buffalo came bellowing and hit the tree and took a big chunk off of it. They had guns so they started to shoot at him, but it seemed they could not kill him. He just kept on hitting the tree. It seemed they could not kill him with a gun.

Everyone was excited because he was taking the tree chip by chip. Of course it was big, but anyone would be scared when he kept hitting the tree chip by chip.

Red Cloud said: "You can't kill that buffalo; the hide is too thick. I will hit one of the legs." He did that; he shot twice and broke three legs. The buffalo could not do anything more, so they all came down and looked at the buffalo. It seemed he did not have any hair on his body. It seemed to be all dirt. That is how they killed that Crazy Buffalo.

They wanted to know how he looked inside so they butchered him. His lungs were nearly dried up. His paunch was the same; there was hardly anything left. There was nothing but dirt in the paunch. Between the skin and hide it was all frothy; he did not seem to have any blood. Those Crazy Buffalo can smell human beings and whether they can see them or not they set out to find them. Red Cloud told this. It must have been around 1844. Red Cloud was very young then.

After butchering the buffalo they continued. As they went along, one of them said: "I think it is bad that we go on. I think that buffalo was holy, and we killed it, so we should go back." Red Cloud said: "No, it is going to be the other way; it's going to be a charm. That is the bravest thing we ever killed, so we will make a big kill. We will go on."

They were going to go north, but the Crazy Buffalo changed their direction, and they went back to the North Platte River and followed it a little direction toward the Rocky Mountains. They came on a ridge and stopped and looked again. There was a valley and another ridge across. A deer was lying there and they all watched it. Pretty soon the deer made the sound—a trilling sound. Pretty soon the deer got up. As they passed by, the deer got up. One of the party looked back and said: "That deer we saw seems to have big hind legs. So let's all turn back and see." They did and the deer was trying to run. They surrounded him and it was a man. He had a deerskin on and had a bow and arrow. He was out hunting that way. It was a Shoshone. If he had not got up, they would not have bothered with him. Red Cloud knocked him over the head, and someone couped him and another killed him and then they scalped him. The party did not do much; when they encountered the Crazy Buffalo it took the braveness out. Half thought something bad would happen; half something good. When they killed the man, they thought it would be best to go home, because they were on foot and the Shoshones had horses. They were afraid, so they all went back home. When they came back, they had a celebration. They had only one scalp, but it was something.[1]

RIVER NAMES

They call the North Platte Duck [*Maǧa*] River. Platte River they call the Pankiska [*Pankeska*], Shell River. The South Platte is called Horse Creek.[2] The shell referred to is not a natural shell but something made out of a buffalo bone. It is white like a pearl, and is a rare thing among the Sioux. There are few who know how to make it. Not all the buffalo have that; once in a while they find a buffalo like that. It is where the leg joins the hip; it is a cup-like thing fitting against the socket bone. Possibly some injury causes a secretion which formed the shell-like formation. Later the white men made some to look like the real ones. There was an old man named this called Pankiska Wakan [Holy Shell]; he died near the Platte.

Niobrara: Minnetanka [*Mnitanka,* Big Water]. Missouri: Minneshoshay [*Mniśośe,* Turbid Water]. White [River]: Maka-izita [*Makizita*], "Smoking earth." There is a place on one of the river banks where smoke came out. That is how they named the river. Cheyenne [River]: Wachpela washte [*Wakpala waśte,* Good River]. Belle Fourche: Forks of the Good River. In olden times it was known as the Sun Dance River because they had a Sun Dance Hill near there [near present-day Sun Dance, Wyoming]. In later years they called it Good River Fork.

LITTLE POWDER RESCUES HIS FAMILY
FROM THE SHOSHONES

It was summer and the people were scattered out. One band moved out. A man named Little Powder had three daughters. The oldest one was quite a girl, nearly a woman. The second one got sick and died. The youngest one

1. George Bushotter, a Teton, recorded a similar story (in Dorsey, *A Study of Siouan Cults,* p. 477). In religious terms, the Crazy Buffalo (*Tatanka gnaśkinyan*) was considered a fearful embodiment of evil (Walker, *Lakota Belief and Ritual,* p. 94).

2. There is apparently confusion here. The Lakotas called both the Platte and the North Platte rivers Shell River. Duck River is reported as their name for the Laramie; both it and Horse Creek are tributaries of the North Platte. The South Platte was called Fat River (*Waśin wakpa*). See Buechel, *A Dictionary of the Teton Dakota Sioux Language,* p. 758.

was two years old. Little Powder told his brother: "I am going out and try to get some meat, and then I will come back. I will go tomorrow early and stay overnight and then come back early the next day."

Next day he took his wife and two children along and they moved camp that day. They selected a place and made camp. He went off hunting. Little Powder had pretty good luck and did not have to go far to get a fine, fat buffalo cow. He butchered in a hurry, because the sun was going down. He had a packhorse, so he packed the meat and at dusk started back for where his family was camped. He could see quite a distance still. When he came there, he saw no tipi and was alarmed. He came and found that the tipi was pushed over, everything scattered, and his family gone. It seemed it was the work of an enemy, so he looked around but could not find anyone. It was dark. In looking for them earlier he could see the horses' hoof marks going a certain direction. He threw the meat away and headed for the main camp on the horse. He reported to his brother that he thought the enemy had got his family. He told that the horses had showed they were heading a certain way. Of course they had taken all his good horses. His brother loaned him some good horses. He told him he was going to follow and for his brother to go back to the camp and look for the bodies of his family. He was going to follow the enemy that same night.

Next morning his brother told everyone, and they got ready and went out to where he had camped. That night he did not know just which way to go, but the tracks had seemed to be heading north. He rode all night. When the dawn came, he happened to be on the tracks. He tracked them until they hit a turn and headed west again. In that country there is nothing but sage and no grass, so it was easy to follow the tracks. He crossed the Platte River. He went on that evening as best he could, but he was afraid he lost track. He rested, and the next morning he found the tracks again and followed them. He rode all day and saw nothing but the tracks. He followed in the moonlight until about midnight, and then rested. At dawn he knew he was pretty close to them. He rode all that day, until it got dark. Then he followed again in the moonlight until it got dark, and then he rested again. That was the fourth day. This was the fifth day, and he came on a big hill and looked down and saw the camp. Just as the party was pulling into the big camp, he got on the hill and saw them. He had nearly caught them.

He waited on the ridge all evening until it got dark. He hid the horses and went up to the camp. He could see the people were excited over something—there was singing and hollering. Then he saw them gathered in the middle where they had a tree. They were hanging up something, and he thought it was probably his little girl. He watched, and did not know what to do. He went back and got his horses and brought them close to camp. He was so mad about it that he did not care whether he died or not. He saw they were Shoshones and so he wore the blanket as they did. He had a gun, and went in with the others. They thought he was a Shoshone and did not notice him. It was so important that he did not care. Every time he saw a Shoshone he felt like shooting him, but he restrained himself. He got near to where they were dancing and saw it was just a coyote hide they had hung up there. They were having a victory dance. He did not see his wife or children and was worried. They were all going back to their tipis so he pretended to be going back to his.

He waited in the brush until he thought everyone was [finished] moving around and going to bed, so he went in and found the tipi where his wife and two daughters were. He thought of going in there, but decided not to. Each time he started to go in, it seemed someone told him not to. Before the tribe went to bed, as he went around, he had picked out some good horses and slipped them down (three) to where he had his horses. The Shoshones wrap their blankets close all the time, so they did not notice him. He waited close to the tent where his wife was and soon everyone was asleep. They did not think anyone was following them, and since they were women they did not tie up the captives. There were guards at the door but they were not watching very carefully. After traveling all those days they were tired.

The tipi was near the creek, and he had his horses hidden underneath the bank. He went up there and took his sharp knife and slit the tipi in the back very carefully. It took a long time to make a hole, and then he got to the bottom. He took two pegs off and opened it up. It was double, and he had another layer to cut, which he did. He reached over and shook his wife by the forehead. She was frightened and grabbed him by the arm. He whispered: "It is me. If the children are all right, you had better hurry." He tied the girl on the saddle of one of the horses. The woman held the little one in a blanket on her back. They led two horses. They did not run, but sneaked out slowly and quietly.

Pretty soon they were over the ridge. Then they started to lope. They rode all night and all the next day and night. The first day they came to flat land and came to a long hill. They looked back and could see the enemies following them. That evening one of the horses tired out, so they changed horses. They rode all night, and at dawn saw the enemies were gaining on them. There was a big bunch of them. He made up his mind they would have to die there. It was a flat, and they would try to reach the ridge where the pines were and stay and fight. Just then one of the Shoshones on a white horse was gaining on them. He looked at him and saw he had no weapon at all. Back at camp they thought the women had gotten away by themselves. The man on the white horse caught up, and he shot him, because the man had only a lance. The others were gaining, and every once in a while he would turn and shoot.

Just as the family was about to reach the hill, the others scattered and tried to get ahead. The woman saw some horsebacks coming. They saw two and then a whole bunch. They were Sioux, and it was lucky that they ran into their own people. The two bands met and started fighting. The Shoshones turned and ran, but the Sioux chased them and killed eight.

Back home his brother and the party had gone to hunt the bodies. They did not find them. They were about two days behind. They expected to meet the man and his family on the way back, and it just worked out right. This is a true story. It happened the same year that Red Cloud found the Crazy Buffalo. That was a kill come back (wakte-agli) and so they had a victory dance.

This is how they have a victory celebration. They go out to look for [the] enemy, and when they make a kill, they scalp the enemy. When they come back, on the way they scrape the skin thin, then they stretch it across a round hooped stick and hang it up to dry. When they come back, they stop near the camp and all blacken their faces with charcoal. They tie the scalp on the end of a stick. One the way back from a kill, the war party gets ready for the celebration. They kill deer and make drums on the way back. They stop a little distance from the camp, then the first kill, the scalper, and the first, second, and third coup(er) get together and the rest stay behind. They gallop into camp and circle around the camp saying, for example: "Black Elk you have said. I met an enemy and I made a kill."

We had just as well finish the story of Little Powder. Those that had made a kill or coup rode around together and then rode back to where the others were, and then they all came back, with the women first and the scalps. Of course Little Powder's experience was quite a thing and would count toward being a candidate. The people were very excited about it. The second time they came they sang. They paraded around with the women in the lead, then the braves with their scalps. Then over and over again, they sang the song referring to the captives:

> Now you shall hear, I bring my captives back.

The relatives of the men in the party, after the first group went around the first time, blackened their faces, too. As soon as they came to the place prepared for that, they had the victory dance. Two events happen at a kill come back. One is joy over the victory. The other—if someone's son is killed over there, that person will cut off his hair and cut his arms. The mother will do the same, cut her arms, and the sisters too. These mourners will circle the village at the same time the victory dance is going on.

In this story no one was killed, but when someone is killed, this is what happens. There is a rule that if a war party goes out and one or two were killed, the members of the party do not blacken their faces. They can have a victory dance anyway, but when the people see the unblackened faces, they know someone was killed, and the mourners get ready. As a rule the mourners keep on mourning as long as there is no revenge. If there was someone in the tribe who had been mourning since the last war party when some relative was killed, they blacken their faces and rejoice when a war party comes back and has made a kill—revenge. Then they blacken their faces and get in on the victory dance and rejoice. When there is a kill come back they get the people who have been mourning and put oil on their hair, which has not been combed since the tragedy; then they comb the hair and give them good clothes and give them one of the scalps. Then they are all dressed up and quit their mourning and start in dancing.

It is an honor to die out in a battle, so when the mourners go around singing they sing:

> Aaah-hey! Aaah-hey!
> (So and so), it is so; it is good to hear about you.
> Aaah-hey, aah-hey, aah-hey!

One reason they sing the song is that any old man will tell a young fellow it is no good to be old. It is good to lie out in the hills or be eaten up by coyotes—that is good; it is better than to be old and feel the old man's troubles. Young men go out to get two great honors—to kill or be killed. Either is an honor.

(Coyote—shunka manitu [*šungmanitu*], "wilderness dog.")

When I grew weary the most encouraging words my father and mother said to me were: "My son, you have grown up to be a man. When you face any difficulties, be brave. Try to be on top of the other man." (For example, if I killed two men, then someone killed me, I would be on top of the two I had killed. You have to kill before you get killed.)

These two stories happened in one season and are true.

SHARP NOSE MAKES PEACE BETWEEN
THE ARAPAHOES AND THE CROWS

The story I am going to tell is about a band of Arapahoes camped at the [North] Platte River going into Wyoming. There is a place called Hide [Rawhide] Butte; it is near Newcastle [Wyoming], on the upper North Platte in the big bend. A long time ago the Sioux found a lot of stretched, dry buffalo hides there; evidently some Indians had prepared them and been chased away. That is why they named the butte Hide Butte. It was right where the river flows north—near the head of the Niobrara River. This story is about the Arapahoes; since they are our allies we know their stories and they ours.

In the winter a whole Arapahoe band was camped, and the next morning there was not one of their horses left; the whole tribe was left afoot. The Crows had taken the horses. A war party was gotten up and they went on foot to get their horses. While they were trailing the horses, it was very slow, because they were on foot and there was a lot of snow. They decided to turn back. One young man named Sharp Nose said: "You men had just as well go back. I will follow them myself and find out where they went to. I will do my best." He thought some would go with him, but they all turned back and let him go on alone. So he got on the top of the hill and watched them going back over the hills. He decided to go on, and then he saw a lone man coming back. He waited for him and it was a brother-in-law—just a very young fellow, not old enough to be a warrior, about fifteen or sixteen years old. I forgot his name but we will call him by a good well-known Arapahoe name: Big Plume.

So Sharp Nose said, "Brother-in-law, what is the matter, why are you coming?"

"I wanted to come in the first place. I thought an older man would volunteer to go with you and I thought I would be among those coming.

When we turned back I thought I would be among those to decide to go with you. Since no one did, I came. I will go wherever you go; I will die wherever you die. That is why I am here."

It was hard traveling, but they went on and on. They came to the Powder River soon. Then they went on and came to Greasy Grass Creek. It took time, but they kept going. Soon they arrived at the Big Horn. They were in Crow country. Right there they got on top of a big ridge. They were careful, since they were in enemy territory. From the top of the ridge they looked down and saw a big camp. They knew it was a Crow camp. It seemed the war party that had stolen the horses did not get home right away—they probably went someplace else, too. It seemed they had just got back. They waited until it was evening. They could see a place near the camp that would be a good place to hide. After dusk they followed the creek and worked their way close to the camp in a gully with many trees and concealed themselves. They began to scheme how they would do it. The older man, Sharp Nose, said: "Big Plume, we are going to steal horses, but we can't steal as many as they took from us. Even if we do, there are lots of people there. Either way we are going to die. I think it would be well for us to die among them. We will wait until the morning and go into the camp. If they kill us, we had just as well die there." The younger man was willing to do that—they were out there to die, anyway.

In the first place, in going back to where the seven camps were dispersed, there were seven things to be given to the Indians. One I am going to mention is the sacred tobacco—in with this is sacred tallow from the animal a man has had a vision of (eagle, bear, buffalo). Sharp Nose had some of that; he was well prepared. He had a [piece of] red flannel and mixed the tobacco and willow bark and tallow and put it in a dried bladder and then in the red flannel. That is a "sacred bundle." All tribes respect that. It is like the white men respecting a white flag. This sacred bundle is used to make peace and to make relationships among the Indians.

So he told the boy: "We are going there. We will die together there." He stripped himself and painted himself with red paint and tallow. Then he put one eagle feather on his head, pointing down. Then he put the sacred bundle on his back. He tied up his clothes, arrows, bow, gun, into a bundle and told the boy to carry it. He filled up his peace pipe with tobacco and held it out in his two hands. The sun was pretty high then. They started from their hiding place and went down to the camp. A Crow going out to look for horses met him and looked at him and hurried back to the camp. When he went back, he told the camp. They all got on their horses and charged out to him. When they came near, they knew it was sacred, so they did not know what to do. The boy was not sacred, so they started couping him—hundreds of times. They took the bow and arrows and other things away from him and couped him. The other one was sacred and they could not coup him.

The head chief of the Crows was among them. He took the peace pipe and shook hands with him and was going along with him. The others wanted to kill him. The big chief took Sharp Nose back to his camp and would let no one harm him. Just before he went into the tipi, Sharp Nose took his bundle and carried it in his hands. The chief motioned for him to sit down. The warriors were still milling around, but a crier was sent around calling for the sub-chiefs and other important men to come in. This happened in the morning and all day they did not feed them. The chiefs had quite an argument. Pretty soon the sun went down. Most of the night they argued. The next morning the chiefs came back again and resumed their council. That went on all day, and they did not offer the two men anything—not even water.

They argued still into the night. I got this from the Crows later and what they were talking about [was]: "This is sacred, and if we kill this man and his helper, something terrible will happen to the tribe. This is sacred and we should respect it, although they are enemies. If we do kill them with this sacred bundle, something evil will happen." The next day they came to an agreement. The chief got up and said: "I am going to accept this sacred bundle. In accepting the bundle I am willing to give up my life for taking the sacred bundle. That I am willing to do. When I accept this, if you want to kill me with this, I am willing." They all cried, "Hi-yeee!" All the chiefs got up and made similar speeches.

[Of] all that volunteered to accept it, one was a medicine man and he was the one who could take the sacred bundle and untie it. To do that he had to have a ceremony and talk to the Great Spirit and offer up a prayer before he untied it. So they got live coals and put some medicine on them and when it smoked they got smoke on it, and then he took the sacred bundle and opened it and gave it to the head chief, who said "Hi-yee!" "Thanks." He touched himself all over with the bundle and kissed it. Then everyone outside yelled, "Hi-yee!" "Thanks!" Then he gave the bundle to the next chief, who did the same and then passed it down, etc. The first one gave a horse to each of the Arapahoes; he also gave them good clothes to wear. When the sacred bundle came back around they each had ten horses and all the good clothes they wanted. Afterward the head chief called for water and gave it to the men. Then he offered them a smoke. Then they fed the men. After that they questioned them. The Crows asked: "What are you? Where did you come from? What business have you? Why do you bring this sacred bundle? Tell us nothing but the truth. You have smoked the peace pipe and must tell the truth."

Sharp Nose said: "I am an Arapahoe. A while back your people went over there and stole every hoof the Arapahoes had and at that moment we chased on foot. But it could not be done, it was very hard for the tribe. The women and children were standing on a hill crying for the horses, and something had to be done. The whole tribe would starve without horses. So the candidates and chiefs got together and told me to bring this sacred bundle. I came here for my people and with this sacred bundle we both came here to die with this bundle. Now you have spared my life and so far I have told you what I wanted to tell you. I have told you nothing but the truth and you have treated me so well that I want to thank you."

The chief asked him how long he would stay there.

"About four days."

Then they all huddled together and the chief said: "What you have brought us is sacred, and I cannot refuse. In four days when you go back you shall take back every hoof that was taken from your tribe. Not even a colt will we keep. Besides you are to take along a Crow and his wife and his son—those three you shall take back." So the Arapahoes got up and stretched out their hands and thanked the Great Spirit. Then they touched the earth. The chief said: "When you take the horses back, thirty warriors will take you part way and help you. From there on a Crow and his wife and son will go back with you."

At the end of the fourth day they got up early. They gave them provisions and gathered the stolen horses in one place and then started out. A sub-chief of the Crows and his wife and son went along. So they started out. The thirty warriors took the party as far as Powder River and then turned back. From there the Arapahoes and the Crow chief and his wife and son started on alone with the horses.

They took their time. Whenever they wanted fresh meat they got a buffalo or deer. When they neared the big camp, they camped and Sharp Nose told them to remain there while he went on in and explained everything. So he rode in himself toward evening. It was winter and they were afoot, so they could not move, and he knew just where his folks were. They were very surprised to see him and wanted to cry but he told them not to. He said, "Father, you get all the chiefs together right away." News traveled and everyone knew he was back and they were curious to know why he had called them all together.

Sharp Nose spoke: "Chiefs, I told the biggest lie in all my life. But in so doing I have done good. I told the Crows that you had made a sacred bundle, which you did not—I made it. But I want to tell them you did make the bundle. I brought a Crow back and I want you to tell him that you told me to go and die with the bundle. It took them three days to decide what to do with us, and they finally gave in and accepted it and I brought back every horse that we owned. They treated me right. Just tell them what I told you. I am going back and when I bring them I want you to bring some blankets—the best you have—and fix a place for them and bring them in in blankets."

They all agreed. That was a rule in the Indian tribe—whoever got horses from a different tribe, they were all his. So the horses belonged to the two Arapahoes not to the tribe. So one chief got up and said: "Sharp Nose you have done a great deed but you can do more. You know that the women and children have cried for the horses, so you should at least give one back to each family." So he said: "No, I cannot do that. The horses belong to the tribe and they can have back the horses that they lost." They all cried out "Hi-yee!" to praise him.

When Sharp Nose was ready to go back to the camp, the Arapahoes had started already. Some brought pemmican and wasna and brought it to the Crows and Big Plume. They ate it, and by that time the Arapahoes were there and helped drive back the horses. As they neared the village, the big chiefs were coming, singing, and they had robes and picked up the Crow woman and put her on a robe and carried her into camp. Another bunch took the Crow man and another bunch took the son. They put up a fine, big tipi and put good things to eat and wear in there and brought the Crows there. They sat down in the tipi and the big chief of the Arapahoes came in and said: "The Crows came on a warpath and took all the horses and the women and children were crying for the horses. It was hard and winter and snow and we knew we would all starve. We made this sacred bundle and told Sharp Nose to go over there and die with it. The boy volunteered to go along. Sharp Nose has already done his mission." He shook hands with the Crow and gave him the pipe of peace and said, "Hereafter we will be friends."

Ever since, the Crows and Arapahoes had no more wars. That is true. It happened when Red Cloud went out on a war party. It happened about one hundred years ago. They gave the Crow many good horses and good clothes. He said he would stay ten days, which he did. I guess Sharp Nose must be a great man; he brought two tribes together and that is the greatest thing a man can do. It is like the two warriors at Pouting Butte. Sharp Nose had won himself the place of big chief of the Arapahoes. They could not elect him right then, but when one of the big chiefs was gone, he was next in line. His son is a chief right now in the Arapahoes— his name is Sharp Nose. Big Plume earned himself the title of sub-chief.

Woyakapi— "They or he told it or them"—They told it or he told it or they told them or he told them. These are not "stories;" they are true experiences. Ohunkakapi—fiction story, fairy tale ("old people tell it"; old people make it up). Ehani Woyakapi— "Long time ago they told it" (legendary story).

TELLING THE FUTURE

There were four ways the Indians knew what was coming in the future;

1. The sun dance—when you go into a sun dance you foresee things concerning the people as a whole. You might be in a coma. Whatever you foresaw it always came true.

2. Lamenting—vigil on a hill. You might be awake in the vigil and see things. If you sleep, in your dreams you will foresee things.

3. There is a place in the Black Hills, also on the Little Big Horn, a bank of solid rock where there are inscriptions that only a medicine man can read. It is a mystery. There is one in the Black Hills that only a medicine man can read (pictograph). We don't know who wrote it, but a medicine man can decode it and get the meaning. We would camp and when we would come back there would be more writing.[3]

4. Any human, man or woman or child, when he is going to die, in his last hours he can see.

3. These are petroglyphs rather than pictographs. The Black Hills site is probably Cave Hills, S.D. The other site is on the Rosebud River, not the Little Big Horn, and is known as Deer Medicine Rocks (see above, p. 198, n. 2). Stuart W. Conner (personal communication, June 29, 1982) reports stylistic similarities between the petroglyphs at these two sites.

[15]

December 12

As far as I know, this story is not confirmed. It is told, but we are not sure it is true. I heard it and wanted to get the details, but it seems that the older people I talked to about it could not tell me much. They know it was a medicine man but don't even know his name. This band of Santees are the ones who have that kind of medicine men. They were camped and somehow a young woman died suddenly. At that time medicine men had the power to do almost anything. Girls would die for no apparent reason. Some would go back and examine the girls. When they put them on the scaffold they were well bundled up. Every time a young girl would die and be bundled up and put on the scaffold it seemed that someone would undo it, especially the head. They got suspicious and the last one that died they examined and [found that] her mouth was pretty wide open and her tongue was gone. Later on another one died; she was undone too; they examined it and her tongue was gone. So they figured a human being was doing it.

Another one died; she was the daughter of a well-to-do chief. They had a ceremonial and feast and buried her with treasures. They thought whoever was doing it was robbing the bodies; but not so. When they found the three with tongues gone, they examined all the others, and all the tongues were gone. They figured that someone in the camp must be doing it. The father of the last one hid himself near the scaffold. They put her in a pine tree. Nearby it was rocky, and he hid with his gun. It is a custom for the mourners to stay there all night the first night. That night her mother and relatives were there. Next night her father went out. He thought he would find something out. Later toward the middle of the night he heard an owl nearby hooting. It sounded more like a human being. He got ready. Sure enough, it was moonlight, and he saw a great big bird flying. It soared above and then landed on the pine tree. It was a bird all right. He looked closely and it was not a bird, but a man. He could not believe that a man could fly like that. So he watched for quite a while, and pretty soon the man went over to the body and started to undo the wrappings. The first time he landed, it was a bird, but afterwards not. As he undid the wrappings from the face, the father said: "Friend, I have been waiting for you. You are the one who has been doing this to the young men and women. You have been getting their tongues. You will not live another day to get another tongue."

The fellow said: "Man, have pity on me. If you let me live I will give you all my power. The power was given to me and I am exercising it. This power was given to me and if you let me live I will give it all to you and you can do lots of things."

"It is just too bad. You killed quite a few of our young men and women."

"I had to do it. It was in order to get the power to fly. With the tongues I made medicine and could fly."

If he would let him go, he would transfer his power so the chief could do those things. But the chief shot him in the head and he fell from the tree. The chief called out to the people camped nearby. They built a big fire and examined the man. He was dressed like a medicine man. He had no feathers except on the ends of his fingers he had some owl feathers tied—every finger—and had little bundles of medicine from the tongues on each finger. Also he had many strung together—tanned hide with medicine made into a necklace—around his neck. His hair was undone. His body was painted but I don't know just how. The chiefs got together and said they should burn him up. Some of them thought he had some medicine on him, and if so, they thought someone else might use it. They all went out and made a big fire and threw him in and appointed men to stay there and keep building up the fire. Toward morning there was nothing left at all.[1]

1. Bushotter recorded a similar Santee story in his collection of Lakota texts (no. 46). Among the Sioux, only the Santee shamans were reputed to take human tongues or other body parts from corpses for use in ritual. See Ruth Landes, *The Mystic Lake*

CARING FOR BABIES

There is a way of bringing children on earth. When it is time for the baby, usually the parents would go out and select two women, good natured and of good character, either young or old. The two will handle the baby. The baby is brought forth on earth and the two women take care of it. The first one—its mouth has to be wiped out, and the woman who puts her finger in the baby's mouth to wipe it out, we believe her character has been transferred to the baby, so the baby will follow the footsteps of the woman. The other woman cleans it with a certain kind of soft weed. They take the inside bark of the chokecherry and soak it, and just before the baby is washed, she tells it she has been a good woman: "So far in my life I have worked hard. I never give in to laziness and try to get along with everybody. I treat my neighbors and everyone alike. So you try to follow in my footsteps. So far I have tried to get along with my people and have raised a family." Then she washes and wipes it and then puts oil and red paint on the baby. She has transferred all her good to the child. If it is a grouchy woman, the child will be that way. We even believe that today. The men do not know all this, but my daughter-in-law probably had something to do with it. After the second one washes the baby, later if the baby cries all the time and is bothersome, they have women medicine men for that purpose. They get those people and pay them and they treat them all over again, and they cure them; the baby stops crying.

In olden times the Indians did better than the doctors and nurses now do. If an Indian woman handles a baby, there is no trouble about the navel, but when the doctors and nurses handle them, there is always trouble. As a rule the navel comes off in four days if an Indian handles it. In olden times it was quite hard to raise a baby, but they used nothing but skins to wrap the baby. With diapers, if it is wet, you have to take it off and put on a clean one. But we used buffalo chips [dried dung]. The women packed them—the old [dried] pieces—and used them for diapers. First they powdered them up and put the powder into the skin. Whenever they wanted to change it, they took out the buffalo chips, which had absorbed everything, and the baby was never wet. Of course we greased them, so they were not irritated. Later the women had cloth and would take it and made a little pad and put the powdered buffalo chips in it and use it that

---

Sioux: Sociology of the Mdewakantonwan Santee (Madison: University of Wisconsin Press, 1968), pp. 59–60.

way. Babies were never wet. They used the softest part of a buffalo hide for the diapers.

In olden times it was hard to raise an orphan, but then a child grew up and developed fully. The Indians had their children three or four years apart, because they want to develop the child fully. Many times the woman would nurse the child for two or three years; the Indians believed that made a husky boy or girl out of them. That is one reason we did not increase as rapidly as white men. Now Indians are more like the white men and they have more children. In olden times the Indians said the four most difficult things in life included the losing of a wife when the babies were still nursing. An orphan baby had to be fed by several different mothers. Later when it could drink soup, that was all right.[2]

TWINS

Indians have a belief that twins are ones that are born again and again. Twins are born four times, but not the others. We don't believe the others were someplace else. Twins might split; there would be only one born and by his actions you could tell he was alone and was a twin. When little twins begin to talk you can hear them telling how the came. They say the twins used jackrabbits for horses before they were born. A twin is thought to select parents; they ride a jackrabbit and go around and pretty soon they find a mother. They wait until she goes for water, and then they get inside her and develop. You have to treat twins very well, because they are easily irritated. If you don't treat them nicely a twin can die anytime if you are not nice. Then they come to someone else.

The way they know: One woman had twin boys. They were two or three months old and she left them in a tipi and two or three other women and she were visiting. Pretty soon a dog yelped in the tipi as if someone kicked or hit him. She ran in and here the twin had crawled out of the cradle and was trying to get back in. Then it was helpless again. Later the two boys told things they had experienced and they overheard them talking about it. When they were little, the dog came and started to eat it [the cradle]. So the one boy got out of the cradle and kicked him. He was trying to get back in when his mother saw him. There is a tribe of twins

2. See Dorsey, *A Study of Siouan Cults,* pp. 482–83; Mirsky, "The Dakota," pp. 417–19; Hassrick, *The Sioux,* pp. 270–75.

someplace. Twin boy and girl were born to some parents. Another twin boy told that the girl had been married to someone in the twin world, but the boy had run away with her and they were born into this world as twins. The twin who told it said that if they did not believe him they would find the boy twin had a wound on his leg, which he received when he ran away with the girl. They looked, and the boy had been born with a scar on his leg.

One incident happened when I was in the Black Hills pageant. A pair of girl twins about fourteen came—white girls. When they first came I was introduced to them. I said: "Yes, I know them. I am a twin myself. In the twin world I know these two. They used to be Indians but somehow they did not treat them right, so this time they tried white people. They are Indians and came here as white people. I know their names. This one was Eagle Shawl." When I said that, the two blushed very much. The other one said, "I guess he is right." To prove that, they usually have odd names. There are two down here three years old. You go over there now and ask one what the other one's name is and he will say "Green Plums" and the other won't talk. You ask him how he came, and they will always say they came riding jackrabbits.[3]

BURIAL AND MOURNING

There are three ways of burying Indians in olden times: you go on a warpath and are killed, there is no burial; you are just left there. Probably coyotes eat you up. The next: scaffold. For instance, if I died, they will prepare me for the burial, dress me in the best clothes and braid my hair. There was no sort of ceremony at that time, but it changed later. They keep the body overnight at the tipi. Next morning the father or head man selects a place to bury the body. Naturally others would come and help to build a scaffold. They took four posts with crotches on the end. Then they put poles across, so they will stand a long time. They were well built, and they used good sized posts. They put strong poles across the top. They wrapped the body in hides and used leather thongs to tie him up securely all over, from head to foot. The body was then ready for burial. If it was a great warrior, then the mother or father would give away. They got a crier to announce that so-and-so had gone on a journey and it would be the last

3. See Dorsey, *A Study of Siouan Cults,* p. 482.

time they would see him, so they were going to give things away. His mother has bid him good-bye. They always give to the needy.

Then they brought a horse with a travois on it. They put the body on the drag. The relatives did not handle the body, but friends did all the preparation. A friend led the horse, and the others all followed the drag in a regular funeral procession, all on foot. Of course no prayers were said there. They arrived at the scaffold all prepared. Two men took the drag and put it against the scaffold. Then two men got on top with ropes and they tied ropes to the body and dragged it up on the scaffold, using the travois for a gangplank. The two men tied the body down to the poles, then the men slid down off, using the travois to get down. The posts had been skinned, the bark taken off, so now they are rather dry. They then painted the post to indicate the things that the dead man had done. If he had killed, they painted the post black, and if he was wounded, they painted a red place. There were other signs for other deeds, such as stealing horses, etc. If there were many honors all the posts would be needed. If he had a good horse they would lead it up to the scaffold and shoot it there, so he could take it along. They cut off the tail of the horse and hung it on one of the posts, so it would swing in the wind.

The Indians believed that such hardships could change people for the better. The people after the burial leave the burial; but the relatives stay there and sing and mourn all night. The next morning at dawn the people from the camp go after them—a warrior or akichita or chief. They prepare a good meal for them, and when they come down the men take a sweat bath and the women wash their faces and smoke. They go into a tipi and sympathizers say a word or two to them. Someone selected to talk says: "Remember it takes four days. Try to see the morning star every morning. Take good care of your horses. Take good care of your gun. In these four days try to get along with everyone. Love your neighbors. In the meantime get out and get a deer or buffalo or something. Remember there are only four days. You should mourn four days."

The Indians believed a man could change his mode of living at this time; he could form a better habit of life than he had before. That is a good time to change to become a better man. If you get up to see the morning star for four days and do your work early and be nice to people, you will form good habits. If you are lazy and can't get along with anyone, that is a good time to change and make a better man out of yourself. The men talked to the men about it and the women to the women. The four days are a time of crying. They should cry those four days; after that you could still mourn but not do much crying. When such things happened, the band would move camp, and the family would stay there for four days, then they moved camp and went roaming for some time, and when they felt like it they went back to the people.

In those days the people were good, but still they bettered themselves at times of mourning. They did not go back to their people, but roamed. They worked and made things and hunted and formed good habits. At the present time we don't go anywhere, and we don't get along.[4]

THE GIRL WHO WAS BURIED ALIVE

I want to tell you just why we put the bodies on the scaffold. The main idea is that they did not want wild animals to eat the flesh. If they put them in the ground, the animals would dig them up. Of course in time the posts would rot and about that time the bundle would have decayed too. By that time the body was dried up, and nothing but bones were left.

Lately over here it happened north of the Black Hills a band of Sioux was camped. A family was coming back there from a band in Canada. They camped several times and came to where the whole Sioux had camped that winter. They saw a scaffold on a hill. There were crows all over and something on the scaffold. They sent a man over there to scare it off. He went up there and was amazed to see it was a human being who had been buried but had come to life. The man who found it was Against the Clouds.[5] He went up there and it was a little girl about twelve or thirteen. She had undone the wrappings and could not crawl out because she was very weak. She tried to cry but was too weak even to cry. So Against the Clouds called out to the others. They all came over and decided to camp there. They did, and brought one of the drags over and put it up to the scaffold and took the girl down. She was very pitiful so they all cried. She could not talk she was so weak. They gave her some medicine and some kind of root pounded. The next day they fed her a little soup. They stayed for about four days. They put good clothes on her and kept her there.

4. See Dorsey, *A Study of Siouan Cults,* pp. 485–87; Tyon in Walker, *Lakota Belief and Ritual,* pp. 163–64; Beckwith, "Mythology of the Oglala Dakota," pp. 425–26.
5. Touch the Clouds (*Mahpiya iyapat'o,* Push against the Clouds) was the name of a leader of the Minneconjou Lakotas.

Before they moved she could just barely talk. They asked her how long she was up there, but all she could remember was that she awoke from a sleep. It took some time to get out of the bundle. She had sat up on the scaffold for two days, but before that she did not know how long she had lain there. As they went along they traveled just a short distance each day. Pretty soon she could walk a little. They got back to the camp of the other Indians. Against the Clouds was an older man and he wanted to adopt her. So he told the members of the family not to tell anyone anything about it. Later a year or so she was a nice-looking young woman again. The girl knew which was her real mother and father. It was hard for her, but she realized that if the man had not picked her up she would be dead. She had a lot of respect for him. She went around on horses for water, etc. Her parents knew nothing about it. She was fat and well.

The tribe was moving camp and at a crossing the warriors were standing on each side to help if any needed help. The girl's father had a friend that saw her. They camped across the creek. That evening he went to her real father and said he had seen a girl that looked like the one he had lost—the same age, everything just the same. "You ought to go over and see her. They [are] camped right over there." It was hard on the girl, for she thought a lot of her mother and father, but she stuck to her foster father because he was so good to her. That evening she was standing outside the tipi, and she saw someone was coming, and it was her real father. She wanted to cry out and run to him, but she thought about the foster parents, so she said nothing at all. She dashed into the tipi and got behind her foster parents. She acted very bashful. Her real father came in and said: "What is the matter with the girl? She is really bashful." The foster father said: "She is. She is very bashful."

The girl hid but her real father spoke and said: "They told me your daughter looks like the girl I used to have. They told me she looks like the daughter of mine who died. I wanted to see her and maybe adopt her." They told her to shake hands with him, which she did. The man cried when he saw her and said: "She really looks like my daughter. If you will let me I will take her home and let my wife see her and we will adopt her. She really looks like our girl." The girl did not want to break down; she knew that if she went she would break down. She wanted to keep it a secret unless her foster parents said it was all right. She said she would go if her mother went with her. They went. As they entered the tipi, her mother came forward and cried, and her relatives and brothers all cried.

She still acted bashful and wanted to tell them, but she was torn between the two and stuck with her foster parents. They sat down and her real father said: "She really resembles my daughter. I swear it is she, but I guess it is your child."

The father said: "I tell you what I will do. I want her to be our daughter, too; she will be our daughter as well as yours." So he gave two of the best horses he had and some good clothes to the girl, who hung on to her foster mother and pretended to be bashful. The real father came again. Against the Clouds made an agreement not to tell, but it leaked out, and the real father found out. So the real parents came over and they cried again. "Against the Clouds, I came here to see you and I want you to tell me the truth. They tell me this is my daughter and you found her and saved her and all that, and that this is really our daughter."

"Yes, I did that. I came upon her as she was sitting on the scaffold. I took her down and my wife and I saved her. It will be up to her to decide to go back to you or to stay with us."

The girl hugged her mother and father and cried and said she would decide. She said: "You are my real mother and father. There was a time when you gave me up as dead. But I came to life and if not for my foster mother and father I would not be alive; I owe my life to them. You bore me once, but they found me and made me what I am today. You be my mother and father, and I will belong to all of you, but I am going to stick by my foster mother and father. That is my decision, but I will come over to see you often. Don't feel bad about it. I am still your daughter, but I owe my life to these two, so I will stay with them."

The foster father had wanted to question her about how she came to on the scaffold, but he had waited until she was normal and well again. So he asked her how it happened. She said: "All I know is that I was asleep. It seemed I slept, and the first thing I heard was a man singing. It was in my sleep. Pretty soon he touched me and said to wake up. 'You are going back to your people. But there are some men coming from this side and they are going to take you back to your people.' When I awoke, to my horror I was on a scaffold. I tried to figure things out and remembered I had been sick and probably died and was buried. I did not see the man but later found out it was a crow talking to me. I was going to get down but was too weak. So I stayed up all day and that night crawled back into the bundle. The next day I got up again but was too weak to get down. Pretty soon I saw a man coming. The crow that talked to me said when I got back to my people I was to do the things I saw. I had visions. You know the rest. You picked me up."

Against the Clouds was not much of a warrior but had raised three boys, one older than the girl and two younger. She was well known for making charms for her foster brothers; later they were famous in killing and getting horses and became great through her medicine. The people realized she had a power. Later her foster brothers, she gave them names. Her name was Plenty White Cows. She named her oldest foster brother Crow Eagle; the second brother, Sees Crow; the youngest one, Last Crow. All became famous. Of all three Crow Eagle was the bravest and became a great chief. This is a true story; I got it from Crow Eagle's grandson, who is about my age. He died lately. He was Minneconjou and lived at Cheyenne [River] Agency [South Dakota].[6]

EATING AND GIVING THANKS TO THE FOOD

The Indians had about two meals a day. They ate any time of the day, but most had two meals. In the morning they ate. When they traveled, they did not eat at noon. I never heard anyone say it was time to eat at noon. If you went to see someone at any time, they would feed you then. In the evening they had a good meal. The main food was buffalo, next the dog. We raised dogs and used them a lot, but we ate them. The dog meat was used in different ceremonies. We cooked the meat different ways, dried, fresh, as soup, roasted on the coals. We also had turnips and berries and chokecherries. We dried them. We scraped the hide and what came off was like flour or shavings. We saved it, and when we made a berry pudding we mixed that with it.

Wasna: meat from the best part of the buffalo (loins) dried. Then you put it on the fire and cook it and pound it. Then you take the bones and boil them and pretty soon the grease comes out. Then you take the grease and mix it with the pounded meat. Some put pounded cherries with it. Later we put some sugar in it. Then they take the outside of the paunch and dry it. Then you put the wasna in it, and it keeps for years in the skin. Some used a bladder.

---

6. A similar story, "The Resuscitation of the Only Daughter," appears in McLaughlin, *Myths and Legends of the Sioux,* pp. 145–50. This story also combines the theme of the woman who brings bad luck to her husbands.

Another mixture is made with acorns. They are thrown in the fire and pop. Then you shell them and pound them and mix them with the fruit.

There were various ways to cook [prairie] turnips: cook them whole, make soup, pound them and make pudding. Woojapi [*wojapi*]—"mixture." We had potatoes; they grew wild and the roots were like sweet potatoes. They grew like peanuts and were small. They grew on a vine like wild sweet potatoes. They were quite sweet.

In a family there is one certain thing they do. Maybe the woman is cooking. When she gets through before she puts it out, she takes a piece of it and says "Wahnaghi [*Wanaǧi*], Spirits, eat this for me, so I may be lucky or have some horses or _____" and she asks for whatever she wants. That was done wherever they were; war parties did it, too. That is an offering to the spirits so they will help them do whatever they want to do. I told about the war party that fed the skull and the woman saved the day for them.

One of the hardest things for the Indians was food. At times some chief would make a feast and call in really old men who were wise and knew a lot and have them give thanks to the food. That is one of the achievements a warrior should have to be a candidate for chief. Food gives life. A warrior should not be stingy with it, and in order to gain a reputation he had to know how to get food and give to the needy. For instance, the food will make a man out of you. Also, it will make a fool out of you. That is the main part. If you want to be a great man, you have to look to the food proposition. Next is the kill, etc., on down. The main thing is food. A good rustler will get out and get meat. When he comes back, he thinks about others unable to get food. He and his wife will get things ready and call for old people to come and get fed. If they know he is a good man, if he goes out hunting, they see him and if they know he is a good one, they say "Hi-yee!" and start sharpening their knives. They know they will have something to eat. But if they know he is no good, they say "Hey, hey, hey" which means he is not good and they won't get anything.

Whenever they were going to give thanks to the food, the warriors that had been feeding the old and needy, they are the ones that make a feast. A warrior who had more than he needed would make a feast. He went around and invited the old and needy. Some would just barely be able to walk. They would be coming and singing his praises. Usually the feast giver had done a great deed of some sort: "Hi-a-he! Hi-a-he! Owns

Sword, you are brave! Hi-a-he!" Maybe they would tell what he had done and say, "It is great!" Then they sat down; each had brought his own cup and knife. The warrior and his wife had food all prepared.

Not every man could give thank to the food. They probably would invite one who could do it. Then they said, "It is time now." The man who could thank the food—some worthy old medicine man or warrior—said: "Grandson, these old people have been in their tipis with their heads down, thinking where to get the next food. They all know you, so they are looking up to your tipi to see if there is smoke coming out. Smoke came out of your tipi and then sure enough you have invited the old and the needy, and they all come rejoicing and singing. You have made them happy. And now we are seated here in a circle and we see the food that you have cooked. It is so nice to look at it. What do you want of the old people, that you have cooked such good food to give to them? You know very well they can't give you anything, but still you feed them. So what do you want from them? They cannot repay you for the nice food. Or maybe it is this war bonnet I wear" (meaning the white head), "maybe it is that you want. And maybe this buckskin" (his own skin) "I wear, maybe it is that you want. Look to the old, they are worthy of old age; they have seen their days and proven themselves. With the help of the Great Spirit, they have attained a ripe old age. At this age the old can predict or give knowledge or wisdom, whatever it is; it is so. At the end is a cane. You and your family shall get to where the cane is." (Meaning he has given him his gray hairs and his old skin—his old age. The warrior feeds them so he can get to be old.)

"The people, the Great Spirit has looked upon them and blessed them and seen that they came to a ripe old age. So whatever comes out of their mouths is sacred. They can help with wisdom that comes out of the mouth. But a warrior, even if he has killed the second or third or fourth, if he does not do likewise, he can't ever make the achievements a warrior should. Food comes first. He must bring food along with his deeds. They say there are four great difficulties. Food is the most difficult thing of all. Any person who lives up to the sayings of the old people and feeds them is a great warrior. Food being the most difficult thing, they say that the food talks. So it talks and says: "He is liberal with me, and so shall he uproot his teeth on me.'" (Meaning that he will have many blessings and live until his teeth drop out.) "'The man who is greedy over me shall not last long.'" Those are the words of the food.

The old man: "Furthermore, someone might say just because he wants to make achievements on mere food, never mind, because he is just a crier for you. This is just like a great many warriors and a buffalo. The buffalo has a shield and starts to circle the tipis. As he goes, the warriors are after him, trying to kill. In vain, [for] the buffalo has a shield and will get back without being hurt. So the buffalo is the food. You cannot do anything with [out] food. Food will always win; it will carry you through. If the food had weapons, it would have many prisoners now. So, Grandson, go as you are. Beyond that hill you will come to an eagle feather. When you get to the feather, go on. On the other ridge beyond you will find a horse standing." (Meaning: the warrior goes on with his deeds. The eagle feather means a kill. He will be lucky on war parties and in bringing back horses.)

That is what is called giving thanks to the food and the warriors. Then the old man says to the young man, if it is his nephew, "Ho, nephew." The young man replies, "How." The next one says, "Ho, son"—"How," and so on around the circle, each greets him in the appropriate manner, according to relationship. When it comes back around the circle to the old man giving thanks, he calls the young man and says: "I am not sending the food down nor up. The people are ready and are hungry, so dish it out." So they dish out the food. That is thanking the food.

Whatever I told you about, that still is among the Indians. Wherever we go we can stop and eat.[7]

MAKING A CANDIDATE (*wicaśa yatapika*)

We will say this fellow that made the feast has made a kill, stolen horses, and scalped. So he has proved himself, but he is not a man yet.[8] Whenever they have a council with three tipis thrown in together, they choose candidates. The akichitas have everything ready. The chiefs and candidates start singing toward the place of the fellow who has done all this saying:

7. For Lakota foods see Ethel Nurge, "Dakota Diet: Traditional and Contemporary," in *The Modern Sioux: Social Systems and Reservation Culture,* ed. Ethel Nurge (Lincoln: University of Nebraska Press, 1970), pp. 35–91; Hassrick, *The Sioux,* pp. 178–80; and Bordeaux, *Conquering the Mighty Sioux,* pp. 122–32.

8. That is, he has not yet been made an "honored man" (*wicaśa yatapika*).

To be a man is difficult you say, but I have looked for this.
Here with great hardships I come.

They have a robe and put him on there and carry him back to where the place is prepared. They give him a peace pipe and a scalp shirt (shirt that has been ornamented with human scalps). No one has a right to wear that unless he is a candidate, chief, akichita, or councilman. Then they give him two eagle feathers to wear on his head.

"So and so, there are a lot of needy ones and plenty old and feeble, men and women both. And if a needy one comes to your tipi and he has no moccasins, take off yours and give them to him. Give him a horse or something. See that your wife has a big pot, so the needy and old will feed out of it. At your tipi a dog will make water on your tipi and if it happens, take your peace pipe and remember these words and your will power." (Meaning there are a lot of things that are insulting, but if I am a chief and someone elopes with my wife, I have to stand it. Take your pipe and control yourself.)

"At your tipi there will be a dog wounded with the arrow still in its body will come back and lie there. But never mind, just hold on to your peace pipe." (That means if my brother got in a fight and was hurt, I should not go and try to revenge him and get in trouble. Control myself.)

"We are going to put you on top of an ant hill, so they will crawl up and bite you. And also we will set you on a beehive, and you are going to go through thorns. This peace pipe is your will power. Hang on to it and remember your will power when you have difficulties."

When they are through with this, they stand him up and sing:

My friends, the candidates have said it is difficult to be a man.
But I looked for him.

Now he is a wichasha yatapika and is a man; wichasha yatapika means "man they praise."9

9. Compare White Bull's account in Vestal, *Warpath,* pp. 231–32; Thunder Bear in Wissler, "Societies and Ceremonial Associations in the Oglala Division of the Teton-Dakota," pp. 39–40; and Calico in Curtis, *The North American Indian,* 3:16.

[16]

December 13

THE TWO MURDERERS

I am going to tell a little story about the candidates [*wicaśa yatapika*].

The worst thing to an Indian is a murder.[1] If there is anything the Indian does not like at all it is a murderer; that is the lowest thing he could do and is considered a dog. He is an outcast. If two fight and one is killed or murdered, they are called dogs. I am going to tell about a murder, because when one takes place, the people do not like the murderer. Even if they do feed him, they throw away the cup he ate from. He has to roam around for three months all by himself before he can be accepted back into the tribe. They felt the murderer brought evil to the tribe or anyone he stayed with. That is why they threw away the cup he ate from. They are not marked, but everyone knows about it, and he has to be out alone. The murderer is just thrown away for three months; even his own folks don't want him. If he is not killed by enemies and survives and comes back, they give him a sweat bath and purify him before he is accepted back into the tribe.

The candidate's name was Charging. He had a brother. Two other warriors killed his brother. I don't know how the trouble started, but the two killed him and got on a hill and were going to kill anyone who came up there. They brought the killed brother back to the candidate's tipi. Charging took the pipe and smoked. He said to the other warriors: "Two

---

1. The best published account on the subject is Ella Cara Deloria, "Dakota Treatment of Murderers," *Proceedings of the American Philosophical Society* 88(5) (November 1944): 368–71.

of you go over there and bring those two back. I don't want anyone to do anything; I want them brought to my tipi."

A murderer is supposed to mourn for the one he killed. Therefore he had three months of mourning and he had to cut his hair short. The two had their hair cut short. Of course they were dressed up to kill. The two warriors went over and brought them back. As they came near, the two murderers threw off their blankets. They threw away their guns and arrows and knives and both cried. They went into the tipi and sat on the body of the man they had killed.

The candidate gave them each a drink of water. Then he got his peace pipe and lit it and offered it to the Great Spirit, Mother Earth, the Four Quarters, and then presented it to the murderers. When they accepted the pipe and started to smoke it, the people knew they were sorry and would accept almost anything, so they all cried "Hi-yee!" "Thanks!" Charging spoke: "Don't fear or be afraid or anything, because you will have me as your brother." They had something to eat and he prepared it for them and even cut it up for them. "All right, brothers, eat."

Then some other candidate got up and spoke: "Today we see something that has been given to candidates when they were elected. It is a hard thing to do, but a candidate must stick to what he has been told. When we were made men they praise, the chief told us that this would happen, saying that a wounded dog with an arrow in his body would be brought to our place, and this is just what he meant. What we saw here is what the chief meant by his words. Now we see Charging; his brother has been murdered and brought back to his place. Charging has remembered the words that were told him. Therefore you have seen him stick to his pipe and remember the words that were told him, and you have seen what has happened. In doing this he has proved himself as a man they praise and has stuck by what he was elected for."

Then he turned to the murderers and said: "Young warriors, you have taken the place of the man you are sitting on. Charging, that is his brother, but you have done away with him and have put yourselves in his place. You must now be brothers to him."

They had a rule and the warriors were told to prepare a sweat bath. Usually when they make one for a murderer they use only four sticks. They are punished and have to face the four corners of the earth by themselves alone. No one owns them; they have no relatives. After they prepared this, Charging had good horses, so he gave each one a good horse and saddle and everything to protect themselves with, food, clothes, guns, bows and arrows, so they could roam around for a few months. The akichita went and (the sweat bath door was facing south) dug a hole right in front of the door in the shape of a man. They took the guns the murderers had killed with and put them on each side of the hole shaped like a man. A medicine man went first into the sweat bath; he was supposed to try to clean them.

When the two murderers went in, the medicine man spoke: "Your Grandfather, the Mysterious One, you have broken his laws. He does not like it; he feels bad. Not only he feels bad, but the four-leggeds of the earth feel bad, too, and now the bad deed you have done will bring evil to our tribe because the four-leggeds of the earth fear what you have done and have left." (This is true because when a murder takes place and the camp does not move, food is very scarce.) "You follow the four directions of the wind and you will depend on them, but the most relative-like one will be where you are always facing, because evil comes from where you are always facing. So when you leave, go where you are always facing, always travel that direction. If you happen to run into a four-legged, kill it and make an offering. Remember the earth is sacred. You have killed the earth. Remember, your brother; you have sent him back to the earth. Remember him. Also have faith in the Mysterious One."

As he finished talking, they both began to cry. In a sweat bath, you put water on the rocks. So he poured all the water on the rocks at once— special for the murderers. This was hard to stand, and the murderers broke through the sweat bath, and they grabbed their guns and shot into the man-shaped hole and threw their guns in there. Then they started to dress. When they were dressed, they went to Charging and embraced him and said "Brother." That was all. They got on their horses and left. They were now outcasts.

As a rule they have to kill four four-leggeds and offer them but not eat anything from them. As a rule they do not stoop down to drink, because if they lean down and drink, they see the murdered man in the water. So they use a wooden cup. They are not supposed to kill and eat for four days, and they are provided with food for four days. After the fifth day they can eat as they want. They have to stay out three moons.

After the two murderers left, Charging had four warriors prepare the burial place for his dead brother. They dug a grave. As a rule if anyone is killed by a man of his own tribe, the mourners do not go along. Also, before he is bundled up, they put a piece of tallow in the dead man's mouth. So the four warriors are the ones who put him on a drag, and take him out to the grave. The parents mourn, but they do not go along with the body and mourn as with the usual burial after a natural death. The tallow is put in the mouth as an offering to the spirit. The two murderers already have their punishment, and they believe the four-leggeds will now come back. The offering of tallow is to ask the spirit to ask the other spirits to induce the four-leggeds to return.

In preparing the burial place, a hole is dug for a grave, and the murdered man is buried face down. A man comes from the earth, and so when a man is murdered he is sent back to the earth. After he is covered up with earth, the four men gather cactus and plant it over the grave.

The two outcasts did their penance. They met enemies, made a kill, and got some horses. Three months passed and one day two men came up on a hill, crying. The people rumored that Charging's brothers had come back. So he prepared a sweat bath and sent two men for them. They brought horses and scalps for Charging, their brother. The two had their sweat bath and a medicine man cleaned them and they were accepted into the tribe. After they were clean, they went to Charging instead of going home. Later the two became famous and became great warriors. One's name was One Horn; the other was called Runs Mountain Sheep. Runs Mountain Sheep's son was on this reservation at Standing Rock; he was a Hunkpapa.

A murderer is called kills home—ti-wichakte [*ti wicakte*], "he kills their home."

INSANITY

We never had dangerously insane people. But we did have some similar to that, though they were not dangerous. Usually they were not called insane; now if we look back we might call them that. But we never heard of that then. Probably the ones we had were born after something, that is, resemble something the mother had to do with before the child was born. For instance, one took after a beaver and was like one. The deaf and dumb are that way because they take after something. We did have people who acted funny and were feeble minded. We called them persons who act funny.

I know of one person whose real name was Afraid of Nothing Bear. He was feeble minded from the time he was born; he had to ask permission to go anyplace. Even when he was a young man he had to ask permission to go anywhere or do anything at all. They had to watch him. Whenever he went he kept on going; sometimes he got lost and they had to look for him and bring him back. Soon they called him Bear Fool, and he was well-known all his life by that name. He was a good worker and would do anything he was told to do. The only trouble with him was he would go along and keep going. They remedied that; his father built a big drum for him. He was always practicing the drum and it was an ornament. Wherever he went he had the drum; when he wandered off he would beat the drum so they knew just where he was. Bear Fool was camped with his grandmother at Wounded Knee. While the fighting was going on Bear Fool was on a wagon. If anyone got killed, he hollered and said: "They got another—woo, woo!" He got up to cheer, and a bullet hit him and killed him. After everything was over, his grandmother was under the wagon, dead. His mother picked up her mother and saw she was not wounded but had probably died from the shock.

FALLING STAR

Ohunka [*ohunkakan*] are not supposed to be told in the daytime, but I will tell this one anyway.[2] There is an old saying that if you tell an ohunka in the daytime instead of in the evening, you will get long hair on your bottom! Whenever a person is asked to tell such a story in the daytime, he

---

2. See the discussion of *ohunkakan* in Deloria, *Dakota Texts*, pp. ix–x, and Beckwith, "Mythology of the Oglala Dakota," pp. 339–40. Black Elk's story combines a number of well-known plains folk tales. This was the usual manner of telling such stories; the storyteller's skill was to combine episodes and keep the audience interested. Such stories would be told night after night to while away the long winter evenings (see Walker, *Lakota Belief and Ritual*, p. 39). Black Elk begins with the story of the women who married stars; one falls to earth and gives birth to Falling Star, the hero. He is raised by the animals (in this case the meadowlarks), then sets off to save a camp of people by defeating *Waziya*, who has been preventing them from getting buffalo (see Riggs, *Dakota Grammar, Texts, and Ethnography*, pp. 83–94, and Beckwith, "Mythology of the Oglala Dakota," pp. 408–11). In the next episode the hero outwits a white crow that has been preventing the people from getting buffalo. This is really an alternate version of the preceding episode, which Beckwith ("Mythology of the Oglala Dakota," p. 409, n. 3) identifies as a Cheyenne variant (see George Bird Grinnell, "Falling Star," *Journal of American Folk-Lore* 34 [1921]: 308–15). The final episode includes the hero's magical journey to rescue the chief's arm in order to marry his daughter (see Deloria, *Dakota Texts*, pp. 133–37). Each of these episodes was told in many variants, with differing heroes, forming part of the corpus of Sioux fiction.

has to have something for the story, so I will have something out of it, and that makes it all right. I am going to ask you to give me a present; you live in a big city and maybe you can find an old overcoat and send it to me. No, I was just joking!

A long, long time ago there was an Indian camp. In one of the tipis there were two young women. They were lying against the tipi outside one night and looking up at the stars, how wonderful they were. They were trying to count the stars. They wondered how high it was, and all that sort of stuff. It was a nice summer night, and the weather was pleasant. While they were looking up there they looked at all the stars and they saw a big star, and right beside it a very little star. One said, "That big star, I surely like that star." The other said, "I like that little star, the one you can barely see. I like that." The other said, "I will marry the big star if you will marry the little one." So the other girl said, "All right."

They lay there for awhile and soon it was bedtime, so they started to go in. They saw two men standing by the door. One spoke: "I heard you wanted to marry me, and the other girl wanted to marry this other man. We heard it so we came after you." The second girl spoke: "All right. You are the one that first suggested it, if you will marry him, I will too." Instead of going into the tipi they started back with the men. It was dark and they could not tell what kind of men they were. One man said, "You wanted to marry me, so come and grab me around the neck, and you," (the other) "grab the other man around the neck." The two men leaned over, so the girls got on their backs and held on to their necks. They told the girls to close their eyes, which they did. Then, away they went.

I do not know which way, but they were traveling. I guess they parted someplace, anyway the young woman who saw the big star was told to open her eyes and they were in a great, beautiful land. She saw she was with a very old man. He was a star all right, but he was very old. The land was beautiful, and the old man was the chief of the big, big camp there. Right beside it was a smaller camp and there the young woman that wanted to marry the dim star had a fine, young, handsome man. When the old man brought his bride to the people, they all rejoiced, for the chief had gone to the earth and brought back a piece of the earth—Star Comes Out's mother.

One day the two villages went together and the women all went out to dig turnips. In digging turnips, sometimes you have to lean against the stick. The girl that married the big star was pregnant. They were both told they should not press the stick with their stomach, they should just push with their hands. Pretty soon the old man's wife was going to press the stick with her stomach. The other said "Don't do that!" But she did anyway and down she fell. She pried the whole ground up. When she landed on the earth she fell very hard and was broken open. The child was developed and did not die.

(At this point usually in olden times when they are telling stories, the listeners are interested and say, "That will be me!" So I had to say that.)

The baby was crying, and pretty soon the magpie noticed it, because he knows everything. He said to the baby: "Wait, I will have to run up some folks to see about this. You wait and I will get the mightiest of the four-leggeds and the two-leggeds." So he flew straight up and made an announcement: "To you the wings of the air, to you the mightiest four-leggeds I am calling, calling you. Come over, you are to decide the destiny of Falling Star." This baby was named in the heavens Star Comes Out, but he fell, so he lost that name and the magpie named him Falling Star.

The magpie was a wing of the air, so he called strongly to the wings of the air, and all kinds of wings came—the eagle, hawk, buzzards, magpies, everything. The meadowlark came last. They all had a council, and the bird chief, the eagle, was there and presided over the council. The question was who should keep Falling Star. The snake was there also. Mr. Owl got up and said: "I think it is proper to let the snake raise Falling Star because he is in a deep place and sheltered and it is nice and warm there, so I think he should raise Falling Star." The snake raised his head and said: "No, I am the most unliked and most pitiful animal of all. I have no legs and have to crawl on my stomach and I eat dirt and can't get around much. I am not liked and I am not fit to raise him." The crow spoke and said: "I will make a suggestion that Mr. Hawk could provide for the baby. He is always roaming around and is a rustler and I believe he could do the job of raising a baby. Mr. Hawk says: "No, I can't do it because I have no relatives at all. Everybody is my enemy and I don't belong with anyone, so I don't think I could do it."

All the animals were there at the convention. The kingbird came in. The reason the birds had first say was that the magpie had found the baby. The kingbird said: "I think the mudswallow should keep it because he has a nice home, it is all well daubed up and there is no way of the baby's catching cold. He has the best home of all of us, and I think he should raise the baby." (The one thing, the birds had the say because most of the animals had no place to stay. The ones that lived in holes and the birds that had nests were the only ones that would come into consideration.) The mudswallow said: "I don't think I could do it. I live high up under the banks and I don't think it is a good place for the baby." The prairie chicken got up and said: "Our big chief the eagle could raise him. He is big and strong and makes a kill always. He is the one to raise him." The eagle said: "It is true I get my prey easily. The food part is all right, but the way I live is not good for the baby. I live high up, and it is cold up there, so I don't think it would be proper to take the baby there."

Mr. Blackbird got up and said: "I know who could raise him. He lives in a hole in a tree. He has a good home in the woods. The woodpecker should raise him." Mr. Woodpecker said: "No, I have not enough room in my house. There are too many of us, so I won't try to keep him." The smallest of the birds, the oriole, got up: "I know who could keep him. In the first place, when we are told to make homes, I think this fellow has a fine home. He is good natured and I think he would be the one to raise this boy. This is the meadowlark." Mr. Meadowlark said: "All right. I will keep him and I will raise him."

I guess you all know how the meadowlark has his nest. It is on the ground and is built up all around. The meadowlark has his doorway facing east. The nest is built all nice and warm with grass.

Mr. Meadowlark took the baby home. His wife was there and he said: "Old woman, they have given me Falling Star to raise, so I am bringing him." The old lady was very glad and said "Hinu, hinu, grandson! Grandson!" He told the old woman to bring the grease, oil, and paint. He washed the baby and greased it and painted it red, and fixed a very nice place for him. He had him all bundled up and put him away to sleep. They fed the baby. The next morning the old lady got up and said: "Old man get up. Our grandson is sitting up." Sure enough, the boy was sitting up. He said: "My grandson, my grandson, hun-hun-hi!" The next night he did the same thing: greased and painted the boy and put him to bed. Next morning the old woman said: "Old man, get up. Our grandson is crawling toward the door!" He got up, and Falling Star was crawling. "Hun-hun-hi, my grandson is crawling!" And he picked the baby up. The couple liked the baby very much and were very glad the baby was already crawling. That night he greased and painted the baby again and put him to bed. Next morning, the old woman got up and called: "Old man, get up, our grandson is walking. He is in the doorway already." So he got up and said "Hun-hun-hi, our grandson is walking!" So he picked him up. That night he greased the baby and put him to bed.

Next morning the old lady said: "Get up, old man, our grandson is gone! He is gone!" The old man got up and looked around but the boy was gone. He was outside playing. He brought him in and said, "Where did you go, grandson?"

"Grandfather, I just went out to play."

Mr. Meadowlark was glad his grandson already walked and talked so he went down in the woods and got him an ash for a bow and some willows for arrows. He made him a good bow and arrows. "Here you are, Falling Star. See how good you are." The old man took one of his hairs and stretched it out and said "See if you can hit that." One of his arrows was blunt and the other sharp. Falling Star got back and took the bow and arrow and split the hair. "That's good" said the grandfather. The boy went out that afternoon in the woods and soon came back with something, and it was a beaver he had shot. They had a good meal. The next day Falling Star went out again and brought back two jackrabbits. The third day he brought back a young deer. Each day he had grown bigger, so he was quite a boy by now. Next day he brought in a buffalo calf.

Of course the meadowlarks were not rich; they were quite poor. When he saw the grandson growing up rapidly, one day he said: "Grandson, one of these days you are going to travel. We are poor and can't give you much. I wish you could have everything you need to travel." He greased the boy and put him to bed. Next morning they found to their amazement that Falling Star was a young man, not a boy any more. Where he lay was a young man, and beside his bed were bow and arrows, clothes, everything he could possibly want or need.

One day the young man Falling Star brought a young buffalo calf in. The liver was good eating. Meadowlark got on top of his tipi and announced: "My grandson brought me a good buffalo calf liver. The calf liver is rich." To this day you hear the meadowlark saying: "pti-hin-chla pinapin [*ptehincala pi napin*], 'calf liver rich!'" They had a lot of papa [dried meat] made, because the grandson had provided so well for them.

One day the meadowlark called him over and said: "Well, Falling Star, you are to travel. You are going to come upon certain things, but have pity on them, when you meet these things." So Falling Star dressed and got ready. He went on his way. Going over a hill he saw a man peeking at him, so he went over to see what it was. The man asked him where he was going, so Falling Star said he was traveling. The man said: "Grandson, I know you are traveling, but you are going to have to meet some hardships. I want you to remember me." He gave him a plume and said: "Remember me whenever you have a hardship, remember me." It was the eagle who presented him with the plume. Then he thanked him, said "How!" and took the plume and went on.

Soon he came to a little grass tipi. There was an old woman there, and she came out and said: "Hun-hi! My grandson is coming. Falling Star is coming. Grandson, you are on a journey but there will be many hardships on your journey. You will meet many difficulties, so I am presenting you this." She gave him a head ornament or cap. On it was a feather of a hawk. She also gave him a long sword. She also gave him a live flying ant. Falling Star had a plume from the eagle, a hat with a hawk feather, a sword and a flying ant. We will have to remember all these things.

It was toward winter now. He came to a big village. Looking down from a ridge he saw a tipi away from the others. It was rather shabby. A little farther on there was another tipi separated from the camp, and it had a lot of dried meat on it. He wanted to go to the shabby tipi, so he did. As he went in, he saw an old man and woman. The old man recognized him and said: "Hun-hun-hi, here is my grandson, Falling Star! He has come to see us. But we are having a hard winter. Grandson, you see this big village. The people here are starving; they are hungry. We, too, are starving. You see this tent away from the village. There is a man there with lots to eat, but he seems to have the people in his hands. They are all afraid of him, and there is no one brave enough to face him." So Falling Star said "How!" Falling Star asked the old man if he ever went to that place, and he said he never did but the man's name was Wazya [*Waziya*]—Where It Always Snows—Source of Snow. The old man said: "Whenever the people go out to hunt, this man goes out and takes away everything they kill. Nobody can do anything about it, and so we are all starving."

As they talked a boy came, and that was the old man's grandson. His mother and father had died, and the grandparents raised him. The old man said: "This is Falling Star, our grandson." So Falling Star turned himself into a boy the same age as the other one. He asked the boy to go over where Wazya lived with him. Wazya had many things to eat, but if the men from the village went there, he would always kill them. But the two boys went over there. As they went into the tipi they saw a great big man with a deep voice, and he said "Hin!" which meant they were not welcome. "Why do you come?" In the corner of the tipi was a little boy who got up and sized one of the boys up and said: "That one is like Falling Star. He has Falling Star's ways."

There was a pole in the middle of the room and on it was a great, long bow. Big, big arrows were there, too, because the man was powerful and a regular giant. Falling Star looked at the big bow and arrows and asked the man: "Kola [friend], do you use these to shoot?" And he said "Sure!" Falling Star said: "Friend, I am going to take a look at it." Wazya said "All right." Falling Star took the bow and arrow. He could just barely reach around the bow, and the string was very big. He tried it out, but Falling Star had so much power that he broke the string and the bow just came all to pieces. Wazya was very surprised and said "Hehhh!"

Falling Star and his friend went out and took some of the papa. Just then the little boy of Wazya came over and the friend said: "You know the little boy that said something in there. He always brings some food to my grandparents and me."

They went back, and the giant did not chase them. Nothing happened. When they walked in, Falling Star's friend was laughing and said: "Grandfather and grandmother, do you know what happened? Falling Star took Wazya's bow and broke it all to pieces."

Just then a crier came around in the village and announced: "Moon Necklace, where you usually go to get your buffalo, that place is just full of buffalo." That meant buffalo came into a certain place. Moon Necklace was the chief of the village. They all went out to kill buffalo. Falling Star said: "Well, grandparents, let's go and get some meat too." The two boys had horses and got out there first. There were many buffalo. Falling Star had just one arrow, but when he shot it, it would go through one buffalo, then another, and another, and killed all in line with the arrow. Then Falling Star would go over and get his arrow and shoot again. Falling Star had made a very big kill, but it was all for the people.

When they butchered, here came Wazya with his children: "Go away, those are mine. Go away!" The Wazya had a big bag and put the buffalo in his bag. His children did just the same. Pretty soon he got to where Falling Star was and he said: "Go on away. Those are mine." Falling Star said: "No, you go away. These are mine." Wazya pushed the boys away.

Falling Star said: "No, you go away" and he took his sword and made one swing and cut Wazya's neck off. Just then the bags flew open and the animals all fell out. Then Falling Star cut off the head of the wife and the children. Finally there was just one little boy left, and he chased him. Pretty soon the earth cracked and he crawled in. You could see where he crawled in, because there was frost coming out.

The people came around and butchered and they all had plenty, and when they returned to camp the old man said: "My grandson Falling Star has come. He came and he is the one who killed Wazya and his whole family. From now on you people will get along fine and have plenty. That is what Falling Star has done for us."

The people went over to where Wazya lived and got all the dried meat. Winter [Wazya] was killed. The little boy that escaped—if Falling Star had killed him, we would not have winter [at all] any more. The chiefs and men they praise and akichita got around and put tipis together and got Falling Star and brought him over. The chiefs got up one at a time and thanked him. The head chief told him that the people had nearly starved because of Wazya, but now that he had got rid of [him] they would get along fine. "Now the people can roam at will, because you have got rid of Wazya. Maybe in the future there may be another man like you, but we will call upon you when the time comes."

They had a big celebration, and Falling Star stayed with the people awhile. They were prospering. One day he came back from hunting and said: "Well, grandma, grandpa, [and] my friend, I am going to leave you. I am really on a journey, so I will proceed. Sometime maybe I can see you again." He went on a very long journey. He traveled all summer, and it was toward winter again.

One day he met a man on a hill. This man asked: "Grandson, where are you going?"

"I am on a journey. I am just traveling."

"Grandson, you are going to meet some difficulties. There are people living a way from here and they are having hard times. You are going to meet some hardships and you will remember me by this," and he gave him a live grasshopper. "When you get to these people, you will have to turn yourself into a four-legged, and if you do get killed, you will come back to life." This man was a meadowlark.

He came again to a big village. He looked it over and selected a shabby tipi where he thought an old man and woman might live. He went there. Inside he was known. The old man said: "Hun-hun hi, here is my grandson! Sit down." There was an old woman there, too. "It is a good thing you came, Falling Star. These people are starving."

"Why?"

"Well, grandson, it seems when they go out hunting, there are buffalo, but there is a pure white crow that talks and it seems he is the one that keeps the four-leggeds away. Whenever they go hunting, the white crow follows and if there are any buffalo he tells them to run. That is how it is that the people are nearly starved." Falling Star said: "Grandpa, I think you had better call the head men of the village. I want to talk to them." They all came, and seemed to know him and said: "Hunhunhi, our grandson has come!" One chief said: "Grandson, we are having a hard time. For years we have tried to get buffalo, but a white crow scares them away, we can't do anything." Falling Star said: "I am going to tell you something. Do it just as I say. There are buffalo near here, and I am going over there. You follow me, and when I get there the white crow will tell the buffalo to go. I will turn myself into a buffalo, and the others will all go. There will be just one buffalo there, and that will be me. When you kill me, just open me up and cut my legs partly off and spread them out. When you come back get a good tipi and put it up in the middle and close it up. Even the top of the tipi, close it up so nothing could get out. I am going to bring the white crow back there."

They gave him a buffalo robe and he took it and went out over the hill. There were some buffalo there, and he went and put the robe on him and rolled around. Then he turned into a buffalo and went with the others and grazed. Soon he heard something, and there was the white crow: "Buffalo, run! Those hunters are coming. They are going to get you." So they all ran, but he stayed there. "You bad one, why don't you run? They will get you." Pretty soon the hunters came and shot him. They opened him up and took nothing and went back. He was not killed and knew everything.

Pretty soon magpies and crows and other birds came and fed on him. The white crow came and said: "Go on get out of here, that is mine. I want to eat it and have it for myself." He seemed to suspect something, because he did not come up, but just sat there and looked after the others had left. He hopped and seemed to be wise to it. He would peek, then the crow jumped. He looked at the buffalo and looked at the eyes. "It looks like the eyes of Falling Star," he said, and kept sidling around. He seemed to know it was a trick. He did not feed on it. He kept looking at the eyes, and then said: "Falling Star, I have your eyes out," when he picked at them. He kept looking around and looked at the eyes and said: "Falling Star has tired eyes." He was just guessing at it; he did not really know, but he was very smart. Pretty soon he was dancing around and he got on a place where there was some nice soft tallow. "Looks like the meat of Falling Star, tastes like the meat of Falling Star." He licked his lips. He was suspicious, so he flew away. Pretty soon the magpies and crows came to feed, but he came back and chased them away. "I am going to eat this time for sure," he said. He jumped around and came to the eyes again. "I guess I better eat the tallow around the eyes. It is nice and soft. Falling Star, one of your eyes is out." So he started to eat.

Pretty soon Falling Star grabbed him by the leg. "White crow, you are not smart enough."

"Friend, let me go, let me go, please." He begged and begged. "If you let me go, you can have my power."

"No, it is too much. You have been mean to the people long enough. I am going to take you back."

All the people saw it and cheered: "Falling Star is bringing the white crow back." They took the crow to the tipi and hung him up by the legs, head down. They built a fire underneath, and the smoke could not get out. He begged, saying they were smoking him to death. Soon he was dead, but he was black from the smoke. Just then someone took the plug out of the top, and the crow kicked one of the feathers off. It flew out and was a crow and got away. He said: "Falling Star, you are not smart. You thought you were smarter than I, but I got away. What about it?"

When he flew away, they all called for Falling Star to do something, but he said as long as the crow was black he had no power. He would never be white again, so he would not have any influence. So they went hunting. The black crow came hollering, but the buffalo would not pay any attention.

After everything was fine again and the people were prospering, he said: "Grandpa, I am going to the next village. I guess they need me over there. There is a woman there I am going to marry."

"Well, grandson, your grandma and your grandpa will be there. When you start don't forget to use what your grandfather and grandmother gave you, especially the hat, the sword, and the flying ant, and the grasshopper. You are going to greater hardships than any you have seen."

So he went on to the third village. On the way, while roaming, he met another man. The man said: "Grandson, where are you going?" Falling Star replied: "I am going to a people over here."

"Well grandson, I hate to see you go there, because you will meet two hardships that will be very difficult. But I am not giving you anything, just remember the things your grandmother has given you—always remember them."

From then on he continued his journey. Soon he came to a very large village. Again he looked the village over and saw a little shabby tipi on the side, so he decided to go there. This time he changed into a young boy and went there. As he entered he saw an old woman. She said: "Grandson, poor grandson, Falling Star, you have arrived. I live all alone here, your grandfather disappeared and I am all alone. It is nice that you came." He did not want the people to know he was there, but they had to eat. Every time he went out he was a young man out hunting and when he came back he turned into a little boy and said: "Grandma, I brought meat back." That went on for awhile, and soon the people knew the grandma had a boy. They called him He Lives with His Grandma.

One day his grandma came back and said: "The chief of the village lost his arm. The Thunder-beings came one day and took his arm and carried it away. Whoever gets the arm back is to marry his daughter." The boy laughed and said: "Well, grandma I think I will take a peek at the woman some time. Maybe she would suit me."

"Another thing I heard, grandson, is that they say the chief lost his arm quite awhile ago and wanted to get it back, and many have tried to get it back, but no one has had any luck. They heard about Falling Star, that some day he would come and retrieve the arm of the chief and marry his daughter. I know they mean you." Falling Star said: "That is one reason I came. Grandma, I want you to keep still about me, because they will know more about me. I want you not to tell anyone I am Falling Star."

That evening he became himself—a young man—again. He went over to see the chief's daughter. The chief's daughter had a tipi of her own, and she lived not in the middle but inside the circle. At night her suitors would come to see her. One by one they stood in line and took turns talking to her. That is the way the Indians really courted. He was toward the last. He waited his turn, then went in and talked to her. "Well, I came

here to find out why you have stayed single so long; there have been a lot
of good warriors eligible to marry you. Why have you not married any for
so long?"

"I am going to tell the truth. I promised when my father lost his arm—
the Thunder-beings took it—that if anyone would get his arm back, I
would marry that man."

All the three villages that he had helped were called the Star People.

That night after talking to her, he liked her, and made up his mind he
would try. So he told his grandmother: "I am going to try for the chief's
daughter. I liked her, and I am going to try to get that arm."

"That is something hard to do. The arm is someplace and is hard to
get." Five powers had been given to him, and he remembered them. The
old woman said: "It is pretty hard for you to go. The things your grandmother has given you, I advise you to leave them here, because you will
have a son, and this son of yours will use these powers. Your son, he too,
will journey, and he too will meet four people having hardships.

He took only the first bow and arrow that his grandfather had made for
him. There were three Star Peoples he had met, and it was up to his son to
meet the other four. That is seven, and that represents the seven stars of
the big dipper. Falling Star had visited three of them, and it was up to his
son to go to the other four. Falling Star went back up into the dipper, and
it is called The Carrier. The Star People—the seven—are the Pleiades.[3]
Later Falling Star went back to his people up there. The four of the
Carrier represent the chiefs, and the big one is the chief of all the star
people that came to get Falling Star—his father, the one his mother
married.

"The first one you will meet going looking for this arm, your grandmother, lives right there just before you get there. You will see her before
you do anything else." He came to the grandmother as he went along a
creek called Rapid Creek. I think it was in the Black Hills. When he met
the old woman she said: "Grandson, where are you going?"

"I am going after the arm of a chief over here."

"Hun-hi, that will be hard to get." She started to feed him some good
things.

3. The Lakotas call the Big Dipper *wicakiyuhapi*, man carrier, and the Pleiades
Tayamnipa, Head of *Tayamni* (Buechel, *A Dictionary of the Teton Dakota Sioux Lan-
guage*, pp. 486, 578). Earlier (p. 292), Black Elk identified the "seven stars" as the Big
Dipper.

"I saw the Thunder-beings when they took the arm; they passed through here, and I saw them." She gave him a sinew ready to sew (thread) and said: "Grandson, if you have to, put a live coal on this end and you will come back like a flash. When you go, on this side of Where the Bears Live, you will meet your grandfather there."

As he went near, he saw the tipi. A man had a blanket on and was doing something around the tipi. The old man looked and said: "Hun-hi, my grandson Falling Star, where are you going? You had better come and have something to eat. My name is Chases Eagle." He went in and saw the tipi was nothing but eagles lying down on the floor.

"Grandfather, I am going after an arm that belongs to a chief over there. If anyone gets it he is to marry the woman that lives in the middle."

"Hun-hun-hi! You are going to run into trouble, but if you do and have to come back, I will give you this. He took one of the plumes off the eagle. "If you get in trouble all you have to do is put this on your head. As you go, there is a place called White Buttes (he ska [*he ska*]). Your grandfather lives there. Be sure to see him before you get where you are going."

As he journeyed he came to the White Buttes, and on top was a tipi and a man hollered to him: "Grandson, I am your grandfather. Come up." So he did.

"Falling Star, where are you going?"

"Grandfather, a woman that lives in the center, her father lost an arm, and I am going after that."

"Hun-hun-hi! That is hard, but you are near now. It is hard to do, but you are close to it now. Grandson, I am not very powerful, but I will give you a feather." The man was a swallow, split-tailed swallow. Now he had the sinew, the eagle feather, and a swallow feather. "Right over there a people live. Just before you get there, on the flats, one of your grandfathers lives, so be sure to go there before you get into the village."

As he went along the flat he came to a very large village with many people. The land was very beautiful and everyone seemed well to do. He heard someone say, "Grandson, come here; I live here." But he could see nothing. It called again. It was in the brush and grass. Here it was the smallest bird in the world—the wren. They are called Holds Buffalo Back. "I am not much of a man; no one notices me, but I can help you. I am going to give you one of my feathers, but I want it back. Better put it on your hair before you start. That arm is right there in the village but it is hard to get. Wear this feather right now and go. Do you see the village?

There is a big tipi right near and that is where the arm is, but it is so difficult to get there. Take my advice and put the feather on right now." He did and turned into a wren. "All you have to do is fly over there. At the tipi is some wood piled up. Light on that and say 'On the warpath I come!' They will hear you and take you in."

So he flew over to the tipi. There were many people around. He got on a piece of wood and said "Warpath I come!" (Zuya wahi). From the tipi a young man, nice looking, came out. He noticed the wren saying that and soon the young man said: "A little bird out there is saying something." So they told him to go out and catch it and bring it in. He caught it gently and took it in the tipi. The tipi was full of men and there was a big pot in the middle, boiling. There was something up there wrapped up, and he thought it was the arm. The young man was holding him and he continued to say "Warpath I come!" Then they made out what he was saying.

The people were Thunder-beings and they had Ichtomi [Iktomi]. The Ichtomi is a smarty who knows everything and can turn himself into other things and fools the people very much. He is known as One Fools the People. He is no good but comes in handy once in awhile. Ichtomi means spider. One of the men said: "You had better get the Black Spider, maybe he knows something about this." The crier went out and called for the Black Spider to come at once. When he arrived he had no shirt on. They said: "Black Spider, we want to know what this little bird is saying. Maybe you know something about it."

"Well, give it to me." And he took the little bird in his hands. When he got it in his hands the bird said "Warpath I come!" and he looked at it and said: "This bird says he came on the warpath, but what could he do? He is so tiny and pitiful, what could he do?" Then Ichtomi threw the little bird in the boiling pot, but Falling Star was prepared and somehow the pot whirled around and the boiling water was thrown all over all the men, especially Ichtomi, who had no shirt. Then the wren turned himself into a man and grabbed the arm. Then he turned himself back into a wren and flew back to where his grandfather was. There he took off the feather. "Here, grandfather, thanks. I am going on." And he put on this split-tailed swallow's feather, and flew like a flash.

About then the Thunder-beings came for him, but he flew ahead of them. He got back to where the swallow had given him the feather, saying: "Thanks for your feather." Then he put on the eagle plume, but did not turn into an eagle but turned into a plume. The lightning flashed but did not hurt the plume at all. He came back to where his grandfather gave him the plume and said, "Here is your plume. Thanks a lot." He then took out the sinew, stepped on it, put a coal on it, it drew together, and before he knew it he was back where he had started from. When he arrived at his grandmother's, she came out with a hatchet and said: "Why are you doing this?" She swung the hatchet and split all the clouds and broke up the storm.

He brought the arm back, but his grandmother said: "You have four things here, but you will have to save them for your son. Now you are getting married so you will have to leave them here for your son to use." (The eagle plume, the sword, the flying ant, and the cap with the hawk's feather.) That night he took the arm and went and stood in the line of suitors. He waited his turn, and when it came he talked to the girl and told her: "Here I am again. I came here the first time and asked you why you did not get married and you said you had promised to marry the man that would get your father's arm. Here it is; this is your father's arm." She took the arm into the tent. The chief had his arm back again.

The next day, early in the morning, they called all the young men. They also called the people. "The chief's arm has been brought back by a young man." There were a lot of warriors there but they did not know which was Falling Star. It was in the night when he returned the arm, so the girl did not know who it was. They told all the young men to put on their best clothes. They lined up the young men and the girl was put in a place so she could pick out the one it was. Finally they all passed and toward the last Falling Star came. When he stepped up to her she said, "Your name is Falling Star," and he said, "Yes, I am Falling Star." One of the chiefs came over and asked him: "Are you Falling Star? The people have talked about you so much, and I want to know the fact that you are Falling Star." Then he said, "I am really Falling Star." Then the announcer said Falling Star had come and had brought back the arm. So they all rejoiced, not because he got the arm back, or because it was Falling Star, but they realized the Star People would put a star up in the heavens that is the biggest star of the universe.

It is like this. Now Falling Star has seen adventures and now just got married, so it will be a whole year before he will have a son and that son will have to go to four Star People. Now I will have to wait a whole year before I can go on with the story.

Appendixes
Bibliography
Index

Appendix A
Concordance

Note: A dash indicates material not mentioned
in *Black Elk Speaks* or *When the Tree Flowered*.

85–90	Red Hail and the two suitors
–	The killing of sixty-six Flatheads
7	Wooden Cup, the prophet
66–72	Pouting Butte
–	The story of High Horse's courting
62–65	The young man who pretended to be a ghost
184–87	Crow Butte
183–84, 187–92	The Shoshones kill thirty Lakotas
144–51	The woman four times widowed
139–41	The dog who saved the people
141–44	The dog whose warning was not heeded
152–53	The Cheyennes run the Shoshones over a bank
–	Flying By's most difficult experience
59–61	The old bull's last fight
–	The Oglala war party that met a Crazy Buffalo
–	River names
–	Little Powder rescues his family from the Shoshones
104–12	Sharp Nose makes peace between the Arapahoes and the Crows
–	Telling the future
65	The Santee owl wizard
3–4	Caring for babies
58	Twins
–	Burial and mourning
224–28	The girl who was buried alive
130–32	Eating and giving thanks to the food
132–34	Making a candidate (*wicaśa yatapika*)
194–201	The two murderers
–	Insanity
153–81	Falling Star

Appendix B
Phonetic Key

Neihardt did not use any systematic orthography to write Lakota words but spelled them as he heard them. Simplified retranscriptions of all Lakota terms used throughout the book have been added in square brackets to guide pronunciation; interested readers can use these to find the words in Buechel's *Dictionary of the Teton Dakota Sioux Language*.

The phonetic symbols used with special significance are the following:

c is pronounced *ch* as in *ch*ur*ch*

ǧ is pronounced as Spanish pa*g*ar

ḣ is pronounced as German a*ch*

j is pronounced as the *s* in plea*s*ure

n following a vowel is not pronounced
   separately but indicates that the
   preceding vowel is nasalized (as
   in French bo*n* or English i*n*k)

š is pronounced *sh* as in *sh*op

glottal stops are indicated by an
apostrophe ('), for example, *k'*

aspiration is not indicated

Bibliography

ARCHIVAL SOURCES

American Museum of Natural History, New York, New York
  Department of Anthropology Archives
    Mekeel, H. Scudder, "Field Notes Summer of 1931, White Clay
      District, Pine Ridge Reservation, South Dakota"
    Sword, George, Unpublished writings
Colorado Historical Society, Denver, Colorado
  James R. Walker Collection: George Sword ledgerbook
Federal Archives and Records Center, Kansas City, Missouri
  Record Group 75, Office of Indian Affairs: Pine Ridge Agency
    Records
      Census records
      Correspondence—Carlisle Boarding School
Holy Rosary Mission, Pine Ridge, South Dakota
  Birth and baptismal records
Marquette University, Milwaukee, Wisconsin
  Records of the Bureau of Catholic Indian Missions: Holy Rosary
    Mission Records
      Correspondence
      Sialm, Placidus, S.J., "Camp Churches"
University of Missouri, Columbia, Missouri
  Western History Manuscripts Collection: John G. Neihardt
    Collection

National Archives and Records Service, Washington, D.C.
    Record Group 75, Office of Indian Affairs:
        Letters Received by the Commissioner of Indian Affairs
        Special Case 188, The Ghost Dance
        Pine Ridge Census Rolls (Microcopy M595, rolls 362–84)
Nebraska State Historical Society, Lincoln, Nebraska
    Gilmore, Melvin Randolph, "On the Ethnogeography of the Nebraska Region"
University of Oklahoma, Norman, Oklahoma
    Western History Collections: Walter S. Campbell (Stanley Vestal) Collection
Sisters of the Blessed Sacrament, Cornwells Heights, Pennsylvania
    Archives of the Sisters of the Blessed Sacrament
Smithsonian Institution, Washington, D.C.
    National Anthropological Archives: Lakota texts by George Bushotter, translated by J. Owen Dorsey.

PRINTED MATERIAL

Aly, Lucile F. *John G. Neihardt: A Critical Biography*. Amsterdam: Rodopi, 1977.
Anderson, Harry H. "Nelson A. Miles and the Sioux War of 1876–77." *The Westerners Brand Book* (Chicago) 16(4) (June 1959): 25–27, 32.
Bad Heart Bull, Amos. *A Pictographic History of the Oglala Sioux*. Text by Helen H. Blish. Lincoln: University of Nebraska Press, 1967.
Badhorse, Beverly. "Petroglyphs: Possible Religious Significance of Some." *Wyoming Archaeologist* 23(2) (September 1979): 18–30.
Beckwith, Martha Warren. "Mythology of the Oglala Dakota." *Journal of American Folk-Lore* 43(170) (October–December 1930): 377–98.
Black Hills Engineer, Mount Rushmore Memorial Issue 18(4) (November 1930).
Blish, Helen Heather. "The Ceremony of the Sacred Bow of the Oglala Dakota." *American Anthropologist* 36 (1934): 180–87.
Bordeaux, W. J. *Conquering the Mighty Sioux*. Sioux Falls, S.D., 1929.
Bray, Edmund C., and Martha Coleman Bray, eds. *Joseph N. Nicollet on the Plains and Prairies: The Expeditions of 1838–39 with Journals, Letters, and Notes on the Dakota Indians*. St. Paul: Minnesota Historical Society, 1976.

Brininstool, E. A. *Crazy Horse: The Invincible Ogalalla Sioux Chief.* Los Angeles: Wentzel, 1949.

Brown, Joseph Epes, recorder and ed. *The Sacred Pipe: Black Elk's Account of the Seven Rites of the Oglala Sioux.* Norman: University of Oklahoma Press, 1963. Reprint (with new preface). New York: Penguin Books, 1971.

Brumble, H. David III. *An Annotated Bibliography of American Indian and Eskimo Autobiographies.* Lincoln: University of Nebraska Press, 1981.

Buechel, Eugene, S. J. *A Dictionary of the Teton Dakota Sioux Language.* Edited by Paul Manhart, S.J. Pine Ridge, S.D.: Red Cloud Indian School, 1970.

————. *Lakota Tales and Texts.* Edited by Paul Manhart, S. J. Pine Ridge, S.D.: Red Cloud Indian School, 1978.

"Buffalo Bill's Goodbye." *New York Times,* April 1, 1887.

Clark, W. P. *The Indian Sign Language.* Philadelphia: L. R. Hamersly, 1885.

Cook, Dorothy. "J. G. Neihardt Made a Member of the Sioux Tribe." *Nebraska State Journal* (Lincoln), Sunday, June 7, 1931, p. 26.

Culin, Stewart. *Games of the North American Indians.* Smithsonian Institution, Bureau of American Ethnology, Annual Report 24. Washington, D.C., 1907.

Cunningham, Leo C., S.J. "Who's Who among Catholic Indians: William Bergin, Sioux." *Indian Sentinel* 10(2) (Spring 1930): 76.

Curtis, Edward S. *The North American Indian,* vol. 3. 1908. Reprint. New York: Johnson Reprint Corporation, 1970.

Danker, Donald F., ed. "The Wounded Knee Interviews of Eli S. Ricker." *Nebraska History* 62(2) (Summer 1981): 151–243.

————. "The Violent Deaths of Yellow Bear and John Richard Jr." *Nebraska History* 63(2) (Summer 1982): 137–51.

Deloria, Ella Cara. *Dakota Texts.* Publications of the American Ethnological Society 14. New York: G. E. Stechert, 1932.

————. "Dakota Treatment of Murderers." *Proceedings of the American Philosophical Society* 88(5) (November 1944): 368–71.

————. *Speaking of Indians.* New York: Friendship Press, 1944.

DeMallie, Raymond J. "Pine Ridge Economy: Cultural and Historical Perspectives." In *American Indian Economic Development,* edited by Sam Stanley, 237–312. The Hague: Mouton, 1978.

————. "The Lakota Ghost Dance: An Ethnohistorical Account." *Pacific Historical Review* 51(4) (1982): 385–405.

Densmore, Frances. *Teton Sioux Music*. Smithsonian Institution, Bureau of American Ethnology, Bulletin 61. Washington, D.C., 1918.

Dietz, Frank T., S. J. "Catholic Indian Congress of 1929: Sioux Catholic Congress Inspiring." *The Indian Sentinel* 9(4) (1929): 151–52, 183.

Dorsey, George A. *The Arapaho Sun Dance: The Ceremony of the Offerings Lodge*. Field Columbian Museum, Publication 75, Anthropological Series 4. Chicago, 1903.

————. "Legend of the Teton Sioux Medicine Pipe." *Journal of American Folklore* 19 (1906): 326–29.

Dorsey, James Owen. "Games of Dakota Children." *American Anthropologist*, o.s. 4 (1891): 329–45.

————. *A Study of Siouan Cults*. Smithsonian Institution, Bureau of American Ethnology, Annual Report 11. Washington, D.C., 1894. Pp. 351–544.

Duhamel's Sioux Indian Pageant. [Rapid City, S.D., ca. 1935.]

Duratschek, Sister Mary Claudia. *Crusading along Sioux Trails: A History of the Catholic Indian Missions of South Dakota*. Yankton, S.D.: Grail, 1947.

Eastman, Charles Alexander. *Indian Boyhood*. New York: McClure, Phillips, 1902.

————. *The Soul of the Indian*. Boston: Houghton Mifflin, 1911.

————. *From the Deep Woods to Civilization: Chapters in the Autobiography of an Indian*. Boston: Little, Brown, 1916.

Friswald, Carroll. *The Killing of Crazy Horse*. Glendale, Calif.: Arthur H. Clark, 1976.

Gilmore, Melvin Randolph. *Uses of Plants by the Indians of the Missouri River Region*. Smithsonian Institution, Bureau of American Ethnology, Annual Report 33. Washington, D.C., 1919. Pp. 43–154.

Goetzmann, William H. *Exploration and Empire: The Explorer and the Scientist in the Winning of the American West*. New York: Alfred A. Knopf, 1967.

Goll, Louis J., S.J. *Jesuit Missions among the Sioux*. St. Francis, S.D., 1940.

Graham, W. A. *The Custer Myth: A Source Book of Custeriana*. Harrisburg, Pa.: Stackpole, 1953.

Gray, John S. *Centennial Campaign: The Sioux War of 1876*. Fort Collins, Colo.: Old Army Press, 1976.

Grinnell, George Bird. "Falling Star." *Journal of American Folk-Lore* 34 (1921): 308–15.

——. *By Cheyenne Camp Fires*. New Haven: Yale University Press, 1926.

Hammer, Kenneth, ed. *Custer in '76: Walter Camp's Notes on the Custer Fight*. Provo, Utah: Brigham Young University Press, 1976.

Hanson, Joseph Mills. *The Conquest of the Missouri: Being the Story of the Life and Exploits of Captain Grant Marsh*. Chicago: A. C. McClurg, 1909.

Hassrick, Royal B. *The Sioux: Life and Customs of a Warrior Society*. Norman: University of Oklahoma Press, 1964.

Hebard, Grace Raymond, and E. A. Brininstool. *The Bozeman Trail: Historical Accounts of the Blazing of the Overland Routes into the Northwest, and the Fights with Red Cloud's Warriors*. 2 vols. Cleveland: Arthur H. Clark, 1922.

House, Julius T. *John G. Neihardt: Man and Poet*. Wayne, Nebr.: F. H. Jones & Son, 1920.

Howard, James H., trans. and ed. *The Warrior Who Killed Custer: The Personal Narrative of Chief Joseph White Bull*. Lincoln: University of Nebraska Press, 1968.

Hurt, Wesley R., and James H. Howard. "A Dakota Conjuring Ceremony." *Southwestern Journal of Anthropology* 8 (1952): 286–96.

Hyde, George E. *Red Cloud's Folk: A History of the Oglala Sioux Indians*. 1937. Rev. ed. Norman: University of Oklahoma Press, 1957.

——. *Pawnee Indians*. Denver: University of Denver Press, 1951.

——. *Spotted Tail's Folk: A History of the Brulé Sioux*. Norman: University of Oklahoma Press, 1961.

Iapi Oaye. Santee Agency, Nebr. 1888–89.

Indian Sentinel. Washington, D.C.: Bureau of Catholic Indian Missions. 1923–1950.

Kadlecek, Edward, and Mabell Kadlecek. *To Kill an Eagle: Indian Views on the Last Days of Crazy Horse*. Boulder: Johnson Books, 1981.

Landes, Ruth. *The Mystic Lake Sioux: Sociology of the Mdewakantonwan Santee*. Madison: University of Wisconsin Press, 1968.

Laubin, Reginald, and Gladys Laubin. *The Indian Tipi: Its History, Construction, and Use*. 1957. 2d ed. Norman: University of Oklahoma Press, 1977.

Laviolette, Gotran. *The Sioux Indians in Canada*. Regina, Sask.: Marian Press, 1944.

Libby, O. G., ed. *The Arikara Narrative of the Campaign against the Hostile Dakotas, June, 1876*. North Dakota Historical Society Collections 6. Bismarck, 1920.

Lowie, Robert H. *The Crow Indians*. New York: Farrar and Rinehart, 1935.

McCluskey, Sally. "*Black Elk Speaks:* And So Does John Neihardt." *Western American Literature* 6(4) (Winter 1972): 231–42.

Macgregor, Gordon. *Warriors without Weapons: A Study of the Society and Personality Development of the Pine Ridge Sioux*. Chicago: University of Chicago Press, 1946.

McGregor, James H. *The Wounded Knee Massacre from Viewpoint of the Sioux*. Baltimore: Wirth Brothers, 1940.

McLaughlin, Marie L. *Myths and Legends of the Sioux*. Bismarck, N.D.: Bismarck Tribune Co., 1916.

McNamara, Stephen, S. J. "Black Elk and Brings White." *Indian Sentinel* (November 1941): 139–40.

Mails, Thomas E., and Dallas Chief Eagle. *Fools Crow*. Garden City, N.Y.: Doubleday, 1979.

Mallery, Garrick, *Pictographs of the North American Indian*. Smithsonian Institution, Bureau of American Ethnology, Annual Report 4. Washington, D.C.: 1886. Pp. 1–256.

———. *Picture-Writing of the American Indians*. Smithsonian Institution, Bureau of American Ethnology, Annual Report 10. Washington, D.C., 1893.

Marquis, Thomas B. *A Warrior Who Fought Custer*. Minneapolis: Midwest, 1931.

Meeker, Louis L. "Oglala Games." *Pennsylvania University Museum Bulletin* 3 (1901): 23–46.

Meyer, Roy W. *History of the Santee Sioux: United States Indian Policy on Trial*. Lincoln: University of Nebraska Press, 1967.

Mirsky, Jeannette. "The Dakota." In *Cooperation and Competition among Primitive Peoples*, edited by Margaret Mead, 382–427. 1937. Rev. ed. Boston: Beacon, 1966.

Mooney, James. *The Ghost-Dance Religion and the Sioux Outbreak of 1890*. Smithsonian Institution, Bureau of American Ethnology, Annual Report 14, pt. 2. Washington, D.C., 1896.

————. *Calendar History of the Kiowa Indians.* Smithsonian Institution, Bureau of American Ethnology, Annual Report 17, pt. 1. Washington, D.C., 1898.

Neihardt, John G. *The Song of Hugh Glass.* New York: Macmillan, 1915.

————. *Poetic Values: Their Reality and Our Need of Them.* New York: Macmillan, 1925.

————. *The Song of the Indian Wars.* New York: Macmillan, 1925.

————. *The Quest.* New York: Macmillan, 1928.

————. "Letter to Julius T. House, August 10, 1930." *Present-Day American Literature* 4(3) (1930): 95–96.

————. "Of Making Many Books." *St. Louis Post-Dispatch,* July 3, 1931.

————. *Black Elk Speaks: Being the Life Story of a Holy Man of the Ogalala Sioux.* New York: William Morrow, 1932. Reprints. Lincoln: University of Nebraska Press, 1961, 1979 (with new preface, introduction, illustrations, appendixes).

————. *The Song of the Messiah.* New York: Macmillan, 1935.

————. "High Horse's Courting." *Indians at Work* 12(5) (January–February 1945): 19–22.

————. "Red Hail and the Two Suitors." *Indians at Work* 13(1) (May–June 1945): 6–10.

————. *When the Tree Flowered: An Authentic Tale of the Old Sioux World.* New York: Macmillan, 1951.

————. *Eagle Voice: An Authentic Tale of the Sioux Indians.* London: Andrew Melrose, 1953.

————. *All Is But a Beginning: Youth Remembered, 1881–1901.* New York: Harcourt Brace Jovanovich, 1972.

Odell, Thomas E. *Mato Paha: The Story of Bear Butte.* Spearfish, S.D., 1942.

Olson, James C. *Red Cloud and the Sioux Problem.* Lincoln: University of Nebraska Press, 1965.

Olson, Paul A. "*Black Elk Speaks* as Epic and Ritual Attempt to Reverse History." In *Vision and Refuge: Essays on the Literature of the Great Plains,* edited by Virginia Faulkner with Frederick C. Luebke, 3–37. Lincoln: University of Nebraska Press, 1982.

Powell, Peter John. *Sweet Medicine: The Continuing Role of the Sacred Arrows, the Sun Dance, and the Sacred Buffalo Hat in Northern Cheyenne History.* 2 vols. Norman: University of Oklahoma Press, 1969.

————. *People of the Sacred Mountain: A History of the Northern Cheyenne Chiefs and Warrior Societies, 1830–1879, with an Epilogue, 1969–1974.* 2 vols. San Francisco: Harper & Row, 1981.

Powers, William K. *Oglala Religion.* Lincoln: University of Nebraska Press, 1977.

————. *Yuwipi: Vision and Experience in Oglala Ritual.* Lincoln: University of Nebraska Press, 1982.

Red Cloud's Dream Come True: Holy Rosary Mission, 1888–1963. Pine Ridge, S.D., 1963.

Riggs, Stephen Return. *Dakota Grammar, Texts, and Ethnography.* Edited by James Owen Dorsey. Contributions to North American Ethnology 9. Washington, D.C., 1893.

Riley, Paul D. "The Battle of Massacre Canyon." *Nebraska History* 54 (1973): 220–49.

Russell, Don. *The Lives and Legends of Buffalo Bill.* Norman: University of Oklahoma Press, 1960.

Sandoz, Mari. *Crazy Horse: The Strange Man of the Oglalas.* New York: Alfred A. Knopf, 1942.

Schusky, Ernest L. *The Forgotten Sioux: An Ethnohistory of the Lower Brule Reservation.* Chicago: Nelson-Hall, 1975.

Sell, Henry Blackman, and Victor Weybright. *Buffalo Bill and the Wild West.* New York: Oxford University Press, 1955.

Sialm, Placidus, S.J. "A Retreat To Catechists." *Indian Sentinel* 3(2) (April 1923): 78.

Śinasapa Wocekiye Taeyanpaha. Fort Totten, N.D. 1907–1912.

Śina Sapa Wocekiye Taeyanpaha: The Catholic Sioux Herald. Marty, S.D.: St. Paul's Catholic Indian Mission. 1936.

"Sioux Prays to Gods from Rushmore Peak." *Rapid City Daily Journal,* August 28, 1936, p. 10.

Smith, John L. "A Short History of the Sacred Calf Pipe of the Teton Dakota." *South Dakota University Museum News* 28 (1967): 1–37.

Standing Bear, Luther. *My People the Sioux.* Boston: Houghton Mifflin, 1928.

————. *Land of the Spotted Eagle.* Boston: Houghton Mifflin, 1933.

Steinmetz, Paul B., S.J. *Pipe, Bible and Peyote among the Oglala Lakota.* Stockholm Studies in Comparative Religion 19. Motala, Sweden, 1980.

Sword, George. "The Story of the Ghost Dance." *The Folk-Lorist* 1(1) (July 1892): 28–36.

Thomas, Sidney, J. "A Sioux Medicine Bundle." *American Anthropologist* 43 (1941): 605–9.

Utley, Robert M. *The Last Days of the Sioux Nation.* New Haven: Yale University Press, 1963.

Vaughn, J. W. *With Crook at the Rosebud.* Harrisburg, Pa.: Stackpole, 1956.

Vestal, Stanley. *Sitting Bull: Champion of the Sioux.* 1932. Rev. ed., Norman: University of Oklahoma Press, 1957.

———. *New Sources of Indian History, 1850–1891: The Ghost Dance —The Prairie Sioux, A Miscellany.* Norman: University of Oklahoma Press, 1934.

———. *Warpath: The True Story of the Fighting Sioux Told in a Biography of Chief White Bull.* Boston: Houghton Mifflin, 1934.

Walker, James R. "Oglala Games, I." *Journal of American Folk-Lore* 18 (1905): 277–90.

———. "Oglala Games, II." *Journal of American Folk-Lore* 19 (1906): 29–36.

———. "Tuberculosis among the Oglala Sioux Indians." *Southern Workman* 35 (1906): 378–84.

———. "The Sun Dance and Other Ceremonies of the Oglala Division of the Teton Dakota." American Museum of Natural History, *Anthropological Papers* 16, pt. 2. New York, 1917. Pp. 50–221.

———. "Sioux Games." *Collections of the Historical Society of South Dakota* 9 (1918): 486–513.

———. *Lakota Belief and Ritual.* Edited by Raymond J. DeMallie and Elaine A. Jahner. Lincoln: University of Nebraska Press, 1980.

———. *Lakota Society.* Edited by Raymond J. DeMallie. Lincoln: University of Nebraska Press, 1982.

———. *Lakota Myth.* Edited by Elaine A. Jahner. Lincoln: University of Nebraska Press, 1983.

Williamson, John P. "Report of Missionary at Pine Ridge Agency." *Sixty-First Annual Report of the Commissioner of Indian Affairs to the Secretary of the Interior.* Washington, D.C.: Government Printing Office, 1892, p. 459.

Williamson, Thomas S., and Stephen R. Riggs, trans. *Dakota Wowapi Wakan: The Holy Bible, in the Language of the Dakotas, Translated Out of the Original Tongues*. New York: American Bible Society, 1880.

Wissler, Clark, "Societies and Ceremonial Associations in the Oglala Division of the Teton-Dakota." American Museum of Natural History, *Anthropological Papers* 11, pt. 1. New York, 1912. Pp. 1–99.

Yost, Nellie Snyder. *Buffalo Bill: His Family, Friends, Fame, Failures, and Fortunes*. Chicago: Swallow, 1979.

Zimmerman, Joseph A., S.J. "Catechist Nick Black Elk." *Indian Sentinel* (October 1950): 101–2.

Index

431